Witchcraft, Witches, and Violence in Ghana

WITCHCRAFT, WITCHES, AND VIOLENCE IN GHANA

Mensah Adinkrah

berghahn
NEW YORK · OXFORD
www.berghahnbooks.com

First edition published in 2015 by
Berghahn Books
www.berghahnbooks.com

©2015, 2017 Mensah Adinkrah
First paperback edition published in 2017

Library of Congress Cataloging-in-Publication Data

Adinkrah, Mensah, author.
Witchcraft, witches, and violence in Ghana / Mensah Adinkrah.
    pages cm
    Includes bibliographical references and index.
    ISBN 978-1-78238-560-8 (hardback) — ISBN 978-1-78533-516-7 (paperback) —
ISBN 978-1-78238-561-5 (ebook)
    1. Witchcraft—Social aspects—Ghana. 2. Witches—Ghana—Violence against.
3. Trials (Witchcraft)—Ghana. 4. Sexism in witchcraft trials—Ghana. 5. Akan
(African people)—Social conditions. I. Title.
    BF1584.G5A35 2015
    133.4309667—dc23

                                                                2014033518

British Library Cataloguing in Publication Data

A catalogue record for this book is available from the British Library

ISBN 978-1-78238-560-8 hardback
ISBN 978-1-78533-516-7 paperback
ISBN 978-1-78238-561-5 ebook

To my parents: Afua Agyeiwaa Boame and Yaw Atuobi Mensah.

CONTENTS

ILLUSTRATIONS

PREFACE

Growing up in Ghana in the 1960s and 1970s, I was immersed in a culture where witchcraft ideology constituted part of the fabric of daily life. The discussions among adults about malevolent witches and the calamities they caused were the background sounds of my childhood that I would be allowed to overhear only while at work doing chores or at play with siblings. I was never invited into such adult conversations and my questions could be met with reprimands. Though less frequent, there were also the accounts of benevolent witches who orchestrated noble deeds for their benefactors. In either case, I heard about the capacity of witches to affect the fortunes of others. Among schoolmates and other compeers, there were the stories shared about witchcraft, witch sightings, and other tales featuring witches and their horrific deeds.

As a youngster, my curiosity and fear for witches, their odious activities and the excesses of witch hunts, would be heightened after I wandered into the local magistrates' court of my hometown one afternoon to find out why a large crowd had congregated outside. The case being adjudicated was both a civil and criminal matter involving witchcraft imputation. A woman in her mid-eighties was narrating to the magistrate the details of her violent victimization at the hands of those making accusations of witchcraft against her. She recounted how her accusers had forcibly bundled her into a taxi and hauled her off before a witch doctor in a small remote village. There, she was given a concoction consisting of a local spirit alcohol mixed with some concentrated bitter herbs and dried, ground coconut meat. She told the court that after being forced to consume copious amounts of this potion, she vomited profusely and then lost consciousness. When she regained consciousness several hours later, her accusers thrust in her lap three notebooks purportedly full of confessional statements she had made after drinking the potion. The statements had apparently been recorded by her assailants and comprised her alleged malevolent witchcraft activities. Standing in the packed courtroom, I was baffled and traumatized to come this close to an accused witch and to hear about the details of a case of witchcraft imputation. The entire experience made quite an impression on me, making me painfully aware of the brutality of witchcraft accusations and witch hunts. I was unable to learn any more about this specific case after leaving the courtroom, while my search for information about the dispositional outcome of the case years later proved futile. But I continued to follow witchcraft-related violence in Ghana and the rest of Africa with keen interest. When, in 2003, I was awarded a Fulbright Senior Scholar Fellowship to study female homicide victimization in Ghana, I elected to focus on witchcraft-related lethal and nonlethal violence. I embarked on a mission to shed light on the subject of contemporary witch hunts in one country to contribute to a broader understanding of the phenomenon. This book is a part of my findings.

Witchcraft accusations and the attendant maltreatment of alleged witches, or witch hunts, constitute one of the gravest and most flagrant forms of human rights abuses around the world. In many African countries scores of persons, mostly women and children, who have been accused of being witches are targets of physical, psychological, or social abuse. Many are subjected to trials-by-ordeal that constitute forms of torture to elicit confessional statements, while some even lose their lives at the hands of public lynch mobs. In several of these countries, newly emergent charismatic churches and their prayer camps along with traditional religious shrines, are at the center of many witchcraft imputations, and are presided over by persons with purely pecuniary motives. In Ghana and many parts of Africa, the congregations of churches swell and church leaders gain in popularity when they profess the ability to catch witches and heal those purported to have been afflicted with witchery.

Contemporary discourse on witchcraft in Ghana has focused almost exclusively on witchcraft-related violence in northern Ghana and the witches' camps in the north. This ignores the major problem, and the very different forms of witchcraft violence that occur in the southern part of Ghana. Available data show that witchcraft suspicions and accusations are rife in southern Ghana as well as northern Ghana, leading to the violent maiming and deaths of many each year. Most of this book focuses on the witchcraft ideology of the Akan, but considers witchcraft beliefs and related violence throughout Ghana.

Acknowledgments

In writing this book, I received assistance from a number of people. As my writing progressed, my mother, Afua Agyeiwaa Boame, directed my attention to several aspects of Akan witchcraft that I had overlooked but was able to address with her guidance. My father, Yaw Atuobi Mensah, was a great source of inspiration throughout my years of formal schooling. It is also from their examples that I have learned social responsibility and the capacity to confront and speak out against social injustice. To my parents, I have dedicated this book. I am grateful to Gladys Lariba and Simon Ngota of Gambaga. The pair, together with Edward Drahamani, helped guide my research in Gambaga and educated me about aspects of the witches' camps in the north, as well as the Presbyterian Church's Go Home Project designed to reintegrate accused witches into their communities. I am also grateful to the numerous Ghanaian informants, including pastors and other religious functionaries, from whom I received valuable information about witchcraft.

During the course of writing this book, I spoke incessantly about witchcraft in Ghana and other parts of the world with my anthropologist wife and academic colleague at Central Michigan University, Professor Carmen White. My young daughter, Hannah Adinkrah, was occasionally privy to some of these conversations from age six. They all patiently bore with me as several hours of witchcraft programs on Ghanaian radio stations permeated the living room at least two days a week throughout the course of writing this book. I am grateful to them for bearing this inconvenience, but know that they also share a common vision of seeing this book written for the role it can play in helping to eradicate witchcraft violence in Ghana and elsewhere.

Finally, my heart goes out to the thousands of people around the world whose lives have been directly and indirectly impacted by the imputation of witchcraft. That victims of violent witchcraft accusations and witch hunts are largely the most defenseless members of societies—elderly women and, increasingly, children—makes this form of psychological, physical, and social violence particularly egregious. I sincerely hope that greater understanding of the problem will pave the way to its end.

INTRODUCTION
Witchcraft Violence in Comparative Perspective

On August 23, 2004, a High Court of Justice in Ghana imposed the death penalty on a 39-year-old carpenter for bludgeoning his wife to death (Amanor 1999a; Sah 2004). The sentence followed a protracted court trial and a guilty verdict for a brutal murder that had occurred five years previously. The assailant claimed he killed his wife after she had transmogrified into a lioness during the dead of night, and was about to devour him. In a sworn deposition given to law enforcement authorities, and later affirmed by the defendant during the criminal trial, the assailant testified that at the time of the murder, he and his thirty-two-year-old wife had been married for six years and together had a five-year-old daughter. He indicated that some days prior to the murder their daughter fell ill and that he had transported her to a local member of the clergy for spiritual healing. The court learned that while at the cleric's house the assailant confided in the pastor that he had been experiencing petrifying nightmares in which he saw his wife transformed into a hermaphrodite, attempting to kill and cannibalize him. The priest reportedly offered him a powdery concoction with instructions to sprinkle the substance in his bedroom for three consecutive days. The husband was advised that he would see "wonders" shortly thereafter. He told police that following his administration of the substance, his nightmares became more graphic and intense. On the night of the murder, he observed his wife morph into several vicious creatures that threatened to kill him. When the police arrived at the crime scene, the assailant told them that he slaughtered a lioness that was charging at him. Only later did he realize that the "lioness" threatening to kill him was indeed his wife.

In another case of egregious violence fueled by suspicion of witchcraft, in January 2001 a 25-year-old unemployed man in the village of Tongor in the Kpandu District of the Volta Region of Ghana used a machete to slash the backside of the head, and to sever the hands of his 75-year-old paralyzed and bedridden paternal aunt (Ephson 2001). He told the police that he suspected the elderly woman of being a witch whose maleficent witchcraft had been responsible for his frequent job losses, protracted unemployment, and his general lack of social and economic advancement in life. In a post hoc crime interview with police, the defendant reported that he had been informed by various witch doctors in his community that the victim was the cause of his economic wretchedness. His well-calculated violent action was designed to extirpate the witch and thereby extricate himself from her spiritual influence. Despite the man's heinous actions, the incident was not reported to the police until a month had elapsed because the victim and her family regarded the assault as a private family matter. The assailant was later sentenced to prison for six years with hard labor.

In October 2009 law enforcement authorities in the capital city of Accra charged a 44-year-old woman with cruelty for force-feeding her seven-year-old nephew a mixture of human excreta and urine (Tenyah 2009). Police investigations revealed that the force feeding was part of a long-standing and systematic pattern of torture to which the child-victim had been subjected while residing with his aunt. Indeed, the torture was aimed at coercing the boy into confessing that he was a malignant wizard responsible for untreatable ailments that were afflicting his grandmother, who was also the mother of the assailant. In addition to the force-feedings, the assailant had applied a heated pressing iron to the face, hands, legs, and chest of the victim to compel him to confess to malignant witchcraft. The witchcraft allegation against the boy was originally initiated by the assailant's pastor who intimated that the boy was a wizard whose witchcraft activities were solely responsible for his grandmother's physical ailments.

In August 2005 a woman in her mid-nineties was nearly lynched in Kumasi, Ghana's second-largest city, on suspicion that she was a witch (Nunoo 2005). The incident unfolded when four young men found the frail, haggardly, and distraught woman sitting atop a boulder located in front of a neighboring house at 1:00 in the morning. The youths surmised that the woman was a witch returning home from a nocturnal witches' Sabbath whose journey was derailed by their witch-sighting. After subjecting her to four grueling hours of physical beatings and psychological torment, the youths frog-marched the woman to the local police station where law enforcement personnel detained her for another three hours while attempting to disperse a fractious crowd that had congregated in front of the police station, clamoring to mete out "instant justice" to the woman. Amidst the commotion, relatives of the elderly woman arrived at the station to appeal for calm and to obtain her release to their care. They informed the police that the woman was psychiatrically impaired and a member of the local royal family and that she occasionally left home at odd hours.

In September 2007 a vortex of suspicions, accusations, and harassment in a small village community led to the suicide of an elderly woman ("Grandma, 85, Commits Suicide" 2007). According to case records, on September 30, 2007, law enforcement personnel were summoned to the lavatory of a small apartment in the town of Nkwatia to recover the corpse of the elderly woman. She had committed suicide early that morning by hanging herself with a stringed sponge tied to her neck from the rafters in the ceiling of her grandson's apartment lavatory. According to the facts of the case, the woman, who lived in Accra, returned to her hometown of Nkwatia to attend the funerary ceremonies of a relative. Following the conclusion of the funeral obsequies, the elderly woman extended an invitation to a grandson with whom she was regularly domiciled in Accra, to come and visit her at Nkwatia. The grandson honored the invitation, traveling with his wife and children to Nkwatia where the family spent a week together. While returning to Accra, the commercial vehicle on which they were traveling was involved in a fatal crash that killed all the occupants in the vehicle. The motor vehicle accident and the deaths triggered a flurry of accusations in which family relations, neighbors, and community members came to perceive the octogenarian woman as a witch who had used her witchcraft to engineer the accident that claimed the lives of her grandson and his family. The intense physical and psychological mistreatment in the form of physical ostracism, gossip, innuendos, and other subtle and overt threats and antagonisms that ensued led the eighty-five-year-old woman to take the drastic measure of terminating her life when she found herself unable to cope with a whirlpool of accusations of witchcraft against her.

In April 2012 a seventeen-year-old girl with an exceptional record of academic performance was forced to abandon her home because of an accusation of witchcraft ("Girl Dumped in Witch Camp" 2012). Under threats of torture and death, the female high-school student fled her home and sought refuge at the Gambaga Witches' Camp in northern Ghana, a sanctuary for accused witches facing persecution and violent attacks from their accusers. Unable to explain the outstanding academic achievements of a female, community members presumptively attributed her academic performance to witchcraft, accusing her of having used her witchcraft power to steal the intelligence of her classmates. The predicament of the student came to the attention of the Ghana's Ministry of Women and Children's Affairs (MOWAC), which retrieved the girl from the witches' sanctuary and transferred her to a school outside her original community.

In 1997 a cerebrospinal meningitis epidemic in northern Ghana that caused 542 deaths led to a spate of public lynchings of suspected witches. During that time, residents in the afflicted communities imputed the disease and its spread to malevolent witchcraft and launched a ferocious campaign to ferret out the witches responsible (Nkrumah-Boateng 1997; "Round Table Conference on the Treatment of Suspected Witches in Northern Ghana" 1998; Safo 1997). In the ensuing weeks, hundreds of women suspected of witchcraft were physically assaulted, occasionally with lethal outcomes. For instance, in March 1997 an angry mob publicly lynched three elderly women in the village of Yoggu, accusing them of spreading the disease through witchcraft. A few weeks later, in the village of Kumbungu, masked vigilantes bludgeoned and stoned to death two women, aged fifty-five and sixty years, on suspicion that the pair had used witchcraft to cause the death of a young man in the town (Hushie and Alhassan 1998).

On November 25, 2010, a 72-year-old woman traveled roughly one hundred miles by bus from her village to visit her adult son in Tema, near Accra (Ocloo 2010a, 2010b). Unbeknownst to the elderly woman, her son had recently relocated to another suburb of Tema. Unable to locate her son's new residence, she found herself stranded, wandering through the neighborhood, and begging strangers for water, food, and money to facilitate her return to her village. Then she strayed into the compound of a thirty-seven-year-old unemployed woman. It was here that she was murdered in cold blood by an evangelical pastor, his sister, and four other accomplices. According to police reports, the pastor had come to visit his sister and was the first to come upon the disoriented elderly woman sitting in his sister's bedroom inside the multi-family dwelling house. The sister had been away from home, having taken her children to school. After raising an alarm that attracted other residents of the neighborhood, the pastor proclaimed the older woman a notorious malefic witch in the community whose flight to a witches' Sabbath had been derailed. The grandmother was detained by the six assailants, and then subjected to four hours of torture during which she was coerced into confessing to malevolent witchcraft activities. After being tormented, she was doused with a mixture of kerosene and gasoline and brutally set ablaze. She was rescued from the blazing fire by a passerby student-nurse and rushed to the nearest local hospital but perished less than twenty-four hours later. A family spokesperson of the victim disputed the imputation of witchcraft, asserting that the victim was an upright citizen who suffered mild and incipient symptoms of dementia resulting from old age. In court, the assailants denied the murder charges preferred against them, claiming that the anointing oil they had smeared on the victim's body during an exorcism ritual had spontaneously erupted into flames amidst intense prayers and repeated chants of "Holy Ghost Fire!."

The above-profiled cases of a spousal murder, maiming, physical and psychological intimidation, as well as vigilantism are not isolated incidents of gratuitous violence. They represent a pattern of aggressive action directed against supposed witches in Ghanaian society. Yet a review of media stories emanating from several societies across the globe in recent years shows that Ghanaian society is not atypical in terms of the violent victimization of putative witches. The physical and psychological brutalization, banishment, and even slaying of alleged witches are not limited to Ghana. Contemporary examples of witch persecutions are found in virtually all corners of Africa (see map 0.1.), from Abidjan to Yaounde, and from Angola to Zaire, illustrating that witch persecution is rampant on the continent (Ashforth 2005; Behringer 2004; Ter Haar 2007; Niehaus 1993).

Witch Persecutions in Africa: A Brief Survey

In recent years, the infliction of violence against suspected or accused witches has emerged as a major form of human rights abuse in Africa. Many local and international media agencies, human rights organizations, and even local law enforcement agencies have reported scores of people being threatened, intimidated, tortured, or murdered on suspicion of witchcraft. It is not known whether the recent proliferation of media reports on the subject reflects a growing incidence of the phenomenon or is merely due to increased interest and expanded coverage in the media. What is certain is that, at present, there is scarcely a society in Sub-Saharan Africa without a record of violent victimization of putative witches. Some of the most severe cases of contemporary witch persecutions documented on the continent have occurred in Republic of Benin, Cameroon, Democratic Republic of the Congo, Gambia, Malawi, Nigeria, São Tomé and Príncipe, South Africa, Tanzania, Uganda and Zimbabwe.

Republic of Benin

Extant reports indicate that belief in witchcraft is also prevalent in the Republic of Benin in West Africa (Behringer 2004; Integrated Regional Information Networks [IRIN] 2005) and is often the basis for severe mistreatment of suspected witches. In the mid 1970s the official government

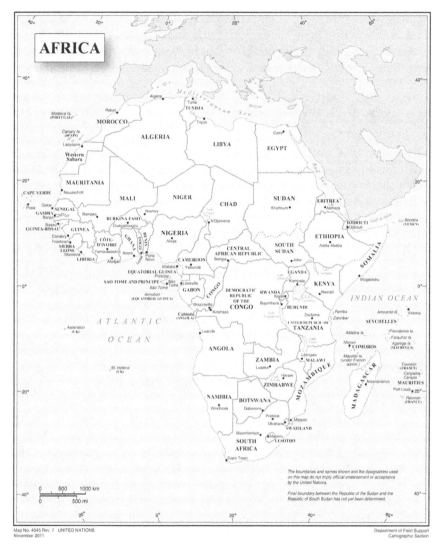

Map 0.1. Map of Africa

was implicated in campaigns of witchcraft persecution contributing to the widespread maltreatment and torture of dozens of elderly women alleged to be witches (see Behringer 2004, 11–12). A July 2005 report issued by the United Nations Office for the Coordination of Humanitarian Affairs (OCHA) suggested that traditional beliefs about childbirth and witchcraft in Benin contribute to the murder of scores of infants in the society annually (IRIN 2005). Among some ethnic groups in the country, there are strong beliefs that infants born in breech positions are witches, and must be killed instantly or abandoned to the elements. Infants whose births are characterized as in any way unusual are killed or left to die in the bush. The report noted,

> Unless a baby is born head first and face upwards, many communities in northern Benin believe the child is a witch or sorcerer. And tradition demands that the infant must be killed, sometimes by dashing its brains out against a tree trunk.
>
> In the eyes of the Baatonou, Boko and Peul people, a child whose birth and early development deviates in any way from the accepted norm is cursed and must be destroyed.
>
> If the parents are compassionate, the baby is simply abandoned to die in the bush or be found and rescued by a charitable soul. . . .
>
> [I]f the parents of an ill-born baby obey the demands of tradition, the infant is handed over to a "fixer." He ties a rope around the child's feet, walks several times round a tree and then dashes its head against the trunk.
>
> Alternatively, the fixer may drown the child or poison it to exorcise the evil which it is deemed to have brought into the world.
>
> It doesn't take much for a child to be sentenced to death in this way. It is enough for the infant to be born feet, shoulders or bottom first or head first but facing towards the ground.
>
> If the mother dies in childbirth, if the child fails to grow its first tooth before the age of eight months, or if its first tooth appears in the upper jaw, it is equally condemned.

Cameroon

Widespread belief in witchcraft and violence against suspected witches have also been widely reported in Cameroon where suspects in witchcraft cases are attacked by individuals or crowds of vigilantes who take the law into their own hands to exact vengeance through beatings and killings of putative witches (Tebug 2004). Discourse about witchcraft in the society depicts witches as cannibals, and as causing death, incurable illnesses, landslides and related environmental hazards, fatal truck accidents, and maternal deaths during childbirth. All manner of misfortune is blamed on the evil machinations of witches (Tangumonkem and Ghogomu 2004). Here, disdain for witches is reportedly pervasive and is responsible for virulent forms of persecution against alleged witches.

The Democratic Republic of the Congo

The situation in the Democratic Republic of the Congo is particularly disheartening as it often involves child victims. Several media and official sources indicate that across the country large numbers of children suspected of being witches are regularly subjected to atrocious violence at the hands of family members and other adults (BBC News 1999; Crawford 2005; Davies 2004; Raghavan 2003). These children are invariably blamed for perceived inexplicable misfortunes such as poor crop yield, job loss, economic hardship, and other personal and familial adversities. According to one report, children who "are too fat or too thin, too quiet or too noisy, wet the bed, or are disabled" are all potentially vulnerable to accusations of *kindoki* (witchcraft) (Crawford 2005). Children who are denounced as witches are commonly subjected to painful exorcisms consisting of physical beatings, torture, and starvation (Blair 2005; Crawford 2005; Davies 2004).

According to one report, "They are often forbidden from drinking water and subjected to such things as anal purges, beatings, and having hot oil poured over them" (Blair 2005, 2). Others are forced to "swallow gasoline, bitter herbs or small fish to force them to vomit out evil spirits" (Raghavan 2003, 2). Indeed, the mistreatment of suspected child witches has grown to such magnitude that thousands of children have been forced to flee their own homes for sanctuaries established expressly for the young victims of such abuse. In 1997 the United Nations Children's Fund (UNICEF) reported that a whopping 60 percent of the children in its shelters in the Congolese capital of Kinshasa were accused witches (UNICEF 2002). And according to a 1999 BBC news report, more than 14,000 Kinshasa children were living in shelters after being accused of witchcraft by family members (BBC News 1999). Children who lacked the relative good fortune of fleeing their assailants were murdered.

Gambia

Belief in witchcraft is endemic to Gambian society. This belief system follows the same pattern observed in other African societies, where the alleged witch is oftentimes a close family member (e.g., mother, aunt, nephew, or niece), cowife, or a neighbor, and is blamed for a variety of misfortunes, including miscarriages, barreness, illness, disease, and untimely death. A recent example of a witch hunt in the Gambia occurred in January 2009, following the death of the aunt of the country's president, Jahya Jamneh. President Jamneh claimed witches were responsible for his aunt's death, and instructed his personal guards and the country's intelligence services to ferret out the culprits. In this government-sponsored witch hunt, scores of witch doctors in neighboring Guinea were contracted to lend their services to the cause of identifying and rounding up the alleged witches. As combined teams of witch doctors, police, and military personnel scoured the hinterlands for witches, scores of individuals were allegedly stripped naked, assaulted, and tortured into confessing to be witches or participating in witchcraft activities.

In the ensuing melee, over a thousand people suspected of being witches were apprehended and imprisoned in secret detention centers for up to five days and forced to drink dangerous hallucinogenic concoctions purported to identify witches. While two people reportedly died from drinking the potion, several others suffered such complications as kidney problems. There were also reports of women being raped and others being robbed of valuables by witch doctors and security forces while the victims were in vulnerable hallucinogenic states after drinking the concoctions. Several people suffered severe physical injuries from the assaults and torture. Hundreds of Gambians fled the country to neighboring Senegal following attacks on their villages by the country's security forces (Rice 2009).

Malawi

Belief in witchcraft is also prevalent in Malawi (Soko and Kubik 2002). Here, as elsewhere, unexplained illnesses, deaths, and other misfortunes are attributed to the workings of witches who are believed to act out of envy and jealousy of the success of their victims (Soko and Kubik 2002). Violence perpetrated by aggrieved individuals or groups against suspected witches is widespread, resulting in extensive property loss, life-threatening injuries, and death. For example, in April 2001 Malawian police apprehended two village chiefs for authorizing the house burnings of suspected witches in villages under their administrative authority. The chiefs' orders came amidst suspicions that the deaths of a child and a village head were caused by the witchcraft of the alleged witches in question. The arsons led to the destruction of houses and property belonging to over twenty family members of the accused witches ("Arrests over Malawi Witchcraft Violence" 2001).

In another incident, in November 2002 Malawi police filed charges against the parents and two other family members of two youngsters—a three-year-old and a two-month-old—for murdering the children on suspicion that the children were witches. According to media reports, several residents, alarmed by loud screams coming from the family's residence, broke into the house unconvinced by the family's claims that they were "praying for the children to remove bad spirits." It was reported that "the four had sharpened a long rod which they shoved into the anus of the two children to rid them of witchcraft" (Martin 2002).

Nigeria

In Nigeria tragic accounts of witchcraft persecution in which suspected witches are burnt, stoned to death or attacked with machetes are legion (Ademowo, Foxcroft, and Oladipo 2010). To illustrate, in December 1989 in the case of *Ezekiel Adekunle v. The State,* the Supreme Court of Nigeria upheld the murder conviction and death sentence of the appellant, Ezekiel Adekunle, for orchestrating and spearheading the murder of one Felicia Ejide, a seventy-year-old woman whom the appellant accused of being a witch. Witnesses described Adekunle jeering at the victim and calling her a witch before jostling her and causing her to fall while she was being carried home on her daughter's back. When the elderly woman fell, the appellant raised a public alarm about a witch being transported away. He led a converging crowd in pelting the elderly woman to death with large pieces of cement block while chanting, "One kills the witch with stones" (International Center for Nigerian Law 2005).

São Tomé and Príncipe

Witchcraft persecution in Africa is not confined to large, populous societies. Even on the small island of São Tomé and Príncipe, off the coast of Gabon, old women are frequently beaten after they are accused of being a *feiticeira* (witch).

South Africa

In South Africa, witch hunts have claimed the lives of thousands of people (Ashforth 2005). In communities characterized by strong witchcraft beliefs, physical assaults perpetrated against persons suspected of witchcraft are legion. Here, "necklacing"—a vigilante-style killing in which old truck tires that have been doused with gasoline are hung around a culprit's neck and set ablaze—has frequently been used to punish suspected witchery (Ashforth 2005). Survivors of witch attacks and their families are forced to seek refuge in witches' sanctuaries, many of which are characterized by material deprivation and squalid living conditions.

Tanzania

From Tanzania comes reports of thousands of elderly women slain in the name of witchcraft persecution. According to one report, more than 3,072 witch killings occurred in the country between 1970 and 2002 (Duff 2005). Meanwhile, a 2002 report issued by the World Health Organization (WHO) estimated that five hundred elderly women accused of witchcraft are killed annually in the country. Reacting to the rapacity of the witch hunts and the massive death toll, one analyst described Tanzania's witch persecutions as a "silent holocaust" (Mfumbusa 1999).

Uganda

Ugandan newspapers are replete with graphic reports of vigilante violence perpetrated by public lynch mobs against persons suspected of practicing witchcraft (e.g., Mambule 2007, 2009; Oloya 2005). These media reports depict numerous instances of witch persecutions, many of which result in the deaths, physical maiming, and forcible displacement of putative witches from their communities. In Uganda, as in other societies profiled, witches are regarded by many as the source of a wide array of personal misfortunes and tragedies that befall individuals and communities. Consequently, witches are widely viewed as a scourge that must be physically exterminated or annihilated to provide a respite in human suffering. These beliefs lead to egregious acts of violence.

A review of Ugandan media reports over the past ten years shows that witchcraft is blamed for myriad maladies and calamities, including strange and inexplicable physical illness, mental illness, alcoholism, HIV/AIDS, and untimely deaths. Forms of witchcraft persecution that follow allegations of witchcraft include destruction or demolition of the accused's home, destruction of crops, forcible eviction from agricultural land, expulsion from village communities, nonlethal physical assaults, and violent homicide. A few cases are provided to illustrate the magnitude of witchcraft persecution in the country.

In September 2005 five families composed of over forty people were evicted from Mabigasa village in Rakai district by residents on suspicion of wizardry. The residents destroyed or appropriated the property that belonged to the suspected witches. The houses and banana plantations of the alleged witches were set ablaze, and their cows and pigs slaughtered and shared by the lynch mob. The violent persecution was triggered by the death of two residents of the village whose demise was attributed to the accused witches (Mambule 2005b).

In the same Rakai district in August 2005, a man and his son had their plantation destroyed, their animals seized, and their house set ablaze because one of the men was suspected of being a wizard. When the accused wizards took refuge at a local police station, a rampaging mob seeking to lynch the father and son attacked the police post, as the police shot and killed a member of the mob who had wrestled a gun from a policeman (Mambule 2005a).

In another incident in September 2005, in Kibenge village in Buwunga, Bukoto East, a fifty-four-year-old woman, Jane Rose Nassuuna, was stoned and hacked to death and her body burnt because she was suspected of being a witch. The daughters of the deceased woman fled for their own lives after attending the local court where their mother was declared a witch and after witnessing the beginnings of the lethal assault on their mother. According to the report, "local officials condemned the woman and let the villagers 'punish' her, claiming she had become a menace to the village" (Ssejjoba 2005, 1). Reports indicated that police had arrested several participants in the attack, including a fifty-six-year-old man who took the woman to court, claiming that the deceased had bewitched his wife who recently died in Kitovu Hospital (Ssejjoba 2005).

In yet another case that garnered widespread media attention, over 150 people attacked teachers at Lukomera Church Primary School, accusing them of using witchcraft to afflict the pupils of the school. According to police, the incident occurred after four female students of the school developed psychiatric problems and collapsed on the compound, a condition the parents attributed to witchcraft ("Locals Bitter" 2005).

Zimbabwe

In Zimbabwe, physical assaults upon suspected witches claim scores of lives annually. When a child or person in the prime of life suffers an inexplicable illness or dies, there is suspicion that malevolent witchcraft is responsible. The aggrieved individual, survivors of a deceased witchcraft victim, or members of the community take retaliatory action against the purported witch, often leading to the destruction of property, maiming, or death (Chavunduka 1980).

Witch Hunts in Non-African Societies

A review of the anthropological and historical literature amply establishes the persecution of alleged witches as a phenomenon that has touched every region of the globe (Behringer 2004). Indeed, the most widely known cases of witch persecution are those associated with the Middle Ages in Europe and during the early colonial period in America when thousands of people were branded as witches or accused of practicing witchcraft, and were subjected to brutal persecution (Jensen 2007). Between the fifteenth and eighteenth centuries, violent retributive action against alleged witches occurred in England, Finland, France, Germany, Holland, Hungary, Poland, Russia, Scotland, Sweden, and Switzerland, among others (Behringer 2004; Jensen 2007; Roper 2004). The accused witches were believed to possess destructive supernatural powers that they used to cause inclement weather, physical injuries, illness, and even death to their victims (Behringer 2004; Jensen 2007; Roper 2004). The resultant public fear about the depredatory actions of witches took frantic proportions while members of the clergy oversaw the purge of thousands of suspected witches. Many accused witches were criminally tried, tortured into confessing to witch misdeeds, and then brutally executed. Persecution of witches in the American colonies occurred in Massachusetts, Connecticut, and Virginia. These trials reached a zenith in 1692 in Salem, Massachusetts, where nineteen persons were executed as witches and 150 more were incarcerated (Jensen 2007). In Europe, as in America, the witches were typically tortured until they confessed, after which they were burned to death. During these infamous witch trials, accused witches were also forced to name their supposed accomplices, who were tortured in turn until additional witches were named.

It is estimated that between the thirteenth and seventeenth centuries as many as half a million people were tortured and executed on the grounds of witchcraft or heresy in Europe. The victims of the European witch persecutions ranged from poor, elderly, unmarried, widowed women to political and social deviants—Jews, Muslims, heretics, and critics of the social, political, and religious order of the time. Examination of the sociodemographic background of witchcraft defendants in Europe reveals that the vast majority of people labeled as witches were women (Oldridge 2002; Roper 2004). According to Oldridge, "the best recent estimates suggest that three-quarters of those executed for witchcraft in Europe were women, though the figures varied considerably from place to place" (Oldridge 2002, 268). These women were generally older, unmarried, and childless, and were thus socially marginalized in their local communities (Roper 2004).

Explanations vary as to the causes of the European and American witch hunts. According to one perspective, the persecution of witches illustrates classic instances of "a search for scapegoats on which fears, hatred, and tension of all kinds could be discharged" (Ginzburg 2002, 122). It was the marginalized—old, infirm, widowed, childless, and other members of the society least likely to fight back—who bore the heaviest brunt of the witch hunts (Midelfort 2002). Gentilcore observes with respect to Italy that "many accused witches were weak and helpless, with no other means of power or influence" (Gentilcore 2002, 104)). According to another perspective, violent actions against predominantly female witches must be seen as retribution in patriarchal societies directed toward women who were either unable or unwilling to conform to gender conventions.

Contemporary anthropological literature and numerous media reports indicate that belief in witchcraft phenomena exists in many societies, although these beliefs remain more entrenched in some places than in others. This literature also shows that violent victimization and persecution of witches commonly occurs in response to allegations of witchcraft. In addition to the cases in parts of Africa profiled above, media reports are replete with documented cases of witchcraft persecutions in India, Nepal, and Papua New Guinea (Ghosh 2013; Ware 2001; "Witch Killings in India" 2000). In Papua New Guinea, as in many other societies where belief in witchcraft persists, witchcraft is invoked to explain misfortune. Witches are believed to be endowed with extraordinary powers that they deploy to cause malefic acts and to bring adversity to their victims. Suspected witches are recurrently accused of afflicting victims with strange, inexplicable, and even fatal illnesses. Here, too, the majority of accused witches are elderly women, often destitute. Efforts by Papuans to rid local communities of reviled, malefic witches in their respective communities have fueled violence against persons accused of practicing witchcraft or harmful magic (Ware 2001). Consider the following case of virulent witch persecution in one Papua New Guinea village:

> Sometime in 1997, Jomani and fellow villagers hauled the women from their homes and questioned them about deaths in the village, including that of an 18-year-old youth whose brain the men believed had been replaced with water by a sanguma [sorcerer]. In villages where belief in witchcraft lingers, such interrogations are brutal: hot metal may be applied to genitals, flesh incised with machetes, or the accused strung up by an arm or leg. In the end, the Mondo One women were killed: three with homemade shotguns, the fourth with knives, because the men ran out of bullets. Jomani says the women had all confessed to being sangumas. Asked why they would do that, he replies coolly: "Because we stab them until they do." And if they hadn't admitted to sorcery? "We stab them anyway." Jomani's village is not unique. Yauwe Riyong, an M.P. from nearby Chuave district, in Simbu province, told Parliament last December that as many as 15 women had been "chopped to pieces" as suspected sangumas. (Ware 2001, 1)

Brutal witch persecutions in India have also been widely reported in contemporary media. A CNN report in 2000 estimated that about 200 women are killed across the country annually on suspicion of witchcraft ("Witch Killings in India" 2000). According to one report, in the Indian state of Bihar, "Women accused of witchcraft are dragged into the forest and hacked, hanged or burned to death. Heads of children have been smashed on rocks. Even nonfatal cases are ghastly. Women suffer smashed teeth, shaved heads or chopped off breasts. Others have been forced to eat excrement or to strip and walk naked through villages" (Misra 2000, 1).

Here, as in many other places where witchcraft persecution has occurred, the overwhelming majority of the accused fit the archetypical image of the witch as an elderly and widowed woman. Among the misfortunes attributed to witches are strange and inexplicable diseases, fatal illnesses, impotence, miscarriage, and unexplained or sudden fatalities. While fear of witches has driven many people to seek traditional remedies against bewitchment, here vigorous persecution of witches has, in recent years, led to the slaughter of scores of women suspected of practicing witchcraft.

Modern-day witch hunts are not confined to India, Papua New Guinea, and societies in Africa. Indeed, there is evidence that contemporary anti-witchcraft campaigns—ranging from isolated incidents by aggrieved parties to systematic patterns of witch persecutions culminating in the lethal victimization of putative witches—have been reported in countries in Southeast Asia, Central America, South America, North America, and Western Europe. In his survey of witch killings in societies around the globe, Behringer (2004) observed that since 1950 witch killings have been reported in Bolivia, Ecuador, Guatemala, Indonesia, Malaysia, Mexico, Peru, and France.

Disturbing Features of Contemporary Witch Hunts

At the most fundamental level, witchcraft persecution involves an accusation of spiritual predation against a putative witch denounced for deploying malevolent spirits to inflict misfortunes and death on others. Violent physical punishment, including death, is then visited on the alleged witch. Contemporary witchcraft persecutions are characterized by a number of distressing features. First, because witchcraft is an occult phenomenon, the alleged acts of spiritual predation that engender witch persecutions are virtually unverifiable by empirical means. The aggrieved parties and other witch labelers (e.g., fetish priests or traditional healers, members of the clergy) have no scientifically demonstrable means for establishing the verity of their claims. In many cases, suspected witches are manipulated, intimidated, or even tortured into confessing to outlandish and imaginary mystical activities. Indeed, studies on witchcraft in many societies have shown that many of the divinatory techniques designed to prove the guilt or innocence of suspected witches, as well as to substantiate claims of bewitchment, are fraught with duplicity, quackery, and charlatanism. Accusations of witchery and the concomitant brutalization and killing of alleged witches typically occur over vehement protestations of innocence by the accused witches. In the frenzied atmosphere of accusations and denials, innocent persons are brutalized, maimed, or even killed.

Another worrisome feature of contemporary witch hunts is the complete absence of due process of law. During the European witch hunts of 1450–1750, witches were executed after lengthy formal trials by ecclesiastical or secular courts (e.g., Roper 2004; Rowlands 2003). In much of the contemporary world where witch persecutions occur, no such trials precede witch killings. The reason is not difficult to fathom. In these societies, witchcraft is not recognized by state laws or criminal codes; witchcraft attributions and accusations are not entertained in state courts. Witch killings are therefore violent extrajudicial acts of vigilantism perpetrated by individuals and groups. Despite their flagrant illegality, witch hunts often generate only minor judicial sentences for the assailants, even in cases of homicide. In many of these societies, the torturing or killing of witches occurs in broad daylight and the perpetrators are well-known in the community. Meanwhile, witnesses to the crime follow a code of silence while law enforcement officers typically lament the absence of witnesses to aid their investigations. In some instances, law enforcement officers themselves pose a hindrance to effective juridical action. Like their compatriots, many police personnel charged with the investigation of witch hunts and the apprehension of criminal suspects hold firm beliefs in the dangers of witchcraft; those law enforcement officials who sympathize with perpetrators of violent witch persecution may even tacitly sabotage official investigations into the crime through insouciance and languidness with the result that their investigations result only in the production of weak evidence that invariably harms the prosecution's case. Similarly, jurors, judges, and other adjudicators in these trials are, themselves, operating under the prominence of witch beliefs. In some instances, community members organize to obtain legal representation for killers of accused witches, reinforcing the community's tacit consent of witch persecution. Where conviction occurs, killers receive only minimal sentences.

Another disquieting feature of witch hunts concerns the double victimization of survivors of such persecution. In some communities, survivors of witch hunts who manage to flee their attackers find themselves consigned to witches' sanctuaries marked by appalling economic and material conditions and social isolation. These individuals are forced to live the remainder of their lives in these sanctuaries, often without the companionship and support of family, friends, and well-wishers who themselves risk charges of witchcraft through their affiliation with the accused witch.

Despite the appalling features of contemporary persecutions, extralegal witch hunts characterized by brutal intimidation, torture, and murder proceed unabated in many communities around the world. Meanwhile, many victims continue to suffer the depredatory actions of their fellow citizens. These crimes warrant urgent systematic study, redress, and remediation, and is one of the central reasons I wrote this book.

Witches, Witchcraft, and Violence in Ghana examines witch persecutions in modern Ghana. It explores how local beliefs about witchcraft fuel violence against suspected witches. It addresses the nature and extent of witch hunts, the causes of witch hunts, and patterns of witch hunts in the society. The book is intended to fulfill two purposes. The first is to contribute to the stock of knowledge about witchcraft beliefs and witchcraft persecution by describing and analyzing modern-day witch hunts that periodically erupt in the contemporary world, using witchcraft-related violence in Ghana as a case study. Second, it is my hope that by highlighting the sufferings that arise from witchcraft accusations and persecutions, individuals and groups will be impelled to channel resources into confronting and eliminating the social, psychological, and physical violence that accompanies witchcraft accusations. This includes establishing policies and programs to assist with the reintegration of individuals ostracized or exiled from their communities as a result of witch persecution. A fundamental premise of this study is that we cannot begin to prevent or control the incidence of witch persecution without understanding its nature and causes.

For many years, both the popular and academic treatment of witchcraft in Ghana has focused almost exclusively on accused witches sequestered in witches' sanctuaries in northern Ghana (e.g., ActionAid 2012; Palmer 2010; Sosywen 2012). Clearly, the witches' camps are the most conspicuous expression of witchcraft persecution in Ghana but are undoubtedly not the only one. The witches' camps of northern Ghana constitute only a small part of the Ghanaian witchcraft landscape, however. Indeed, the witches' camps are a northern Ghana phenomenon only; they do not encompass patterns of witchcraft accusations, witch hunts, and the treatment of putative witches in the southern sector of the country where the majority of the Ghanaian population currently lives. A broader and more complete analysis of witchcraft in Ghana should include analysis of witchcraft beliefs and practices as well as the treatment of putative witches among Ghanaian ethnic groups in the southern sector of the country. For example, accused witches in southern Ghana are never transported to witches' camps located in the north. Instead, they are dealt with in their local communities or sent to Christian prayer camps and exorcists. In sum, focusing exclusively on witches' camps in northern Ghana leads to a skewed discussion and interpretation of witchcraft in Ghana. This book offers a comprehensive analysis of witch hunts in the entire country.

Plan of the Book

This introduction gives the reader insight to contemporary witch hunts in Ghana and throughout the African continent, as well as in India, Papua New Guinea, and other select countries around the world. This comparative, empirical excursus provides some evidence of the scope and nature of contemporary witch hunts.

Chapter 1 provides a general description of Ghanaian society in order to contextualize the phenomenon of witch hunts in Ghana. An understanding of and familiarity with Ghanaian society—including its people, cultures, values, and social and economic development—is necessary to understand the place of witchcraft beliefs and witchcraft-related violence in the society.

Chapter 2 is a comprehensive overview of witchcraft beliefs among Ghanaians, with a strong emphasis on Akan witchcraft beliefs. This chapter illustrates the extent to which witchcraft beliefs are entrenched in Ghanaian society. This is essential in fully understanding the forces that shape witchcraft-related violence.

Chapter 3 is an exploration of how witchcraft beliefs are acquired by Ghanaian citizens through various institutions involved in their socialization, or agencies of socialization. To this end, this chapter explores in detail the role of such major institutions as family, school, and the mass media in purveying witchcraft beliefs in the country.

Some Ghanaian songs focus directly on witchcraft while some give them a prominent place and yet others merely broach the subject. In chapter 4 the lyrical texts of eight songs with witchcraft references or themes are analyzed and used to illustrate this pattern. While such songs are performed to entertain, the songs unwittingly serve as mediums for reinforcing witchcraft ideology in the country.

There is a corpus of proverbs dealing with witchcraft in the Akan language. Analysis of these proverbs reveals a great deal about witchcraft beliefs in Akan society. To some extent, they are also another key influence in transmitting witchcraft beliefs and promoting attitudes in Ghanaian society. In chapter 5 thirty-four such proverbs are cited, translated, and their meanings given, demonstrating how they provide insights into witchcraft beliefs in the society.

In Ghana, imputations of witchcraft occasionally lead to charges of slander and prosecution of the accusers. In addition, witch killings and other forms of nonlethal violence against putative witches are prosecuted in the criminal courts. These witchcraft trials typically generate widespread public interest and extensive media coverage, providing information that further affirms Ghanaian witch lore. Chapter 6 explores four witchcraft-related trials that occurred in Ghana in recent times as well as their implications for socialization into Ghanaian witchcraft beliefs.

Although they are rare, in Ghana horrific murders are occasionally committed against putative witches. These types of homicides range from incidents involving a single victim and a single offender, to vigilante-style mob killings. In Chapter 7 case histories of thirty-five homicides perpetrated against accused witches are analyzed and used to illustrate how witchcraft beliefs contribute to fatal violence in the society.

In addition to homicide, other forms of violence and cruelties are suffered by some Ghanaians in the name of witchcraft persecution. Chapter 8 focuses on cases of nonlethal abuse meted out to persons accused of witchcraft. These abuses include threats with various weapons, physical assaults, and banishment from communities.

Women and girls are the most vulnerable to witchcraft accusations and associated violent victimization. Chapter 9 explores women's vulnerability to lethal and sublethal violence in witch hunts. The chapter explores the relationship between societal patterns of misogyny and gynophobia as well as female subordination and patriarchal arrangements in contributing to witchcraft accusations and witch hunts as a form of gendered violence.

A primary goal in writing this book was to give exposure to witchcraft related violence and to suggest strategies for curtailing its occurrence. The conclusion is a discussion of programs and policies that can be instituted to control witchcraft-related violence in Ghana with broader applicability to other countries.

Chapter 1

GHANA
The Research Setting

Located on the west coast of Africa, Ghana is a country occupying a total land area of 239,538 square kilometers (Ghana Statistical Service 1998). It is bordered on the east by Togo, the west by the Ivory Coast, the north by Burkina Faso, and the south by the Atlantic Ocean (see map 1.1.). Situated just north of the equator, the country has a tropical climate with average annual temperatures of about 26 degrees Celsius (about 79 degrees Fahrenheit). The average monthly temperature rarely falls below 25 degrees Celsius (77 degrees Fahrenheit). Spatial temperatures, rainfall, and vegetation vary depending on distance from the Atlantic coastline and land elevation. The northern part of the country, which is closer to the Sahara Desert, has a rainy season that commences in March and lasts until September; for the remainder of the year it is hot and arid with temperatures reaching as high as 38 degrees Celsius (100.4 degrees Fahrenheit). In the southern tier, two rainy seasons occur, spanning from April to July and again from September to October (Ghana Statistical Service 1999). Temperatures in the southern half of the country range from 21 to 32 degrees Celsius (70 to 90 degrees Fahrenheit).

History and Politics

From 1844 to March 6, 1957, a time of Portuguese, then Danish and British encroachment, the area that comprises Ghana was known by Europeans as

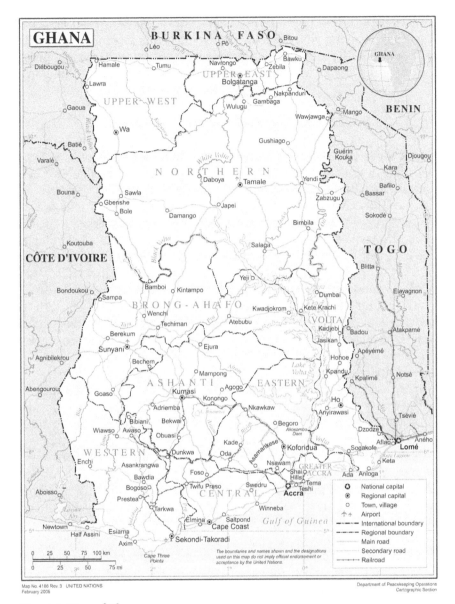

Map 1.1. Map of Ghana

the Gold Coast due to its rich reserves of the precious metal. It was chris-
tened Ghana following the attainment of political independence from
Britain on March 6, 1957. Ghana is currently a parliamentary democracy,
having experimented with scientific socialism in the late 1950s and early
1960s, series of military interregnums and dictatorships between 1966 and

1990, and a couple of recent civilian administrations (Adinkrah 1983, 1988; Osei 1999). Barring violence and coercive incidents associated with military putsches, the country has generally been spared the turbulent political crises and warfare that have wracked several countries in the region.

Population

According to the 2010 census, Ghana had a total population of 24,658,823, with females constituting 51.2 percent and males comprising 48.8 percent (Ghana Statistical Service 2012). The age structure of Ghanaian society reflects characteristics typical of other developing nations, with a disproportionately large representation of youth and a markedly smaller proportion among the aged (Ghana Statistical Service 2012). According to the 2010 census, the young (fifteen years old or younger) composed 48.9 percent of the population while the elderly population (sixty-five years or older) constituted a mere 4.6 percent (Ghana Statistical Service 2012).

The country is divided into ten administrative regions, each with its own headquarters or capital: the Greater Accra Region (Accra), the Ashanti Region (Kumasi), the Eastern Region (Koforidua), the Western Region (Sekondi-Takoradi), the Central Region (Cape Coast), the Brong-Ahafo Region (Sunyani), the Volta Region (Ho), the Northern Region (Tamale), the Upper East Region (Bolgatanga), and the Upper West Region (Wa). With urban locale defined as a community exceeding five thousand in population, about half of the Ghanaian population (49.1 percent) resides in rural communities (Ghana Statistical Service 2012). The Greater Accra and Ashanti Regions are the two most urbanized administrative regions in the country, with the Accra-Tema metropolitan area alone having a population of approximately 3 million people. The level of material poverty is higher and the overall standard of living, including access to a range of basic services, is significantly lower in rural communities than in urban areas.

The concentration of a range of goods and services, including government offices, hospitals, tertiary institutions, airports, entertainment centers, and other infrastructural facilities in the major cities have encouraged bristling migration into urban areas (Oppong 2004). As in many societies, the rural areas and small towns in Ghana are bastions of traditional cultural beliefs. Here, norms and values embedded in the culture are very strong and superstitions pervade many facets of daily life. Among rural dwellers, there is no demarcation between the spiritual and public realms as independent spheres. Religious beliefs and practices permeate the entire social fabric including marriage, education, economic affairs, and politics.

Ghana is a society characterized by ethnic, linguistic, and religious heterogeneity. The Akans are the numerically dominant linguistic and ethnic group, constituting 47.5 percent of the population. Other ethnically distinct and numerically significant groups include the Mole Dagbani (16.6 percent), the Ewe (13.9 percent), and the Ga-Dangme (7.4 percent) (Ghana Statistical Service 2012). While English remains the official language and the medium of instruction in schools, presently more than one hundred local languages and dialects are spoken. The main local languages are Akan, Ga, Ewe, Hausa, Nzema, and Dagbani.

Religious diversity in Ghana is reflected in the various traditional religions and organized churches with which Ghanaians identify. The religious landscape is mapped onto the country regionally. The northern part of Ghana is overwhelmingly Muslim, while in the rest of the country, Christian churches and traditional faiths predominate.

Education and Literacy

Literacy rates in the country are comparable to that of many developing nations. The most recent census indicates that 74.1 percent of the population aged eleven years and older is literate. Slightly higher than 67 percent of the total population is literate in English, while 53.7 percent is literate in at least one Ghanaian language (Ghana Statistical Service 2012). The percentage of children enrolled in primary and secondary school is undergoing rapid expansion (see Figure 1.1). Although available evidence shows a narrowing gender gap, literacy rates for females (68.5 percent) lag behind that of males (80.2 percent) (Ghana Statistical Service 2012). Based on the most recent census data, the level of illiteracy is higher for females than it is for their male counterparts in all regions of the country (Ghana Statistical Service 2012). Gender differences in literacy are a reflection of marked gender disparities in educational attainment. Females have a median of 2.3 years of formal schooling compared with males, who have 4.9 years of schooling (Ghana Statistical Service 1999). These disparities are most apparent at the tertiary level. During the 2008–9 academic year, women and men made up 37 percent (38,328) and 63 percent (64,220), respectively, of the total 102,548 students enrolled in Ghanaian public universities (Ministry of Education 2010). Available data indicate dramatic increases in enrollment in the country's universities in recent years. Official data show that total enrollment in the public universities rose from 93,973 in the 2007–2008 academic year to 102,543 in the 2008–9 academic year, representing an increase of 9 percent in one year (Ministry of Education 2010).

Figure 1.1. School Children

Economy

Four major occupations dominate Ghana's economic sector: agriculture and related work (49.2 percent), production and transport equipment work (15.6 percent), sales work (14.2 percent), and professional and technical work (8.9 percent) (Ghana Statistical Service 2002). As in many developing nations, unemployment is a major social problem, with nearly 11 percent of the economically active population without employment. And as in many developing nations, social programs that subsidize such goods and services as housing, food aid, health care, and child care are nonexistent.

Women constitute 51.4 percent of the working age group and 56.3 percent of the economically active population in Ghana. Data on the distribution of female economic activity and labor participation indicate that the overwhelming majority of working women, or 92 percent, are concentrated in nonwage labor or self-employment. By contrast, only 69 percent of working men are in nonwage employment (Asmah 2003). Females who do participate in the paid workforce are marginalized, confined primarily to low-paying occupations.

Emigration has been a major trend over the past three decades as Ghanaians seek economic opportunities elsewhere. It is the dream of many a Ghanaian to obtain a travel or immigrant visa to emigrate to a country abroad, with the United States, Canada, the United Kingdom, Germany, the Netherlands, Italy, and other European countries being the most preferred countries of destination (Oppong 2004). For those unable to emigrate to the United States or Europe, Asian countries such as Japan and South Korea, or other African countries such as South Africa, Zimbabwe, or Libya are considered viable alternatives to pursue better economic fortunes (Oppong 2004).

Communications

In 2001 Ghana had forty-nine FM stations, three shortwave stations, and ten television broadcast stations. Nearly every Ghanaian household owns at least one radio. In 2002 it was estimated that there were 12.5 million radio and wireless sets and 1.5 million television sets in the country. Internet usage in the country is relatively low. In 2009 it was estimated that there were only 1.3 million Internet users (The World Factbook 2012).

Health Indicators

As with most parts of the world, available data reveal that the life expectancy of Ghanaians has increased significantly in the past few decades, increasing from forty-five years in 1960 to fifty-seven years in 1998 (Ghana Statistical Service 1999). In 2009 the average life expectancy for females was 60.7 years, and for males it was 59.0 years (Ghana Health Service 2010). The infant mortality rate is fifty-seven per one thousand live births, while the current total fertility rate is 4.5 children per woman (Ghana Statistical Service 2002). High premium is placed on having children in Ghanaian society, with "prolific childbearing generally encouraged in traditional Ghanaian society" (Ghana Statistical Service 1999, 71). For instance, among Akans, when a wife bears a tenth child, she is traditionally honored in a ceremony in which a *badudwan* (sheep) and other special gifts are bestowed on her. In secular and religious rituals such as those accompanying puberty, marriage, and births, Ghanaians pray for fertility and plenty of children. The high value placed on prolific childbearing follows from a number of factors. First, in agrarian communities additional children are prized resources who provide additional farm-hands. Second, the absence of official social insurance programs means that children represent a source of security as future caregivers of elderly parents. Additionally, although attitudes are changing, in some communities large family size is emblematic of wealth and reflective of high social status. Conversely, childlessness, whether voluntary or otherwise, is frowned upon and a source of shame. Neither males nor females are inclined to espouse a desire to be childless and those who do are likely to face scorn and ridicule (Obeng 2004).

As is characteristic of many low-income countries, Ghana faces a paucity of basic medical facilities, personnel, and services. In 2009 the total number of doctors and nurses in the country was estimated at 2,033 and 24,974, respectively (Ghana Health Service 2010). In 2009 the physician-population ratio in Ghana was estimated at 1:11,929 with a corresponding nurse-population ratio of 1:971 (Ghana Health Service 2010). Psychiatric care is also limited (Ewusi-Mensah 2001; Laugharne and Burns 1999). There are currently only three psychiatric hospitals in the country. A recent report estimated that there was one psychiatric bed for every 15,000 Ghanaians and one qualified psychiatrist for every 1 million to 1.5 million residents (Appiah-Poku, Laugharne, Mensah, Osei, and Burns 2004; Ewusi-Mensah 2001).

The dearth of medical resources and personnel, and the concomitant high medical costs, coupled with a heavy reliance on traditional herbal medicine and orientation toward the occult and divination, have spawned a plethora of herbalists and myriad ritual specialists (Appiah-Kubi 1981). The scarcity of health-care resources contributes to heavy reliance on faith healers, occult practitioners, fetish priests, and diviners to diagnose and treat physical and psychiatric maladies. The predominance of rural residence in Ghana presents an additional complication in the delivery of health-care services. Presently, it is extremely difficult for rural residents to receive regular medical attention, further enabling the emergence of a thriving rural industry of herbalists, Christian faith-healing prophets, and other practitioners of traditional medicine, along with untrained persons posing as medical specialists who purport to have the ability to diagnose and treat all manner of illnesses (Obeng 2004).

With the advent and recent proliferation of Christian fundamentalist or Pentecostal churches, prayer houses and healing temples have also increased in many parts of the country. These are founded and staffed by spiritualists who claim to exorcise evil spirits, or who serve as earthly intermediaries between the Christian God and their human clients. These spiritualists often trace the etiology of disease to demonic affliction and spiritual oppression. Many Ghanaians who are faced with adversity utilize these services for physical, mental, and spiritual healing. Media reports exposing and condemning religious fraud have become ubiquitous ("Beware of False Prophets" 2000; Kyei-Boateng 2000; Mensah 2000; "Rawlings Slams at False Prophet" 1997).

It should be stressed that faith healers, herbalists and other traditional practitioners have large clienteles among the sick and afflicted, due to culturally based interpretations that attribute illness and misfortunes to supernatural forces. For example, Ghana reportedly has one of the highest fatality and injury rates related to road accidents in the world. While investigations of these fatal accidents typically identify such factors as poor road conditions, speeding, reckless driving, failure to use seat belts, and driving while under the influence of alcohol as causal factors, many Ghanaians will contend that the actual cause is supernatural (Mensah 2011). Similar explanations follow from any death of a young person and other calamities affecting individuals and communities.

Common Diseases and Illnesses

Ghana has the full spectrum of diseases characteristic of countries in Sub-Saharan Africa. According to the WHO, commonly occurring diseases in the country include anthrax, buruli ulcer, cerebral spinal meningitis, cholera, chicken pox, dysentery, infectious hepatitis, *dracunculiasi* (guinea worm), malaria, measles, pertussis or whooping cough, pneumonia, polio, *schistosomiasis* (bilharzias), *onchocerciasis* (river blindness), tetanus, trachoma, tuberculosis, typhoid, yellow fever, and venereal diseases. While the vast majority of preventable diseases in the society are waterborne, malnutrition and diseases acquired through insect bites continue to be common.

In 2010 Ghana's Ministry of Health identified malaria as one of the leading causes of death in the country (Ghana Health Service 2010). In 2001 an estimated 17,143 cases of malaria were reported for every 100,000 population (U.S. Agency for International Development [USAID] 2004). According to official figures, 3 million cases of malaria were recorded in the country during 2004 alone. Officials estimate that a total of 15,000 children under five and 2,000 pregnant women died of malaria during 2004 (Kofoya-Tetteh 2005). In children less than five years of age, it is estimated that 70 percent of deaths are caused by infections aggravated by malnutrition.

Maternal mortality claims the lives of thousands of Ghanaian women each year. The maternal mortality ratio (MMR) is defined as the number of maternal deaths per 100,000 live births. The 2010 Ghana Population and Housing Census established that Ghana's MMR was 485 per 100,000 live births (Ghana Statistical Service 2012). That means more than 33,000 Ghanaian women die annually in childbirth (Ghana Statistical Service 2012). Although almost all expectant women seek antenatal care from a health professional, only one in two women delivers in a health facility, and barely three in four women seek postnatal care (Ghana Health Service 2007).

Another major cause of morbidity and mortality among the Ghanaian populace is automobile accidents. According to 2004 statistics published by Ghana's National Road Safety Commission (NRSC), an organization created to reduce automobile accidents and fatalities, "six people die on Ghana's roads every day, while on average an additional 34 suffer injury daily in accidents involving over 21,000 vehicles" (NRSC 2005). Ghana's Ministry of Road and Transport announced that in 2004 a total of 649 persons died in 14,854 road accidents in the country ("Six Forty Nine Died" 2005). In 2007 2,043 people died in road accidents while 1,858 perished in road accidents in 2006 (Mirror Reporter 2008, 35). In 2008 it was estimated that 1,518 persons died in road accidents and 8,037 were injured (Yirenkyi 2009). A recent report noted, "The peak period of road accidents is during the Christmas period and at least one person is killed daily and scores more suffer incapacitating injuries in these accidents" ("Medical Association Advises" 2003). In 2001, Ghana's cabinet minister for Transportation and Communications noted, "Virtually every family in [this] country has been struck by sudden death and suffering due to a road accident" (NRSC 2005, 7). According to the NRSC, the country's "atrocious road safety record compared to other African countries" that claims 2 percent of the country's GDP annually is caused by a multiplicity of factors: speeding, driving while intoxicated, not wearing seat belts and helmets, inability by drivers and pedestrians to read or interpret road signs correctly, and a lack of emergency medical care (NRSC 2005).

Alcohol and Illicit Drug Use

It is reported that a large and growing number of Ghanaians are currently using illicit drugs (Salia 2009). The magnitude and the rising trend in the illicit production, demand for, and traffic in narcotic drugs and psychotropic substances, as well as the threat they pose to the health and welfare of Ghanaians have been stressed in the local media (e.g., Salia 2009). According to an official in the country's Narcotic and Drug Control Board, "In Ghana today, drug abuse has ceased to be an urbanization issue, but a nationwide canker eating deeper and deeper into the fabric of our society. Drug consumption has become so rampant in almost every educational institution in Ghana, filtering down from tertiary institutions to the junior high schools in the country; indiscipline at home, in schools, in society are all products of drug abuse" (quoted in Salia 2009, 16).

Despite the growing problem, enforcement agencies face inadequate resources, both human and logistical, to deal with the problem. This is compounded by the fact that most drug users decline to seek medical, or especially psychiatric, interventions given the stigma attached to visiting psychiatric institutions as well as the attribution of drug-related psychiatric symptoms to supernatural causes (Ohene-Asiedu 2008b). Statistics at the nation's psychiatric hospitals are striking. According to one report, out of the 594 drug-related cases admitted to the Accra Psychiatric Hospital in 2007, 400 were cannabis-related, 141 alcohol-related, and 53 involved cocaine and heroin use (Salia 2009). It is notable that between 2007 and 2008 the Pantang Hospital, well known for providing extensive psychiatric care, recorded an increase of 88 percent in the number of admissions directly related to substance abuse (Ohene-Asiedu 2008b).

Mental Illness and Mental Health Services in Ghana

According to official estimates, in 2010 about 2.4 million of Ghana's roughly 25 million people suffered from some form of mental illness (Awenva et al. 2010). Despite official acknowledgment of an increase in the diagnoses of mental health and neurological disorders in the population, health services for the mentally ill remain scarce (Awenva et al. 2010; Ewusi-Mensah 2001; Ministry of Health 2007; Wozuame 2010). According to one estimate, only 2 percent of the mentally ill population in the country receives professional mental health care treatment (Atitsogbe 2014). Concurrently, several people with psychiatric and neurological disorders such as schizophrenia, manic depression, neurosis, epilepsy, and other severe and common mental disorders do not receive any medical care (Yeboah 2009). Outpatient psychological counseling services for those suffering from emotional distress and minor psychiatric disorders are severely limited, while the country has no nationally based suicide prevention programs (Adinkrah 2011a, 2011b, 2012a, 2012b; Awenva et al. 2010).

The dearth of psychiatric services available to the mentally ill is attributable to insufficient resources. According to one estimate, only 1 percent of the country's health budget is allocated to mental health care (British Medical Association 2013). There are at present only three psychiatric hospitals in the country, all of them located in major cities in the southern part of the country (Edmonds and Morley 2010; Ministry of Health 2007). The uneven distribution of psychiatric services has serious implications for accessibility as roughly 50 percent of the Ghanaian population currently lives in rural communities. Compounding issues of accessibility is the scarcity of service personnel. There is currently a national shortage

of psychiatric doctors, psychiatric nurses, mental health and clinical social workers, clinical psychologists, and other mental health–care providers (Awenva et al. 2010; Ewusi-Mensah 2001; Ministry of Health 2007). In
March 2009 it was reported that there were only four full-time and eleven
part-time psychiatric doctors working in the country's public health sector (Yeboah 2009). In 2008 the country's health ministry reported that
there were only five hundred psychiatric nurses for the entire country, a
ratio of one psychiatric nurse for every 44,000 people. That same year, the
government ministry reported the ratio of consultant psychiatrists to citizens in the country to be 1:2,000,000 (Ministry of Health 2007). The shortage of mental health practitioners is partly attributable to insufficient
financial remuneration and difficult working conditions. Additionally, it is
attributable to the stigmatization of the mentally ill in the society, which
reportedly extends to practitioners working with mental health patients.

Mental health–care delivery in the country is also hampered by a shortage of essential psychotropic pharmaceuticals, basic psychiatric medicines,
and other important medical supplies (Awenva et al. 2010). To illustrate,
in April 2010 all three public psychiatric hospitals in the country experienced an acute shortage of major psychiatric drugs (Yeboah 2010). Individually or collectively, these shortages can result in lack of treatment or
undertreatment of certain psychiatric illnesses, premature termination of
treatment, clinician frustrations, patient dissatisfaction, delays in treatment, and the resort to alternative and often ineffectual treatment modalities (Oheneba-Mensah 2010; Osei 2010). In a few instances, drug shortages
resulted in nonlethal and lethal assaults on residential patients and medical staff by violent inmates (Yeboah 2010).

Many Ghanaians attribute psychiatric illness and neurological impairments to a range of malevolent supernatural forces, including witchcraft
and sorcery (Ewusi-Mensah 2001; Ohene-Asiedu 2008a). Others attribute
mental disorders to family curses, while others consider psychiatric impairments as evidence of ancestral or divine punishment for violations
of social or cultural taboos. For this reason, some place greater faith in
spiritual cures than in medical interventions directed by health-care professionals. Family members of the psychiatrically impaired often dispatch
mentally ill relatives to residential Christian prayer camps, traditional
herbalists, fetish priests, traditional healers, and a myriad of magicoreli-
gious functionaries (Clemence 2009). Some, however, resort to traditional
and indigenous healers because of the unavailability or unaffordability of
the services in medical facilities. Surveys of treatment modalities at these
healing centers reveal flagrant human rights abuses, including physical
assaults, forced confessions, and mental coercion. Some mentally ill patients are reportedly shackled in restraints, flogged, and forced to fast or

ingest sand and other substances. Many patients are referred to modern psychiatric hospitals only when their conditions worsen or when it is determined that their condition is not amenable to spiritual or traditional curative regimens (Vervynckt 2009).

Given the stigma that surrounds psychiatric disorders, those suffering from mild forms of psychiatric illness (e.g., depression, anxiety) often shun treatment at both modern and traditional treatment centers. The patients that typically present at these facilities are those exhibiting violent or paranoid behavior. For overtly ill patients who receive treatment at psychiatric hospitals, recovery, wellness, and discharge are associated with, and compounded by, stigmatization and rejection. Oftentimes, extended family relations and society at large refuse to accept their return to their communities, forcing their continued stay in these facilities. In January 2010 it was reported that the Accra Psychiatric Hospital—the country's premier and largest psychiatric hospital—had 1,200 patients on admission although the facility was built to accommodate only 600 (Gobah 2010; Osei 2010). A significant proportion constituted discharged patients refused by kinsfolk. Those who attempt to return to society face enormous challenges with employment, given massive prejudice and discrimination against the mentally ill ("Sad Case of Cured Mental Patients" 2011; Salifu 2010).

Ghana's North-South Developmental Divide

Ghana is divided into two major geographical parts—a relatively developed South and an undeveloped North. This geographic divide coincides with major differences in health, infrastructural development, and socioeconomic indicators. The developmental chasm between the North and the South has been attributed to myriad factors. These include colonial policies that targeted the southern sector for development and neglected the northern sector, as well as social and economic marginalization by successive political regimes since independence. Given its proximity to the Sahara Desert, the northern part of the country is also affected by severe climatic conditions such as sparse rainfall and shorter growing seasons. These factors contribute to periodic droughts, crop failures, and famine. Now, as in the past, the three major regions of the north exhibit higher rates of unemployment than the relatively affluent South. In response to this, each year many young men and women abandon the harsh conditions of the North and migrate to the South in pursuit of employment and a higher standard of living. Statistics on domestic migration patterns in the country show that the Upper East and Upper West Regions, located in the north, are among the four administrative regions in the country characterized by the highest net outmigration (Ghana Statistical Service 2002).

The North also exceeds the South in levels of illiteracy. With a national illiteracy rate for persons fifteen years and older estimated at 46.9 percent, the three regions of the north surpass the national level with a 2000 census data indicating illiteracy rates for the Northern, Upper East, and Upper West Regions as 78.7 percent, 78.1 percent, and 75.5 percent, respectively (Ghana Statistical Service 2002). In terms of urban residence, the 2000 census established that 43.8 percent of the national population was living in urban areas. The three regions of the north were the least urbanized, with 26.6 percent, 15.7 percent, and 17.5 percent of the Northern, Upper East, and Upper West Regions, respectively, being defined as urban (Ghana Statistical Service 2002). These three regions also recorded the highest average household size (Ghana Statistical Service 1998). While the 2010 census reported a national average household size of 4.4 persons, the three regions of the north—the Upper East, the Upper West, and the Northern Regions—had household sizes of 5.8, 6.2, and 7.7 persons, respectively (Ghana Statistical Service 2012).

Northern Ghana continues to lag behind southern Ghana across all health indices. Life expectancy is considerably shorter and infant mortality is relatively high. Poor conditions of sanitation contribute to dramatically higher incidences of infectious and parasitic diseases. Medical disorders and diseases currently endemic to the North, and far less common in the South, include buruli ulcer, cerebrospinal meningitis, elephanthiasis, guinea worm, hookworms, hydrocele, measles, mumps, polio, river blindness, roundworms, sleeping sickness, tuberculosis, and whooping cough. Available data indicate that the Northern, Upper East, and Upper West Regions of the country also have the highest rates of malaria and cholera (Alhassan 2004). According to another report, "The percentage of stunted children in urban Upper East Region (60.7 percent) is about five times that of urban Greater Accra Region (12.3 percent)" (Ghana Statistical Service 1998, 36).

The health crisis of the North is exacerbated and perpetuated by limited access to medical care. Health-care professionals such as doctors, surgeons, nurses, psychiatrists, and pharmacists tend to refuse postings to public hospitals and government facilities in the North because of the harsh climatic conditions, lack of social amenities, and undeveloped infrastructure (Quaye and Nunoo 2009). In 2009 it was estimated that the doctor-patient ratio in the Upper West Region was 1:91,083 and 1:29,000 in the Upper East Region, although the national average was 1:13,000 (Beacom 2008; Quaye and Nunoo 2009). In one study, it was found that "While more than half of Ghanaians take 30 minutes or less to reach the nearest health facility, about 80 percent of households in rural Northern, Upper East and Upper West regions have to travel over 30 minutes before reaching the nearest health facility" (Ghana Statistical Service 1998, 33–34). The percentage of children born at a health facility is lowest in the Northern Region (8.2 percent) and highest in the Ashanti Region (54.3 percent) (Ghana Statistical Service 1998, 35). While 26 percent of children under five years old in Ghana were underweight in 1997, the proportion of underweight children was highest in the three regions of the north, with about 50 percent of the children in both rural and urban Upper East Region being underweight (Ghana Statistical Service 1998, 37).

Statistical indicators that reflect general living standards reveal a markedly lower quality of life in the North than in the south. The north faces a relative lack of potable water. Based on 1997 data, only 1 percent of Upper West residents and 1.8 percent of Northern Region residents had access to a pipe-borne, protected well, or tap water supply (Ghana Statistical Service 1998, 50). As was noted in one study, "[T]he south is endowed with many rivers and lakes unlike the north, where the main natural reservoirs are dams, whose sites are determined by their ability to withstand the dry season rather than nearness to the community" (Ghana Statistical Service 1998, 50). Educational disparities are also dramatic between the North and the South. Students in the three regions of the north have only minimal access to secondary and tertiary education and experience the highest school dropout rates (Ghana Statistical Service 1998).

A number of traditional cultural practices in the northern part of the country impact the quality of life for women and girls. These include female genital mutilation, child betrothal, child marriage, polygyny, and leviratic marriage. According to the 2000 national census, polygynous unions were more common in the three northern regions than any other part of the country.

The harsh living conditions in the north are greatly compounded by periodic outbreaks of internecine warfare based on interethnic conflicts, and protracted chieftaincy disputes (Kpiebaya 2009). Of particular notice is the Nanumba-Konkomba ethnic conflict and the Yendi chieftaincy crisis. In the past two decades, periodic outbreaks of violent conflict have claimed several lives, creating a social, political, and economic climate that has stymied development. In 1994 a land conflict between two major ethnic groups, the Kokombas and the Nanumbas, resulted in the massacre of 2,000 people and the displacement of 150,000.

The northern regions have been the sites of the worst excesses of violence committed against suspected witches in contemporary Ghana (Adinkrah 2004, 2011d; Palmer 2010; Round Table Conference on the Treatment of Suspected Witches in Northern Ghana 1998). The use or threatened use of force against putative witches is commonplace. Ruthless attempts to extirpate witchcraft from the communities often fuel mob lynchings of suspected witches. The northern regions are also home to the largest witches' sanctuaries in the country. Many a suspected witch is lynched without a trial. In 1997, during a massive cerebrospinal meningitis epidemic, the disease and its spread were attributed to witchcraft. That year, organized and unorganized groups of youths and other aggrieved persons tried to quell the disease by using swift and brutal force against those suspected of being witches. Natural disasters such as droughts, famine, and disease epidemics are often imputed to witches.

Status of Women

The social, economic, and political circumstances of Ghanaian women vary from one ethnic group to another. Among patrilineal groups such as the Ewe and ethnic groups of the North, patriarchal values are more staunchly emphasized, with the subsequent subordinate status of women in their social relationships with men. Conversely, women of the matrilineal Akan-speaking groups (e.g., Ashantis and Kwahus) have the relatively higher social status and greater economic independence that come with the organization of descent and inheritance around the matriliny. However, overall and across ethnic groups, Ghanaian women occupy a subordinate social status vis-à-vis their male counterparts in virtually every social domain (Amoah 1987; Latimore 1997). Indeed, there is a general cultural expectation that women demonstrate respect, obedience, and acquiescence toward men, particularly in respect to their husbands' wishes and demands.

In Ghana, as in many societies, gender-role socialization commences at birth, continues throughout the lifecycle, and involves all the major institutions of the society. Cross-gender play is met with disapproval. Gender-norm transgressions are negatively sanctioned; children who deviate from stereotypical gendered behavior are punished through vituperative teasing and name-calling. Among the Akans, girls who resist or rebel against traditional gender expectations are called ɔbaabarima (the equivalent of the Western tomboy), while males who set out to challenge or reject traditional men's gender-role patterns are mockingly referred to as ɔbaafadie (sissy). Boys and girls are expected to pursue academic subjects and occupations considered appropriate for their gender. For instance, males are stereotyped as being innately more proficient in mathematics than girls. Females who excel in mathematics and the physical sciences in school are often branded as witches (Wojtas 1998). Women who attempt to enter nontraditional professions such as medicine, engineering, and architecture are similarly labeled.

Differential socialization perpetuates a highly gendered division of labor (Amoah 1987; Oheneba-Sakyi 1999). Women's activities are centered on the domestic realm, with primary responsibilities in raising children, preparing meals, laundering clothes, and performing other household chores (Chao 1999; Oheneba-Sakyi 1999). The significance of the domestic role in Ghana is suggested by the concerns of women troubled about their future prospects for marriage if they have not wed by the age of thirty. By contrast, men are expected to be the primary economic providers of the family and heads of the household, with activities centered on engagement in the public sphere (Oheneba-Sakyi 1999). This has not precluded women's participation in the labor force. However, women are overrepresented in nonwage labor, or the informal sectors of the economy, such as in small-scale farming; market vending of produce, prepared foodstuffs, cloth, and other goods; or as bakers, seamstresses, and hairdressers (Chao 1999; Clark 2001; Okine 1993; Prah 1996). Those in salaried or wage employment are concentrated in low-paying, temporary, and part-time jobs, particularly in stereotypically female occupations such as nursing, teaching, and low-level clerical work (Chao 1999; Prah 1996). Very few women currently occupy upper-echelon positions in the civil service. The predominance of women in the highly volatile informal sector, marked by unpredictability of earnings and low-wage occupations, coupled with high female unemployment rates, contributes to the economic marginalization of women, many of whom must rely on husbands, common-law partners, boyfriends, or male relatives for material support or financial supplementation (Chao 1999; Pellow 1978).

Polygyny, or marriage involving a husband and two or more wives, is a culturally accepted practice among many ethnic groups in the country. The 1998 Ghana Demographic and Health Survey (Ghana Statistical Service 1999) revealed that 23 percent of married women in the country were in a polygynous union in 1998 compared with 28 percent in 1993. The data further show that older women were "more likely to be one of several wives to a man than younger women" (Ghana Statistical Service 1999, xxi). Available data show that polygyny is more likely to occur in rural than in urban areas (Ghana Statistical Service 1999). While many Ghanaians are revising their views on the practice, having multiple wives is still denotative of male power, prestige, and virility.

Currently, intrafamily decision-making processes are dominated or controlled by men. Aggressive actions between spouses or other intimates, with males dominating as perpetrators and women as victims, occur with relative frequency, occasionally culminating in femicide, or lethal victimization of women (Adjetey and Ofori-Boadu 2000; Adinkrah 2008a, 2008b, 2008c, 2012, 2014a, 2014b; Ampofo 1993; Appiah and Cusack 1999; Offei-Aboagye 1994; King 2001). An estimated one in three Ghanaian women is a victim of intimate-partner violence (Donkor 2000). Rape and other forms of sexual violence against women are widely reported in the local dailies (Armah 1999; Clay 1999; Hudson 1999; Mensa-Bonsu 1994). A sexual double standard prevails. Female adulterous behavior is disapproved. Infidelity by females, real or imagined, is a common complaint in divorces and is commonly offered by battering and uxoricidal men to justify their aggression (Adinkrah 2008a, 2008b, 2008c, 2012, 2014a, 2014b).

Among some ethnic groups, oppressive cultural traditions and exploitive norms of patriarchy conjoin to bolster male domination and female subordination. In the northern part of the country, clitoridectomy and other forms of female genital mutilation persist despite their present legal proscription (Amuzu 2000; Dorkenoo 1994; Odoi 2002; Odoi, Brody, and Elkins 1997; Osei-Boateng 1998). In recent years women's political activity and responsive governmental legislative actions have contributed to the outlawing of the *trokosi* system, which placed young girls in total servitude to traditional religious shrines (Boaten 2001). However, anecdotal evidence suggests that this practice also continues. There are other cultural practices that reinforce the subordinate status of females (Appiah and Cusack 1999; de Graft-Johnson 1994). Among some ethnic groups, following the death of a husband the surviving widow undergoes ritualistic baths in cold water three times daily as part of the mourning rites (Appiah and Cusack 1999). Subtle pressures are brought to bear on the grieving widow to shave off the hair on her head, don the traditional mourning colors (red and black) for a year, and to avoid wearing earrings and sandals on her feet. In some communities, the woman is forbidden from remarrying for a designated period of time and to abstain from sexual relations for a period of up to two years. There are no such corresponding requirements for a widower (Shroeder, Danquah, and Mate-Kole 2003).

Ghanaian women are significantly underrepresented in government and in political decision-making, comprising only 9 percent of elected parliamentary representatives and 3 percent of membership in district assemblies (Asmah 2003; Sam 2004). Compared with men, only a handful of women serve as cabinet ministers. Many commentators conclude that women are equally marginalized in the decision-making associated with traditional institutions, including the family. In 2001 the New Patriotic Party government established the MOWAC to promote a "harmonious society with equity and equality between the male and female genders and in which the survival, protection and development of the child are guaranteed" (Asmah 2003, 27).

Status of Children

Children make up a sizable proportion of Ghana's population. In 2010 48.9 percent of the population was aged newborn to fourteen years old (Ghana Statistical Service 2012). Ghanaian society places a high premium on childbearing. Voluntary childlessness is unknown while barrenness in females and sterility and sexual impotence in males are regarded as pitiable conditions (Agyekum 1996; Mends 1994; Wiafe 2008). The high social esteem accorded to childbearing contributes to the fertility rate of 4.5 births per woman reported in the 2000 census (Ghana Statistical Service 2002). As noted previously, among the Akans, a woman who gives birth to her tenth child is honored during the *badudwan* ceremony, a public ceremony in which a sheep that is offered by the husband to congratulate the wife, is slaughtered, amidst elaborate celebratory festivities (Enos 2002).

Despite the high regard for fertility, children in Ghana occupy a subordinate social status vis-à-vis adults in virtually every domain of social life. Among the Akans, for example, children are regarded more as the property of their parents and members of their *abusua* than as distinct and autonomous individuals with special needs, rights, and entitlements that must be given priority (Mends 1994). Throughout the society, there is a universal expectation that children demonstrate respect, obedience, submissiveness, and acquiescence toward adults at all times. Most Ghanaian families are patriarchal, with fathers holding the final authority and exercising control over the social, economic, and physical well-being of the wife and children (Sarpong 1974). The lower social status of children finds expression in the lesser allocation of such domestic resources as clothing, food, and other provisions toward children in the household (Sarpong 1974; UNICEF 2002).

Corporal punishment is a common form of discipline in many Ghanaian homes. It is widely believed that enforcing physical forms of discipline is a parental duty and that sparing the rod will only spoil the child (Ashiagbor 2008). Despite a statutory prohibition in the public school system, the use of corporal punishment is rife within schools. This is particularly the case in rural regions of the country where flogging is the primary method of discipline. Students who are tardy, disobey teachers' instructions, demonstrate moral lapses, or perform poorly academically are subject to severe physical punishment (Ashiagbor 2008). Excessive cases of corporal punishment have resulted in serious injuries and even deaths (Kyei-Boateng 2009).

Reports of child neglect and abandonment are commonplace (Afrifa 1994; Ansong 2009; Plange-Rhule 2008). Current rates of births to unwed mothers are also high and many noncustodial fathers fail to provide cash and material resources for their wards. Children who come from large and indigent families often suffer hunger and other deprivations due to stretched economic and financial resources. Frequent media reports regarding neonaticidal and infanticidal killings, child abandonments, child neglect, and the actual sale of children further reflect the difficulties that confront some parents in providing for the maintenance and care of their children (Afrifa 1994; Ansong 2009; Owusu 2010; Plange-Rhule 2008). Due to poverty and financial constraints, some children drop out of school early and are enlisted by their parents or guardians to sell wares or take up a trade to contribute to the family's maintenance (Ansong 2009; Dykes 2008).

There is a common practice in Ghana whereby rural parents send biological children to reside with extended kin in urban areas. While some parents do this out of conviviality of extended kin relations and to strengthen extended kin ties, others are motivated more by material interests. Unable to materially provide for their children, these parents choose to select affluent or at least financially better-off relatives for this practice. These kinfolk can include grandparents, aunts, uncles, and other family members. Some children who have been sent to live with kin to further their education and to take advantage of economic prospects in the cities actually find themselves forced to abandon their schooling as relatives transform them into domestic servants, consigning them to cooking, cleaning, child care, and other domestic chores for the household. Other children are forced to assist their relatives as trading vendors, peddling everything from ice water on the streets to yams in the market. In some arrangements, parents actually formally hire out their children to wealthier nonkin as domestic servants. While some children fare well under these arrangements, there are several reports of such children suffering material neglect, as well as physical, emotional, psychological, and sexual abuse at the hands of relatives. Many children who are sent to live with relatives are second-class citizens in these homes, easily becoming victims of scapegoating for myriad problems in the home. In these instances, they also readily become victims of witchcraft accusations.

Official law enforcement data, as well as media reports indicate a growing incidence of rape, defilement, incest and other forms of sexual assault against children (Akyea 2009; Atakpa 2009). At present, child sexual abuse constitutes a significant proportion of all crimes committed against children. Assailants include parents, relatives, and strangers (Akyea 2009). Cases of adolescent prostitution have also been reported (Akyea 2009; Aziz 2008; Boateng 2009).

Although the country's constitution guarantees children protections and safeguards against abuse and exploitation (Dankwa 1994), certain traditional, cultural, and social practices subvert these ideals. For example, Article 28, Section 3 of the 1992 constitution states that "a child shall not be subjected to torture or other cruel, inhuman or degrading treatment or punishment" (Constitution of the Republic of Ghana 1992). However, there is evidence that children suffering from severe physical disabilities and mental disorders are stigmatized and regarded as expendable by their families; such children are occasionally abandoned in public places to die, with some of them rescued and sent to orphanages (Oliver-Commey 2001). Traditional cultural practices that physically and painfully mark or denigrate children include tribal scarification and skull shaping. Some practices that specifically disenfranchise female children include infant betrothal, child marriage, female genital mutilation, and *trokosi,* or the placement of young girls in servitude to fetish shrines to atone for the misdeeds of families and relations (Afrifa 1994; Duodu 2008). Meanwhile, the government lacks the requisite resources to establish programs to ensure the effective realization of constitutional provisions and other legislative enactments that protect children (Dowuona-Hammond 1994; UNICEF 2002).

Status of the Elderly

Consistent with demographic trends in many societies across the globe, Ghanaian society is currently experiencing a graying of its population. The most recent census report indicates that the segment of the population comprising persons sixty-five years and older rose from 4 percent in 1984 to 5.3 percent in 2000 but fell slightly to 4.7 percent in 2010 (Ghana Statistical Service 2002, 2012). Further evidence of the aging of the population is reflected in the rise in the median age of the population from 18.1 years to 19.4 years over the same period. Both data reflect improvements in health care and life expectancy. The higher female life expectancy raises the median age of the female population to 19.8 years compared with the 18.9 years for males (Ghana Statistical Service 2002).

Concordant with the spatial distribution of the general population, the elderly population is primarily rural (Darkwa 2000). Although there is evidence of occasional migratory flows toward urban centers as some elderly join adult children residing in urban areas, this phenomenon is far less common than aging urbanites returning to the rural hometowns and villages following retirement or during their twilight years. Whether in urban or rural settings, the vast majority of elderly Ghanaians live in multigenerational or extended family households. Given the combination of polygyny and gerontogamy, some elderly men live with younger brides and children in nuclear family settings. Elderly women tend to live with their spouses, or if widowed or divorced, reside in extended-family house-holds with their older children and their families. Nursing and retirement houses, assisted living facilities, and other forms of institutional care for the elderly found in industrialized nations are virtually nonexistent in Ghana.

Throughout Ghana, there are ethnic communities that, historically, have valued their elders' purported wisdom that comes with lifelong ex-perience. The elders are also valued as the guardians and keepers of oral tradition, history, and cultural heritage, and as sources of counsel for youth (van der Geest 2002). As repositories of history and accumulated knowledge, they are regarded as human archives or libraries to be con-sulted for knowledge on matters of cultural importance to the group. In Ghana today it is not uncommon for people to travel long distances to go to the rural areas to consult elderly relatives about some aspects of historical, religious, or technical knowledge. Many Ghanaian youths seek advice from elderly relatives about marital, health, and nutritional con-cerns. The importance accorded the elderly in this realm is epitomized in the oft-repeated Akan proverb, "Sɛ wonni ɔpanyin a due" (those without an elder suffer), emphasizing the poverty of not having an elderly relative.

Other ways in which communities pay homage to the traditional wis-dom of elders is through the forms of gerontocratic governance found in many ethnic communities around the country. Particularly in rural settings and traditional institutions, elders tend to occupy the executive, adminis-trative, and judiciary positions of the society. As is evident in Ghanaian chieftaincies and traditional practices pertaining to them, in selecting the Akan chief preference is often given to the most mature and physically active adult male candidate. Additionally, in day-to-day governance and administration, the chief is assisted by a council of elders that invariably comprise chronologically aged men. Such tendency toward gerontocratic rule finds evidence in modern politics and national governance where many leaders are aged fifty years or older.

Still, it is possible to romanticize the position of the elderly when dis-cussing their respected role in traditional settings. Increasing modern-ization, Westernization, the spread of formal education, the introduction of the printed word, computers, and other electronic media have signifi-cantly altered the emphasis placed on traditional knowledge and, hence the place of elders as repositories of that knowledge (Brown 1999). Rapid technological change is diffusing into the developing nations. The emer-gence of new forms of knowledge and increasingly easier access to this knowledge about complex social issues has presented avenues for youths to question the validity of traditional beliefs about religion, kingship, and ritual.

The economic status of the Ghanaian elderly is precarious in several respects. The statutory retirement age in Ghana is sixty years old and although retirees are eligible for a pension from the Social Security and National Insurance Trust, pensions and retirement payments are meager, contributing to a significant reduction in their standard of living. Meanwhile, for those who labored in the informal sector such as farming and fishing, there is no income at all following cessation of those economic activities. Needless to say, old age and attendant physical problems make it impossible for the elderly to engage in economically productive activities.

Currently, there are no welfare services such as supplemental income, food, health-care, and housing assistance for the elderly and other categories of deprived populations to address their material needs. In the absence of these social security or social insurance programs, the elderly poor often face a bleak future as they age. Many elderly people slowed down by age and unable to work at jobs they did in the past are relegated to the economic margins of society, forced to rely on the financial support of their adult children and other relatives. However, given the current socioeconomic realities that include unemployment, inflation, rising costs of living, and general economic malaise, the elderly are increasingly being regarded as burdensome by their children and other care providers (Brown 1999). Even among the elderly, there is a growing perception of being forsaken and abandoned by their children and other kindred (van der Geest 2002).

Elderly females suffer the double jeopardy of being female and aged, a status characterized by greater social, economic, and political marginalization. Following from limited work experience in the formal employment sector, many women have little to no guaranteed income or financial resources by the time they reach old age and are entirely dependent on spouses, children, grandchildren, and other familial support for economic maintenance. Additionally, old age fails to confer on elderly females the same political advantage garnered by older males. Older females find no concurrent representation in governance or on governing boards of elders in the community. Lower rates of literacy among the aged female population also hampers their active participation in civic society. As previously noted, the vast proportion of the illiterate population in Ghana is female while most of the female elderly population is illiterate. While they are revered, respected, and sought out for their counseling roles and assistance in socialization of youth within their families, they are also vulnerable to accusations of witchcraft when regarded as excessively meddlesome, inquisitive, and loquacious.

Although less youth-oriented than many Western societies, Ghanaian society is one in which ageism and other ageist biases are growing. Ageist beliefs are expressed in jokes and negative labels and terms. Elderly people are, for example, described as *kolo* (old-fashioned), rigid, accident-prone, loquacious, cantankerous, evil, and witchlike. Contrary to popular assumptions, even in a traditionally oriented, developing society like Ghana, the elderly do not relish the prospects of growing old. In a recent study, Brown (1999, 112) observed that over 76 percent of a sample of elderly Ghanaians characterized their experience as marked by hardships and misery, a period of financial problems, a period of social ostracism, inadequate care, lack of respect, ill-health, pain, weakness, and being a burden on others. Estimate of depression in the general Ghanaian population has been put at 20 percent (Flaherty et al. 1982, cited in Ingram, Scott, and Hamill 2009). Available research suggests that depression is one of the most prevalent psychiatric disorders in the older adult population of Ghana (McCarthy n.d.).

The universal drive to maintain a youthful appearance finds empirical support in Ghana where hair dyes are used liberally to alter visible signs of aging. The saying "yoomo bɛ Ga" (there is no old lady in Accra) reflects the pervasive practice of covering gray hair by using hair dyes.

The Disabled in Ghana

According to the 2010 Ghana Population and Housing Census, 3 percent of the Ghanaian population is afflicted with some form of disability. Numerically speaking, this is 739,764 persons in a population of 24,658,823. In terms of gender breakdown, the census established that 52.5 percent of the disabled population was female while 47.5 percent was male. Regarding type of disability, the census information indicated that visual or sight impairment was the dominant form of disability with 40.1 percent of the disabled population suffering from this form of disability. The next most common form of disability was physical challenges, which characterize 25.4 percent of the disabled population. Other forms of disability enumerated in the census data included emotional/behavioral disability (18.6 percent), intellectual disability (15.2 percent), hearing disability (15.0 percent), speech impairment (13.7 percent), and other forms of disability (10.4 percent). Regarding the spatial distribution of disabled persons in the country, the 2010 census data show that five of the ten administrative regions of the country exceeded the national average in terms of the percentage of the population living within the administrative region. These were Central Region (3.4 percent), Eastern Region (3.6 percent), Upper West Region (3.7 percent), Upper East Region (3.8 percent), and Volta Region (4.3 percent) (Ghana Statistical Service 2012).

In Ghana the disabled population suffers considerable social stigmatization. Disability is commonly believed to be symptomatic of supernatural punishment imposed by the ancestral spirits and other deities of the land for infractions committed by the afflicted individuals or their forebears (e.g., parents, grandparents). In other instances, disability is held to be evidence of a generational curse imposed by an aggrieved person on the family or lineage of the disabled person. Many Ghanaians also ascribe disability to bewitchment, in which case a witch has used a spirit medium to afflict the impairment on the disabled person.

Although the human and civil rights of the disabled population of Ghana are guaranteed by the constitution of Ghana and the international conventions of which Ghana is signatory, in practice the disabled population faces substantial prejudice and discrimination from relatives, neighbors, and the larger communities of which they are a part. In some ethnic communities, disabled persons are said to be evil or spirit persons that must be avoided at all costs. In some communities newly born disabled infants are surreptitiously murdered and discarded. Some disabled infants are poisoned or simply discarded in the bush or thrown onto refuse dumps to perish (Oppong-Ansah 2011). Sometimes the pressure to eliminate the child comes from community members who see the child as an evil contaminant capable of infecting the entire community. Some families of disabled children refuse to enroll them in school, keeping them hidden from the public purview out of shame and disgrace. Reports of disabled persons being neglected or sequestered in cages meant for domestic and farm animals are occasionally reported in the mass media. As adults, disabled persons in Ghana face employment discrimination and other forms of exclusion ranging from denial of driving privileges to having difficulties attracting suitors (Azu 2011). In the area of employment, it was reported that in 2001 only 31 percent of the disabled population of working age were employed; that is, a whopping 69 percent did not have employment. Conversely, 80.2 percent of the nondisabled population was employed (Commonwealth Human Rights Initiative 2007). Quotidian life for the disabled can be traumatic. Disabled students are taunted and abused by their colleagues. There are inadequate infrastructural resources to help the disabled to get around. At present, it is difficult for the disabled to gain physical access to many facilities in the country.

Contemporary Ghanaian Ethos

Observers and analysts of Ghanaian society note that a consumerist ethos has gripped the society. This ethos is marked by an unbridled quest for material success and the ostentatious display of opulence in the form of handsomely furnished mansions, luxury automobiles, electronics, clothes, jewelry, and other material trappings (Agyeman 2009). Many Ghanaians covet the awe, admiration and respect that come with having a large home, the latest model luxury car, designer clothes, designer jewelry, a range of electronics including cellular or mobile phones, and ready cash to dispense to relatives, acquaintances, and strangers. The means by which this conspicuous consumption is enabled is regarded as less important than the ultimate ends (Clegg 1981). This social context, where wealth is sought by any means necessary, intersects with traditional religious belief systems where it is widely believed that supernatural entities have an interest in, and influence upon, human affairs, including material prosperity. The link between an unconstrained pursuit of material success with ritual homicide and occult medicine in Ghana (Adinkrah 2005) finds parallels in other contemporary societies (Kabba 1992; Smith 2001; Sanders 2001). Smith's (2001) analysis of ritual murders in Nigeria shows that ritual homicides in the society were instrumentally motivated acts designed to attain fast wealth. Sanders (2001) similarly found in his analysis of ritualistic killings in Tanzania that these homicides were motivated by a desire to procure fast wealth by means of occult medicine produced with human body parts.

Religion

Ghana is a deeply religious society. Although there is very little statistical data and few published records that document the full extent to which religion permeates the social fabric, it is not difficult for any observer to be keenly aware of the significance of religion in the social and cultural landscape of the country. In the urban centers and most rural communities, church steeples and, increasingly, the domes of Islamic mosques are a backdrop on the horizon of distant rolling hills. Thousands of signposts along major Ghanaian highways direct citizens to the country's hundreds of prayer or healing camps where religious specialists allegedly exorcise demons and conduct spiritual healings.

Presently, no statistical information exists regarding the extent to which the populace subscribes to various religious beliefs or participates in religious activities; however, it is axiomatic that the overwhelming majority of Ghanaians believe in some supernatural phenomena and participate in religious rituals. None of the Ghanaians interviewed and informally surveyed in the course of this study claimed agnosticism or atheism.

Religious heterogeneity in Ghana is reflected in the various institutionalized and traditional religious faiths with which Ghanaians identify. According to the 2010 census, 71.2 percent of the population identified an affiliation with a Christian denominational church, followed by Islamic adherents (17.6 percent) and subscribers of traditional faiths (5.2 percent). Another 5.3 percent of Ghanaians reported no affiliation with any religion (Ghana Statistical Service 2012). Among Christians alone, there is a high degree of denominational and sectarian pluralism, with dozens of Christian denominations, sects, organizations, and new religious movements operating in the country. All mainline religions—the Catholic Church, the Presbyterians, Methodists, Anglican, Baptist, AME Zion, Seventh Day Adventists, and the Jehovah's Witnesses—are represented. The Church of Latter Day Saints has recently emerged as a growing presence in the country. In addition, new sects such as apostolic and other evangelical sects are represented. Another notable development is the phenomenal growth of Christian evangelical denominations. At the same time, mainline religious groups such as the Presbyterians, Methodists, and Catholics are facing declining membership. It is believed that the shifts in religious affiliation have come about because of the appeal among Ghanaians of the overt miracles identified with Pentecostal churches (see Figure 1.2.).

Islam has also been an established religion particularly in northern Ghana as the second-largest organized religion in the country. Presently,

Figure 1.2. Church Building

adherents of the Islamic faith constitute about 18 percent of the population. A significant proportion of the remainder of the population comprises those who subscribe to traditional religious beliefs and practices. In recent years such new age religions as the Ba'hai faith have established a following in the country. It needs emphasizing that in Ghana conversion to Christianity, Islam, or any of the new age religions does not necessarily mean the complete abandonment of traditional religious beliefs and practices. Many a Ghanaian Christian still maintains traditional beliefs in animism, ancestor veneration, witchcraft, ghosts, and other supernatural forces. For instance, in his study of Asante Catholicism, Obeng (1996) observed that some Asante Catholic priests and the laity alike, held ancestral beliefs as well as belief in witchcraft. For some Ghanaians, the power of ancestors is regarded as more immediate and effective than other religious faiths.

Traditional Religion

Traditional Ghanaian religion comprises largely ancestor veneration and animism. Belief in the existence of ancestral spirits is universal in Ghana. Ghanaians of all ethnic persuasions believe that following a physical death and burial of bodies, souls travel to the ancestral world to join other ancestral kin who have preceded them. This spiritual world of the ancestors, known in Akan as *asamando*, has no determinate geographical location. As spiritual beings ancestral spirits maintain close, constant, daily connections to the living, although they remain invisible to them. Complementary beliefs in reincarnation suggest that newborns of the clan or lineage come from this band of ancestral kin. Importantly, not everyone can become an ancestor. There are strict meritorious criteria for membership into the ancestral body of spirits. Membership is reserved for people who have led exemplary lives on this earth. A person must also have died what is referred to as a good death as distinguished from a bad death. Bad deaths include those resulting from childbirth, accidents, homicide, suicide, or highly stigmatized illnesses (e.g., leprosy, tuberculosis, HIV/AIDS) and are said to generate bad spirits. Among the Akans, these spirits are referred to as *asaman bɔne* (bad ghosts) or *asaman twentwen* (wandering spirits). By virtue of their supposed evil deeds, it is believed that upon death, witches and wizards are precluded from membership in the group of ancestors. These spirits supposedly hang around the earth because they cannot reach, or are denied entry into, the spiritual world of the ancestors.

Throughout the year, special festivals, religious celebrations, and other acts of reverence are conducted to remember the ancestors and help reunite the living with their departed kin. This may involve the slaughtering of a sheep or the pouring of libation to invoke the ancestors. During these solemn occasions, ancestral spirits are solemnly and reverentially asked to intervene on behalf of the living to bestow such special favors and blessings as good health, fertility and successful births, economic and material prosperity, success in all earthly undertakings, and physical protection from evil spirits and evil forces such as sorcery and witchcraft. On certain occasions ancestors are enjoined to come and wine and dine with the living on specially prepared food left at special vantage points. Indeed, the ancestors can diurnally be invoked by mere words, without libation, to assist the living. It is believed that the power of the ancestors to bestow largesse on the living stems from their location. As spirits, departed ancestors are closer to God, the Creator and supreme deity of the universe, and are capable of interceding for their living kin. Prayers or petitions routed through them have a shorter distance to travel to God and the other superior deities.

Belief in ancestral spirits and their power to sanction the behavior of their living kinfolk has implications for social control. While ancestral spirits have the capacity to bestow blessings and good favors on the living kin who lead morally upright lives, in the same way they have the power to negatively sanction or punish those with whom they are dissatisfied through the withdrawal of their protection from their living kindred, thereby rendering them defenseless to all manner of tribulations. Apprehensions about the loss of spiritual protection from the ancestors, as well as fear of retributive sanctions for personal misdeeds, make people extremely diligent about observing social norms.

Sacrifices and offerings of food, drink, money, and live animals are a central feature of many traditional religions throughout the country. These sacrificial practices are intended to invoke supernatural entities to control those forces over which practitioners feel they lack control. By making sacrificial offerings to the gods, believers hope to obtain the blessing of their ancestors and gods, ensure the well-being of their families, and ward off diseases, accidents, deaths and other misfortunes. Proscribed and suppressed during the colonial epoch, ritualistic practices of human sacrifice continue to occur in contemporary Ghana according to empirical and anecdotal reports (Adinkrah 2005; Asiedu 1992a, 1992b; Gocking 2000; Meyer 1998, 2002).

Accompanying the high degree of religious pluralism in the society is a high level of ritual involvement. Despite predictions in some quarters regarding the global tendency toward secularization, Ghanaian society appears to be experiencing a religious revival. Church attendance and religious observances appear to be on an upward swing. Over the past few decades, Bible-study groups have proliferated, schools operated by religious organizations remain vibrant, publications with religious foci have burgeoned, and all-night prayer meetings have become commonplace.

In the urban settings, grand religious rallies marked by zestful singing, sonorous preaching, drowning wails, and excited worship have become regular fare. Also gaining in popularity are religious meetings marked by intense preaching and "miraculous spiritual healings." Religious processions, conventions, festivals, and assemblies have also become legion. Although no national statistics exist on frequency and patterns of church attendance, most Christians attend church service regularly. Sundays in Ghana are marked by a throng of adherents to morning, afternoon, and evening worship, as well as other religious observances. Some religious denominations hold services at least twice on Sundays. During the week many Christians attend worship services, spiritual growth seminars, Bible classes, and prayer and healing services. The all-night religious services held from about 7 P.M. until 7 A.M. the following morning have become an important feature of Christian devotional worship and healing. Particularly in the urban centers the air is punctuated by the singing and preaching emanating from churches and other centers of worship, from sun up to sun down.

The importance of religion in the lives of Ghanaians is further evident in the time, energy, and resources allotted to religious activities. Many Christians spend several hours each week engaged in the upkeep and maintenance of church facilities, such as weeding the church compound and helping with the construction of new church buildings. With the evolution of several churches into faith healing centers, the actual number of people living on church premises for religious healing purposes has also increased.

There are a variety of religious organizations and clubs that extend the association and fellowship of church members. Religious-based organizations currently constitute a large proportion of social clubs, self-help groups, women's organizations, youth clubs, and other voluntary organizations operating in the country. In addition, many churches and religious bodies are actively involved in the provision of social services for the poor and the needy. These services range from the provision of shelter for orphaned youths and the homeless to providing leadership training for women in the church. Religious-based organizations also provide personal counseling and pastoral education to their congregation while many churches also offer vocational training to youths or supporting neighborhoods (see Figure1.3.).

The influence of religion in Ghana extends to the incorporation of religious rituals into daily activities and mundane features of life. This is evi-

Figure 1.3. Youth at a Church Service

dent in many Ghanaian homes, where upon arising and before leaving for work, school, and other activities, there is morning devotion. Each meal, whether consumed in such public settings as restaurants or in the privacy of the home, begins with a prayer of blessing and thanks. At government offices and other official workplaces, Bibles and other religious tracts can be found conspicuously displayed atop desks of Christian devotees. In many public as well as private establishments, the day's work begins with morning devotion consisting of religious songs, reading of Biblical texts, short sermons, and prayers. In commercial vehicles operating around the country, many a driver bows down his head or rests his head on the steering wheel and says a prayer before embarking on a journey. The conclusion of the trip is marked by prayers of gratitude for a successful journey.

In Ghana it is amply evident that religion is not consigned to the private sphere. Links between religion and the state are strong, and nearly all public functions commence with solemn prayers or religious devotions. Christian and Muslim clerics are often invited to public functions to read scriptural passages and offer prayers befitting the occasion. Religious holidays dominate the government calendar. In 2012 six of the thirteen public holidays were for religious observances. The most sacred days of the major religions—including Christmas, Good Friday, and Holy Saturday for Christians, and Eid al Fitr and Eid al Adha for Muslims—are observed as public holidays with the closure of schools, businesses, and public offices.

Religious work constitutes one of the fastest-growing spheres of employment in the society. With religious groups mushrooming along with the associated prayer houses and healing temples, several Christian faith-healing prophets and apostles have emerged on the local scene. Itinerant preachers relying on public offertories for daily subsistence can also be spotted at major truck parks, bus stops, and street corners and other public settings and facilities, preaching the gospel and trying to win converts. On the campuses of various tertiary institutions, religion provides the rationale or basis for students to congregate in groups for religious worship and fellowship. These groups are fast replacing ethnic affiliation as a basis for group identification.

Religious programs dominate the national airwaves. Religious radio stations currently abound, featuring sermons, personal prayers, testimonials, or spiritual counseling for life's problems. These programs are interspersed with gospel and other religious music. Over the past few years gospel music and songs with specifically religious themes have proliferated. Many of these songs describe God as omnipresent and omniscient.

The dominance of religion in the society is also well illustrated by the frequent use of religious messages and symbols in daily intercourse. This includes the use of religious messages on signposts of commercial enterprises. Inscriptions on commercial vehicles profess the same religious messages. In an analysis of inscriptions appearing on Ghanaian public transport vehicles, Adinkrah (2006) noted that more than 90 percent had religious themes. A sample of the religious inscriptions included God Is King; God's Time Is the Best; Trust in God; No Jesus, No Success; God Is Great; God First; Oh! My God, Have Mercy; and In God We Trust.

Consonant with the growth of religious influence on the society, religious leaders in Ghana command considerable respect and wield immense political and social influence. Church leaders are granted forums to express opinions about major and controversial social and political issues, including national unity, tribalism, religious tolerance, poverty, human rights, and environmental issues. International religious leaders on the lecture circuit have found Ghana to be a particularly receptive location and make regular visits to the country. But pastors have also been implicated in debauched activities. Media reports feature stories of religious leaders charged with various forms of deviance and criminal transgressions ranging from charges of fraud to forcible rape (Adjokatcher 1989; Aklorbortu 2012a; Kyei-Boateng 2011). In one high-profile case, a renowned pastor was prosecuted, convicted, and sentenced to prison for sexual abuse of his own daughter ("Jesus One Touch Jailed" 2011). Increasingly, rumors of fraud, financial mismanagement, embezzlement, and adultery allegedly committed by religious leaders have also surfaced. Fraudulent claims of divine powers or supernatural intervention have featured prominently in newly emergent crimes in the country. Today, a growing market has developed for soothsayers, sorcerers, occultists, and other religious specialists who promise wealth, power, influence, and foreign visas in exchange for money from their clientele (Sah 2005).

Witchcraft, Organized Religion, and the Law

Belief in witchcraft, sorcery, and other occult forces is a fundamental feature of traditional Ghanaian religious beliefs. While Christianity and Islam may have attenuated traditional supernatural beliefs, they have not completely erased them. For example, decades of proselytizing by Christian missionaries have failed to eclipse witchcraft beliefs. The vast majority of Ghanaians profess a belief in witchcraft. For many Ghanaians, witchcraft continues to evoke awe, horror, and fear. Contrary to the expectation that higher levels of formal education is associated with a secular orientation and the abandonment of traditional religious beliefs including witchcraft, in Ghana the educated often profess as much a belief in witchcraft as do those with limited formal schooling. An unlettered farmer and a medical physician are both likely to profess beliefs in witchcraft and the power of witches.

Admission that one is a witch or wizard does not constitute a criminal offense under the Ghanaian penal code. Even a person who publicly confesses that he has used his witchcraft to kill another person cannot be held legally responsible for those deaths. A person can, however, be held criminally liable for offenses he commits against a suspected or an alleged witch. For example, a person who murders or commits battery or physical assault against another person whom he suspects to be a witch commits a criminal offense of murder, battery, or aggravated assault, respectively, against the person and is legally liable for prosecution. If convicted, he or she can expect to be criminally punished and to suffer death by hanging or to receive a long custodial sentence. It is notable that although capital punishment is still legal in Ghana, judicial executions have not been carried out since 1993.

Why has witchcraft imputation not spawned numerous lawsuits in the country? The answer is simple. There is no legal punitive sanction for witchcraft. Thus, when law enforcement officers receive a report of confessed bewitchment or imputation of witchcraft, they urge the parties to return home and informally resolve the matter. Informal resolution is recommended because witchcraft is not recognized by law. Moreover, individuals are prudent about making direct accusations of witchcraft. Nonviolent witchcraft-related civil lawsuits go to court only when an alleged witch has exhausted informal options available outside the legal process. If the aggrieved party believes that the case is beyond informal resolution, and warrants a judicial solution, he or she may seek redress in the court of law. The next chapter provides a detailed description of witchcraft ideology in Ghana.

Chapter 2

WITCHCRAFT BELIEFS IN GHANA

Understanding witchcraft-related violence in Ghana requires intimate familiarity with Ghanaian witchcraft beliefs, as these are the belief systems that guide and influence the behavior of many Ghanaians. This chapter provides a detailed description of the most salient features of witchcraft beliefs and practices in Ghanaian society, focusing on the core witchcraft beliefs of the Akans, the largest ethnic group in the country.

A considerable body of literature, both popular and academic, has accumulated on witchcraft beliefs and practices in Ghanaian society (e.g., Adinkrah 2004, 2008a; Akrong 2007; Amoah 1987; Anderson 1999; Assani 1996; Assimeng 1977; Bannerman-Richter 1982; Blay 1968; Boakye-Sarpong and Osei-Hwedie 1989; Brempong 1986, 1996; Debrunner 1961; Donkor 2010; Dovlo 2007; Drucker-Brown 1993; Field 1955; Gray 2000; Grindal 2003; Nabila 1997; Osei 2001; Owusu-Ansah 2000; Parish 1999, 2000; Wyllie 1973). This literature shows that witchcraft beliefs are entrenched and pervasive in the society. Although to date no national surveys have been conducted that focus on the nature, extent, and patterns of witchcraft beliefs among Ghanaians, evidence from a variety of sources suggests that witchcraft beliefs are prevalent, with the vast majority of Ghanaians professing a belief in the reality of witchcraft and the existence of witches (Adinkrah 2004, 2008; Assimeng 1977; Bannerman-Richter 1982; Debrunner 1961). As Max Assimeng (1977, 54) aptly describes the Ghanaian witchcraft scene, "[T]here appears very little disagreement over the fact that witchcraft beliefs are now embraced by people of all segments of Ghana's social and economic system." While one may perchance encounter citizens who deny or even mock the reality of witchcraft and witches, and who denounce witchcraft beliefs as irrational or mere superstition, most Ghanaians fear witchcraft and witches as real phenomena (Grindal 2003). As a researcher in sociology born and raised in Ghana, I grew up hearing stories of witches, bewitchment, witchcraft accusations, and witchcraft ideology. In the course of ten years of ethnographic research in Ghana I encountered numerous individuals who not only espoused a fervent belief in witchcraft phenomena and the activities of witches, but who could recount riveting and mesmeric tales of personal encounters with witches and witchcraft phenomena.

Witchcraft Phenomena in Ghanaian Society

A cursory survey of Ghanaian society reveals the pervasiveness and resiliency of witchcraft beliefs in the society. Various mass media depict a profusion of witchcraft phenomena. Mainstream newspapers, popular magazines, and local tabloids regularly carry news reports of witchcraft accusations, witch confessions and the violent victimization of alleged witches (e.g., Amanor 1999a, 1999b; Buabeng and Kofoya-Tetteh 1998; Kyei-Boateng 1997; Mensah 1997; Nkrumah-Boateng 1997; Safo 1997; Seini 1998; Yeboah 2001). In addition to regular reports of witch hunts and other witchcraft-related violence, detailed analyses of local witchcraft issues contained in page-length articles in major newspapers abound, covering such themes as veracity of witchcraft, the nocturnal activities of witches, and the overrepresentation of elderly females among accused witches (e.g., Agyako 1998; Donkor 2008, 2011; Dornoo 2009; Osei 2011). Additionally, witch beliefs are prominent in the "Letters" and "Features" sections of local dailies, where animated exchanges occasionally occur between ardent believers of witchcraft and a few impassioned nonbelievers (e.g., Mensah 2012; Yeboah 1977). Among Christians, religious sermons regularly focus on witchcraft and the malevolent activities of witches, as well as what "good" Christians can do to ward off or conquer the evil forces of witchcraft (Adinkrah 2004, 2008).

Witchcraft beliefs and ideas are also prevalent in music. Lyrics of the popular Ghanaian music genre known as "highlife" and its more contemporary variant "hiplife" contain frequent refrains about witchcraft beliefs and the role played by witches in stultifying other people's progress in life (Adinkrah 2008; Brempong 1986). Similar themes suffuse locally produced soap operas and dramatized plays that are regularly featured on local television as well as in a cottage industry of locally produced movies on DVD. Furthermore, inscriptions on local commercial vehicles and the signposts of commercial establishments are saturated with messages depicting witch fears or witchcraft beliefs (Adinkrah 2008).

Descriptive Terms for Witchcraft and Witches

It is axiomatic that witchcraft beliefs exist among all ethnic groups in Ghana (Debrunner 1961; Ghana Education Service 1988; Nukunya 2003). Consequently, there are, at a minimum, as many terms for witchcraft as there are ethnic groups in the country. Ethnic distinctions in the terms used to describe witchcraft and witches are provided in table 2.1. Among Akans (e.g., Ashantis, Kwahus, Akims, and Akwapims), witchcraft is *bayie*, *beyie*, or *bayi* while the witch is *ɔbayifo*, *ɔbayifoɔ*, or *beyifo* (Adinkrah 2004; Amoah 1987). The Fante-speaking group of the Akans refers to witches and witchcraft as *ayɛn* or *anyɛn*. Among the Ewe, witchcraft is known as *adziwowo* and the witch *adze*, while the Ga witch and witchcraft are both called *aye*. The term for witch among two northern ethnic groups, Kasena and Gonja, are *chorro* and *egbe*, respectively (Ghana Education Service 1988). In local English parlance, Ghanaians fastidiously distinguish between the male and female witch, using wizard for the male witch and witch for the female equivalent.

Table 2.1. Witchcraft Terms in Ghanaian Ethnic Communities

Ethnic Community	Witch	Witchcraft
Akan/Twi/Fante	*Bayifo/Anyɛn*	*Bayi/Anyɛn*
Ewe	*Adze*	*Adziwowo*
Dangme	*Hialolaze*	*Hia*
Ga	*Aye*	*Aye*
Nzema	*Ayene*	*Ayene*
Kasena	*Chorro*	*Cherro*
Gonja	*Egbe*	*Kegbe*
Dagbeni	*Sonya*	*Sobugim*
Sisala	*Hila*	*Hingling*

Source: Ghana Education Service, 137; Grindal 2003.

Diversity of Witchcraft Beliefs

Witchcraft beliefs in Ghana are far from monolithic, varying across ethnic groups (Assimeng 1977; Mullings 1984; Nukunya 2003). Hence, although there are some fundamental similarities in witchcraft beliefs across ethnic groups, there are myriad differences in the intricacies of witchcraft beliefs among different groups. For example, among the ethnic groups of northern Ghana, it is believed that a witch can bewitch anyone—relatives, neighbors, friends, schoolmates, workmates, or strangers—whereas among the Akan-speaking groups the notion is prevalent that a witch can only bewitch maternal relatives (Adinkrah 2004; Gray 2000). Also, among the patrilineal Tallensi of northern Ghana, witchcraft is believed to be transmitted through the *soog* (matrilineal kinfolk). Among the Anlo-Ewe, another ethnic group that traces descent and transmits property through patrilineal lines, witchcraft power is believed to be inherited from and transmitted through mothers (Nukunya 2003).

Given the predominance of the Akan-speaking ethnic groups in Ghana, Akan witchcraft beliefs are the most pervasive in the country and will provide the core for most of the discussion of witchcraft beliefs in this chapter. Even within one ethnic community such as the Akans or a linguistic cultural Akan group such as the Ashantis, there are some variations in the details associated with witchcraft beliefs, ideas, and practices. This is illustrated by the disagreements that often characterize discussions on *Etuo Mu Wɔ Sum*, a weekly 90-minute long radio program broadcast on Peace FM 104.3 that focuses on witchcraft beliefs, sorcery, and other occult phenomena in Ghana. Guests on the show, including self-proclaimed witches and wizards, express divergent ideas about witchcraft and witchcraft activities. Call-in listeners of the show also express contrasting views about the reality of witchcraft and the power of witches. Despite these variations in some details, there are some common themes that can be discerned as a core set of Akan witchcraft beliefs.

What Is Witchcraft?

As is the case with many ethnic communities in Ghanaian society, Akans regard witchcraft as a form of mystical, supernatural, or spiritual power possessed and used consciously by some individuals, either to protect and promote the welfare of or to cause harm to unsuspecting members of the witch's *abusua* (matrilineage) (Adinkrah 2004; Debrunner 1961; Mensa-Bonsu 2001; Nukunya 2003; Obeng 2004). Although typically regarded as a malevolent spirit that is employed to wreak havoc on its victims, it is believed that some witches utilize their witchcraft power in beneficent ways to advance their personal interests and the welfare of selected loved ones (Amoah 1987; Bannerman-Richter 1982).

Like many other ethnic groups in Ghana, Akans distinguish between *bayie* (witchcraft) and *aduro* (sorcery). While *bayie* is a mystical, spiritual, or supernatural power inherent in particular individual carriers and used consciously to assist or harm others, *aduro* is medicine obtained from a sorcerer who consciously and purposefully prepares the potion by combining herbs, household objects, worn items of clothing, and bodily substances such as hair and nail clippings or a range of other materials in order to produce harm to the intended victims. In Ghana there are specialized practitioners of sorcery who receive monetary imbursement to prepare sorcery or potions that can bring about harm to individuals, groups of persons, or entire communities.

It is commonly believed that a witch's mystical power usually derives from a recipe of bodily excrescences (e.g., human hair, fingernail parings), human skulls, human teeth, kola nuts, herbs, beads, cowries, sea shells, and blood (Debrunner 1961; Kuada and Chachah 1999). This concoction is usually stored in a *bayi kukuo, bayi kuku,* or *bayi sɛn* (pot), a gourd shell, or some other container that is then buried in the earth or hidden atop, under, or beside a big tree in the forest. The container may also be kept under a bed in the witch's bedroom (Debrunner 1961; Gray 2000). Another popular belief is that the *bayi kukuo* or *bayi sɛn* contains not only the witch's witchcraft powers, but also the souls of her victims (Korankye 1997). Discourse on Ghanaian witchcraft beliefs show that in many instances when a witch has been caught, apprehended, or arrested by a fetish shrine, a member of the clergy, or any of the myriad ritual specialists, the alleged witch directs the audience to a spot where such witch substances are found (Debrunner 1961). It is believed that in some instances the witchcraft power is contained in such items as *ahweneɛ* or *aheneɛ* (stringed waist beads), ankle bracelets, or a necklace that the witch wears on her or his person (Bannerman-Richter 1982). Some female witches are believed to regularly or occasionally carry their witchcraft spirits in their vaginas in the form of snakes, scorpions, centipedes, and frogs (Bannerman-Richter 1982; Kuada and Chachah 1999; Soku 2000) or as a fibroid growth in their stomachs (Kuada and Chachah 1999).

It is believed that when witches are attending church services they leave the witchcraft substance at the entrance of the church building. They then pick it up at the close of the church service, thereby escaping detection. Some deliberately go into the church building with the witchcraft substance or power, ostensibly to challenge or test how powerful the pastor is. These witches are said to risk being caught if they underestimate the power of the pastor.

Is the Witch Aware or Conscious of His or Her Witch Status?

While in some cultures it is believed that a person can be a witch without knowing it (Mair 1973), according to Akan beliefs the witch is always conscious of or aware that he or she is indeed a witch (Korankye 1997; Ntim-Korsah 1988). Yet in his monograph, *From the Coven of Witchcraft to Christ*, proclaimed as a "true life testimony," the Ghanaian author Reverend Leonard Soku (2000), a Ewe, offers an alternative viewpoint:

> Initially a person can become a witch without knowing it. He or she may just be having bad dreams, having nightmares, seeing snakes and monsters. A nice person inviting them to a particular place. Sometimes one dreams that one is flying. One begins to eat a good meal in dreams often with good meat in the meal. All of this time, one is a witch, without knowing. One may finally find that one attends parties very often, meeting known friends and new people. Gradually it would be announced to you that you are now one of them. By this time, some creatures have come to dwell in you. To the best of my knowledge, every witch has snakes plus either frogs, scorpions, centipede or a bird in his or her stomach. This is the source of one's power to do anything against mankind. (Soku 2000, 49)

The "Good" and "Bad" Witchcraft

As alluded to above, Akans believe that there are two types of witchcraft: *bayi pa* (good or beneficent witchcraft, also known as *bayi fufuo* [white witchcraft]) on the one hand, and *bayi bɔne, bayi borɔ,* or *bayi kwasea* (bad or malevolent witchcraft, also known as *bayi tuntum* [black witchcraft]) on the other hand (Korankye 1997; Obeng 2004; Opoku 1982). Akans believe that *bayi pa* is used by their carriers to promote the social advancement of the witch's progeny and other loved ones. *Bayi bɔne,* as the name suggests, is used conversely to cause harm to persons and their property. Many people, however, consider witchcraft as inherently evil, noting that even the good witch will bring ruination to some in order to advance the welfare of others. For example, a good witch who wants to bring academic success to her children will have to remove her victim's brain and then deposit such inside the skull of the loved one, concurrently causing imbecility or idiocy in the victim whose brain has been removed.

It is believed that some good witches use their good or beneficent witchcraft to secure traveling visas for their children to go overseas. Concurrently, a witch can spoil the efforts of others who are less favored by the witch. Hence, those who fail to secure visas for foreign travel often blame it on the evil machinations of a purported witch in their lineage. For those who secure visas, witches are believed to have the capacity to change the photographs in passports, resulting in the victim's repatriation or being denied entry in foreign countries.

It is popularly believed that beneficent witches and wizards make up only a minute fraction of the total witch population in the society; they do not belong to witch covens, and are very rarely caught, arrested, or exposed by traditional witch doctors. As one informant told me during an interview, due to the beneficent purposes of their witchcraft "people with *bayi pa* are not exposed or caught by witch doctors." Korankye (1997, 16) writes of beneficent witches in the Ajumako traditional area: "Those who are suspected of having good witchcraft are treated fairly well than the bad ones. Those [good] witches, according to the people of Ajumako traditional area, do not belong to any witch society. They are also feared in the society but not like the bad ones."

Number of Witches in the Society

How many witches are purported to exist in Ghanaian society? The Akan saying "Efie biara bayie wɔ mu" (there is a witch in every lineage) suggests that the country is full of witches. If one goes by that popular Akan saying, then one can rightly claim that there are thousands of witches in a country of about 25 million people. Some lineages are said to have more than one witch or wizard operating independently or in concurrence.

Dreams, Nightmares, and Witchcraft

According to Akan witch beliefs, dreams provide a window into deciphering who in the family or community is a witch. Dreams are also believed to expose the activities of witches and provide forewarnings of actual or imminent bewitchment. According to Akan dream interpretations, if someone dreams that he was flying through the air, then that is an indication that the person is about to receive witchcraft or witchcraft powers from a matrilineal kinfolk. Having recurrent nightmares is also associated with witchcraft. Some men who are sexually impotent or who suffer from erectile dysfunction disorders claim to have developed their affliction after dreaming of engaging in sexual intercourse with a close family member such as a sister, mother, or aunt. Mettle-Nunoo (1994, 67) notes, "[I]f a pregnant woman dreams of having sexual intercourse with a stranger and not her husband, it is believed that she has been seduced by evil forces and in most cases, miscarriages result. It is also widely believed that when a person dreams of being chased by a bull or a cow, it is interpreted to mean that witches are haunting him."

Food and Witchcraft

Among Akans, certain local foods are strongly linked with witchcraft, witchery, or witchcraft activity. Palm oil, with its red color and viscous consistency, considered to be similar to blood, is oftentimes associated with witchcraft. Given the widely popular belief among Akans that witches drink blood and eat human flesh, people in the community who are extremely fond of palm oil and meat may be suspected of being witches. Similarly, women who sell palm oil, palm fruits, or pork may be branded witches (Amoah 1987). As will be elaborated in a subsequent section on modes of transmitting witchcraft, it is widely believed that the witchcraft substance can be hidden in these foods and passed on to the unsuspecting victim who consumes the food (Ntim-Korsah 1988).

Witches Are Nocturnal

Among the central themes of Akan witchcraft beliefs is the notion that witches are nocturnal. They are described as traveling secretly through the air as balls of fire at night to remote locations where they cavort with other witches and spiritually feast on the flesh of unsuspecting relatives, thereby causing physical and psychological harm, and even death, in the process (Adinkrah 2004; Debrunner 1961; Gray 2000; Korankye 1997; Nukunya 2003; Soku 2000; Wyllie 1973). The belief in the ability of witches to fly through the air is so strong in the Akan witch belief system that a common nickname for witches is *atufaa* (flies smoothly), signifying the ability of the witch to glide through the sky with ease.

Witches' Guilds

Among many ethnic groups in Ghana, the belief is widely held that individual witches belong to local witches' guilds, covens, associations, or companies (in Akan called *fekuo* or *fekuw*) that meet regularly (Debrunner 1961; Gray 2000; Korankye 1997; Mensa-Bonsu 2001; Mettle-Nunoo 1994; Ntim-Korsah 1988). Witch covens are believed to be variable in size but membership is believed to range from about a dozen to about a hundred and fifty. These witches' guilds hold clandestine nocturnal meetings in remote locations, arriving by their own flight or by riding on such animals as buffaloes, antelopes, leopards, and owls (Debrunner 1961; Soku 2000; Bannerman-Richter 1982; Mensa-Bonsu 2001).

The witches' guilds are believed to be highly structured, well-organized hierarchical organizations with officeholders and followers (Debrunner 1961; Mettle-Nunoo 1994; Soku 2000). As Debrunner (1961, 29) described, "The whole thing is a society, in which they have elders, messengers, chiefs, policemen and executioners." Activities and behavior of members of the witch-company are believed to be governed by explicit rules and guidelines, infractions of which can incur the wrath of other members. Decisions reached are binding and are enforced by witch police and their military personnel. Consider the following excerpt from Soku's (2000) "true life testimony" of witchcraft:

> Every witchcraft coven has a King, a Queen, a Linguist. Various departments are organized with department heads e.g. chief messenger supervises those who will go out in the night to bring victims for slaughter. Victims could be brought from any part of the world. On satanic computer they know the city, the street, the house number and room number. The computer could be a small mirror or water in a cup or container. There is the Head of the Executioners' Department. They took interest in killing the victims. Witches do not succeed in killing true Christians, though they may influence their businesses or lives. The victims are not normally killed in human form. They are mostly changed into animals and killed and feasted on. The person dies physically. Harsh disciplinary actions are taken against those who failed to accomplish their assignment or tasks. (Soku 2000, 46)

Soku (2000) further asserts the belief that members of witch companies are allotted specific tasks or assignments that are distributed at witches' meetings:

> Assignments are given at witches' meetings. Nice girls who are members are the deadly weapons used against mankind. Most are given power to lure men into sexual relationships to steal their money, prosperity, break marital homes, make the men alcoholics and sexual perverts. Some of the pretty girls lay with twenty or more men a day. The mystery is that they gave creatures, especially snakes to their victims to have the affair with. This is spiritual power. That is why their victims become hopeless in life. We have some of these girls who are saved on our teams who testify to glorify God for delivering them. Some are sent to distribute sickness. Some members are asked to break marriages of their friends and relatives. Some are assigned to break down prosperous companies and businesses. (Soku 2000, 47)

Another element of Akan witch belief is that among witch companies, most of which are spiritually cannibalistic, the distribution of human body parts at ritualistic feasts is based on one's position in the witch company, with those occupying positions in the top echelons of the guild receiving the most prized parts of the meat (Debrunner 1961; Mensa-Bonsu

2001; Ntim-Korsah 1988). As Debrunner (1961, 37) documents, "[T]he meat is shared according to rank, the chief getting the best part." According to Mettle-Nunoo (1994, 65), "The king receives the head, the queen takes the trunk and other members take the other parts. The blood of their victim is however shared equally among them."

Nocturnal group gatherings of witches are described as not exclusively devoted to cannibalistic feastings. Other activities commonly engaged in include consuming alcoholic beverages and social dancing. Witches are also said to play such games as soccer (Debrunner 1961), the most popular Ghanaian sport. In playing soccer, witches are believed to spiritually cut off the head of their victims for use as soccer balls. At the end of the game, the head is restored to the unsuspecting victim who may suffer headaches, neck pains, fatigue, or some other physical affliction the following day, due to his or her head having been used all night as a soccer ball (Gray 2000, 278). For student victims, this may cause low academic achievement and an overall dulling of intelligence. It is believed that the umpires or referees of these games use the bones of their witchcraft victims as whistles for umpiring the soccer games (Mettle-Nunoo 1994). In his study of witchcraft beliefs among the Ajumako people, Korankye (1997, 11) noted that the people believe that "the farm which is used by witches as their playing ground suffers low production."

Witch Familiars

In order to facilitate their nocturnal flights to witch covens, witches are believed to transform themselves into certain animals, insects, or birds (Debrunner 1961; Soku 2000). Akans refer to animal witch familars as *bay-iboa*. Soku (2000, 31–32) notes, "A witch could change into a bird such as an owl or a vampire bat, a vulture or any bird. She or he could change into any animal, flies (e.g. housefly, tse-tse fly) or birds. Some powerful wizards turn into [the] common housefly or wind." He further notes, "Most of the times the witches call each other for the meeting. Sometimes owls cry around the area to inform friends that time is up for the meeting" (Soku 2000, 48). Soku (2000, 47) notes, "On arrival at a meeting place, they [the witches] transform back into human form. At such a meeting place you can identify each other." Witches are generally believed to regularly assume animal forms to conduct their evil machinations:

> The more violent the witch the more violent the animal whose form she assumes; thus, less evil witches generally assume the forms of animals which are relatively benign. One of the animals which harmless witches change into

is a bird. One witch may change into a vulture and feed on rubbish in garbage dumps, and another may transform into a marine fowl and prey on aquatic life. After changing into astral animals, witches materialize on the physical plane to indulge their appetites, and in sparsely populated regions of the country, they can be seen as balls of fire on lagoons, rivers, and the sea as they feed at night. (Bannerman-Richter 1982, 31)

Another form that witches assume is that of grazing animals. A witch may turn herself into an antelope and graze on the vegetation close to home. But a diabolical witch can assume an antelope's shape not just to feed, but also to destroy farms. For example, a jealous cowife who is a witch may transform herself into a herbivore and ravage her rival's crops. If that woman materialized in the physical dimension to do so, then the farmer would wake up in the morning to find her farm laid waste, but she would attribute the damage to natural animals. If the damage occurred astrally, however, then the victim might ascribe it to inclement weather, for the crops would wilt as if from natural causes. Witches with aggressive natures assume the forms of animals such as snakes and large carnivores like the leopard or the hyena. These are the witches considered to be the most dangerous threat to human life, for they are cannibals and relish the ethereal flesh of human beings (Bannerman-Richter 1982, 31–32).

Given the belief that witches have the capacity to transform into certain types of animals, particularly those that facilitate access to their victim, the following animals and insects are feared by Ghanaians for their association with witches: ants, bats, birds (especially owls), cats, centipedes, cockroaches, crocodiles, dogs, fireflies, goats, hyenas, leopards, millipedes, mice, mosquitoes, pigs, and snakes. The presence or even the hoot of an owl in the vicinity of one's abode or living quarters in the dark of night causes panic in residents. People outdoors will quickly retreat indoors at the sight or sound of an owl due to its perceived link to witches. Many believe that when an owl lands on the roof of one's house, it is a bad omen of the highest order. The firefly (lightning bug) and its flickering night light evoke similar fears. A firefly in one's bedroom is suggestive of bewitchment.

The belief is also commonly held that witches are capable of traveling under the sea in the form of marine life to set traps for potential victims who may be traveling by boat or ship. These traps can be used to cause boats to capsize, causing deaths. The witches then feast on the dead and drink the blood of injured survivors. Witches are described as causing problems for many a professional hunter. The witch can turn a bewitched individual into a game animal. If the hunter shoots at the animal, the dying animal turns into a human being and the hunter is charged with murder and his life is destroyed either by criminal execution or by long-term incarceration. To avert such disasters, the hunter is advised to cut off the tail of the hunted animal immediately after its death. This will prevent the animal from morphing into a human being.

Meeting Grounds for Witches

Common meeting grounds described for witch companies include the local marketplace, uncompleted buildings, abandoned warehouses or factories, cemeteries, major refuse dumps, farmlands on the outskirts of a village or town, mountain tops, and the banks of a river (Debrunner 1961; Mettle-Nunoo 1994; Soku 2000). A common belief is that witches' meetings are sometimes held atop tall trees (Debrunner 1961; Soku 2000) that, according to one writer, "turn into sky-scrapers in the night with soft furniture [and] with all facilities for conferences and game rooms" (Soku 2000, 48). Some witches are believed to use cobwebs or spider webs as a means of transport to witch gatherings while some use spider webs as telephones to communicate with other witches. Thus, in Akan symbolism being entangled by a spider web anywhere—at home or in the bush—may signify bewitchment.

Witch Sightings

It is fairly common for Ghanaians to share stories about witchcraft phenomena that include accounts of actual witch sightings. How does one know that one has encountered a witch? According to Akan witch beliefs, a witch manifests itself at night as a giant ball of glowing light or fire bouncing up and down or hopping from place to place. Several informants who claimed to have seen or encountered a witch at night described having seen a giant sparkling ball or balls of fire sitting atop a tree or on a grassfield. The ball of fire can dissolve into sparks, then regenerate into another huge, glowing ball of fire. Some eyewitness accounts claim that these balls of fire moved toward them gradually or at top speed as if preparing to attack them, or simply hopped on the grassfield unconcerned about their presence in the vicinity. Such accounts are typically accompanied by warnings to quickly move away upon sighting a witch because the witch may violently attack anyone who peers at it for too long.

Anthropophagous or Cannibalistic Witchcraft

What happens at the meetings of the witch covens? One of the prevailing beliefs regarding Akan witchcraft is that witches are primarily anthropophagous, practicing a form of spiritual cannibalism (Adinkrah 2004; Awedoba 2002; Debrunner 1961; Gray 2000; Mensa-Bonsu 2001; Mettle-Nunoo 1994; Nukunya 2003; Soku 2000). Mensa-Bonsu (2001, 507) notes, "The meetings are cannibalistic feasts: the bodies of the witches' victims are cut up, cooked in a pot (the *bayisɛn*) and eaten. The ranks of a witch in the company or covens (*fɛkuo*) determines whether he or she shall receive the head, the trunk, the hands and so on. Some believers in the cult maintain that the reason for co-operative group is to enable witches to share in eating victims of other kinship groups, since any one witch can kill only from among her flesh and blood."

In his book, *From the Coven of Witchcraft to Christ,* Soku (2000) avers, "Water and food in the meeting of witches is human blood and the human flesh" (Soku 2000, 46) while the legs of bewitched individuals are used as chopping boards or logs for cutting meat, hence the protracted sores on their victims' legs (Mettle-Nunoo 1994). It is believed that pacts are made between participating witches stipulating that any witch who partakes in a ritualistic cannibal feast must at some point provide a human victim. Failure to comply, it is believed, carries severe penalties for the errant witch; he or she could be killed by the witch company that would, in turn, feast on the witch. Other beliefs indicate that any witch who partakes in the cannibal feast of human flesh provided by other witches but is unable or unwilling to supply similar human flesh of their own is forced to forfeit a finger, a toe, a limb, or some other body part to his or her witch comrades for their own feasting (Bannerman-Richter 1982). Belief in this mystical forfeiture of body parts as penalties in witch covens probably explains the common perception among Akans that individuals in the community who suffer from one or more of a number of physical deformities must be witches who have relinquished parts of their own bodies to witch comrades under such circumstances.

In supplying a human victim for the cannibal feast, witches are expected to sacrifice a very close or intimate family relation or loved one rather than just any matrikin. Given that witchcraft is essentially a malevolent power designed to wreak destructive deeds, in selecting targets for death or destruction witches target individuals whose death or destruction will cause the greatest pain and suffering to their immediate family or community. These include financially or academically successful children, grandchildren, nieces or nephews, and brothers or sisters. To illustrate, witches may kill a final-year medical student, a successful lawyer, or a pregnant woman. As a corollary, witches are also known to select potentially successful marriages for destruction by rendering one of the spouses infertile, to thwart prospects for the acquisition of a visa for foreign travel, or to bring about other forms of ruination. It is widely believed that when the time comes for a witch to supply a victim for ritualistic feasting, members of a witch coven can reject a fellow witch's choice of a victim if they think the demise or destruction of the victim will not cause sufficient anguish or suffering for the survivors.

As a first step to cannibalizing their victims, witches transmogrify their human victims into such animals as goats or sheep, which are then slaughtered and consumed (Debrunner 1961; Soku 2000). Soku (2000, 46) writes, "The victims are not normally killed in human form. They are mostly changed into animals and killed and feasted on. The person dies physically."

Noncannibalistic Witches

Traditional beliefs about witches and witchcraft also include noncannibalistic witches (Bannerman-Richter 1982; Soku 2000). Noncannibalistic witches are those who do not wish to imperil the physical lives of their relatives or loved ones. As noted above, cannibalistic covens of witches operate on principles of reciprocity. Partaking in a cannibalistic feast requires submission of a victim for a future feast. Noncannibalistic witches are the equivalent of vegetarian witches, abstaining from the ritualistic consumption of meat. Noncannibalistic witches, it is believed, oftentimes self-describe as vultures who scavenge for food on refuse dumps. In *The Practice of Witchcraft in Ghana* (1982), Bannerman-Richter describes the activities of noncannibalistic witches: "During the night, while other witches gather in groups to indulge their appetites, she may change into a vulture or a centipede and feed on garbage at garbage dumps" (Bannerman-Richter 1982, 85). In the social world of witches, noncannibalistic witches are not accorded the same degree of respect as are cannibalistic witches; they occupy the bottom rungs of the witch social hierarchy. Some beliefs suggest that noncannibalistic witches are witches who have been temporarily or permanently expelled and excluded from cannibalistic witch covens for violating normative practices of the coven.

The Spiritual Witch

Another common Akan witchcraft belief is that a witch conducts all nocturnal deeds in spirit form while her physical body sleeps (Bannerman-Richter 1982; Fisher 1998). Thus, people who tend to attain a very deep sleep are suspected of being witches. The assumption is that difficulties in rousing a person from their sleep indicate the soul or spirit has departed the body, leaving the physical body behind. It is believed that before a witch undertakes the nocturnal aerial flight to attend the witches' Sabbath, she must perform magical rites to put members of her household to sleep so that they will not notice her absence from the house (Ntim-Korsah 1988). Consider the following excerpt from Ntim-Korsah's study of witchcraft beliefs among the people of Techiman in the Brong Ahafo region of Ghana, regarding rituals performed by witches prior to departure for nocturnal meetings:

> If a witch wants to fly in the night, he or she hypnotizes all people sleeping in the room by any method that is preferable. A pillow can be laid on the head of the one sleeping next to him or her and this is supposed to keep watch so that nobody gets up before the witch comes back. Lotion could also be dropped on the sleeping partner so that he sleeps soundly throughout the witch's absence. At Hansuah near Techiman it was narrated to me by a witch doctor that once, a witch in an attempt to put lotion into the eyes of those sleeping, one of them almost opened his eyes so the lotion went on the eye balls. This later resulted in a severe eye trouble which could not be cured scientifically at any hospital. An advice was given by an older woman that the eye problem was a spiritual disease and that the oracles should be consulted. When this was done, it was then known that it was due to the lotion of a witch. The eye trouble was in a form of punishment for attempting to challenge the witch so the plan by the witch was that the person would have been rendered blind so that he was unable to trouble the witch again. (Ntim-Korsah 1988, 14–15)

Another popular Akan belief suggests that witches strip themselves naked before undertaking their nocturnal flights to witches' meetings. Ntim-Korsah (1988, 15) describes the Techiman-Brong belief: "They strip themselves naked and after that, talisman and rings including the witch substances are taken. Some are believed to besmear their body with some pomade, some drink some lotions or syrups, some sit on particular chairs and then, charged with the witch power, they emit fire so that even if a person is awake, it would take time before the one can see clearly, and after that, they fly away."

Who Is Bewitched?

There is a common Ghanaian belief that ungenerous, uncaring, and non-sharing behaviors may precipitate bewitchment of the person who exhibits such behavior. As a corollary, it is believed that witches generally do not kill persons who are kind, caring, compassionate, and generous toward their relatives, financially or materially. This belief is associated with the local Ghanaian value of sharing. A popular Akan proverb illustrates this worldview: "ɔbayifoɔ kum wadi-wamma-me na ɔnkum wama-me-na-ɛsua" (the witch kills the person who eats and does not give me any, not the one who eats but gives me only a little). Importantly, a fundamental Ghanaian value is sharing. People who are wealthy are enjoined to share their wealth with their more economically marginal relatives. People who are wealthy but are heartless, uncaring, or selfish with their wealth are said to stand a good chance of suffering death through bewitchment.

Can Witches Bewitch Spouses and Other Nonkin?

Can a wife bewitch a husband or can a husband bewitch his wife? Can a witch ever bewitch any nonrelative? Among some ethnic groups in the country, the bewitchment of spouses and other nonkin is said to not only be possible, but also to regularly occur. Yet Akans generally believe that direct bewitchment is only possible between persons who are members of the same *abusua* (Adinkrah 2004; Bannerman-Richter 1982; Gray 2000). Concurrently, a person cannot be directly bewitched by a stranger, friend, acquaintance or any nonrelative. This is illustrated by the Akan proverb, "ɔbayifoɔ anum yɛ nnam a, odidi asuogya na ɔntumi mfa ntwa asuo" (however sharp or destructive the power of a witch, she cannot cross the river with the witchcraft power). That is, however sharp a witch, she cannot attack a stranger but can use witchcraft to attack only a maternal relative. Other Akan maxims illustrate the close familial relationship between the witch and her victim: "aboa bi bɛka wo a na ɛfiri woara ntoma mu" (the insect that is biting you is located inside your own clothes). This stresses the Akan notion that one can be bewitched only by a close relative. Another maxim is "nku me fie na ɛnkɔ su me abɔnten," which castigates the witch relative not to kill a person at home and then go to mourn that person in public.

While Akans hold direct bewitchment of a spouse or other nonmatrikin to be impossible, Akans consider it possible to indirectly bewitch nonkin. This requires working through a witch colleague who belongs to the *abusua* of their intended victims (Bannerman-Richter 1982; Brempong 1986). An Akan proverb, "sɛ abɔbonten so ni bɛnya wo a, na efi wo fie nipa" (an outsider can harm you only with the connivance of your own family member) reflects this phenomenon.

While witch lore contains little on the subject of husbands bewitching wives, references to wives bewitching husbands, directly or indirectly, are common. It is believed that such husbands can be identified by the nature of their behavior toward their wives. Such husbands are identified as exceptionally subservient and submissive to wifely control. In traditional Ghanaian society, men are the economic providers in the family on whom wives and dependent children rely for their material sustenance and economic survival. In most instances, the husband is the sole or dominant breadwinner of the family. Along with this economic role, the man is the effective head of the household, responsible for making final and authoritative decisions regarding major matters that affect the family. Households that significantly deviate from this model are regarded with considerable suspicion. Particularly in instances where it is the wife who is the dominant personality in the household and the husband is regarded as inordinately obsequious, it is commonly alleged that the wife is a witch who has appropriated her husband's intelligence, knowledge, will, and prestige and turned him into an animal that she commands during the night. It is explained that some female witches transform their husbands into horses or donkeys at night and ride them to travel to their regular witch conferences or Sabbaths. These types of suspicions are most rampant in the case of households where the man performs such work as chopping firewood, providing child care, or engaging in any food preparation, all of which are considered to be women's work. For example, Korankye provides the following on the Ajumako traditional area and their beliefs about the possibilities of wife-husband bewitchment:

> Among the people of the Ajumako traditional area witches cannot bewitch a person outside her clan but a witch can cause harm to her husband. A husband who pays no attention to the needs of his wife can be punished by his wife who is a witch. Husbands are ridden as horses to witch meetings by their wives who are witches when they fail to fulfill their obligations as husbands. Sometimes they suffer chronic headaches, waist pains and stomach troubles. They cause their husbands to obey their commands. It is not uncommon to see husbands submitting to their wives. The wives therefore become heads in marital homes. (Korankye 1997, 19)

In many instances, men have divorced wives accused of witchcraft or who have confessed to being witches. Men who divorced wives branded as witches often did so out of fear of bewitchment by the wife. Some men also appeared to be attempting to avert the shame and stigma attendant to having so close an association with a witch. For unmarried women, accusations of being a witch potentially dims their prospects of finding a husband. An unmarried woman whose sister or mother has been accused of witchcraft may find it hard to obtain a suitor.

Symptoms of Bewitchment

How does one know that one is being bewitched? Akans believe that particular types of nightmares are symptomatic of bewitchment (Debrunner 1961). Dreams or nightmares in which the dreamer is being pursued or attacked by wild animals is considered a sure sign that one is being bewitched (Debrunner 1961). A nightmare in which a person is being attacked by a *onwansan* (bushbuck) is considered particularly indicative of bewitchment. Regarding the linkage between dreams and suspicion of bewitchment, consider the following:

> A person infers bewitchment if he/she dreams of being chased by a close relative such as an aunt or a grandmother. If at the same time he falls ill, and all of a sudden the sickness is one of a mystery, for instance severe headache which he had never experienced before and which orthodox medicines have failed to cure, he begins to suspect that he is being bewitched by the one he dreamed of. Among the Mamprusis, a person who suspects bewitchment discloses his/her suspicion to the family head. A meeting of the household is convened and the suspect is confronted with the allegation. If she denies the allegation, which often happens, they send the matter to the chief's palace who will then direct them to the Gambarana [custodian of the witch sanctuary in Gambaga, or witch doctor] who through a fowl ordeal is able to ascertain whether the person is indeed a witch. (Assani 1996, 4–5)

There is another particular type of dream experience that is taken as unquestionable proof of bewitchment. This type of dream, called *omununkum* in Akan, involves some form of physical paralysis. The dreamer has a vivid, intense nightmare and has difficulty awaking from the dream. The dreamer typically feels incapable of moving, and is unable to shout or scream for assistance. Recurrent experience of such sleep paralysis is diagnosed by fetish priests or healers as an indicator of bewitchment.

Modes of Preserving and Transmitting Witchcraft

Given that witches bequeath their witchcraft power to their favorite children (usually daughters) and favorite grandchildren (usually granddaughters), one can safely infer that witches regard witchcraft as a good or precious thing worth transferring only to beloved relatives. According to Bannerman-Richter (1982, 36), "witches often regard witchcraft as a kind of heirloom." The witchcraft power does not die with the death of the carrier or practitioner. Such an important family heirloom must be preserved at all costs. "Occasionally, however, the transfer is made to a non-relative, but this happens only when the dying witch has no relatives of her own to whom she can transfer her witchcraft. When this is the case, she may give her witchcraft to her closest friend's daughter or granddaughter" (Bannerman-Richter 1982, 36).

A review of the witchcraft lore of various ethnic groups in the country indicates that there are several modes for the transmission of witchcraft power to other persons, including intrauterine or congenital transfer, ingestion of food laced with the witchcraft substance, commercial purchase of the power, and insertion of the witchcraft power in trinkets and jewelry that are bequeathed to one's progeny or offered as gifts (Bannerman-Richter 1982; Debrunner 1961; Mensa-Bonsu 2001; Nukunya 2003).

Akans believe that children inherit witchcraft from their maternal relatives, particularly such close relations as the mother and grandmother. In some instances, the witch substance is given to the child in utero if the mother herself is a witch (Bannerman-Richter 1982; Kuada and Chachah 1999; Mensa-Bonsu 2001; Mettle-Nunoo 1994). In these cases, the witch substance or *bayie* is transmitted naturally via blood and other bodily fluids in the womb from the witch-mother to the developing fetus. In instances of intrauterine witchcraft transfer, some assert that the witchcraft power becomes activated following birth. Other observers (e.g., Mettle-Nunnoo 1994, 64) maintain that "such children do not realize that they are witches till they attain puberty." According to Bannerman-Richter (1982, 33), "the natural born witch, is by far the most evil witch in Ghana, but despite the keenness of her type of witchcraft, she is herself usually ignorant of how she came by it. Asked how she got her powers, she might reply that she 'came with it from the sky,' meaning that it was God-given; she was born with it."

There are those who believe that a woman who is not a witch is capable of producing an infant who is a witch: "This is because it is believed that witches wash their filth in nearby streams before returning home after their nocturnal activities. The stream thus becomes infested with witchcraft. Therefore, the first woman who steps into the stream to fetch water for her household chores would have her next issue infested with the witch spirit" (Mettle-Nunoo 1994, 64).

Akans also maintain that witchcraft substance may be transferred through food or drinks, without the knowledge or consent of the potential inheritor or acquirer of witchcraft (Kuada and Chachah 1999; Mensa-Bonsu 2001). The most common foods used in the transmission of witchcraft substance are those prepared with red palm oil or palm fruits. For instance, among Akans there is a common belief that the witchcraft spirit is usually transferred through *aprapransa,* a local food prepared from corn, palm fruit soup, and red palm oil. It may also be transferred through such foods as *abεnkwan* (palm fruit soup) or *garifɔtɔ* (a dish consisting of *gari,* which is grated, dried, and fried cassava, cooked beans, and red palm oil). A self-avowed witch might say, "The ɔbayi was given me by my aunt. When she came to stay with me she cooked some soup one day and gave some to me. Some weeks or months after she had gone home, I began to feel ill and miserable and then I knew that [she] must have given me a *bayi* in the soup" (self-avowed witch quoted in Mensa-Bonsu 2001, 509). People are therefore implored to be wary of accepting food from persons they suspect to be witches and from whom they fear bewitchment.

Both children and adults are considered capable of acquiring witchcraft as gifts from close kin within the *abusua*. Witchcraft may be transmitted through trinkets like earrings, waist beads, necklaces, and other types of jewelry (Mettle-Nunoo, 1994). It is not uncommon to hear such witch confessions as "My grandmother was a witch and when she died she left me some earrings. Later on, when I became a witch, I realized that the ɔbayi must have come to me from my grandmother's earrings" (Mensa-Bonsu, 2001). Given that this is another popular mode of transmission, young girls and women are counseled against accepting beaded bracelets, waist beads, jewelry, trinkets, and other types of jewelry as gifts from elderly relatives that could be using such objects for transmitting their witchcraft power.

There are strong incentives for witches to pass on their witchcraft power. There is a strong belief among some Akan groups that witchcraft power cannot to be taken to the netherworld (Ntim-Korsah 1988). A witch must shed his or her witchcraft spirit before death. For this reason, people are cautioned to stay away from a witch who is on the verge of death. Facing imminent death, a dying witch can transfer her witchcraft to a favorite daughter or granddaughter by simply breathing the witchcraft spirit into the child or spitting it into the child's mouth. It is not uncommon to hear self-confessed witches describing their mode of acquiring witchcraft by such methods: "My mother had been a witch, when she was dying and I bent over her she breathed her ɔbayi from her mouth into mine with her last breath. I became very sad and ill after her death, and soon I knew that I was a witch and the ɔbayi had come from my dying mother" (quoted in Mensa-Bonsu 2001, 509).

Other Means to Acquire Witchcraft

Akans also believe that witchcraft may be purchased from a sorcerer in the same way that a person acquires personal property (Bannerman-Richter 1982; Mettle-Nunoo 1994). The motive for purchasing witchcraft spirit is always considered to be instrumental.

> Driven by greed and quest for power, some people seek out necromancers and panderers of witchcraft and buy it from them. The necromancer is usually

only a middleman who introduces the prospective buyer to the evil spirits who distribute witchcraft to buyers. Most sorcerers who participate in this kind of activity are men, and while they sell the powers to others, they themselves refrain from using them, as they are very much aware of the terrifying consequences of dabbling in witchcraft. A sorcerer who sells witchcraft is like a dope pusher who abstains from taking dope himself. Sometimes an occultist who panders witchcraft may even warn a prospective buyer of the dangers involved in the practice and might sell it to her only after all efforts to dissuade her have failed. (Bannerman-Richter 1982, 38)

It is believed that witchcraft that is purchased is far easier to dispose of by the carrier than is inherited witchcraft (Awedoba 2002; Bannerman-Richter 1982). Bannerman-Richter (1982, 21) theorizes why hereditary witchcraft is difficult to shed: "Inherited witchcraft is not so easy to get rid of, for usually a witch who inherits her witchcraft would not know how to get rid of it herself, because in most cases the donor would be deceased by the time she goes through a change of heart, since witches usually bequeath their witchcraft to their favorite relatives while on the verge of their own death; it is some kind of parting gift."

Does the mode of acquisition of the witchcraft substance affect the potency of the witch power? Some observers suggest the affirmative. Mensa-Bonsu (2001, 509) notes, "A few people, it is held, are born witches. The *bayi* comes from the mother into the pregnant womb. Such congenital witches are the worst kind and little can be done to cure them. 'Curing them is like plucking a live fowl: after a time the feathers grow again.'" Writing on the transmission of witchcraft among the Kasena, Awedoba notes,

Kasena believe that some people acquire at birth the ability to "see"; that is to say, they can see spirits and people's souls and be able to harm others by snatching their souls which they can eat or destroy in some other way. Such are the *chera* or witches. They are believed to have acquired the propensity from their mothers and the concept of *ka fo da yia* (to deny one another's eyes) confirms this. It is an axiom that within the full sibling group, if one is proved to be a witch, the other full siblings are also witches since the propensities inheres in the matriline. It is also believed that a mother who is a witch will not fail to feed the witchcraft substance to her children. The *chera* or witches are believed to be more powerful than ordinary people but that power compares in no way with the greater power of the ancestors (*chira*) and the local gods or *tangona*. This is evidenced by the tendency to call upon the gods to deal with the witches. One rule observed by witches is not to transgress lineage boundaries. A witch can only prey on his or her lineage members. Parents may catch their children or present them to the other witches in the clan settlement in settlement of witchcraft debts. Marriage severs the right of a woman's lineage to catch her or use her or her children in settlement of witchcraft obligations. To do this would provoke the anger of the ancestors. On the other hand, after marriage, a woman witch becomes eligible for recruitment to the coven of witches in her husband's clan settlement. (Awedoba 2000, 23)

Akans believe that not everyone is capable of receiving and properly nurturing the witchcraft substance. Some *sunsum* or *kra* (personalities, spirits, or life souls) may not be compatible with the witchcraft substance. This can cause the recipient to suffer serious psychological problems that may manifest as madness or chronic physical maladies.

Gender and Witchcraft

Patriarchal attitudes, misogynistic beliefs, and ageist values mediate witchcraft beliefs in Ghanaian society. It is believed that the overwhelming majority of witches are female (Adinkrah 2004; Amoah 1987; Bannerman-Richter 1982; Gray 2000; Kuada and Chachah 1999; Wiafe 2001). Indeed, the majority of persons suspected of, accused of, or allegedly caught or arrested for witchcraft by fetish shrines and pentecostal churches or, yet still, banished to witches' sanctuaries throughout the country, are women or girls (Amoah 1987). So widespread is this association of witchcraft with females in many Ghanaian minds that some authors equate it exclusively with females. In *The Practice of Witchcraft in Ghana* (1982), Bannerman-Richter justifies the use of the female pronoun, she, throughout the text because, as he puts it, "though not exclusively a female phenomenon, most witches are females" (ii).

Why are there gender differences in witchcraft involvement? Ghanaians commonly attribute males and females with innate differences that are invoked to explain greater female proclivities toward witchcraft activity. They maintain that females are spiritually weaker than males, and are therefore more prone to be utilized by malevolent spirits for evil ends. As Amoah writes,

> In a traditional society, women were considered weak, both physically and spiritually, for it was believed that they have light or weak *sunsum*. *Sunsum* is one of the spiritual elements present in a human being, and it is believed to be transmitted to children through the father. It yields certain personality traits, such as bravery, and sometimes acts as a protective aura for the individual. Because women have weak *sunsum*, they are said to be easy prey to outside spiritual powers and influences. This belief in women's special susceptibility accounts, in part, for the frequency of witchcraft accusation against women. (Amoah 1987, 86)

Akans perceive witchcraft to stem from feelings of *anibrε* (jealousy or covetousness) (Debrunner 1961; Obeng 2004). Some observers maintain that, compared with men, women are more inclined toward resentment, jealousy, vengefulness, and envy, and are generally morally deficient. These characteristics, they claim, make women vulnerable and more susceptible to the influences of witchcraft (Gray 2000).

Some Ghanaians believe that females are more likely than males to become witches because of their lower intelligence and emotionality, compared with men. Although attitudes are changing, throughout Ghana in all ethnic groups there is a tendency to perceive women as childlike, more emotional, and of lower intelligence than men. There is widespread perception that while men are oftentimes occupied with matters of real importance, women are more concerned with the trivial and the petty. As Amoah (1987, 85) describes it, "In most of the deliberations concerning the welfare of the community, women are left out. If men are present, the views of women are not needed; it is said, ɔbaa deɛ onim nyansa bɛn? "What wisdom has a woman?" It is precisely because women are considered unintelligent that their views are rarely sought in decision making."

Female witches are also believed to be much more active practitioners of the profession than are their male counterparts (Bannerman-Richter 1982). They attend meetings more regularly and are more involved in the activities of the witch coven. Relative to male witchcraft, female witchcraft is also believed to be more frequently used for destructive ends. Female witchcraft is believed to more likely be used to kill, cause infertility, blight neighbors' crops, cause financial ruination, cause alcohol dependence, and cause long, incurable illnesses. Male witchcraft, on the other hand, is more often directed toward such beneficent ends as protecting their progeny, advancing prosperity in their children, and facilitating bountiful crop yields. However, when male witchcraft is used for destructive ends, its potency is said to be much greater than female witchcraft. Indeed, although only a small minority of witches is believed to be male, it is widely believed that the potency of male witchcraft, whether used for benevolent or malevolent ends, is far greater than female witchcraft. It is believed that the power of one *baribonsam* or *barima bonsam* (male wizard) is equivalent to the power of seven female witches combined. This makes wizards more dangerous than witches; wizards, therefore, inspire greater fear (Bannerman-Richter 1982, 74). Debrunner noted (1961, 73-74): "Wizards are reputed to be more dangerous than witches. Two of them, I have frequently been told, are strong enough to destroy a town." However, because it is believed that wizards use their witchcraft for constructive ends while witches use their witchcraft for destructive purposes, people are more fearful of the bewitchment potential of elderly female relatives than they are of elderly male relatives.

Old Age and Witchcraft

Many cultures believe that old age and the possession and practice of witchcraft are strongly linked. In Akan witchcraft discourse, witches are typically portrayed as elderly persons (Adinkrah 2004; Bannerman-Richter 1982). Among the Mamprusis of northern Ghana, too, elderly persons are at greatest risk of being accused or branded a witch. At the Gambaga Witches' Camp, a sanctuary for witches fleeing familial or community persecution, I found a large number of senior citizens and elderly persons in the population of residents. Old men and women were particularly vulnerable to witchcraft accusation and subsequent banishment from their communities. This common tendency to link old age with witchcraft in Ghanaian society has spelled doom in many instances for many an elderly person, but particularly elderly women. Bannerman-Richter (1982, 17) notes, "The secrecy about witches' identities has created in most people a sense of paranoia and suspicion to such a point that an innocent person may be suspected of being a witch and harassed unduly just because she was fortunate enough to live to a great old age. This stigma is usually reserved for old women; longevity in men carries no such suspicion."

Why are the elderly, particularly the very elderly, so vulnerable to witchcraft accusations? One answer is that, in a society with high rates of infant mortality and where life expectancy is low, the aged have reached an age less commonly attained and are suspected of having used witchcraft power to achieve it (Korankye 1997).

Child Witches

While elderly females are most often identified as witches, Akan witch beliefs acknowledge the existence of child witches. The belief is strong among Akans that witchcraft power can be given to an infant or newborn at birth or even while still in the mother's womb. Generations ago when it was more common for elderly female relatives to assist in birth deliveries as midwives, it was believed that if the birth attendant was a witch, she could change the newborn's fate to something less desirable, particularly if it was perceived, spiritually, that the child would grow up to become successful in life. Given that elderly females are perceived to be the source of witchcraft transfer, children who reside with maternal grandmothers are perceived to be at an acute risk for receiving witchcraft because of their physical proximity to the source, which makes it easier for the transfer. Being the favorite child of a grandparent or a parent who is a witch also places the child at risk for the receipt of *bayie*. This tendency for alleged witches to transfer the witch substance to a favorite child or grandchild affirms the belief that witches perceive witchcraft as a good thing that is worth passing on to favored wards. As earlier discussions indicated, the witch substance can be passed on to the child via food or drink or given to the child as gifts of adornment such as bracelets or as waist beads.

There is a widely held belief in some Ghanaian communities that extreme precociousness in children is evidence of witchcraft possession. A child who is considered *aperɛwa* (speaks like an adult) or one who is *mpanyinsɛm* (acts like an adult) or one who is *pɛ nsɛmkeka* or *kasa dodo* (loquacious) is most likely to be tagged with a witch label. Children who are verbally or behaviorally disrespectful toward adults are also often suspected of being witches.

Precociousness in behavior and language is interpreted as children carrying a witchcraft spirit older than their chronological age that pushes them to unconsciously act the way they do. Among school-aged children, the witch label is more likely to be placed on female peers who excel academically or demonstrate aptitude in mathematics and the sciences. A boy who excels academically does not face such accusations because it is expected that boys will naturally excel academically, as well as in athletics.

Disabilities and the Witch

Traditional beliefs in Ghana commonly impute the causes of disability to such evil influences as witchcraft and sorcery; others attribute it to a curse on the individual or his family (Oliver-Commey 2001). For this reason, disabled persons can be regarded with compassion by some and with complete disdain by others; they often encounter discrimination in society (Hagan 1981).

People with disabilities, particularly if they are elderly, are likely to be considered as witches. Instead of seeing disability as an impairment or disease, some Ghanaians commonly conceptualize disability in the elderly, particularly elderly females, as a manifestation of witchcraft practice. This stems, in part, from the belief that witches tend to offer their own body parts to the witches' coven when they are unwilling or unable to supply a human victim for cannibalistic feasts.

Specific physical features are interpreted as indicative of witchcraft possession, particularly when conjoined by other factors. Elderly women with physical features considered extraordinary are most susceptible to witchcraft accusations. These include physical deformities or abnormalities, emaciated bodies, wrinkled facial skin, toothlessness, yellowish or reddish eyes, stooped or hunched posture, flaccid breasts, shriveled stomachs, and facial or chest hair (Adinkrah 2004; Assani 1996; Debrunner 1961; Nukunya 2003). Young or old persons with six or more fingers are also likely to be suspected or accused of being witches (Debrunner 1961). In a small town in the Eastern Region of Ghana, the story was related to me of an elderly female suspected of witchcraft who was arrested or caught by a fetish shrine. In her confessional statement to the shrine, this peasant farmer, known throughout the small village community for her affliction with leprosy of the fingers and toes, allegedly confessed that spiritually she was a witch queen. According to her own testimony, at night during her revels with other witches in her witch coven, what appeared to ordinary eyes as leprosy were in fact jewelry and ornaments made from unadulterated gold; these ornaments sparkled at night and symbolized her queenly status in the witch company.

Behavioral Characteristics of Witches

Also vulnerable to the witch label are elderly women whose behavior or outward demeanor is considered eccentric. This includes women who regularly talk or mutter to themselves or who are regarded as inquisitive, meddlesome, garrulous, and cantankerous (Assani 1996; Bannerman-Richter 1982; Gray 2000).

Any woman whose children have achieved exceptional success or failure in any realm may be suspected of being a witch (Adinkrah 2004; Amoah 1987). Elderly women with either financially successful or unsuccessful children can become the target of witchcraft accusations, with the attribution of success or failure placed squarely on the witch (Adinkrah 2004; Amoah 1987). Indeed, suspicions of witchery by and witchcraft accusations against women—particularly elderly women—are so common that it is almost impossible to find a Ghanaian who is unaware of any elderly woman in his or her community accused of being a witch (Adinkrah 2004).

Low socioeconomic status and poverty are additional risk factors for imputation of witchcraft and victimization for violence related to witchcraft accusations. Indigent, elderly widows with little formal education are subject to witchcraft accusations in greater proportion to their peers in the higher socioeconomic classes. Older women who are economically well-off are seldom targets of witch accusations.

Suspicion of witchery, witchcraft accusations, and risk of violent victimization are also greatest for elderly women who live alone. Elderly women who are socially isolated and have few relatives are often branded witches, the assumption being that they have used supernatural afflictions via witchcraft power to decimate their families or to have killed and eaten them spiritually (Amoah 1987). In Amoah's study, a sixty-year-old woman who had been twice widowed was divorced by her third husband when he discovered that she had outlived two previous husbands. She was later accused by the husband and the wider community of witchcraft because she had been twice widowed and had two alcoholic grown-up children (Amoah 1987).

Malevolent Witches and the Evil That They Do

If there is one thing that Ghanaians share in their witchcraft beliefs, it is the notion that witchcraft is an evil, malevolent force employed to afflict all manner of misfortunes on another person. Concurrently, witches are regarded as inherently evil and depraved and therefore deserving of severe censure, including death. According to Bannerman-Richter (1982, 13–14), witches are "believed to derive great pleasure in harming and killing people. The more innocent their victims the greater pleasure they derive from their wickedness." Most Ghanaians believe that witchcraft is always used for malevolent purposes (Bannerman-Richter 1982; Kondor 1991a; Kuada and Chachah 1999). There is a common belief that witches cause automobile accidents, plane crashes, and train derailments. Witchcraft can also be used to afflict epilepsy and cause blindness and madness in others. It is further believed that witches can morph into ferocious animals and destroy other people's farms. In the minds of most Ghanaians, the major or sole preoccupation of witches is to maim, kill, or destroy. As one informant, a local Ghanaian pastor, ardently expressed to me in one interview, "Witches are the agents of Satan. Human flesh is their food and human blood their drink. They are evil spirits so they don't like good things. When they see good things, they like to destroy it. Witches are afraid of Christians because they fear the word of God. Witches are afraid of prayers. So if you are a Christian and you like prayers, witches cannot deal with you to destroy you or harm you."

Although it is believed that a small minority of witches use their mystical powers to good ends, Akan witch beliefs focus on the malefic witch (Debrunner 1961). Witches are blamed for myriad maladies and disorders (Bierlich 1995; Debrunner 1961; Ghana News Agency 2012; Gray 2000). No disease, illness, or physical affliction escapes attribution of witchery. As later sections of this chapter illustrate, in Ghana witchcraft has been used to explain anemia, breast cancer, debility, hepatitis, HIV/AIDS, leprosy, meningitis, rheumatism, scabies, stroke, hypertension, insomnia, senility, and a number of other illnesses (Kwamin 2008; Ghana News Agency 2012; Yankah 2004). Bierlich (1995) observed from the study of citizen perceptions of guinea worm infestation in northern Ghana that on a few occasions witchcraft, fueled by the envy of fellow citizens, was mentioned as the cause of guinea worm infestation.

It is popularly believed that witches have the ability to cause a range of accidents. For instance, a witch may cause a tree to fall on a person or cause a victim to suffer a snake-bite (Mettle-Nunoo 1994). More notably, witchcraft is used to explain truck accidents and associated injuries and deaths. Fatal automobile accidents, particularly those occurring around Christmas, New Year's, and Easter holidays, are perennially blamed on the maleficent activities of witches and wizards. As Soku (2000, 46) writes, "To have human blood, accidents are planned on roads, in the air, on the sea, in factories and natural disasters." In Ghana, traffic accident fatalities have become so rampant that some observers have utilized the term "epidemic" to underline their prevalence. Indeed, national data show an upsurge in vehicle crash rates and automobile accident mortality figures during holidays. While road traffic experts attribute these accidents to drunk-driving, driver fatigue, defective vehicles, poor roads, and excessive speeding on the nation's highways and on urban and semi-urban roadways, the Ghanaian public often blames the accidents on supernatural causes, including witchcraft. Therefore religious leaders, churches, individuals, and entire communities invest hours in prayers for protection against supernatural forces to avert road crashes during these peak seasons. The perennial attribution of road accidents to demonic and negative spiritual forces such as witchcraft caused the following public awareness announcement to be inserted in a conspicuous section of a local daily newspaper just two days before Easter:

> The Executive Director of the National Road Safety Commission (NRSC) Mr. Noble Appiah sees things differently and says the gods, witches and evil spirits are innocent of all accusations of involvement in accidents that occur in the country during such periods and other occasions. . . . Fatigue, drunk driving and overspeeding are the main culprits in the road accidents that occur during periods such as Easter. It is common knowledge that during such periods, there are many more passengers who intend traveling to various destinations to spend the occasion with families and friends. The passengers who crowd the lorry [truck] stations become attractive to commercial vehicle drivers who try to cash in to make as much as they can. Drivers try to do as many as possible without rest. The second cause of accidents during Easter periods is drunk driving, and this trait is said to be more associated with private car drivers. Due to the festive occasion, many people take friends and relatives out for a drink and most often over-indulge. This leads to accidents. The next cause of accidents is over-speeding. Commercial vehicle drivers intent on cashing in on the occasion would want to over-speed in order to make more trips in a day and this leads to accidents. In the situation where vehicles

in the country are not well maintained and the roads are generally in poor shape, over-speeding could be dangerous. Over-speeding and over-taking are the twin evils that cause accidents most but these are not demons but the result of poor driver behavior. ("Avoiding Accidents" 2004, 17)

Witchcraft and Chronic Abuse of Alcohol

Witchcraft is also invoked to explain chronic alcoholism (Amoah 1987; Appiah-Kubi 1981; Awedoba 2002; Mettle-Nunoo 1994). It is commonly alleged that in the case of an alcoholic the witch has mystically placed a large metal container, locally called *grawa* (gallon) or *bare* (barrel), inside the alcoholic's stomach to collect the liquor consumed. Due to the enormous size of the container, no amount of alcohol that the bewitched alcoholic drinks is ever sufficient to fill it up. So the alcoholic continues drinking, never reaching a level of satiation (Mettle-Nunoo 1994). It is believed that until the container is spiritually removed from his stomach, alcoholism or excessive alcohol consumption will persist for the afflicted individual.

Witchcraft and Untimely Deaths

Witchcraft is often used to explain *mpatuwuo* (sudden or untimely deaths). People who die in their youth or suffer sudden deaths are assumed to be victims of bewitchment (Awedoba 2000; Debrunner 1961). In a society where very few deaths are autopsied, all deaths except those of the aged tend to set in motion all manner of speculation about the witch or sorcerer responsible, particularly if the death involves a very young person, a wealthy person, or a highly educated person. According to Akan belief system, witches slowly consume the flesh and internal organs of their victims (Kuada and Chachah 1999). It is only after the essential or vital organs such as heart and lungs have been devoured that the afflicted person dies. What seems to the uninitiated to be a sudden death may have been a slow death spanning days, weeks, or even months. Since witchcraft is considered primarily malevolent and destructive and its purpose is to cause the greatest pain or havoc to its victims, witches target people in the prime of their lives who are successful in their fields of endeavor or who have promising futures, rather than the old, frail, or unsuccessful.

There is a perception in this part of the world that if someone who is apparently well dies suddenly, then there must be more to it than meets the eye. This feeling is so ingrained in our thinking that it is very common for one to say that there must be some "domestic forces" at work. Some people then go to the extent of "consulting oracles and deities to find out what might have caused the death. It appears people cannot imagine that a person can die "just like that." I have heard and seen the reactions of relatives and the puzzled look of utter disbelief on their faces. Due to our ignorance, and some might say, superstition, we are often tempted to believe that this is not something that can be explained medically. Even when post mortems have been conducted, which clearly explain the cause of death, people still doubt the doctor's report. (Clay 2003, 11)

Witchcraft and Infertility

Impotence and sterility in men is often ascribed to witchcraft (Appiah-Kubi 1981). In traditional Ghanaian communities, a man who is incapable of fathering a child is typically assumed to have been a victim of witchcraft machinations. Given the high premium the society places on bearing children, depriving a man of his ability to father children is regarded as one of the most egregious afflictions that a witch can visit on a man. Not only does infertility in men cause disgrace in the community, but it also guarantees that the afflicted man will have no biological children on which to bequeath wealth and property, making his nephews and nieces in the matrilineal line automatic inheritors of his wealth. It is believed that such deprivation of the ability to father children is often accomplished through the spiritual removal of a bewitched male's testes or penis (Appiah-Kubi 1981). Confessional statements of witches often include claims of the removal and discarding of testicles of afflicted males in pit latrines, burying them in the ground, or hanging them atop huge *onyina* (silk-cotton) trees. The *onyina* tree is noted for its great size and height and for its finger-length thorns protruding from every angle of the tree. Access to the top of the tree via climbing is impossible. There have been some instances where confessing witches claimed to have removed and used men's penises as *abɔsoɔ* (a woman's belt or money bag worn around the waist).

In recent years it has also become common for Ghanaian men suffering from erectile dysfunction to invoke witchcraft as the cause of their affliction. This has prompted increasing numbers of men suffering from the condition to seek supernatural cures, remedies, or protection, through the services of shamans and other ritual specialists, rather than through medical treatment. Meanwhile, the alleged witches believed to be responsible are sought out and beaten, maimed, or even killed. The following account was provided by a columnist in a 1999 issue of the *Mirror*, a popular Ghanaian weekly:

In my hometown, Breman Asikuma, a school mate of mine, a policeman suffered four marital divorces because he was impotent and could not have sexual affair with any of his wives. He discovered later from some spiritual men that his impotence was due to his mother who had spiritually taken it away, owing to the fact that he (the son) had failed to remit her [i.e, had failed to send her money]. All spiritual efforts to regain his manhood had failed. So this policeman-victim did not go soft on the issue any longer, but went openly to the mother threatening to kill her with a sharp cutlass he wielded in his hands. The threat paid off. The mother confessed, gave him some herbal concoction to drink; and lo and behold, he was healed. He is now married with four children. (Ahinful 1999, 12)

Infertility and barrenness in women is equally an ignominious condition (Agyekum 1996; Sarpong 1977; Warren 1973). Given the Akan's matrilineal system of tracing descent, a woman who is incapable of bearing children cannot contribute to the continuation of her *abusua*. Innuendos and insinuations are often cast against the barren woman, suggesting her worthlessness. Again, witches are implicated through such acts as inverting the barren woman's womb to ensure that sperm from the male sexual partner cannot proceed to fertilize her ovum, or removing the uterus and burying it in the ground or hanging it atop an *onyina* tree. As in the case of the removal of men's testes, unless the witch returns the uterus, the bewitched woman has no chance of ever becoming pregnant.

Other explanations for how female infertility can be caused by maleficent witchcraft include suggestions that witches use a broom to sweep the uterus and then remove the victim's ovaries, thereby making conception virtually impossible (Brempong 1996). Stories also abound indicating that, following conception, witches occasionally remove the fetus for their own consumption, causing miscarriage or stillbirth in the expectant mother (Assimeng 1981; Brempong 1996). Additionally, consistent with their ability to morph into various forms, witches are believed to have the ability to change themselves into prospective male suitors and have sexual intercourse with the woman victim, therefore causing infertility or barrenness in her. Witches can assume the physical and facial form of the husband, have sexual intercourse with a pregnant woman, and cause her to suffer a miscarriage. Given the prevalent belief that barrenness, infertility, and sterility are caused by the maleficent activities or powers of witches, infertile couples frequently consult nonmedical practitioners for treatment such as Christian prayer houses, herbalists, traditional healers, and spiritualists, as a first-line measure (Kwawukume 2004).

Witchcraft and the Etiology of Stigmatized Conditions

Among Akans, *etwa or etwere* (epilepsy or epileptic seizures), euphemistically called *abonsam yaree* (disease of the devil), is one of the most stigmatized and dreaded of diseases. Akan speakers are exhorted to avoid all verbal references to the disease "because of the fear that the speaker can contract it when he mentions its real name" (Agyekum 1996, 176). It is strongly believed that witches have the capacity to spiritually cause epilepsy through witchcraft or bewitchment. Consider the following excerpt provided by a medical doctor with an established medical practice in Ghana: "Many people do not believe that epilepsy is a medical problem like any other and act as if this is caused by supernatural forces. During history taking when the doctor asks if a patient has ever had a seizure, at once the attitude of the patient changes. The Akans will say '*daabi, daabi, Nyame mpa ngu*' which means, no, no, God forbid" (Clay 2004, 12). Belief in the supernatural cause of epilepsy is the foremost reason people turn to prayer camps and spiritualists for spiritual assistance in the treatment of epilepsy.

Mental illness is another highly stigmatized condition in the society. Among the Akans, verbal discourse of any kind about mental disorders is taboo, given the immense fear and superstition that surrounds the disease. For example, many people believe that one can become insane by laughing at a mentally ill person or by merely uttering the word for madness or insanity (Agyekum 1996). Also in the context of witchcraft and bewitchment, among Akans the invocation of witchcraft as the supposed cause of severe or long illness is not confined to physical maladies alone but extends to insanity and other forms of psychiatric disorders. At present, many Ghanaians believe that mental illness is primarily the result of bewitchment (Agyekum 1996; Debrunner 1961; Obeng 2004). During my research tenure in Ghana, the story was related to me of a putative witch who placed a centipede inside the brain of her son, causing incapacitating sensations and mental illness in the purported victim. It was alleged that the man could not engage in any productive venture as he found the crawling sensations in his brain debilitating. The man consulted a fetish priest or shaman who promised an effective cure, indicating that the source of his condition was his mother. The fetish priest told the afflicted man that he would treat him but that an effective treatment would lead to the death of his mother, the alleged witch. The man acquiesced to the treatment. The centipede was said to have been spiritually removed from his brain. According to the informant, the condition of the young man improved immediately and his mother expired within hours of his return from the fetish priest.

Because psychiatric disorders are attributed to witchcraft, family and friends of the mentally afflicted often take their psychiatric patients to Christian prayer healing camps and traditional healers rather than have them committed to mental or psychiatric hospitals for treatment (Appiah-

Poku et al. 2004; "Psychiatrist Calls" 2005). Lamptey's (1977) research on inpatients with a psychotic illness in Accra yielded the finding that 92 percent of the patients had consulted traditional healing centers before seeking hospital treatment. In most prayer or healing camps, frequent and intense prayer and fasting are invoked to facilitate the deliverance of the mentally ill from the shackles of malevolent forces blamed for their condition. It is only when the prayer camps fail to heal the patient that they are sent to psychiatric hospitals. Even when patients are cured of their illness and are subsequently discharged from psychiatric hospitals, they are victimized by the prejudices of communities and even relatives with stigmatizing views of mental illness.

Agyekum (1996, 172) notes, "Among the Akan, *kwata* or leprosy is considered as one of the most dreadful diseases in the society. It is a disease that must not be mentioned in public; even at home, it must not be mentioned in normal conversations." Even cured leprosy patients and their families face stigmatization and ostracism (Agyekum 1996; "Leprosy Ambassador" 2010; Obour 2012). Bewitchment is often considered a source of leprosy. Others believe that leprosy is the result of a curse imposed on an individual or entire lineage by an aggrieved individual seeking vengeance. Others believe leprosy is punishment from the gods for some serious infraction against the community. For all of these reasons, lepers are shunned.

According to one report, Ghana records about 14,000 new cases of tuberculosis every year, and that an estimated 10,000 Ghanaians die of the disease annually (Amanor 2008). Many myths surround tuberculosis. Among these is the belief that tuberculosis is the work of witches and other malevolent spiritual forces. The multiplicity of euphemistic references for tuberculosis is denotative of the dread surrounding the disease in the Akan social realm. Among these, Agyekum (1996) mentions three: *owabɔne* (bad cough), *yarebɔne* (bad disease), and *nsamanwa* (ghost cough), in reference to the belief that the disease will eventually kill and turn the victim into a ghost (Agyekum 1996, 176). Given that tuberculosis is a stigmatizing disease and tuberculosis patients are among the most stigmatized groups in the society, it is widely believed that the witch deliberately spiritually infects her victim with the disease to cause the victim *animguaseɛ* (shame and dishonor) (see "Time to Eradicate TB" 2009). An April 2005 newspaper article appearing in the *Daily Graphic* titled "TB Is Not a Curse from the Gods" (Bonsu 2005) attempted to refute the prevalent notion that tuberculosis is the result of malevolent spirits.

Blindness is also perceived to be *abonsam yareɛ* (a disease of the devil) and is attributed to witchcraft or the malevolent activities of witches. Sores that are *kisi kuro* (chronic or slow to heal) are also believed to be caused by witchcraft. It is believed that witches use the part of the body bearing the sore, usually the leg, as a chopping board, hence the resistance of the sore to healing. As long as witches use it as a chopping board, the sore festers. Western medicine is deemed ineffective in treating ailments that are identified with supernatural etiologies. Snake bites, addiction to drugs, hemorrhoids, disabling injuries, business downturns, poverty, relationship failures, parenting problems, conjugal discord, and divorce may all be attributed to the actions of witches (Bannerman-Richter 1982; Ghunney, Greer, and Allen 1999; Gray 2000).

Medical Doctors and Witchcraft Beliefs

The pervasiveness of witchcraft beliefs among Ghanaians has implications for medical practice. Some Ghanaian medical practitioners, by virtue of having been socialized into Ghanaian norms and values, can hold views about the role of witchcraft in causing illness and disorders that are not countered by extensive years of scientific education, socialization, and training in Western medicine. Doctors who believe in witchcraft and witches are apt to attribute unusual or undiagnosable illnesses to the workings of witchcraft or sorcery and to advise patients to seek treatment for their ailments outside of formal medical establishments (Akosah-Sarpong 2012).

Witchcraft and Academic Failure

Some Ghanaians believe that witchcraft power can be used to make school-aged children fail in school, play truant, and to drop out altogether (Korankye 1997; Ntim-Korsah 1988). Witches are said to occasionally cause school-aged children to underachieve in school by turning their heads into soccer balls that witches kick around at night during their nocturnal meetings. It is also believed that a witch can use her witchcraft power to remove the brains of one child in order to add them to the brains of her own children to heighten their intelligence while creating dullardness in other children.

Witchcraft and Inability to Find Marital Partners

It is also widely believed that witches can deliberately use their powers to negatively affect a person's prospects for finding a romantic partner or spouse. Both male and female witches are said to have the capacity to spiritually marry an individual in whom they are sexually or romantically interested, surrounding this spiritual partner with an invisible shroud or aura that is impenetrable and that makes them literally unapproachable and unavailable to the opposite sex. Many women, in particular, who have yet to be married by their thirties or forties may blame their inability to secure a mate on a (female) witch or wizard who has married them spiritually. Such women even describe rousing from their sleep with such telltale signs as vaginal wetness, as if they have just completed a sexual act. Another form of bewitchment that makes women in particular unmarriageable includes the witch who spiritually smears female matrikin with urine, feces, garbage, and other malodorous agents that selectively emit their foul odors in the presence of members of the opposite sex, unbeknownst to the bewitched herself. The bewitched cannot comprehend or address the source of social rejection that she experiences from prospective mates since she cannot detect the odors that surround her. Witches can also turn the faces of such females into that of males so men see them as fellow males and therefore take no interest in them.

Witchcraft, Poverty and Financial Problems

Many Ghanaians believe that witchcraft can be used to cause poverty or financial ruin in their victims (Kuada and Chachah 1999; Mettle-Nunoo 1994). Witches are considered to have a variety of techniques or mechanisms at their disposal to accomplish this. They can, for example, use their spiritual powers to perforate the pockets of their victims so that whatever amount of money the bewitched individual earns disappears mysteriously or is frittered away through unnecessary expenditures (Kuada and Chachah 1999). They can put physically invisible holes in their victims' palms so that whatever amount of money falls into their palms is drained away. It is also believed that witches can cause their victims to fritter away hard-earned money on unnecessary, doomed-to-fail litigation. They can transform males into wanton womanizers who spend all of their money on women, and they can cause individuals to spend all of their money on alcoholic drinks to the point of becoming alcoholic and penurious. They can cause people's houses or cocoa farms to burn, bringing about significant financial loss. They can destroy the businesses of owners of commercial vehicles by causing their vehicles to suffer major truck accidents. They can bring well-to-do individuals to financial ruination by causing gambling and lottery addiction. They can lead thieves to steal their victims' assets so that they lose all of their wealth. Some Ghanaians also attribute job losses to the activities of witches. A civil servant or other worker who loses a job from dismissals, retrenchment, or any other factor may attribute such a job loss to a putative witch. The attitude is that everything happens for a reason, and that misfortune is caused by witches.

It is commonly believed that another mechanism for witches to cause financial mishap to farmers is by causing crop failure. Witches are believed to be capable of spiritually rendering a farm's topsoil impotent by using a broom to sweep minerals and other nutrients off of the soil. Alternatively, they may spiritually transform themselves into wild animals and graze on the crops, causing the crops to wilt or yield poorly (Ghana News Agency 2011).

Given the strong belief in witches' ability to hamper financial success, many Ghanaians who suspect that they are not reaping the financial benefits commensurate with their toils or who suffer sudden loss seek *abisa* (divination from fetish priests) to determine the source of their misfortunes or lack of financial success. Many are told that their lack of financial prosperity is due to the evil machinations of an alleged witch in their *abusua*. The story was related to me of a taxi driver who plied the streets of Accra. It was alleged that he would often drive his vehicle for hours without procuring a single passenger—a real mystery, given the number of people often hustling for taxis and other public transportation to get to their destinations. According to the story, a witch had caused the driver's empty taxi to always appear full to the ordinary eye so that nobody would hail his taxi. Given the strong belief in the role of witches in causing financial ruination, many young people who are starting life but fear financial ruination by witches go to witch doctors to obtain antiwitchcraft charms for spiritual protection.

Witchcraft and Criminal Behavior

Witchcraft is said to be capable of inducing some victims toward criminal and deviant behavior, particularly criminal recidivism and serious criminal offending. Deviant and criminal conduct—including rape, murder, and child sexual molestation—are explained in supernatural terms as symptoms of bewitchment. Witches are said to turn otherwise normal, conforming individuals destined for greatness into criminals who bring disrepute onto themselves and their immediate relatives. In a small town in the Eastern Region of Ghana, the story was related to me of a witch that was responsible for creating a classic kleptomaniac beginning in infancy. According to the story, a maternal grand aunt had visited the newborn and his mother at the hospital and commented about the infant boy's purported destiny to become a great person. The grand aunt was alleged to be a witch who had spiritually altered the boy's destiny, implanting a new destiny of thievery, and criminality. The bewitched child began his career of criminality pilfering pens, pencils, and erasers in primary school and escalated to major theft from family, neighbors, and strangers by the time he attained adulthood.

Witchcraft and Destiny

Among Akans, there is a belief that one's *nkrabea* or *hyɛbrɛ* (destiny) is determined prior to birth but can be altered through witchery. Thus, while whether one will be a success or a failure in life is established prior to one's birth, witches can change things for better or for worse. In Akan witch stories, one recurrently hears accounts where such negative alterations in destiny occurred. In the most common form of destiny alteration, the child is born great and witches in the family, spiritually aware of his greatness, use witchcraft to alter such destiny. The lyrics of Akan highlife songs are replete with themes about the use of witchcraft in changing a person's destiny. Both Brempong's (1986) and Adinkrah's (2008a) studies of Akan highlife songs provide fascinating cases of such musical lyrics.

The Good Witch

Some witches allegedly use their witchcraft to protect or facilitate the success of their children (Bannerman-Richter 1982). Good witches use their witchcraft to make their children healthy and prosperous, or to assist their children in securing visas for overseas travel. The story was related to me of a woman who had ten children, all girls. She used her witchcraft to aid each of her daughters to get a "good husband." In fact, so successful was she said to have been in this venture that each of the daughters was, at the time, married to a financially successful man living overseas in such countries as Britain, Germany, the Netherlands, Norway, and the United States. Contrast this with another story I was told concerning a maternal grandmother who was alleged to be a witch. In this family, all three daughters returned to their natal homes after brief marriages. Their maternal grandmother allegedly confessed that she had used her witchcraft to ensure that the marriages of her granddaughters would fail. According to Akan witchcraft beliefs, the witch can use witchcraft to secure successful marriages or wreck them at will. Consider the following letter that appeared in an advice column of a Ghanaian weekly. In an article, "Did She Bewitch Me?," the writer laments his current marriage and seeks the newspaper columnist's advice. The letter is reproduced in toto for purposes of illustration:

Dear Nana Ama,

I am a 42-year-old Muslim in a relationship with a woman I am not happy with. I have therefore decided to share my problem with you. In the first place, I did not propose love to this woman. A sister brought her from Nigeria to me after my university education. Because of the relationship between my sister and I, I couldn't say no to her. The woman became pregnant that very year and gave birth to a daughter who is now five years old. Now I'm convinced the woman bewitched me because people from her tribe are notorious for their juju practices but like all such things, after a while the effects wear off. Now, I believe whatever she used on me is gone. Nana, what on earth would have caused me to go in for an illiterate, a divorcee with four children and an old lady, if I had not been bewitched? It doesn't make sense at all. I have sleepless nights so I've left her in the village while I'm resident in the city. Meanwhile, there are single, fresh-looking young ladies looking for men to marry them. I am looking forward to finding a young lady of my own taste of whom I will be proud to marry. I need your help or I will sack her but keep my child. (Razak 2003, 13)

Black People's Witchcraft, White People's Witchcraft

Ghanaians generally believe that witchcraft is not the exclusive preserve of Africans or black people. However, they believe that while black people's witchcraft is malevolent and destructive, white people's witchcraft is benign, benevolent, and productive. The Akans call good or white witchcraft *bayi pa* or *bayi fufuo,* and black or bad witchcraft as *bayi tuntum, bayi bɔrɔ, bayi bɔne,* or *bayi kwasea* (Mettle-Nunoo 1994). It is commonly asserted that while white people use their witchcraft or *bayi fufuo* for socioeconomic development, black people use *bayi tuntum, bayi bɔrɔ,* or *bayi kwasea* to devour human flesh, and to cause accidents, illnesses, warfare, crop failure, earthquakes, famine, and countless other physical, social, and psychological ills. Simply put, black people's witchcraft is used to stymie others' progress in life. People point to the invention of the automobile, airplane, television, computer, and the discovery of electricity as manifestations of the use of white people's witchcraft for development and progress. In chapter 4 I examine in depth the lyrics of one song about the subject that are contained in a very popular Ghanaian highlife song "Devil" by A.B. Crentsil, a famous Ghanaian highlife musician.

What Motivates the Witch?

What does the witch gain from bewitching others? What value or benefit could a witch derive from the use or practice of her witchcraft? Among

Akans, as among many other local ethnic groups, it is widely believed that bewitching is the result of jealousy, resentment, and hatred of the fortunes of others. In the words of a fetish priest I interviewed in a small village, "A witch is envious of other people's happiness. A witch does not want you to be the best you can be, to have all you can possibly have and to be as successful and as gorgeous as you have the potential to be." According to Akan witchcraft beliefs, witches do not randomly or capriciously select their victims but purposely harm only people they hate or envy, or those with whom they have a conflict (Adinkrah 2004; Debrunner 1961; Obeng 2004). The purpose of witchcraft assault is to attack and destroy people they are jealous of or annoyed with, or who they envy. Among Akans, a witch who is jealous of the material advancement of her siblings, nieces, and nephews may use her witchcraft to cause their downfall or undercut their success. Among some ethnic groups in the north for whom bewitchment is not confined to relatives, witches may use their witchcraft to destroy a cowife and her children in a polygynous marriage through the infliction of illness, for example.

Good witches, on the other hand, use their witchcraft to protect and promote the good health, success, and overall well-being of their loved ones, and to prevent illness from afflicting loved ones. The following story was related to me of a Ghanaian professor teaching at a university in the United States. The professor's mother was suspected of being a witch who had used her witchcraft to remove the brains of several members of her *abusua,* including her own brothers and sisters, and then to implant the brains in her son's head. This created his success in all academic subjects, culminating in his winning numerous academic laurels. The professor was described as having obtained a bachelor's degree, two master's degrees, and a doctorate degree; as having published extensively; as having received several prestigious research grants; and as being a highly successful teacher. According to the story, the son had reciprocated his mother's spiritual assistance by bringing her to live with him in the United States in order for her to share in the bounty of her witchcraft machinations. The informant reported that the professor, fully knowledgeable that his many achievements were the result of his own talents, hardwork and discipline, dismissed the rumors as offensive and preposterous.

When to Fear Bewitchment the Most

Although witch activities are believed to occur throughout the year, the activities of witches are said to reach an acme during the weeks or days preceding Christmas and Easter when the festivities of witches involve grand feasting. In preparation for those festivities, witches are believed to send their representatives to go and stand in the middle of busy roads or major highways to cause accidents and to procure bodies for drinking human blood and eating human flesh. The story was related to me of a woman who suffered recurrent leg swellings in the weeks leading to Christmas, swellings that healed after the Christmas festivities. According to the story, upon divination the woman was told that her afflicted leg was being used by witches as a chopping board in the weeks leading up to and during Christmas.

Identifying the Witch

While divination is believed by some Ghanaians to be the most reliable way to identify a witch, others believe that personality characteristics and behavior in ordinary social intercourse afford opportunities for identifying the witch. Informants regularly mentioned a person's *suban* (character) or *nneyɛɛ* (behavior) as indices that could reveal the individual's identity as a witch. For example, a person considered uncongenial, garrulous, meddlesome, or cantankerous is often branded a witch (Amoah 1987). Children who chronically exhibit disrespectful behavior toward adults are suspected of being witches. Persons who are extremely covetous are readily accused of being witches. In one small town in the Eastern Region of Ghana, several informants were quick to point out a particular woman who they presumed to be a witch. Popularly known in the community as Abɔyɔ killer (the killer from Abɔyɔ) or *bɔɔla so pete* (the vulture or scavenger of the garbage dump), many people recounted tales of extraordinary behavior by this person, confirming or reinforcing their suspicions of her witchery. The woman identified to me looked to be about eighty years old and physically strong, short, and wiry. Unlike many women her age, she did not walk with a limp or with the aid of a walking stick. Among behavioral characteristics commonly noted by the informants, she was said to be inquisitive, garrulous, talkative, loquacious, and argumentative. She was said to have verbal altercations regularly with her adult children. She was alleged to collect things regularly from the garbage dump located near her house, a behavior that earned her the name *pete* (vulture or scavenger) of the garbage dump. While most women traders specialize in the sale of a single item or a limited range of items throughout their working lives, this woman was said to sell every imaginable item, including kerosene, cloth, imported second-hand clothes, fried yams, and *konkonte* (cooked powdered dry cassava). Particularly extraordinary to observers was her sale of kerosene during broad daylight. In Ghana many kerosene sellers peddle their wares in the evening, at dusk, or during the entire evening, between 6 P.M. and midnight when most people purchase kerosene for their paraffin lamps.

There is a general perception that one can physically identify a witch or distinguish a witch from a nonwitch. Witches are said to be physically ugly with black or discolored teeth and unkempt fingernails. There is also a belief that witches walk upside down—that is, with their heads on the ground, with their feet projecting upward (Debrunner 1961). To the ordinary eye, however, they appear to be walking normally. Given this perceived tendency for witches to walk in this inverted fashion, it is believed that one can identify a witch by kicking sand on his or her heels. If the person responds by rubbing or wiping his or her eyes, the assumption is that the sand went into the eyes of the inverted witch.

Who Cannot Be Bewitched?

Persons with strong *sunsum* or *kra* are said to be immune from spiritual assaults by witches. The Akan have a saying: "abayifoɔ ntumi obi a ne sunsum yɛ den or sɛ wo sunsum yɛ duru a, abayifoɔ ntumi nha wo" (witches cannot harm someone with a strong spirit) (Fisher 1998; Mettle-Nunoo 1994). The belief is also widely held that people who deny the existence of witchcraft and witches cannot be harmed by witchcraft. For this reason, there are persons in Ghana who profess that they do not believe in witchcraft. Others contend that while they believe in the existence of witches, they do not believe in the power of witches to harm them as individuals. A third category of persons believed to be spared bewitchment are strong Christians: it is said that witches cannot harm people with strong Christian convictions (Soku 2000). Regular prayers and fasting are said to be efficacious in warding off witch spirits. For this reason, it is commonplace for people fearing bewitchment to join pentecostal churches, sleep with Bibles under their pillows, display angel figurines at their bedposts, wear a crucifix as part of a necklace, or carry a rosary (see Figure 2.1.).

The Stigma of the Witch Label

The witch label carries tremendous social stigma in Ghana. Witches are demeaned and vilified in their communities. The supposed witch is invariably bitterly condemned and rejected by family, neighbors, and their wider community. As Mettle-Nunoo (1994, 66) notes, "The witch is seen as a bad person—she is antisocial, full of envy, spite and malice. She is there-

Figure 2.1. Angel Figurines and Bibles near a Ghanaian Sleeping Bed

fore far removed from the good people who are virtuous, unselfish and kind-hearted and who are not associated with witchcraft."

Throughout Ghana, alleged witches are perpetually viewed with suspicion. The witch label becomes a master status that engulfs the individuals and overshadows everything they do. Women traders who are suspected of being witches will find that their goods are no longer salable. Consider the case of a woman who successfully sold boiled rice with stew at a local market prior to an accusation of witchcraft. The accusation fueled rumors that the rice was sand, the stew was fecal matter, the oil was blood, and the meat in the stew was human flesh being peddled as beef or chicken. A similar story was related to me about a market vendor who peddled vegetables in a local market. After the accusation of witchcraft was made, it was alleged that the eggplants the woman sold in the market consisted of stones transformed spiritually into eggplants. Another story was related to me regarding an apprenticed seamstress, twenty-one years old, who was terminated from her employment because of witchcraft suspicions. The 21-year-old reportedly went to a church prayer meeting where she was allegedly caught by the presiding apostle. Several days later when information about the incident filtered to her boss, she was dismissed. The manager feared that the young woman's witchcraft would be used to destroy her business.

Stigmatization of the witch can extend beyond her person, affecting her children as well. In the Abɔyɔ killer case described earlier, a daughter and granddaughter of the alleged witch were presumed to be witches as well and suffered the same ostracism.

A witch label is extremely difficult to shed if such labeling was the result of divination. However, women who are exorcised of witchcraft and subsequently go to Pentecostal or spiritual churches are perceived to be clean or born again, and to have undergone genuine conversion from witchcraft. They are also believed to be genuinely remorseful for all of their witchcraft deeds and therefore deserving of forgiveness.

Exorcism

Witches are said to be permanently malevolent unless exorcised. Exorcism is believed to be doomed to fail unless the alleged witch voluntarily submits to the process. The alleged witch who is coerced into undergoing exorcism rituals will kɔ fa (pick up) the witchcraft later. In Akan witch lore, every witch has a witch name known only to those within her witch coven. It is believed that witches cannot be exorcised of their witch spirits unless they make full disclosure of the name to the dewitching specialist or to the public (Mensa-Bonsu 2001).

Many Ghanaians hold that a successful exorcism of witchcraft can be performed only by a shaman or witch doctor whose witchcraft power exceeds the potency of the witch being exorcised. In one account provided to me, an elderly woman once engaged the services of a witch doctor for the purpose of being exorcised of her witchcraft. The octogenarian witch claimed to be uninterested in trying to take her witchcraft to the netherworld. According to the account the witch, accompanied by the fetish priest, went into a remote forest where the exorcism was to be performed. At the initiation of the exorcism, the priest asked the woman to demonstrate how she usually prepared for her nocturnal trips with other witches. The woman allegedly began to morph into a tigress. The witch doctor, terrified by the turn of events, immediately fled from the site.

Historically, witch-cleansing rituals were performed exclusively by fetish priests schooled in the art of exorcism, but in Ghana today the exorcising role has increasingly been usurped by Christian pastors, apostles, evangelists, or prophets affiliated with spiritual or faith-healing churches (Kondor 1991b).

The latest addition to witch-hunting experts in Ghana are the numerous Christian spiritual churches. Invoking the Bible as their authority in fighting evil spirits, the ministers of these churches play a major role in the effort to eradicate witchcraft. Many of these preachers call themselves prophets and prophetesses, claiming psychic as well as exorcist powers. They claim the ability to identify witches in their congregations and call on them to step forward to confess their witchcraft; when the witch confesses, the minister then lays his hands on her head and calls on the Holy Spirit to free her from witchcraft. (Bannerman-Richter 1982, 10)

There is a belief that following an exorcism some "ex-witches reestablish connections with their witch-spirits and return to cannibalistic witchcraft, for they claim that once a witch tastes human flesh, it is not easy to break the habit" (Bannerman-Richter 1982, 73).

Divination

As a form of religious practice, divination is a way of seeking and obtaining information from the supernatural realm by religious or ritual specialists or diviners. Following an accusation of witchcraft, a divination is conducted to establish the veracity of the accusation. The diviner or fetish priest (see Figure 2.2.) may slaughter chickens or sheep, or cast bones. In

Figure 2.2. Advertisement for a Fetish Priest

the Gambaga Witches' Camp, the *gambarana* (the custodian of the witch sanctuary in Gambaga, or witch doctor) uses the chicken or fowl ordeal to ascertain whether or not someone is a witch: The chicken is slaughtered and allowed to flutter to its death. If it falls on its belly, it is a sign that the accused person is a witch; conversely, if it falls on its back, the accused person is innocent. By falling on its back and baring its belly, it reveals that the accused witch has not eaten any human flesh. By falling on its belly and exposing its rump, it reveals that the alleged witch has something in her belly—human flesh—that she is concealing.

Individuals who suspect that they have been bewitched may consult an oracle or witch doctor who, through divination, may reveal or confirm the identity of the offending witch. Fearing bewitchment, many individuals also consult various ritual specialists to obtain protective charms, amulets, and talismans to forestall any bewitchment (Bannerman-Richter 1982; Gray 2000; Owusu-Ansah 2000; Parish 2000).

Witch Finders and Witch Catchers

Some individuals are identified as possessing powerful antidotes to witchcraft. In the Gambaga area of northern Ghana, the *gambarana* is believed to have the means to render witches powerless or to neutralize the witchcraft power of any witch who sets foot in his compound. Following divination, he prepares potions for the witch to ingest. This is believed to render any witchcraft ineffectual.

Some fetish shrines and fetish priests in Akan communities specialize in the catching of alleged witches. They are known as *abosommrafoɔ* (witch finders). It is said that witches who are arrested by these fetish shrines must provide detailed confessions about the source of their witchcraft power and their witchcraft activities or they will die (Konadu 2007).

There is a common belief that witch doctors or witch finders are themselves witches. It is commonly said that one must be a witch to catch a witch (Assimeng 1977; Bannerman-Richter 1982; Ntim-Korsah 1988; Obeng 2004), and that ordinary people are not capable of catching witches. This is reflected in the Akan saying, "ɔbayifoɔ na ohu ne yɔnko ɔbayifoɔ" (it is the witch who recognizes his witch colleague). Witch doctors who are witches or wizards, however, are believed to possess witchcraft of the beneficent genre (see Figure 2.3.). They use their witchcraft merely to catch or arrest witches and to free their bewitched clients from the clutches of purported witches. During my trip to the Gambaga Witches Camp in February 2004, the *gambarana* openly boasted about being a wizard. He claimed that he had the power to detect a witch and exorcise witchcraft powers because

Figure 2.3. Signpost Advertising an Herbal and Spiritual Center

his witchcraft power was superior to that of the witches he catches. "You can step outside my hut and take a photograph of the exterior walls of this hut and you will be guaranteed that I will appear in the photograph while still sitting inside the hut," he professed. I did not take him up on this challenge. In his sociological excursus of the Ghanaian witchcraft scene, Assimeng describes the witchcraftly activities of a witch doctor who served as his informant:

> She is usually convinced that most causes of misfortune originate from a person's lineage network. In such a case, what she does, therefore, is to promise to visit the client's hometown *witchcraftly,* i.e. between 1 A.M. and 3 A.M. to enquire from other witches in that town about the social and kinship background of the client. Her next move is to identify the person who is responsible for the client's misfortune. This done, she then asks what the assailant's complaints are, and what she wants the bewitched person to do in order to regain health and deliverance, etc. It should be borne in mind that this is some kind of a soul-to-soul encounter, which could often give rise to doubts in the mind of the client as to possible collusion between the witchdoctor and the assailant. The technique throughout is to be able to elicit the co-operation of the bewitcher who might even ultimately indicate the medication that is appropriate for the sickness or misfortune. In cases of intransigence (after per-

suasive entreaties had failed), what the witchdoctor does is to mobilize the support of other local witches in the town for her bargaining efforts. If they, too, are unable to help, she then seeks support from her "own resources" for what could then become a conflict-stuffed bitter encounter. (Assimeng 1977, 72)

Protection against Witchcraft

Ghanaians employ a variety of protective mechanisms and adopt several preemptive or counter strategies to shield themselves from potential bewitchment. These strategies include the wearing of protective charms, amulets, or talismans on their bodies, usually around their waists, in their clothes, or around their necks to ward off malevolent witch influences. Roving shamans, witch doctors (fetish priests attached to antiwitchcraft shrines), or *mallams* are sought out for charms and amulets. One such protective talisman is the *bansere* or *sɛbɛ* (a leather pouch containing passages from the Koran along with an Arabic magic formula). When worn on the finger, around the waist, or as a necklace, the amulet is presumed to have the capacity to protect the wearer against the evil machinations of witches. Other protective antiwitchcraft devices include what are called wonderful rings or magical rings worn by believers (Mettle-Nunoo 1994). These rings are regarded as offering potent protection for the wearer against a variety of calamities, including the malevolent activities of witches and wizards.

Closely related to antiwitchcraft amulets and other protective charms are the protective medicines provided by witch doctors, fetish priests, or herbalists. These concoctions often consist of a black powder that is smeared into small incisions made into the body of the person seeking the protection against witchcraft. The powder is put in drinking water or *koko* (corn porridge), and the person swallows it. These medicines are believed to make a person's flesh and blood bitter and therefore unattractive to anthropophagous witches. Some Ghanaians travel far and wide in their bid to ward off bewitchment, seeking protection from allegedly powerful antiwitchcraft shrines. In Ghana it is widely believed that medicines provided by the Akonnedi, Tigare, and Okomfo Nyamekye antiwitchcraft shrines are particularly efficacious in stemming the malevolent activities of witches. In recent years a number of herbalists and spiritualists have introduced specially formulated anointing oils, creams, and herbal concoctions to the Ghanaian market that promise to protect the wearer from witchcraft and fortify them against other spiritual attacks (see Figure 2.4.).

Many Ghanaians also believe that issuing strong verbal threats and regularly casting insinuations against a putative witch will ward off bewitchment. In some instances, verbal threats are accompanied by physi-

Figure 2.4. Sample of Spiritual Protection Oils and Creams Being Sold on the Ghanaian Market

cal joustling or assaults of the putative witch. Threats to kill, maim, or beat the putative witch accused of using, or attempting to use, witchcraft against the accuser is believed to render any witch spells cast against the accuser ineffective.

Joining and maintaining active membership in a spiritual church is believed to afford protection from bewitchment. Many Ghanaians believe that a witch who attempts to enter a spiritual church will be confronted by powerful spiritual forces that will arrest or catch the witch, and cause him or her to confess to witchcraft activities. Pentecostal churches also offer their congregants holy water and holy oil that members are enjoined to sprinkle in their homes to ward off witches and their malevolent activities. Pastors of pentecostal churches are believed to possess the spiritual powers to reveal to their congregants signs (*oyikyerɛ*) of current or imminent bewitchment and to stave off the spiritual assault of witches. It is also believed that people who worship certain deities collectively receive protection against witchcraft from these gods. The deities are believed to despise witches and witchcraft.

Smudging, or the burning of special herbs and spices, is believed by many to prevent the entry of witches into one's home by smoking out witches. The fumes from burning garlic are believed to have the capacity to drive out evil spirits, including witches. According to Mettle-Nunoo

(1994, 70), "Among the [Ga] Adangbes, fumigation [smudging] is carried out with leaves and sharp pepper."

The performance of good deeds is believed to provide an antidote against bewitchment. People who are kind-hearted philanthropists do not evoke ill-will from others. Since bewitchment is typically precipitated by jealousy, envy, and ill-will, persons who share their wealth with their poor relatives or share some of their wealth with community members in a variety of ways are generally thought to be spared bewitchment. The Akan proverb "ɔbayifoɔ kum wadi-wamma-me na ɔnkum wama-me-na-ɛsua" (the witch kills the person who eats and does not give me any, or the witch does not kill the one who eats but gives me only a little) illustrates well this idea of sharing as a preemptive strategy against bewitchment. Hence, financially successful people who wish to avert bewitchment are advised about the blessings that follow from generosity.

While individuals can engineer forms of protection against witchcraft, there are also communal or collective means to obtain protection from witchcraft. Some villagers erect small or dwarf walls around the entire circumference of their village. These walls are believed to effectively hold witches at bay. According to Mettle-Nunoo (1994, 70), an example of "such magic fence is the 'pampam': a low fence of obstruction over the foot-path near a town or village used to prevent the entrance of evil spirits."

Witchcraft Beliefs and Social Change

The impact of social change on witchcraft beliefs is reflected in shifting Akan beliefs regarding witchcraft. Let us consider Akan witch beliefs regarding the ability of witches to journey to overseas destinations. Roughly thirty years ago, prior to the large-scale migration of Ghanaian citizens overseas, it was believed that Ghanaian emigrants living abroad were immune from bewitchment from their witch relatives living in Ghana. It was believed that the power of the witch was neutralized by direct or indirect contact with the salty waters of the oceans. Now, barely three decades later, and with thousands of Ghanaian citizens living abroad (Ghana Statistical Service 2012; Oppong 2004), these ideas appear to have changed. Stories have proliferated about Ghanaian witches living in Ghana traveling overseas purposely to harm their relatives living and working in the United States, Canada, and in European countries. During an episode of the radio program *Etuo Mu Wɔ Sum,* a caller living in the United States related an incredible tale to the listeners. According to the story, a Ghanaian emigrant who was living temporarily in the United States was a witch and had brought her witchcraft to that country. During the night, she went on a flight to a witches' Sabbath and was knocked down en route by an airplane. The caller said he had seen the alleged witch and could testify to the extent of the witch's injuries. Indeed, many Ghanaian citizens resident abroad are increasingly spending large sums of money for protection against the harmful machinations of witch relatives living in Ghana.

Further evidence of the transformation of Ghanaian witchcraft beliefs are the current ideas about the capacity of witches to use new technology to perform their misdeeds. Ghanaian witches are now said to use computers, compasses, and GPS maps to locate their victims living in Ghana and abroad. They are presumed capable of boarding airplanes to travel overseas, using credit cards, and evading customs and immigration. Soku (2000, 46) writes, "Victims could be brought from any part of the world. On satanic computer they know the city, the street, the house number and room number."

The incorporation of current events in Ghanaian society into witchcraft ideology is subtly transforming witchcraft beliefs. For example, witchcraft is now invoked to explain the incidence of HIV/AIDS (Dornoo 2009; Kwawukume 2008; Yankah 2004). Many Ghanaians now believe that HIV/AIDS is spread through witchcraft and that witches have the capacity to give a person AIDS (Dornoo 2009; Yankah 2004). Concurrently, some believe that the prevention and control of the disease is dependent on the containment of witches. The following story, written by journalist Ohene Foster, appeared in the February 26–29, 2004, issue of a newspaper *People and Places,* which is published in Ghana. It is reproduced here verbatim.

Woman Gets AIDS after Eating AIDS Victim

Wonders, they say, will never cease in the world. A self-confessed witch, 15, who decided to use her evil forces to render her parents poor at long last revealed the cause of her enlarged and abnormal stomach and her deformed appearance, which was the major worry of her parents who fought to get her cured. Narrating her diabolical agenda to her parents at the Ebenezer Worship Centre at (Island City) Ahenema Kokoben, a town near Kumasi in the Ashanti Region, Ama Bio (the self-confessed witch) in a very deplorable state disclosed that about a year ago, she and her coven of witches went out to feast on a human flesh. That night, she being the queen of her group, was given the head of the trapped human being-turned goat in recognition of her leadership position. After eating the said human head, Ama Bio said her condition started to deteriorate after four days, though she spiritually knew that something bad would happen to her later. After six months, Ama Bio realized that the head she ate did not 'digest' thus, making her stomach swell. That was not all; Ama further shocked the congregation when she told the Head Pastor Reverend Ebenezer Adarkwa Yiadom on Sunday, 15 February 2004 that the person they killed and spiritually enjoyed the flesh was an HIV/AIDS patient. She further told him that the person's spirit had transferred AIDS virus to her, hence her deteriorating condition. In an answer to a question, Ama told Reverend Ebenezer Adarkwa Yiadom that although she was aware of the cause of her predicament and also saw the efforts of her parents to ensure her recovery, she did not pity them because she wanted them to become completely poor even to the point of stealing. This was after she revealed that three other people living in the house were members of her coven who embarked on the operation with her which led to her contracting AIDS and her over-sized stomach. True to her word, at home, Ama exposed three other people before she died that very night. In an interview, Madam Abena Mboro, her mother, confirmed the story and said the confession from Ama and her death brought some relief because they had financially suffered for a very long time because of her. On his part, Reverend Ebenezer Adarkwa Yiadom also confirmed the story, saying, such miracles are from God, who deserves praise and thanksgiving. (Foster 2004, 3)

Presently the belief that HIV/AIDS is caused by, or spread through, witchcraft has prompted some sufferers to seek cures in prayer centers rather than medical establishments (Kofoya-Tetteh 2008). Consider the following news item that appeared in the *Daily Graphic* of July 16, 2004:

People Living with HIV/AIDS (PLWHA) have been advised not to spend most of their time and resources in spiritual homes at the expense of their clinical treatment. A nurse at the St. Martin's Hospital at Agomanya in the Eastern Region, Mrs.Theresa Tetteh, who gave the advice said, a lot of the PLWHA used to have the notion that they were being bewitched and therefore tend to spend all their time and monies looking for cure at spiritual homes and only go for clinical care when their situation deteriorates. Mrs. Tetteh said it was disturbing that sometimes during visits to communities, the health team found a lot of PLWHA who have abandoned their monthly clinical attendance and devoted all their time to praying at spiritual homes. She said although God's intervention was key in the treatment process, it was indeed necessary for all people diagnosed with the HIV/AIDS virus to constantly seek medical attention through which God also worked. (Osei-Edwards 2004, 23)

Witchcraft Is Used to Explain Exceptional Talent

In Ghana, witchcraft is often used to explain exceptional skill or talent. In the area of soccer, the most popular Ghanaian sport, witchcraft was used to describe the exceptional skills of one of its famous players, Osei Kofi. In a short biography about this soccer player who retired from the sport to become a minister of religion, a newspaper columnist wrote,

Rev. Osei Kofi, one of the most prolific goal scorers with exceptional dribbling skills during his days with the senior national team, the Black Stars, and with Kumasi Asante Kotoko, had all the attributes of a great player. He dazzled fans and hypnotized players from opposing teams with his dribbling skills. More often than not many players found no antidote to his moves anytime he initiated them. Osei Kofi was well known throughout Ghana and Africa at large, and was a real thorn in the flesh of many defenders whom he often left bemused and reduced to dummies. His skills par excellence compelled the fans to bestow the name, "Wizard Dribbler" on him. (Azu 2004, 31)

In another feature story appearing in the *Daily Graphic,* a newspaper columnist recounted the tale of a blind farmer with exceptional skills:

If ever a disabled person excels academically or demonstrates any human prowess such as topping a group or class, or winning a prize, they are either witches or wizards, or that their parents used underhand deals to enable them achieve the feats. I once knew a blind man who made a cocoa farm. He planted the seeds and nurtured the seedlings. The gossip was that he had four eyes—he was a wizard. All of us children looked suspiciously anytime we saw him. So instead of admiring him for his hard work, we were made to detest him. (Boadu-Ayeboafoh 2004, 7)

Also, witches are believed to possess incredible supernatural powers that can be utilized to accomplish all manner of feats within a short period of time. In story after story informants attributed unusual prowess and extraordinary feats to witches. Soku (2000) writes, "Wizards have real supernatural powers to operate. They could travel to any part of the world and back between 12 midnight and 3.30 A.M." And according to Bannerman-Richter (1982, ii–iii), "a witch can transmogrify herself into a half-human, half-animal form; she can undergo sexual changes and age transformations, and she can transmute natural objects into different substances. In that world, a witch can ride on the back of a leopard, and like a wingless Pegasus, the leopard can transport her across the sky to witch gatherings; in that world, a witch and beast can talk to each other and team up in diabolical activity." In one village in the Eastern Region of Ghana, the story was related to me of a middle-aged man who developed a swelling in his neck that appeared to be a case of goiter. The man, who previously was living in one village but later moved to another, confessed that he was a wizard and had one time attempted to swallow the entire river flowing through the village so as to deprive the inhabitants of the village the use of the water from the river. In the process, he choked on the river that remained lodged in his throat.

Witchcraft Confessions

Another major element of Akan witchcraft ideology is witchcraft confessions (Bannerman-Richter 1982; Debrunner 1961; Gray 2000; Soku 2000).

Witches believed to have been caught, arrested, or apprehended by a fetish priest, minister of religion, member of the clergy, pastor, shaman, prophet, or witch doctor must describe the sources and manifestations of their power. They must also provide a full account of their witchcraft and their witch deeds, including a list of their victims and what the witch did to them. This, it is believed, is necessary for the alleged witch to be freed or delivered from witchcraft powers. Failure to make complete disclosure of one's misdeeds or sins in the confessional statement can lead the witch to become severely ill or mentally deranged, or to die (Korankye 1997; Ntim-Korsah 1988; Obeng 2004).

Several informants related stories of being physically present when a witch was arrested or caught. According to the accounts, following an arrest, witches offer confessional statements detailing the names of their victims, how they afflicted them and why, in addition to revealing how they acquired the witchcraft power, who initiated them into witchcraft, the source of their witchcraft power, and where it was hidden. According to Debrunner (1961, 126), "In order that their witch spirits may lose their power, they may then reveal their secret names, and sing their 'witch song.' They must hand over the objects in which the witch spirit was supposedly kept—beads, towels, pots, stools, cloth, etc." In their confessional statements, witches are also often said to identify others in the community who are involved in the witch company. Based on her review of the confessional statements of purported witches appearing before the Akim Abuakwa courts, Gray concludes, "Witchcraft confessions tended to follow very similar plot lines. The witch presented herself as the victim of the *bayi* or witchcraft substance within her. She had not sought to become a witch but had been pressured or tricked into becoming one by other witches. These witches then drove her to attack her own kin by entrapping her into debt" (Gray 2000, 259).

Many people in Ghana also believe that, once caught, witches can be prevailed upon to heal the afflicted or bewitched individual, curing those they have made ill or restoring to the impotent or barren lost fertility as well as ensuring the financial recuperation of those who have incurred financial losses. This healing must involve reversing the witchcraft spell used to cause the afflictions.

Witchcraft Beliefs Cut across the Entire Society

It needs emphasizing that witchcraft beliefs cut across all sectors of Ghanaian society and are held by persons from all walks of life, regardless of their educational background, occupational status, social standing, or religious affiliation (Awedoba 2002; Assimeng 1977). As Awedoba (2002, 160) correctly puts it, "Both urban and rural folk, educated and non-educated, Christian, Moslem, and 'pagan' all continue to be conditioned by witchcraft beliefs." Anecdotal evidence indicates that university academics, medical doctors, engineers, scientists, judges, and all manner of professionals are among those who share the beliefs and fears regarding the destructive powers of witches and witchcraft, making such beliefs pervasive in the society (Assimeng 1977; Mensa-Bonsu 2001). Commenting on the multiplicity of social backgrounds of witchcraft believers who came to consult a witch doctor he studied, Assimeng noted,

> As for the social and economic status of clients, one can say that there is no imaginable status group in Ghana from which clients do not appear before witchdoctors. . . . The range could be from university teachers seeking witchdoctors' support over university council decisions affecting such teachers, to taxi drivers who want their vehicles to be "spiritually cleansed" against what they fear to be the prospects of enemies misusing such vehicles during bewitching rides in the night. . . . I have often seen highly respectable men and women waiting for their turn in queues [to see a witch doctor], very openly parking their cars, in some cases. (Assimeng 1977, 75–76)

Even ministers of religion are not immune from harboring strong beliefs about witchcraft and seeking protection from bewitchment. Rumors of Christian clergy visiting local fetish shrines and those of neighboring African countries to obtain protection against bewitchment and sorcery are rampant in the society. The following passage is excerpted from an interview conducted with a Ghanaian medical professional. The quotation encapsulates some of the essential features of the putative Ghanaian witch—that witches are elderly females who fly across the sky to congregate at a secret location where they kill and cannibalize their unsuspecting human victims, and that Christian prayers have the capacity to neutralize the power of witchcraft and witches:

> There are certain things that one cannot explain unless you believe in it. I just want to tell you a personal experience. I was in a church, a spiritual church. We were praying all night. It was about 2 or 3 A.M. The place we were praying was not covered; there was no roof. An old woman just fell down from nowhere. I am telling you that I was not hallucinating. We were not hallucinating. The lady fell naked and started begging. All that she said was that she was going somewhere and when she got there, where we were praying, a force pulled her down. So people lay hands on her for her to confess and started praying. How do you explain this? Was she traveling by helicopter? Did someone catapult her somewhere? There was no tree around. So if that was not witchcraft, it is something that one cannot explain. (B. Asare, Interview)

In the documentary *Healers of Ghana* (Dodds et al. 1996), Ghanaian university academic and scholar Dr. Kofi Asare Opoku of the University of Ghana offers the following:

> Belief in witchcraft is not a mark of an uneducated or illiterate person. There are many educated Africans who believe in witchcraft because it is a fact. It is a force which is experienced daily in their own lives and in the lives of Africans. It helps them to explain events that would otherwise remain inexplicable. My own research for the past 15 years has brought me to a belief in it because I have ample evidence to show that there is a force called witchcraft, or any other word that one may want to use, that is at work in human society which brings about untold suffering and hardship on people and that there are in the society people like herbalists and priestesses who can actually combat this evil force. Diseases go to the hospital which are caused by witchcraft which doctors cannot handle and those patients are often sent back to these herbalists who know how to handle such diseases and treat such people successfully. (Quoted from "Healers of Ghana," 1996)

If witchcraft beliefs are pervasive in Ghanaian society, it is critical to identify the processes and institutions involved in promoting witchcraft ideology. The following chapter discusses the transmission of witchcraft beliefs in Ghanaian society.

Chapter 3

SOCIALIZATION INTO
WITCHCRAFT BELIEFS

The preceding chapter provided an in-depth description of Ghanaian witchcraft beliefs. It seems fitting at this juncture to begin a discussion of how Ghanaians acquire beliefs in and ideas about witchcraft. Sociologists use the concept of socialization to denote the process of learning the norms, values, belief systems, and customs of a particular group or society. Through socialization, people also acquire the behavior protocols, ways of knowing, and worldview of their community or society. As will become clear from this chapter, socialization into witchcraft beliefs takes a variety of forms and involves various institutions in Ghanaian society. The process of socialization into witchcraft ideology is often subtle and beyond conscious awareness. As with many forms of social learning, while socialization through a number of institutions during the formative years proves to be a particularly critical phase for inculcation, in Ghana exposure to ideas about witchcraft occurs throughout a person's life.

Socialization by Family

An important agent of early socialization into witchcraft beliefs in Ghana is nuclear and extended family interaction, an institution that is central to the social fabric of life in Ghanaian society. Many Ghanaian households are multigenerational, with grandparents, children, and grandchildren often residing under the same roof. Parents, siblings, aunts, uncles, cousins, and other adults and children serve as conduits for the transmission of witchcraft ideology. Given the level of institutionalization of witchcraft beliefs within all institutions of Ghanaian society, including the family, children are exposed to the range of discussions that revolve around the subject of witchcraft in most households. Family members often invoke witchcraft to explain family, community, or societal misfortunes or tragedies. Attributions of witchcraft regularly surface in efforts to explain infertility, mental illness, prolonged or severe illnesses, the death of a young person, and other misfortunes. Family conversations occasionally focus on alleged witches and the benevolent or malevolent activities of such witches. In the family setting, one also learns through gossip, rumor, and innuendo about those members of the extended family, dead or living, who are alleged to be witches. One hears family members make reference to persons in the community who are regarded as witches or who have been bewitched, as well as to the mechanics of bewitchment.

Peer Socialization

Peer groups also provide a forum for learning about witches and witchcraft phenomena. Classmates and neighborhood play groups are often key transmitters of knowledge about witchcraft beliefs. Peer groups reinforce beliefs encountered in the home setting and provide an additional source of gossip and rumor about alleged witches in the community. In fact, children's play groups provide one of the first significant institutions in which witchcraft accusations are utilized as a form of social control. Among children, the word ɔbayifoɔ (witch) is regularly used as an insult for recalcitrant group members considered quarrelsome, or who gossip or display behavioral patterns inconsistent with group norms. In children's play groups, girls who are highly argumentative, engage in games normally played by boys such as soccer, or engage in physically aggressive behavior such as hitting other children are labeled witches or abayifoɔ.

For school-aged children attending boarding schools, what has been described as the "hidden corridor curriculum" (e.g., Hemmings 2000, 1) provides almost as significant a source of information about witchcraft as the family. In Ghana a significant proportion of second-cycle educational institutions are boarding schools, where students spend three to seven years in residence. These boarding schools are organized as full or quasi-total institutions where students sleep, play, eat, learn, and worship together. Life with peers in such intimate quarters creates strong social bonds, providing numerous opportunities for students to confide in each other. This often includes sharing stories about witchcraft phenomena. The author's own seven years of experience in an all-boys boarding secondary school in Ghana amply confirms this. A favorite pastime among friends, roommates, and classmates was discussions of alleged witches and their malevolent activities. Indeed, as recently as August 2004, the Ghanaian Ministry of Education issued a memorandum suggesting a growing incidence of occultism in secondary and tertiary institutions in the country (Mantey 2004).

Student subcultures in both boarding and nonboarding schools often employ witchcraft accusations to explain differential academic performances of individual students or groups of students. Female students with exceptional academic achievement, particularly those who excel in courses in mathematics, statistics, and the physical or natural sciences such as chemistry or physics may be branded as witches. At tertiary institutions, women who pursue what are designated male professions such as engineering and medicine, or who major in the natural sciences are suspected of being witches. Many Ghanaians believe that academic excellence in general, and success in mathematics and the physical sciences in particular are exclusively male preserves, and that it is unnatural for females to distinguish themselves in these areas. It is therefore presumed that females who outshine males in these areas can do so only via the supernatural interventions of witchcraft.

Women and girls who defy traditional Ghanaian gender-role socialization, gender roles, and general cultural norms of femininity in terms of physical appearance, clothing, sexuality, and sports are also branded witches. Girls who are regarded as inordinately physically or verbally aggressive, particularly toward or in comparison to males, are also likely to be labeled witches.

Witchcraft Socialization and the Official School Curriculum

The formal or official school curriculum in Ghanaian schools provides another milieu for acquiring knowledge about witchcraft phenomena. A review of Ghanaian school curricula shows that the topic of witchcraft is covered in considerable detail in social studies and religion courses at the junior and senior secondary school levels. Here, students learn basic knowledge about what witchcraft is and what witches do. The textbook for junior secondary school students, *Cultural Studies for Junior Secondary Schools: Pupils Book Two,* includes an entire unit on witches and witchcraft. Developed by the Curriculum Research and Development Division of the Ghana Education Service, the textbook provides information to students about "the nature of witchcraft; how witchcraft is acquired and how witches work" (Ghana Education Service 1988, 137–39). Exercises at the end of the chapter ask students to "(1) Mention some of the sources of witch power; where can this be found; (2) how the different ethnic communities call a witch and to; (3) describe some of the good or bad things a witch can do" (Ghana Education Service 1988, 139). The implications of teaching and quizzing youth about witchcraft phenomena in a school setting include reinforcing and cementing witchcraft beliefs. For purposes of illustration, I reproduce verbatim excerpts from the aforementioned textbook:

> In most Ghanaian communities, some people are said to practice witchcraft. The source of the witch's power is found in strange things: human hair, human nails, herbs, human blood, skulls and cola, etc. They are usually kept in a pot, a gourd, a shell or any other container. These containers are usually hidden in the farm, under big trees, under beds, in the hearth and so on. . . . It is generally believed that a person may be a witch but may not be aware of it until at a later stage. In some communities, many people's problems are said to have been caused by witches, e.g. sickness, death, barrenness, lack of prosperity, failure in work. . . . It is believed that there are several ways by which one can acquire witchcraft or become a witch. It can be inherited. A relative who is a witch can pass it on to a member of the family as he dies. He does this by presenting an object or something that contains the witchcraft as a gift to the person. People also say that others get theirs through eating certain kinds of food already prepared with the substance in it. And still others acquire theirs through presentations made to them in the form of money. Witchcraft may also be acquired through picking certain objects or swallowing objects which contain witchcraft. For instance, a person might pick a jewel on the ground and use it. If it contains the substance, he will become one as soon as he puts it on.
>
> Witchcraft, according to the traditional believer, can be put into good or bad use depending on the nature of the substance. But the activities of the bad witches appear to be more widely known than those of the good ones. Good witchcraft can be used, for example, to make one's children grow well and prosper. However, it is believed that the bad witchcraft may be used to harm others. For example, it can make people barren, sick or poor. It may even kill people. A witch is therefore a threat to the society and no one wants to be considered one. . . . It is said that a witch moving at night glows like fire and can fly. Witches are also said to walk with their heads down and legs up. . . . It is believed that a witch does not work alone. Witches work in teams or groups. In the group, every member has a special duty. There is a chief, a queen-mother, a linguist and so on. They have rules to obey. It is believed that witches can change into such animals as birds, snakes and so on when they are on duty. It is believed that they meet on tree tops, refuse dumps, banks of rivers and so on. It is at such meeting places that they decide what to do. (Ghana Education Service 1988, 137–38)

Students who pursue the subject *West African Traditional Religion* at the advanced levels or Senior Secondary Certificate Examination levels are inundated with information about witchcraft beliefs and phenomena. The syllabus prescribes the acquisition of knowledge and information about witchcraft concepts, ideas, and beliefs. Students learn about the stereotypes of witches, how witchcraft is acquired, witchcraft confessions, activities of witches, and the evils attributed to witches (Mettle-Nunoo 1994).

College or university courses in anthropology and sociology provide another source of information about witchcraft. The main purpose of these courses is to present academic concepts, offer theoretical insights, and review extant scholarly research and theoretical paradigms from a purely academic perspective without proposing a position about the veracity of witchcraft phenomena. Nevertheless, students complete the course enriched in ideas about witchcraft phenomena in their society as well as in other societies discussed in the course. Courses such as Traditional Ghanaian Social Institutions, Social Structure of Modern Ghana, and Societies and Cultures of Africa offered at the University of Ghana, Legon, are among those courses that devote some discussion to witchcraft ideas in Africa in general, and in Ghana in particular. At the Kwame Nkrumah University of Science and Technology in Kumasi, the Sociology Department offers a three-credit course, "Social Structure of Ghana." As listed in the university bulletin, the course explores, "[t]he concept of social structure; the peoples of Ghana—ethnic groups and their spatial distribution, migration history; kinship—terminology, importance, descent systems; the family types and functions; cosmological ideas—rituals, myth, witchcraft, ancestral worship and their functions" (Department of Sociology and Social Work 2014, 2). Other academic disciplines that offer courses with detailed or focused analyses of witchcraft and related topics include psychology, religion, history, and political science.

The Mass Media

Another powerful influence in the acquisition of local witchcraft ideology are the mass media. Newspapers, popular books, magazines, radio, movies, television, and the Internet are all prevalent forms of mass media in Ghana. Through these media, Ghanaians are exposed to their society's conceptions of who witches are, what they do, and what society does to control them. Ghanaian media messages are suffused with witchcraft ideology and phenomena. Whether through television, radio, locally produced movies, or music, one is surrounded by media forums to learn about witchcraft beliefs, witchcraft stories, witchcraft practices, witchcraft values, and the activities of witches.

In the past few decades the problem of witchcraft-related violence has been publicized through the news media. Hence, increased media attention has become a significant means for people to become aware of beliefs about witchcraft and witches. The 1997 witch killings in the Northern Region of Ghana was one of the most widely publicized cases of brutality against alleged witches in the country. The killings prompted calls for the investigation and prosecution of the culprits responsible. It also prompted a host of newspaper articles, television programs, and other media reports. In the interim, a number of television documentaries were aired to dissuade the public from taking hostile measures against suspected witches in their communities. By 2003–4, I observed, while I conducted ethnographic research on violence against women in the country, that these documentaries were still being aired.

Because the roles of different media are so significant, it is worth focusing on each medium's specific impact.

Television and Video

Television provides a powerful medium for the reproduction and dissemination of witchcraft ideas and imagery of witchcraft phenomena. As previously stated, there were ten television broadcast stations in the country in 2001. Concurrently, a large percentage of Ghanaian homes had television sets. Television news broadcasts carry stories of lethal and nonlethal attacks on putative witches. Ghanaian television soap operas recurrently present witchcraft themes. From this medium, one learns about the characteristics of alleged witches, witchcraft accusations, and the lethal and nonlethal treatment of supposed witches. Such dramatizations also convey how witches influence everyday behavior. The viewer is exposed to alleged sources of witchcraft powers, the essential characteristics of witches, and the havoc that witches can wreak upon individuals, the local community, and the larger society.

The ever-proliferating number of Nigerian- and Ghanaian-made movies or videos also continue the process of socialization into witchcraft. Many of these movies have themes that focus on the subject of witchcraft (see Figure 3.1.). Movies actively perpetuate the local beliefs about witchcraft. My own analysis of witchcraft themes in films and movies broadcast on Ghanaian television during ten years of ethnographic research revealed that women usually are cast as witches, implying female tendency toward witchcraft. Men, by contrast, are more frequently presented as witch doc-

Figure 3.1. Sample of Ghanaian Witchcraft Movies

tors. In November 2009 the Ghanaian cabinet minister for information ex-coriated the staff of a Ghanaian TV station for regularly screening films with witchcraft content ("Minister Condemns" 2009).

In recent years there has been a major proliferation of video shops in the country. From the most rural of locations to urban centers, one will find a multitude of video shops lining side streets and open market areas. The typical video shop specializes in the sale of hundreds of DVDs featuring both locally produced and Nigerian movies that either focus on or include witchcraft themes. Videos can be purchased cheaply for a price roughly the equivalent of US$2.00. Unlike television programming, which requires living within range of a satellite connection, all that is required for viewing DVD films is a DVD player and a monitor. Such accessibility and affordability have made DVD movies a widely popular form of enter-tainment that can be enjoyed by those in even the most remote locations with access to electricity. In the privacy of their homes, Ghanaian individuals and families invest hours of their day engaged in the viewing of DVDs where they are exposed to repetitive imagery and stereotypical notions about witches and the machinations of witchcraft.

Popular Dramas

Locally produced dramas in the theater, at concert shows, and on television serve a valuable function in disseminating and reinforcing witchcraft ideology. Dramatizations expose viewers to a range of ideas and themes around witchcraft beliefs, including what an alleged witch looks like, the mechanics of witchery, and the misfortunes that witches are capable of causing in their wake. Through the actions of protagonists, dramas also often include prescriptions or solutions for victims of witchery to pursue to extricate themselves from the alleged clutches of a suspected witch.

Newspapers

Newspapers constitute another important source for learning about witchcraft phenomena. Public perceptions and attitudes about witchcraft are shaped by what people read from the print media, including newspapers and magazines. In Ghana hardly a week goes by without a local newspaper carrying a story about a witch, witchcraft, or sorcery (see Figure 3.2.). Reports about witchcraft accusations, divinations, trial by ordeal, and the lethal and nonlethal assaults of alleged witches and witch confessions are often featured in the front pages of local newspapers (see Figure 3.3.). A review of the *Daily Graphic*, the *Ghanaian Times*, the *Weekly Spectator*, and the *Mirror* over a thirty-year period (1980–2010) uncovered a massive collection of news articles, feature stories, and editorials about witchcraft (e.g., Donkor 2008, 2010; Gyan-Apenteng 2007, 2010). For example, the Kobua witchcraft case, elaborately profiled in chapter 6, received tremendous coverage in local newspapers. The *Daily Graphic*, the *Mirror*, and the *Weekly Spectator* covered the trial in its entirety, providing daily or weekly reports to the Ghanaian public. As another case in point, following the murder of several elderly women accused of using witchcraft to spread a cerebrospinal meningitis epidemic in the Northern Region in 1997, it was revealed that scores of women expelled from their homes and villages were being kept in captivity in witches' camps following their witch confessions. The initial media exposure of the witches' camps prompted a host of newspaper articles, television programs, and other media reports as news reporters from all over the country and abroad descended on the Northern Region to provide the public an account of these camps and the events surrounding the witch hunts. More than a decade since this event the witches' camps are still newsworthy as local and international journalists continue to publish case reports of witches in the Northern Region (e.g., Donkor 2011; Palmer 2010).

Figure 3.2. Newspaper Stories of Witchcraft

Local tabloids such as the *People and Places* and the *Chronicle* routinely carry stories about witchcraft, ritual murders and occultism. My review of local newspapers from 1980 and 2012 yielded over one hundred cases of lethal and nonlethal assaults inflicted on purported witches. These cases are profiled in chapters 7 and 8 of this book. Many of these media case reports provided detailed information about the crime as well as the phenomenon of witchcraft. Readers of these newspapers are unlikely to escape the stories with their sensationalist titles. Feature articles and columns of newspapers address witchcraft phenomena and beliefs in Ghana. Consider this prominently displayed exchange published in the Mirror Lawyer column. Here, in a segment captioned "Can Witches and Wizards Be Prosecuted?," the columnist responds to the earnest questions of a reader concerning witchcraft.

Question:

Dear Lawyer,

Why do witches and wizards do their evils and confess to them while the government sits down without raising a single finger at these criminals? Can't there be enacted a law or decree that punishes witches when there is sufficient proof of their evil deeds, especially when they confess to them? If armed robbery is punishable by death why can't the government punish the witch who confesses having killed 72 people etc.? In some countries, witches or wizards are punished by law when there is sufficient evidence of their nefarious acts. Why can't Ghana follow suit but looks on and allows the wizards and witches to harm the society which we are all trying to bring up? Remember, the witches and wizards are aware that they are the cause and source of most of the evils that happen in society. What is wrong with punishing them by law when they are exposed, especially when they expose themselves?

Answer:

Criminal jurisprudence deals with facts that can be proved and not with myths, beliefs and opinions. Witchcraft is a superstitious belief that a human being can turn him/herself into a bird or an animal flying off to places and kill a human being. These beliefs have been with man since creation and I have no doubt at all in my mind that they will be with us till the day of judgement. Whether one believes in such myths or not, is not the issue here. The issue here is whether a person who confesses that he/she practices witchcraft through which persons have been killed or babies "been eaten up" in the womb of their mothers before birth or that they have eaten up the fertile glands and hormones of a woman causing barrenness or have eaten up the bones of a person's legs causing paralysis can be prosecuted under Criminal Code in Ghana. My answer is no. No because such claims cannot be proved in court nor disproved by producing contrary facts in opposition or defence. Murder being a capital offence is not tried on confessions. Such confessions must be proved to have been made under certain circumstances to the satis-

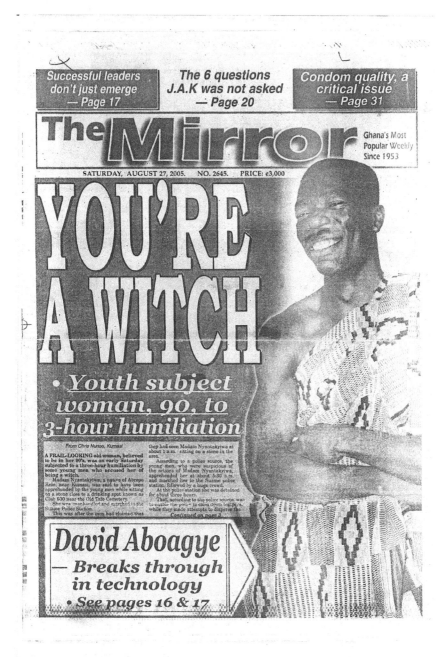

Figure 3.3. Front Page of a Ghanaian Newsweekly Depicting a Story about Witchcraft Violence

faction of the court before they can become admissible. In criminal law, independent evidence must be led to corroborate such admissions or confessions. If a man or woman goes to a fetish priest or priestess and makes a general statement that he/she practices witchcraft, I find it difficult to see how such a statement can be proved to enable a jury [to] convict that person of murder. Mr. Owusu-Ansah uses the correct word when he says "when there is SUFFICIENT EVIDENCE" in the problem. That is the gravamen of the case. Several factors have to be "sufficiently" proved in court before a jury can convict or acquit a person charged with murder. It is my submission that no such evidence can be produced in witchcraft cases to warrant the use of precious time, money and energy in trying such cases. The criminal law must be certain. Witchcraft cases cannot and do not have any such certainty. It is just a bundle of beliefs and since such beliefs cannot be proved with concrete facts, it is impossible to try practitioners of witchcraft on their affirmations of their possessing supernatural powers to do all manner of mischief to their victims. As I have already stated, the criminal law must be certain and in order to do this, every case must be investigated, evidence gathered and the accused must be connected with the CORPUS DELECTI that is to say the main object which formed the basis of the charge of the crime. None of these things can be done in cases involving witchcraft.

Radio

Radio may have a greater impact on teaching about witchcraft than television and video. This stems from the greater accessibility of radio in the country, as nearly every Ghanaian household owns a radio. Currently, there are over fifty radio stations (The World Factbook 2003) and an estimated 12.5 million radio and wireless sets in the country. Radio broadcasts a variety of news, educational, and entertainment programs, and have a significant effect on the attitudes and behavior of the Ghanaian populace. News stories about witch murders are carried by all media outlets, including radio. Radio news stories on witchcraft-related murders include information about the victim, assailant, modus operandi, circumstances of death, and the spatial and temporal aspects of the incident.

There are certain radio programs in Ghana that are renowned for their wealth of witchcraft themes. For example, the radio programs *Etuo Mu Wɔ Sum* and *Ewiem Wiem* play an increasingly important role in socialization into witchcraft ideology. These Tuesday and Thursday evenings programs respectively are dedicated to discussions of witchcraft issues. The call-in segments at the end of the programs offer listeners the opportunity to ask questions about witches and witchcraft phenomena and to share their own experiences with the host and other listeners. For example, during the March 28, 2006, *Etuo Mu Wɔ Sum* program, the host relayed the account of a man who tied up his mother with a rope and was about to murder her because, according to him, the mother had turned him into a teetotaler. There is little question that public perceptions about witchcraft are often formed on the basis of what is heard in a few celebrated cases that receive widespread media attention, including on the radio. As Korankye observes:

> Another cardinal factor accounting for the strong belief in witchcraft in the area is some radio programmes. These include "Odomankoma Asem/Akan Belief in Creation and "Beenu Nkombo" Food for thought. These are Akan magazine programmes held in Ghana Broadcasting Corporation 1 (GBC). These programmes are held on Tuesday 9:30 P.M. and Wednesday 10:30 P.M. respectively. In these programmes, certain stories are told concerning various spirits such as [mmoatia], ghosts, monsters and witches. During these hours both children and adults are seen around radios listening. (Korankye 1997, 26)

Internet

In an age of ubiquitous Internet news outlets, Ghanatoday.com, Ghanaweb. com, Ghanamma.com, Ghanacrunch.com, Ghanareview.com, Myzongo.com and Accra-mail.com are among Ghana-based Web sites that have given visibility to witchcraft-related violence in the country. These Web sites serve as a vehicle for the dissemination of media reports on violence perpetrated against alleged witches and other witchcraft-related crimes. Media reports disseminated through Internet news outlets help to bring the abuses of witches out of obscurity into the national and international arena of public concern.

Religious Sermons on Radio and Television

Broadcasts of Christian sermons constitute another important source of information about witchcraft in Ghanaian society. Analysis of sermon content on Ghanaian radio and television reveals that the menace of witchcraft is a central theme. Although the manifest function of these sermons is to teach about the mechanics of bewitchment and provide direction to believers on ways to conquer witchcraft, the latent consequence has been to affirm the public's palpable fear of witchcraft. During these sermons, scriptures from the Bible are quoted copiously to certify the existence of witches. The sermons reflect popular societal conceptions of witchcraft. Witchcraft is described as a powerful yet invisible and malevolent force. It is emphasized that God is all good but that witches, as agents of Satan, are engaged in an insidious campaign to wreak havoc on God's children. Witches are portrayed as evil and depraved and responsible for much of the suffering in society. Most suffering is attributed to individual witches or conspiratorial actions of witch companies or witch groups. Poverty, business failure, broken homes, insanity, crime, and drunkenness are all attributed to witches. Witchcraft victims are defined as innocent and unsuspecting. These sermons promote notions that witch attacks are clandestine, pervasive, and insidious, and that everyone is potentially at risk of victimization from these assaults by lineage members unless they intensify their prayers, fasting, tithing, and their will to do good. Sermons also include dream interpretations. Nightmares are interpreted as indicative of bewitchment. All unusual and recurrent dreams are explained within the context of witchcraft.

Between 2001 and 2012, automobile accidents claimed the lives of numerous people in Ghana, including prominent Ghanaian politicians, entertainers, medical doctors, and student leaders. The rate of fatal and nonfatal road accidents in the country remains high. Many sermons attribute these tragic accidents to witchcraft. In Ghana many people blame witchcraft for the spate of automobile accidents that typically occur during the Christmas and Easter holidays when there is a massive volume of traffic associated with the holiday festivities as people living in urban areas travel to their home towns. In the days leading up to holiday seasons, sermons are laden with warnings against powerful, conspiratorial witch gangs. Speeding, drunk driving, and driver fatigue are rarely mentioned while the holidays are characterized as a time of witch feasts. Christians are thus implored to intensify their prayers to avert falling prey to the evil machinations of witches. In recent years, with the intensification of witch hunts against elderly women, some sermons make a point of cautioning listeners against assuming that every elderly woman is a witch and to be circumspect in their accusations.

Etuo Mu Wɔ Sum Radio Program

The Akan phrase "etuo mu wɔ sum" (the inside of the barrel of a gun is dark), is the name of a weekly, two-hour-long radio program that explores all facets of witchcraft and other spiritual phenomena (e.g., ghosts, mmoatia, reincarnation, sorcery, magic) in Ghanaian society. The program is broadcast throughout Ghana with Web radio streaming also transmitting to such overseas locations as the United States, Canada, the United Kingdom, Germany, Japan, France, and the Netherlands. For ten years the program was hosted by Agya Birifa, a popular disc jockey and radio personality affectionately known in Ghanaian broadcasting circles as the priest of the airwaves. The program regularly features interviews with self-proclaimed witches, alleged witnesses, victims of bewitchment, and representatives of various religious organizations. Etuo Mu Wɔ Sum is carried on the Peace

FM 104.3 radio station that has about 70 percent of countrywide coverage and has media correspondents stationed around the country. These correspondents call in each week to report witchcraft-related incidents that occurred around the country during the preceding week. The program concludes with a call-in segment where listeners are invited to ask questions and offer comments. Given its macabre content, the program has been described with some affection in some circles as the most terrifying program on radio. In the ten years that the program has been on the air, it has explored such topics as the meaning of witchcraft, the distinction between witchcraft and sorcery, typologies of witchcraft, motivations behind bewitchment, patterns of bewitchment victimization, identifying characteristics of witches, typical behaviors of witches, explanations for the overrepresentation of women among accused witches, how witches execute their deeds, the deleterious effects of witchcraft, insider perspectives on witchcraft through interviews with self-professed witches, anti-witchcraft methods and safeguards, the impact of witchcraft on families, and exorcism. Featured programs on *Etuo Mu Wɔ Sum* are often the topic of discussion among listeners and the general public for days following the program. Incidentally, one of the most commonly posed questions is how one might identify a witch, to which the answer given is almost invariably, "hwɛ onipa no nneyɛɛ" (examine the person's behavior or actions). An important question to ask is whether or not the program shapes people's interpretation of reality, beliefs and behavior or, even more explicitly, it encourages violent acts against suspected witches? In accounting for a perceived upsurge in accusations against suspected witches in recent years, some analysts have pointed accusing fingers at radio programs such as *Etuo Mu Wɔ Sum*. Has *Etuo Mu Wɔ Sum* served to strengthen witch beliefs? Has it raised fears about witches?

Audiocassette Recordings

Many members of the clergy in Ghana regularly sermonize on the subject of witchcraft, acknowledging that witchcraft is a potent force capable of derailing a good Christian from a path toward salvation. One enterprising preacher by the name of Abraham Obugyei (n.d.) has made an audiocassette with a sermon devoted exclusively to the topic of witchcraft. Titled "Bayie Ho Asɛm" (discourse on witchcraft) and delivered in Akan (Twi), the sermon is a detailed treatise on Akan witchcraft ideology. Apostle Obugyei begins the sermon with a prayer, and then proceeds to discuss the characteristics of witches and the nature of witchcraft more generally. The sermon is interspersed with biblical quotations. Enlisting the assistance of a colleague who reads the relevant passage, Obugyei follows with an expatiation on each biblical verse, using it to affirm, validate, and buttress points made throughout the sermon. He cites and explains the following biblical verses: Ephesians 6:10, I Corinthians 2:11, Deuteronomy 18:10, James 2:18, Mark 5:1, Ezekiel 19:1, Micah 3:2, Isaiah 33:1, Job 7:4, Acts 16:16, Psalm 59:6, Psalm 37:4, Mark 7:31, Mark 9:14, Luke 20:1, Proverbs 30:13, Hebrews 4:12, Revelations 3:1, and Psalm 91:1.

Throughout the sermon, he refers to witches as *ewiem mu atumfoɔ* (powers of the sky) and *esum mu atumfoɔ* (powers of darkness). He characterizes *bayie* or witchcraft as wild. He describes the world as *ewiase yɛ sum* (the world is dark) and inscrutable, meaning that there is so much that is unknown to mere mortal humans.

On the nature of the relationship between the witch and the bewitched, he quotes the popular Akan saying regarding bewitchment: "aboa bi bɛka wo a na ɛfiri woara ntoma mu" (the insect that is biting you is located inside your own clothes). This illustrates the idea that one can be bewitched only by someone with whom one has an intimate physical or social relationship.

The sermon also emphasizes the surreptitious and decadent tendencies of witches. Obugyei cites, for example, how a person could be eating food from the same bowl with a witch but unbeknownst to the victim, the witch has turned the other's portion of the food into human excreta while the witch enjoys her own portion of real food. To buttress the point about the devious nature of the witch, he further refers to a witch in flight as having the speed of a jet fighter, capable of traveling long distances undetected. He describes how a witch in aerial flight can set off on a journey from Ghana to the United States at midnight, arrive safely to capture and devour its human victim, and return to Ghana before daybreak.

He also emphasizes the notion that one must be a witch to catch a witch. Obugyei asserts that every *ɔkɔmfoɔ* (fetish priest and priestess) is a witch (*ɔkɔmfoɔ biara yɛ ɔbayifoɔ*). By the same token, anyone who can perform wonders, including professional magicians, is a witch.

He contends that witches are capable of bewitching Christians, but qualifies that they can only bewitch lukewarm Christians. Conversely, he reiterates that witches are fearful of very strong Christians such as born-again Christians ("okristo ni papa biara ɔbayifoɔ suro no") and tremble at the sight of a picture of Jesus Christ ("ɔbayifoɔ biara hu yesu a na ne ho popo"). Obugyei personalizes the statement by saying that because of his status and spiritual strength as a solid, unwavering Christian, "ɔbayifoɔ biara hu me a osuro me kɔkɔkɔkɔ" (all witches fear me immensely). He argues that with Christianity, if a witch sets out to entrap a person, God ensures that the trap is unsuccessful or frees the person from the trap ("ɔbayifoɔ sum wo fidie a Onyame bɛyi wo afiri mu").

In a discussion regarding exorcism of witch power, listeners are informed that before a member of the clergy can exorcise a witch spirit, the witch has to confess to all evil deeds that he or she has perpetrated through witchcraft. Meanwhile, a successful exorcism by a Christian pastor will require that the pastor fortify himself or herself with potent prayers and fasting to ensure protection from the witch's evil power.

On the subject of witch covens and nocturnal witch activities, the listener is told that witches belong to an association, society, or coven (*bayie ye ekuo* or *bayie ye society* that meets nightly. The sermon also includes the idea that witchcraft power is an heirloom—*bayie ye agyapadee* (prized property) that has been in an *abusua* for several generations and that it is impossible to extirpate or totally eradicate witchcraft from a lineage ("bayie ase ntu wɔ abusua mu"). According to the sermon, witches do not cross over after death carrying their witchcraft power, but leave it on this earth, bequeathing it to someone in their *abusua* prior to their own death.

The sermon describes witchcraft as inherently evil. It is reiterated throughout the sermon that witches love evil and hate goodness, with the statement "obayifoɔ biara tan papa dɔ bɔne." Witchcraft is also referred to as a highly terrifying phenomenon ("bayie ye adeɛ a eye hu paa") and most despicable for humanity ("bayie ye adeɛ a onipa kyiri paa"). To exemplify the cruel and heartless nature of witches ("abayifoɔ tiri mu ye den), Obugyei tells the story of a witch who used witchcraft to kill her own son who was a final-year university student. Obugyei asserts that as an itinerant preacher, he occasionally encounters people who state that if they ever had witchcraft, they would use it in the service of good. He vehemently counters with the statement that witchcraft is anathema to goodness since it is impossible to use it for positive ends. He emphasizes that it is the witchcraft power that controls and directs the person who carries it to do its bidding and therefore the carrier has no control over that power because it is a force independent of human will and cannot be consciously used for a given purpose.

Obugyei refers to witches who claim to use their witchcraft to good ends, based on never having had to sacrifice family members of their own, as rich in the spiritual realm. These wealthy witches participate in the consumption of other witches' meat, but when the time arrives for them to bring a victim of their own, they use their wealth to purchase nonrelative victims to make their contribution to the coven's feast. Wealthy witches purchase nonrelatives actively sold by other witches, who emboss "For Sale" signs on the clothing of bewitched family members, along with the residential address where the witch can be contacted for the purchase of the bewitched victim. At night, the wealthy witch travels to the house of the other witch to negotiate the price for the bewitched. In this way, the wealthy witches spare their own family members, giving the appearance that they have good witchcraft since none of their own relatives have suffered any of the ill fortunes that are signs of bewitchment. By contrast, the witches who sell off their own relatives in this manner are the poor witches. In Obugyei's own words, "bayi hiani na ɔyɛ bayi kwasea" ("It is the poor witch who is the foolish witch").

According to the apostle, women are inherently prone to be witches: if there are one hundred women in a lineage, then no fewer than ninety-nine of them are witches. A male witch or wizard is called *bari bonsam* or *bayi bonsam* in Akan. *Bonsam* in Akan language refers to the devil, while *bari* is a shortened form of *barima* (male). Listeners are told that male witches (wizards) are very dangerous indeed, and far more destructive than a female witch. One male witch, he tells the listener, has witch power that is the equivalent of that of one hundred female witches. He further tells the listener that if there is one wizard in the family, all the males in the *abusua* will turn into nonentities or *akwasampafoɔ* (drifters). To illustrate the enormity of the power of wizards, Obugyei states that when a wizard or male witch sneezes, all the children in the *abusua* will contract measles.

Much of the sermon is devoted to a description of the machinations and outcomes of malefic witchcraft. Many people who awake feeling weak with bodily pains have been battered in the spiritual realm by a witch while sleeping. In cases of persons who complain about pains in their eyes, he says it is because the witch has removed their eyeballs in the night and used them as toffee, sucking on them and then placing them back by morning light. The dull student has had his or her brain removed by the witch, who has hidden it. At night, the sound of dogs barking is not what it appears to be: it is actually witches calling each other for their nightly meeting. The existence of a *akyakya* (hunchback) is explained through witchcraft: the witches have used a rope to twirl the person's body, making it impossible for the legs to grow straight, which, instead, are folded into his or her back. The stutterer has literally had his or her tongue tied by the witch, making speech difficult. *Etware* (epilepsy) is purely a witch disease; every person with epilepsy is a victim of bewitchment, according to the sermon. This also applies to *agyemirekutu* (mumps). Some people who wake up in the morning convinced that they have developed mumps have actually been pummeled in the face by witches as they slept. Those who face difficulties finding a spouse or romantic partner have been married to a witch in the spiritual realm. If a vendor or retailer continually loses money despite having a productive business, this is the result of witches whittling away the money of the vendor, for example by placing holes in the palm of the unsuspecting vendor and snatching the money away through the spiritual realm.

Obugyei describes instances of sudden death involving apparently healthy, young individuals. He attributes these deaths to witchcraft. These were persons who had been living while, unbeknownst to them, their essences had been consumed by witches; that is, their various bodily organs had been eaten by witches in the spiritual realm. These individuals, completely unaware of their physically vulnerable state, felt healthy, but when hit or struck in any way, suddenly fell dead.

On the subject of child witchcraft, he tells the story of a three-year-old girl who was bequeathed witchcraft power by her ninety-year-old grandmother immediately before the elderly woman passed away. After relating this account, however, the apostle cautions against the presumption that all old women are witches with the statement, "aberewa bi wɔ hɔ a n'anim sɛ akorɔma nanso ɔnkye nkokɔ mma" (there are some elderly women who look like hawks but do not catch chicks).

In one segment of the sermon, Obugyei poses the rhetorical question, "Can a witch go to Heaven?," then answers that a witch cannot go to Heaven until he or she confesses and renounces his or her sins.

He concludes the sermon by providing an account of his own personal encounter with a sixty-year-old wizard. The wizard felt his death was imminent and wanted to have his witchcraft exorcised so that he could go to Heaven. The man confessed that he participated in nocturnal flights with other witches. In the witch coven to which he belonged, the trunk of a plantain tree, when felled, was used as an airplane. He and the other witches sat on it and were able to travel from Ghana to the United States in seconds. He confessed that his index finger was where his witch power resided. He could, for example, point his index finger at a car, bursting the tires and causing the car to have an accident. He confessed that he would then proceed to drink the blood of the accident victims as they lay dying.

Witchcraft in Popular Music

Music is another powerful medium for socialization into witchcraft phenomena. Whether it is traditional folk songs, highlife, or its more contemporary derivative hiplife, lyrics in Ghanaian music are suffused with vivid or subtle references to witchcraft and the malevolent activities of witches. Brempong (1986), in his analysis of popular Ghanaian highlife music, observed that the lyrics of several popular highlife songs focus on the influences of witchcraft in shaping a person's destiny in life on earth. Such lyrics reinforce beliefs in the existence of witches, wizards, and witchcraft, and that witches are responsible for heinous and notorious offenses. The lyrics of several popular hiplife songs also discuss witchcraft themes.

For example, Batman's hiplife album *Dankwasere* features a song called "Di Wo Line Mu." Here, the lyricist sings, "me nya nwuu yɛ nso wore yɛ me ho ayie, wo mmerɛ na ebɛ ba ama y'abɔ wo bayie" (I am not dead but you are mourning me; your time will come for you to be accused of witchcraft). In Kwaadee's song "Aborɔ ne Bayie" profiled extensively in chapter 4, he sings about cases of alleged witchcraft, witchcraft suspicions, bewitchments, and the use of malevolent witchcraft to perpetrate nefarious deeds, including "aborɔ ne bayie nti yɛse ɔbarima nyem" (a man who became pregnant via witchcraft).

Children's Literature

Story books written for Ghanaian children can perpetuate witchcraft beliefs and ideas by exposing young minds to witchcraft ideology. This ensures the entrenchment of witchcraft beliefs and ideas by the time children reach adulthood. Moreover, that witchcraft themes would be considered appropriate material for chidren's books suggests the extent to which witchcraft ideology pervades Ghanaian society. During a visit to the University of Ghana Bookstore at Legon and other smaller bookstores in July 2009, I had no difficulty picking out several children's books with witchcraft titles and themes, including *Witches Night Club* by Buabeng Boahen Foster; *Witches in Paradise* by Buabeng Boahen Foster, *The Witches and the Hunter* by Williams Asamoah, *Christian Witches* by Pascal Kafu Abotsi, and *One Blow: You Devil, Leave Me Alone!* by Ike K.F. Tandoh (n.d.).

To demonstrate the concordance between themes covered in these children's books and Ghanaian witchcraft ideology, I offer an in-depth exploration of the contents of one such book. From the local literature series *Stories Grandma Told,* I examine the story in Kofi Brenya's (1992) children's book *The Ungrateful Friend.* In this story, the cat family and the mouse family were once best friends. However, suspicions and accusations of witchcraft, following the death of the mouse's child, turned them into sworn enemies. Suspicion of witchcraft, divination, accusations of witchcraft, the development of antagonistic relations between the two families, and Mrs. Mouse's brutal physical assault on Mrs. Cat, following the death of the mouse's child, all mirror the phenomena of witchcraft accusations, assaults on putative witches, and the subsequent marring of relations between persons and families:

> In ancient times, Cat and Mouse were very good friends. They lived in one house. They did everything together. . . . The friends and their families lived happily together. . . . Unfortunately, Mrs. Cat became sick. She was confined to

bed. One day, Cat, Mouse and the children of Cat went to their farm. The two wives and the twins were left in the house. Mrs. Mouse cooked food. She gave some of the food to her twins to eat in the kitchen. She then carried some of the food to Mrs. Cat in her room. While she was returning to the kitchen, she heard her children yelling. She rushed to the kitchen. One of her twins was severely burnt. She quickly took him to hospital for treatment. Cat and Mouse came back from their farm to hear this sad news. They went to the hospital to be told that the child had died. They were shocked by the news. The death marked a turning-point in the cordial relationship between Cat and Mouse.

A week later, Mrs. Mouse consulted a fetish priest to know why her son died. The fetish priest surprisingly told her that Mrs. Cat used her witchcraft to kill that child. Initially, Mrs. Mouse became confused. She thought the fetish priest was wrong. "How can this good friend kill my child? Her family helped me to get the drugs which enabled me to produce these children. She has been kind enough to care for me and the children. She can't kill him." She told the fetish priest. "You argue well. But listen to me. A poultry farmer painstakingly feeds his chickens with very good food and clean water. He keeps the hen-coop neatly. But when these chickens are grown, what happens?" the fetish priest asked her.

Mrs. Mouse was still confused. She, therefore, went to a friend to discuss what the fetish priest had told her. This friend was an old lady. Everybody believed that that lady was highly experienced in life and would always give good advice. "Do you believe in witchcraft?" The old lady asked Mrs. Mouse. "No," Mrs. Mouse answered. "I see. I also did not believe in witchcraft until witches killed all my children. Now, I believe that witches can kill any creature. What the fetish priest told you is true. There is no doubt about that. By the way, do you know that Mrs. Cat is a powerful witch?" The old lady asked her. "But I am sure that she was in her room. Only the two children were in the kitchen. How could she kill my child who was far away?" Mrs. Mouse asked. "In the spiritual world, it is possible to travel thousands of kilometers within one second. This means that the evil spirit Mrs. Cat has can move from her room to the kitchen and back within one second," the old lady explained. "But Mrs. Cat was weak and moved slowly with much pain. How could she move all that fast?" Mrs. Mouse anxiously asked the old lady. "It is the evil spirit she has which she sent to kill your child," the old lady explained further.

Mrs. Mouse became satisfied that Mrs. Cat killed her son. And so the trouble began. She went to Mrs. Cat and asked: "Are you asleep?" "No. I can't sleep. I feel pains all over my body," Mrs. Cat answered in a friendly tone. "I am happy you can't sleep. Why don't you use your witchcraft to cure yourself? You think you can kill my son and have peace? Not at all," Mrs. Mouse shouted. Mrs. Cat became confused. She slowly moved from her bed and sat on a stool. She was sweating profusely and was in great pain. She had grown very weak. "My friend, what is happening?" Mrs. Cat asked. "Who is your friend? You have killed my son and you call me your friend? A witch cannot be my friend. You are my enemy. You either use your witchcraft to kill me or I will kill you and your witchcraft today," Mrs. Mouse shouted. Mrs. Mouse then dragged

Mrs. Cat out of the room and started to whip her repeatedly with a cane. Mrs. Cat was too weak to resist or defend herself. (Brenya 1992, 2–13)

Adult Fiction

Novels for adults by local authors often incorporate themes involving witches, witchcraft, and the power and influence of witches to affect human affairs. Asare Konadu's novel, *The Wizard of Asamang* (1964), has been widely popular among Ghanaian youths as well as adults since its first printing in 1964. The protagonist, Kwabena Asare, at age seven dreams about being chased by two bulls, cultural symbolism denotative of bewitchment. He relates the dream to his parents who respond by taking him to Mununkum's antiwitchcraft shrine to obtain protection to ward off witchcraft and evil spirits. At the shrine, the boy is given a rancid potion made of blood and herbs to drink, which he spits out. He is immediately branded a wizard by a fetish priest affiliated with the shrine and is forced to endure a painful exorcism ordeal. In chapters 6 and 7 of the novel, "My Visit to Nantan" and "I Was Declared a Wizard," respectively, the author provides a detailed discussion of Akan witchcraft beliefs and practices including witchcraft accusations, divination, confessions of witches, the role of witch doctors, exorcism, purification rituals, and the use of amulets and other protective charms to fend off witchcraft and other malevolent spirits. The reader is exposed to the exorbitant fees and fines imposed by witch-finding fetishes and the mistreatment of suspected witches. Consider the following discussion between Kwabena Asare and his father about a mentally deranged man who was also brought before the anti-witchcraft shrine for suspected bewitchment:

> I turned and looked at my father and asked, "Papa, is this man too being troubled by a witch?" "It is possible, my son. Witches are very crafty. They can be responsible for many ills, including madness." "If this is what witches can do then I'm thankful I came," I said. "You must be thankful to me your father. You could easily have become like that madman, you know," said my father. "It is a pity, isn't it, papa, to see that man suffer like that." "He is not responsible. Witches have made him so. They have taken his brain away and that is the result of the man's madness," my father said with emphasis as if he had himself been a victim of witchcraft. (Konadu 1964, 53)

Consider, as well, the mission statement of Kwabena Asare's mother when she appears before the shrine of the fetish priest of Mununkum followed by the chicken divination performed at the anti-witchcraft shrine:

"I'm here, my lord, as you might have known, being a great fetish before whom nothing in this world is hidden, to ask you something. You know, first I had suffered from witches and therefore I had never had any children apart from the only one I have. Then last week my only child dreamt and from the nature of the dream it appeared some witches are after him. They want to kill him. My husband and I are also here to ask for your protection. We must also mention the plight of my mother-in-law who is suffering from rheumatism, and my grandfather who has been bed-ridden for over five years." My mother then turned to my father who all along had been nodding his head. It appeared she wanted to be reminded of other things she had not mentioned. My father quickly got the cue and added as an appendix the case of his sister who was barren and also of his younger brother who was epileptic. I knelt there quietly gazing at the fetish priest. He looked straight into our faces. When my father had concluded, the priest uttered a loud noise, "Hi, hi." The hen was strangled and left to flutter its wings on the ground. It was this fluttering of wings that came through faintly as we waited outside in the queue. After a few seconds the fowl stopped struggling and lay on its back. The priest then shouted, "Thank you, thank you." The linguist exchanged glances with the priest and then passed on to my father some black powder. He asked papa to use some of it in my food when we returned home. He was also to get some herbs and bathe me in them. We were now ready to leave the hut. I held tightly to my father's cloth and soon we were in the open again, much to my relief. But other things were yet to come. (Konadu 1964, 53–54)

The confessional statements of those who were branded witches by the fetish also reflect various themes around Akan witchcraft beliefs that have been outlined in this book. For example, there is the predominance of older women offering confessionals, the attribution of myriad physical and mental maladies to witchery, and the motivation of witches acting out of anger, revenge, jealousy, or greed.

The elderly woman fell down on her knees and asked that her life be spared for she had committed grievous crimes. "I have killed my brother, taken the womb of my daughter and made her barren and I was going to kill my younger sister when I met you." (Konadu 1964, 65)

"I used my finger nails as beans to cook for my husband. I have snakes in my stomach which come out at night. At one time they chased and bit to death a man in our village who quarreled with me. Indeed, I have wronged you, Otumfuo Odomankoma." (Konadu 1964, 65)

"My brother had on the previous day refused to take me in his lorry [truck] to Asukokoo but when his wife asked him to take her to visit her mother he agreed. So I crossed the road with cobwebs which blinded him and he drove straight to his death. I also drew blood from the ulcer on my niece's foot and that is why it has never got healed. When my husband never had money for meat, I turned flies into fish and cooked them for food." (Konadu 1964, 67)

This book undoubtedly reinforces witchcraft beliefs already acquired through such sources as family, school, and children's peer associations.

Aside from popular fiction, dozens of books have been published containing themes of witchcraft, sorcery, and magic, some of which claim to be based on actual facts. Readers are treated to a cornucopia of scenes of witchcraft, sorcery, and the role of witches in influencing daily life. Reading such books not only reinforces established witchcraft beliefs, but also induces fear of witchcraft and witches.

Folk Tales

Oral traditions, including folk tales, provide another medium for the dissemination of witchcraft ideas. In multigenerational families, older siblings and cousins relate folk tales to younger members of the family while older adults commonly gather young children around them and tell them fictional tales in the evening hours before bedtime. Hence, many Ghanaians grow up with stories of witchcraft, the *sasabonsam* (forest monster), *mmoatia* (short, elf-like creatures with supernatural powers), and the power of the devil. Tales featuring witch stories with witch characters and themes parallel local witchcraft beliefs. Physical and behavioral stereotypes of witches, their flights to secret nightly assemblies, the malevolent female witch, the vile deeds of witches, cannibalistic witches consuming their offspring or kinsfolk, the alteration of *hyɛberɛ* (destiny or fate), the thwarting of other people's progress, and how witches bequeath their witchcraft to family members may be included in such tales.

Religious Organizations and Practitioners

Religious organizations and institutions play a particularly critical role in socializing their members about witchcraft phenomena. In the Christian churches, sermons often center on the malevolent powers of witches and how Christians must fight to vanquish witchcraft and other evil forces. Prayer sessions frequently take up the issue of witchcraft and its malevolence. Testimonials from the congregation often center on the attribution of witchcraft to a host of financial, marital, and health problems and how such individuals managed to utilize the power of prayer, fasting, and faith to conquer such dark forces, thereby extolling the power of the Christian faith. Any sign of sinful behavior is considered symptomatic of wavering faith and the devil's triumph.

Periodic religious conventions are held in the course of the calendar year in several communities. Depending on the congregational size of the diocese, conventions attract hundreds of congregants seeking treatment or relief from variant forms of suffering and distress. Officiating ministers perform exorcisms and remove bewitchments from those with illnesses or other alleged afflictions brought on by witchcraft. At some of these conventions, there are episodes of witches being caught and confessing to their spiritual crimes. Following a witch confession, information is rapidly circulated via gossip in the community regarding which new witch has recently been caught, and the nature of their maleficent deeds.

Some evangelists also disseminate information about witchcraft through their own published books (e.g., Simpson 2009). Scriptural passages from the Christian Bible are copiously cited in support of arguments about the reality of witchcraft. These books often cover such themes as how the devil, through the medium of witches, can inflict harm and death by supernatural means; the alleged testimonies of born-again witches; maleficent deeds that witches have confessed to; methods for identifying witches in one's lineage; and protocols for Christians to protect themselves from the actions of witches.

Witchcraft Trials and Witchcraft Cases

Over the past few decades, a number of witchcraft-related civil and criminal trials have been held in Ghana. The issues litigated have included defamation cases in which plaintiffs sought redress in civil court as well as cases of criminal assaults and homicides in which defendants were prosecuted by the state for criminal actions against suspected witches. In Ghana, formal witchcraft trials in the country's judicial system provide ample opportunities for the dissemination and perpetuation of witchcraft beliefs. Through the various media (e.g., radio, television, newspapers, magazines, and the Internet), the public learns about the cases and their outcomes. Indeed, given the widespread public interest in the subject of witchcraft, witchcraft trials are invariably well attended by the general public. From the initial apprehension of criminal suspects by law enforcement officials to the conclusion of the formal trial, enquiring citizens throng the corridors of local police stations and hallways of court buildings, trying to catch glimpses of the defendants and plaintiffs. Invariably, curious spectators arrive several hours before the commencement of proceedings to ensure they will have standing space, with some spectators leaving only after the proceedings have ended. Such trials provide opportunities for spectators to gossip, theorize about what happened in the case, and compare and contrast notes about the ongoing and unfolding drama before them and previous witchcraft trials to which they have been exposed. Those who cannot be at the trial inform themselves by reading media reports that are presumed to accurately and exhaustively capture the facts.

An example of one high-amplitude witchcraft case was that involving one Abena Kobua. This case caused considerable national sensation and was of enormous popular interest. In chapter 6 of this book, I describe this 1975 witchcraft-related trial in extensive detail to demonstrate how the trial proceedings served to reinforce witchcraft ideology as well as to educate the Ghanaian public about the nature of witchcraft and the activities of witches. In this case two accused witches took legal action against their accusers in a bid to defend their reputations that they felt had been blemished by an imputation of witchcraft. The defendants were found to be civilly liable in a magistrates' court and ordered to pay compensatory damages to the plaintiffs for the torts that were committed. As evidence of the newsworthiness of witchcraft trials in the society, journalists from each of the major newspapers in the country at the time—the *Daily Graphic*, the *Ghanaian Times*, the *Sunday Mirror*, and the *Weekly Spectator*—diligently covered the trial proceedings daily, from the inception to the conclusion, relaying to the curious public pictures and briefings on what transpired in the courtroom. Retrospective reviews of media coverage of the trial reveal that several special feature sections and columns in newspapers and magazines around the country were devoted to coverage of the case. Photographs accompanying the news stories showed courtrooms teeming with observers. News reports showed a raucous crowd with the magistrate issuing intermittent orders for the public to remain silent and not to disrupt the proceedings.

This chapter has demonstrated that there exists a diverse array of sources for the learning of witchcraft lore in Ghanaian society. Witchcraft imagery is omnipresent in Ghanaian culture, in both material and nonmaterial culture. Throughout life, the average Ghanaian is surrounded by information concerning witchcraft and witches. I have documented several types of sources for acquiring this information. Witchcraft imagery is available in the jokes that people tell, the folktales that are told and retold, the newspapers the literate public reads, in the videos and films people watch, in the inscriptions written on commercial vehicles in which they travel, in the proverbs that adorn speech, and even in children's literature. This chapter also included a brief reference to popular music as one among several forms of mass media that socialize Ghanaians into witchcraft ideology. The following chapter explores in greater depth the prominent role of popular music in promoting witchcraft ideas in Ghanaian society.

Chapter 4

WITCHCRAFT THEMES IN
POPULAR GHANAIAN MUSIC

Music has a vital role in all societies, serving as a major conduit for the expression and transmission of cultural values, beliefs, and norms. To investigate music's role in the acquisition, dissemination, and perpetuation of Akan witchcraft ideology in Ghana, this chapter explores the representation of witchcraft in highlife and gospel music through the example of eight songs. Content analysis of the song lyrics reveals prevailing Ghanaian beliefs about witches and witchcraft, suggesting that music may play a supportive, if not pivotal, role in the reinforcement and dissemination or transmission of witchcraft beliefs.

It is axiomatic that song lyrics often relate to the social, cultural, or political events and happenings in a society. As any ethnomusicologist would note, the music of any society, in its capacity as a communicative and expressive art form, can provide a window into the society, often affirming, reinforcing, and critiquing the prevailing values, beliefs, norms, and aesthetics of the times. A diachronic analysis of musical genres within the same society can give a window into cultural continuity and change. As in most societies, music in Ghanaian society provides salient information about the core values, beliefs and concerns of the society (Asante-Darko and van der Geest 1983; Brempong 1986; Yankah 1984). Here, musicians of varied musical genres have used song to communicate societal views on births, destiny, witchcraft, gender relations, and death (Asante-Darko and van der Geest 1983; Brempong 1986; van der Geest 1980, 1984; Yankah 1984).

Among the major musical genres that have enjoyed tremendous popularity in contemporary Ghana are highlife, hiplife, and gospel. With origins that date back to the late nineteenth and early twentieth centuries, highlife music has long dominated the Ghanaian music scene as the most popular musical form (Collins 1994). As a musical genre, highlife is described as a "fusion of indigenous dance rhythms and melodies and western influences, including regimental music, sea shanties and church hymns" (Graham 1988, 76). Contemporary highlife is played with such modern instruments as the guitar, saxophone, piano, electric organ, cymbals, and drums. It is estimated that there are currently over one hundred highlife bands in the country. Today, highlife musical compositions are found in English, pidgin, and all Ghanaian languages, particularly Akan and Ga. Hiplife, which is a hybrid musical genre with roots in highlife and heavily influenced by hip-hop and reggae rhythms, entered the Ghanaian music scene in the early 1990s and has become the dominant musical form in youth pop culture. Highlife and gospel music have a more extensive history in Ghana. Ghanaian gospel music, like its variants around the world, involves Christian themes that regularly invoke scripture to convey messages of hope, comfort, and redemption, as well as moral instruction. Both highlife and its more recent offshoot, hiplife, give voice to the issues of the day, as well as to values and belief systems in Ghanaian society—from gender conventions to more general notions about human nature.

Witchcraft beliefs remain a vast part of the lyrics of Akan highlife and hiplife; many song texts make reference to witchcraft and the supernatural. In song after song, protagonists invoke witchcraft to explain infertility, alcoholism, conjugal problems, child sickness and deaths, multiple divorces, economic ruination, and a multitude of other personal misfortunes. Anyone who spends time listening to Ghanaian popular music becomes aware of the extent to which lyrical texts make reference to witchcraft and the dynamics of bewitchment. Three of the eight analyzed songs were the title tracks on the albums on which they was released, further suggesting a centrality of the witchcraft theme.

Each song was sung in Akan, the dominant non-English language spoken in Ghana, which makes for widespread dissemination of lyrics that are instantaneously accessible to most Ghanaians. The lyrics of all eight songs were transcribed from audiocassette tapes purchased in Ghana, then translated into English from the Akan language. Transcription and translation were done by the author, a native Akan speaker. These were cross-checked for accuracy by another native Akan speaker. Excerpts from the songs are occasionally provided and analyzed for illustrative purposes.

Each of the eight songs has been a phenomenal success as measured by airplay time on local radio and as televised music videos. When it was first released, "Bayi Kwasea" (Foolish Witchcraft) became a theme song for the popular weekly radio program about witchcraft, *Etuo Mu Wɔ Sum,* receiving play time as background music to discussions on the show as well as during program breaks. Although the number of albums, CDs, and audio-cassette tapes sold is indeterminable in the absence of officially collated data on the subject, each song has a tremendous popular appeal with audiences, evident by the extent to which the song is played on radio, television, in public transportation, and in private homes. In Ghana, popular highlife, hiplife, and gospel songs are frequently played in myriad venues, including birthday parties, outdoorings or baby-naming ceremonies, graduation parties, weddings, and funerals. They are also played at markets and in commercial vehicles such as taxis and commercial minivans plying Ghana's roads. In each of these venues, the songs under study have passed the test. For instance, "Anadwo Bogya" (Lightning Bug), a gospel song with an upbeat tempo, enjoyed massive popularity in the summer of 2005, as I became well aware while conducting ethnographic research in Ghana; this song was being sung by school children and adults alike. Released in the late 1970s, A.B. Crentsil's highlife song "Devil" has become a classic, continuing to generate tremendous airplay some forty years later.

Although all eight songs focus on the subject of witchcraft, the thematic details conveyed in the text of each song vary. For this reason, I have analyzed each song separately.

"Devil," by A.B. Crentsil

In the song "Devil," which is the title track of his late-1970s highlife album, A.B. Crentsil focuses on the distinction between two types of witchcraft. According to the lyrical text, the possession of witchcraft power, as well as the practice of witchcraft, is not restricted to Africans. Westerners, Crentsil proclaims, are also invested with the capacity to acquire and possess witchcraft power. However, Western witchcraft is defined by its beneficent, positive qualities, utilized for constructive purposes or good ends. He notes that Westerners—code for white people—invariably employ their prosocial, constructive witchcraft for the benefit of their societies. Here, A.B. Crentsil specifically ascribes the invention of airplanes and trains to the powerful, beneficent European witchcraft, emphasizing that trains and airplanes are useful, facilitating physical mobility and allowing one to traverse expansive geographical distances with ease.

In contradistinction with the beneficent witchcraft of Westerners, Crentsil decries black people's witchcraft as inherently destructive, motivated by greed, jealousy, and envy, and used principally to wreak havoc on society and afflict misfortunes and incalculable harm on individuals. He sings, "The black man's witchcraft is used for destruction. When he sees his fellow human being making progress, he says, this person, I am going to destroy him, make him blind, cripple; he will never make money." Crentsil beseeches Ghanaian witches in the opening lines of "Devil" to use their *anyɛn* (witchcraft powers) to assist their children in attaining material success. Then, in the final stanza of the song, he forcefully commands the devil to leave, with the refrain, "Go away from me, you devil; Go away from me, you devil."

Crentsil's lyrics reflect deeply entrenched Ghanaian views about witchcraft and its role in explaining disparities in material resources and technological development between African and Western societies. As emphasized in chapter 2, popular Ghanaian witchcraft beliefs include a clear distinction between two categories of witchcraft (Adinkrah 2004; Bannerman-Richter 1982). The first type is known as *bayi pa* or *bayi fufuo.* The second kind is called *bayi borɔ* or *bayi kwasea,* or *bayi tuntum.* Maleficent witchcraft is the use of witchcraft power to cause harm to another person while beneficent witchcraft is used to provide protection or promote success for oneself or loved ones (Adinkrah 2004; Bannerman-Richter 1982).

For many Ghanaians, the technological and material developments of Western societies remain something of a mystery that begs an explanation. The perceived relatively greater social stability and prosperity of the Western world is linked to the beneficent activities of European or American witches, whereas persistent warfare, famine, and poverty in Africa are attributed to the maleficent, harmful, or diabolical witchcraft of African peoples. Thus, the preponderance of good witchcraft in Europe, Canada, and the United States is the underlying explanation for white people's progress. White people not only use their witchcraft for development, but also for the benefit of their immediate communities and humankind. They use it to protect their families and their communities from evil and to cure illnesses and disease. By contrast, black people use their maleficent witchcraft to cause physical and mental disabilities in people they envy or despise. In the 1982 publication *The Practice of Witchcraft in Ghana,* Bannerman-Richter underscores the maleficent nature of Ghanaian witchcraft: "The so-called white witch, that is, a witch who, as a principle devotes her powers solely to combat evil and to benefit mankind, rarely occurs in the Ghanaian witchcraft cosmology, even though some traditional doctors and fetish priests and priestesses who are dedicated to fighting witchcraft are themselves witches" (Bannerman-Richter 1982, 90).

This dichotomy between white witchcraft as good and constructive versus black witchcraft as bad and destructive is captured in a popular Akan saying: "sɛ wo rekɔ asɔre na sɛ wo hyia oburoni a na w'ahyia wo Nyame" (when you are going to church and you meet a white person, there is no need going anymore for you may have met your God). The implication is that the white person embodies wealth and riches that will be bestowed on you through your connections with them. It also signifies their proximity to the goodness found in God.

Galia Boneh's (2004) study of the conceptions and attitudes toward the material success of *mbroni* (white people) among the Gonja people of northern Ghana yielded findings that could be generalized to the mass of Ghanaians. She noted that attributions of white peoples' material wealth or success were invariably and directly linked to the perceived tendency for Westerners to use their witchcraft powers for constructive purposes. Gonjas ascribed Western inventions of "spaceships, rockets and technological abilities such as creating dolls, robots and other simulations of human beings" to white people's *kigbe* (witchcraft). Conversely, lack of material development and technological advancement of Gonjas were blamed on the latter's tendency to use their witchcraft to maim, kill, or destroy (Boneh 2004, 60–72). Incidentally, Boneh (2004, 67) quotes four lines from the lyrics of Crentsil's "Devil" to illustrate the parallel between the lyrical text and the attitudes expressed by her informants.

Ghanaian interpretations of Westerners' material prosperity are consistent with a broader understanding of the role of witchcraft in generating wealth in Ghanaian culture. For many Ghanaians, the wealth and overall good fortune of humans in general can only derive from the ritualistic machinations of witchcraft. Affluent or materially successful Ghanaians are commonly perceived to be the direct beneficiaries of either their own beneficent witchcraft or the salubrious witchcraft of their kinfolk. Hence, as many Ghanaians regard Westerners as the epitome of abundant wealth, material prosperity, and success, they have concomitantly invested Westerners with a superior or higher grade of witchcraft that has made this wealth and success possible.

What is the source of self-deprecating witchcraft beliefs harbored by Ghanaians? In the absence of a systematic investigation of the issue, the following explanation is conjectural at best. These self-denigrating beliefs appear to have their roots in Ghana's colonial past where European people and cultures were extolled while African people, their institutions, and history were impugned. Under British colonial rule, for example, Ghana's formal education was characterized by a Eurocentric curriculum. The Nkrumah years (1957–1966) that initiated Ghana's status as an independent nation were associated with educational reforms designed to encourage Ghana's development toward self-sufficiency and a distinct national identity independent of their colonial past. Yet the emphasis on national pride was systematically rolled back following Nkrumah's ouster and has yet to experience any significant resurgence. Hence, more than fifty years of political independence has not significantly minimized negative and disparaging attitudes. There has been very little effort on the part of post-Nkrumah Ghanaian governments to shed colonially inspired images that juxtapose the elevation of Europeans and the denigration of Africans. Indeed, the overall post-independence Ghanaian experience has not been dramatically different from the colonial experience. Denigrating and self-depreciating attitudes have been further exacerbated by the strong influence and popularity of contemporary Western mass media. Ghana has not escaped the plethora of films from Europe and North America that perpetuate the glamorization of European cultures with corresponding images of Africa as a continent mired by warfare, political corruption, hunger, and abject poverty (Adinkrah 1992).

"Bayi Kwasea," by Emmanuel Amponsa

In the song "Bayi Kwasea," the lyricist, Emmanuel Amponsa, focuses on malevolent witchcraft as a dominant theme. The Akan word for witchcraft is *bayi* while *kwasea* in Akan translates as foolish or stupid. Here, the singer focuses on a prevalent notion in the Akan witchcraft belief system, that malevolent witches employ their witchcraft powers for cannibalistic purposes, to kill and devour their human victims (Adinkrah 2004; Bannerman-Richter 1982; Debrunner 1961). In the lyrical text, the witch is chastised for eschewing chicken, beef, goat meat and other meats while showing a preference for human flesh. The lyrics remind the malefic witch about the plenitude of chicken, beef, and goat meat in the stanza, "nantwie nyɛ nna, nkokɔ nyɛ nna, mpɔnkye nyɛ nna" (cattle are plentiful, chicken are plentiful, goats are plentiful). At the same time, the lyricist decries the foolishness of the malefic witch who cannot envision that a predilection for anthropophagy or cannibalism will lead to the decimation of his or her own progeny since in Akan beliefs one can consume the flesh only of one's own kinfolk. The cannibalistic witch is then implored to be wise (*sua nyansa*) by refraining from anthropophagous practices that will lead to the demise of his or her own children.

In the next stanza, *bayi kwasea* (the foolish witch) is compared to a ɔkwadwofoɔ (lazy person). Here, *bayi kwasea*'s idiosyncratic preference for human flesh as well as her concomitant repudiation of chicken, beef, and goat meat is apparently interpreted as a lack of discipline and an attempt to avoid the hard work necessary for acquiring the financial resources for purchasing other meats. The flesh belonging to one's kinfolk is meat available for unfettered appropriation via witchcraft. The lazy, foolish witch is exhorted to go to the ant to learn its wisdom. By implication, failure to go to the ant to learn wisdom will lead to the continued consumption and eventual decimation of one's offspring and other maternal relatives. Importantly, several Ghanaian folktales extol the attributes of the ant, whose perceived virtues include sagacity, industriousness, meticulous organization, and deferment of immediate gratification. These are the antithesis of the stereotypical image of *bayi kwasea* as indolent, improvident, egotistical, and hedonistic. Following the example of the ant should promote a good work ethic and, ultimately, the cessation of anthropophagy.

As noted in chapter 3, in Ghana leaders of the myriad Christian churches pontificate on the evils of witchcraft in their sermons and biblical teachings, condemning witches as malevolent beings who perpetrate odious crimes against humanity. Ghanaian discourse on witchcraft is also replete with references to biblical scripture that convey the redemptive forces of Christianity (Soku 2000). In the song "Bayi Kwasea," the lyricist makes references to the scriptural content of I Samuel 28: 7–19. Here, the singer recounts a story to illustrate the Christian God's abhorrence for witchcraft and witch spirits, underscoring the antithesis between witchcraft and Christianity. Listeners learn of the story of King Saul who had failed to heed Prophet Samuel's solemn warnings. While in distress and hoping to obtain some counsel and encouragement from the departed prophet, King Saul seeks the assistance of a witch, asking that she use her powers to conjure the spirit of the departed prophet. When Samuel's spirit appeared, it excoriates King Saul for dabbling in witchcraft, saying that by his actions he has committed a major sin against God. The text is used not only as a basis for counseling *bayi kwasea* to reform his or her ways, but also to condemn those who would seek associations with witches or witch doctors. Once again, Christianity is offered as a remedial measure to witchcraft activities. The witch is implored to confess all of his or her witch deeds to the Lord God in exchange for forgiveness of his or her sins. The witch is then told that he or she will be exorcised of evil powers and receive full redemption.

The textual message of "Bayi Kwasea" is consistent with witchcraft beliefs in Ghanaian society, past and present. Among Ghanaians, there is a well-ingrained idea that the death of a young person is the result of witchcraft, sorcery, or other supernatural forces. Youthful death is simply regarded as unnatural or supernatural. Accordingly, suspicions that cannibalistic witchcraft is at the root of a child's death of unknown etiology are ubiquitous in the society (e.g., Adinkrah 2004). Such allegations are often leveled against women who have suffered multiple miscarriages, stillbirths, the death of an only child, or the death of more than one child. Sudden deaths occurring after a short illness or through automobile accidents tend to heighten these suspicions. In most instances the alleged witch is the biological mother while fathers are rarely accused of using cannibalistic witchcraft to victimize their offspring. During my research in Ghana, there were a number of occasions when informants pointed out, or made references to, women who had consumed some, most, or all of their children through witchery. Additionally, numerous Ghanaian folktales focus on women with many children who lost all or a substantial number of their progeny through their cannibalistic witchcraft activities (e.g., Asamoah 2004).

"Anadwo Bogya," by Joseph Mensah

In "Anadwo Bogya" (Lightning Bug), the title track of a popular gospel album, Joseph Mensah sheds light on the nature and the dynamics of bewitchment. The song title is a play on words that encapsulates several meanings related to witchcraft ideology. In the Akan language, the word *anadwo* refers to nighttime while *bogya* is the word for firefly. Reference to nighttime is consistent with Ghanaian conceptions about witches and witchcraft. It is widely believed that witches are nocturnal, transmogrifying themselves from human form into nonhuman creatures and traveling through the air as balls of fire to attend nightly witch gatherings. The firefly is particularly popular as a witch familiar. Consequently, fear of the firefly is rife among Ghanaians (Bannerman-Richter 1982; Debrunner 1961).

Witches' proclivity for nocturnal activities is a recurring theme in the lyrics of "Anadwo Bogya." The lyricist repeats the phrase "eduru anadwo a na ɔyɛ me" (it is during nighttime that he or she bewitches me) to emphasize the point. Here, the surreptitious tendencies of the witch are conspicuously evident in the song lyrics. The witch is portrayed as invisible while committing evil deeds. Indeed, so clandestine are the witch's actions that the identification of the witch is well nigh impossible despite constant and close physical association maintained with their victims during the daytime. In Ghana, as in many societies, witchcraft is identified with a code of secrecy among its practitioners; witches are admonished to keep their activities covert. Their secret meetings are held at night, usually from midnight to cockcrow at venues unseen by the outside world. It is hard to identify witches because their activities are concealed by visibly normal activities. Take the example of a woman who sells red palm oil at a Ghanaian market. It will be believed that such a woman is a witch actually selling human blood which has been spiritually transformed into red palm oil. By stressing the clandestine nature of witches and their activities, the song reinforces popular societal fears of witches and witchcraft; listeners are concurrently counseled to remain vigilant about witches and the horrors of witchcraft.

Another significant theme that finds recurrent emphasis in the song is the issue of intimate relations between the witch and the bewitched, followed by betrayal of the latter by the former. Although the specific nature of the relationship between the witch and the bewitched in the song is not disclosed, one can infer that the relationship is a personal one. Phrases such as "ɔbɛn me ho pɛɛ" (he or she is physically very close to me) emphasize emotional as well as physical proximity between the bewitched and his or her tormentor. Further evidence of this intimacy is provided in the characterization of the witch as one who is very familiar with the bewitched's roots (onim m'ase paa)—perhaps from infancy, childhood, or adolescence. The lyrics portray the witch and the bewitched as virtually inseparable during daytime; they travel to and fro together. The witch and the bewitched are presented as commonly sharing meals and eating from the same bowl. Moreover, the bewitched shares his deep, personal secrets and intimate details of his life with the witch; together, they commiserate about life's challenges, difficulties, and injustices. The witch, in turn, offers him encouragement and succor in times of personal distress and in the midst of these challenges. Yet the witch betrays the protagonist, carrying out nocturnal witchly assaults against him. In a dramatic reversal one stanza later, after describing the solidarity between the witch and bewitched, the witch is portrayed as a lecherous creature residing deep inside the bewitched's knee joint, inflicting debilitating injury on him or her. The close physical proximity between the witch and the bewitched allows the witch to gain unhindered access to his or her victim, both physically and spiritually. Thus, it is personal intimacy with a witch that makes one most vulnerable to becoming a host of the witch and thereby a victim of bewitchment. This is particularly consistent with prevailing Akan notions regarding witchcraft that recognize that a person can only directly bewitch a close matrikin (Adinkrah 2004; Bannerman-Richter 1982; Debrunner 1961).

The cunning and treacherous nature of the witch is prominent in the lyrical text throughout the remainder of the song. In one stanza, the character of the witch is likened to that of anomaa konekone, a proverbial bird in Akan folktales whose actions are characterized as traitorous. Anomaa konekone flies clandestinely upstream along a flowing river to muddy the waters of the stream, then, to hide its actions, hurriedly flies downstream to raise a fuss about someone muddying the waters. The listener is invoked to compare the witch with the treacherous bird, commiserating with the bewitched and sharing in life's activities, offering advice, yet ultimately assaulting and betraying the witchcraft victim. To further reinforce the duplicitous nature of the witch, the singer offers another analogy, equating the witch's behavior to the notorious Ghanaian house mouse that simultaneously bites its victim and blows on resulting wounds. Some Ghanaians sometimes wake up from a night's sleep unable to walk because of sores that have appeared on the soles of their feet. Some believe that these sores are caused by a house mouse, a breed of rodent found in Ghana, which has a reputation for nibbling on the soles of their sleeping victims while soothingly blowing on the feet to avoid rousing the person. The treachery and double-dealing nature of the witch is further emphasized with yet another analogy in another stanza. Here, the witch's behavior is likened to a tiny insect in Ghana called *kanea kaba*. Usually found at night flying around electric lights, it has the capacity of getting into one's clothes and inflicting several painful tiny bites on its victim. One may shed all of one's clothes in pursuit of this creature but will have difficulty locating it because of its minute size and ability to elude detection.

The lyricist expresses pessimism about life and calls on listeners to exercise circumspection in this world. As most Ghanaians who claim to have been bewitched or to know others who have been bewitched note, "ewiase yɛ hu" (the world is a dangerous, threatening place). The singer employs the same phrase to reiterate the idea that no one is safe and that everyone is vulnerable to witch assaults. Therefore people should exercise caution and beware the machinations of their supposedly close relatives.

The singer ends the song on an optimistic and hopeful note, discussing a strategy for overcoming witchcraft—belief in Agya Onyame (God the father) who is depicted as the master and great conqueror of all evil. He asserts that the blood of Jesus Christ the redeemer that Christ spilled on the cross has saved him, the singer. With the Christian God on his side, he has overcome the evil machinations of the witch and has been saved from the witch's nefarious deeds. Because of this, "ne nwuma nyinaa ara ayɛ kwa" (all the witch's destructive actions did not come to fruition). In Ghana acceptance of Christianity, joining a spiritual church, trusting completely in the Christian God, regularly fasting, and praying are perceived to provide protection in warding off witches. By contrast, lack of faith in the Christian God makes one particularly susceptible to bewitchment.

A number of questions emerge from an analysis of the lyrical text of "Anadwo Bogya." First, is the lyricist providing an account of an actual witchcraft allegation or is it merely a fictional account? Second, the lyrics make the personal characteristics of the witch indeterminable; the witch is not identified as male or female, young or old, rich or poor. Such ambiguity is intriguing, given the predominance of poor, elderly women among persons accused of malefic witchcraft (Adinkrah 2004).

"Beyie Nnim Omeni," by Super Yaw Ofori

In this 1993 highlife song, musical artist Super Yaw Ofori sings about the cruel and indiscriminate witch who shows no mercy or pity toward his or her own kin. As is the case with all songs reviewed in this chapter, the lyrics of "Beyie Nnim Omeni" (a witch does not recognize a close relation) offer the listener a glimpse into some of the central narratives of Akan witchcraft beliefs.

The song opens with a rapid, jovial exchange between two female witches, one named Aso and the other Takyiwaa, who are busily making preparations for an impending nocturnal witches' secret gathering. When Aso asks about the location for the secret assembly, Takyiwaa answers that the meeting will occur under a big bridge. Aso expresses surprise, inquiring thus: "Isn't this the same location we went the other night where we were nearly apprehended and exposed?" Takyiwaa responds, "We are still going there for the meeting because we are great," referring to the fact that their particular witch coven is so powerful as to have the capacity to elude detection once again. The discussion then shifts to who they will select to be consumed during their cannibalistic witch feast. Aso asks Takyiwaa "Who are you bringing to the Sabbath tonight?" "I am bringing my biological child," she replies. Aso offers, "I am bringing my grandchild." When asked which part of her victim's body she will consume during the witches' gathering, Takyiwaa replies, "I am going to eat her forearm." Aso announces that she will eat her victim's liver. Then, Aso tells Takyiwaa that they are causing so much mischief with their witchcraft. Takyiwaa responds by expressing insouciance, stating "yε mmine" (we don't care/ we don't mind). When Aso tells Takyiwaa that their witch activities would preclude their entry into Heaven, Takyiwaa responds with hilarity, saying that Heaven had long passed them by. The dialogue ends and fades away with the raucous joyous laughter of the two witch accomplices.

The main text of the song that follows this prelude focuses on three basic themes: (1) the cruel nature of the witch and the destructive nature of maleficent witchcraft, (2) the invariably close or intimate nature of the relationship between the witch and the bewitched, and (3) the double-dealing nature of the witch. In the following, I expatiate on all three themes.

There are repeated references to the witch causing the spiritual death of the bewitched through "yε we wo nam" (the consumption or devouring of the victim's flesh). The singer also alludes to the infliction of pain, suffering, and other social and psychological afflictions. References to "ɔno na ɔre yε wo" (he/she is the one doing it to you) implicates the witch in deploying witchcraft power to cause strange or inexplicable illnesses, impeding fertility in females, rendering men sterile or impotent, causing infants and children to sicken or die, and creating other forms of misfortune for victims.

The second major theme is the use of witchcraft power to bewitch persons whom the witch has close physical association or blood ties to, particularly the witch's offspring, brothers, sisters, mothers, or grandchildren. Phrases such as "nea ɔbɛn wo paa na ɔnya wo a ɔbɛ yɛ wo" (the one who is very close to you physically or relationally is the one who will attack you) and "nea ɔne wo didi na ɔwe wo nam" (the one you share the same eating bowl with is the one who will eat your flesh) reflect the close social proximity between the witch and the bewitched. The ruthless nature of the witch in victimizing close blood relatives is expressed in the title of the song: a witch does not recognize a close relation. This means that only an *obayifoɔ* (a person who is utterly merciless) would employ *beyie* (witchcraft) to destroy his or her own progeny and other close relations.

The third major theme is the treacherous nature of the witch. The singer laments his bewitchment by a very close relation who shared his home. The witch was the first person he saw upon waking up each day. The witch was the first person to greet him and ask about his well-being. In an insincere expression of sympathy, the witch even routinely commented on why he, the victim, was suffering so much in this world. In his lament, the bewitched further notes that the witch was also the same person who chaperoned him from spiritualist to spiritualist in search of a cure for his physical, financial, and psychological woes. Yet it was the witch who stymied his treatment by deliberately avoiding those places where he would receive an effective cure. This was because the witch's witchcraft power would be exposed by the spiritual healer. In the words of the singer, the witch takes him in the wrong or negative direction, not only to elude detection, but also to enable the witch to continue wreaking havoc on the bewitched.

In another stanza, the treacherous nature of the witch is analogized with the actions of the *ohuruyɛ* (tsetse fly) that, in Akan folktales and proverbial sayings, presumably bites and blows on its victims simultaneously in order to prevent the victims from noticing that they are being bitten. In this analogy, the victim is so close to the witch that it is difficult for the former to identify the witch as the source of his or her woes. The singer also invokes the imagery of the proverbial bird *anomaa konekone* to underscore the two-faced nature of the witch. As noted in the previous discussion of "Anadwo Bogya," the *anomaa konekone* goes upstream of a flowing river to muddy up the waters and returns downstream to inquire about the source of the muddying waters.

The heartless, pitiless nature of the witch is another recurrent theme. The witches are portrayed as so ruthless and cruel in their destructive deeds that they fail to show mercy even toward close relatives and other intimates. The incessant use of the refrain, "beyie nnim omeni," which is repeated twenty-two times in the song, is designed to give particular emphasis to this aspect of Akan maleficent witchcraft.

In conclusion, the song text is replete with references to several elements of Akan witch beliefs. First, there are the cannibalistic tendencies of the witch. That witch cannibalism was the focus in the brief prelude to the song is worth noting since, as earlier observed, it is widely believed by most Akans that most witches are of the most malefic kind. In cannibalistic witch companies, participants spiritually bring human victims who they spiritually cannibalize during nocturnal witch gatherings, resulting in the spontaneous death of their victims as they devour their essences. Second, events at the witches' Sabbath are featured. The consumption of the blood, flesh, and bones of witch victims is described as a central feature of these gatherings. Third, we learn of one example of witches' meeting grounds: under a big bridge. Fourth, the listener learns of the close nature of the relationship between the witch and the bewitched: Takyiwaa plans to take her own child while Aso will bring her grandchild. Fifth, one learns that witches are aware that they are witches, recognize the destructive nature of their actions, and are gleeful about what they do. The hilarity and joyous tone with which the witches revel in their dialogue and relish their planned activities illustrates this. They know that God disapproves of what they do and that they will likely not make it to Heaven and yet are not deterred. Sixth, most witches are presumed to be female. That the opening witch dialogue involved two women is consistent with popular Ghanaian notions of who a witch is. As noted in an earlier section of this book, most accusations of maleficent witchcraft are directed against elderly women. One cannot, however, ascertain the ages of the women involved in the opening dialogue.

"Bayi Kyiri Mani," by Nana Ampadu I

The song "Bayi Kyiri Mani" ("Witchcraft Despises the Intimate") is a track on the highlife album, *Abusua Bɛsi Wo Konko* by Nana Ampadu I and the African Brothers International Band. Similar to Super Yaw Ofori's song, "Beyie Nnim Omeni," the lyrics of this song underscore the destructive nature of witchcraft in Akan society. *Bayi bɔne* (maleficent witchcraft) is equated with *honhom fi* (bad spirit) and is described as directing its animus toward intimate family members. In a refrain that is interspersed throughout the song, *bayi bɔne* or *honhom fi* is said to *kyiri* (despise) the *ɔmani* (the intimate). The listener is told repeatedly that *honhom fi* or *bayi bɔne* takes pleasure in engineering the destruction or downfall of *ɔmani*. Two phrases, "*ɔmani bɔ fam a na wopɛ*" (you relish in the downfall of the intimate family member) and "*ɔmani hwe ase a, na wo bo adwo*" (you're happy about the downfall of the intimate family member) are repeated throughout the song to emphasize the evil machinations and malevolent nature of *bayi bɔne*. The evil witch is also said to delight in bringing about dishonor or shame on *ɔmani*.

In one segment of the lyrical text, the malefic witch is castigated for using witchcraft to decimate her entire family while actively seeking social affiliations with *ɔhoho* (strangers or nonrelatives). This is a veiled reference to cannibalistic witchcraft, which in the Akan context primarily involves the spiritual killing and consumption of matrikin at nocturnal witch gatherings. Also in the song, the lyricist accuses the malefic witch of rejoicing in the success of the stranger while using her witchcraft to turn her own family members into *akwatia* (midgets) and chronically ill persons. The maleficent witch is also rebuked for using her witchcraft to cause barrenness in her own daughter—this, despite the fact that this daughter is the same person who cares for the witch financially and materially. Finally, the malefic witch is chastised for using her witchcraft to destroy her own son, reducing him to a perpetual failure and drifter (*w'abɔ asesa*) who moves aimlessly through life, unable to achieve success in anything he sets out to accomplish.

"Aborɔ ne Bayie," by Okomfo Kwaadee

The song "Aborɔ ne Bayie" ("Witchcraft and Ruination") is a two-part song that tells a story about witchcraft and bewitchment, with part one appearing on the album *Okomfoɔ Kwaadɛɛ*. The lyricist ends the song on a suspenseful note, vowing to resume the story later, which he does on his subsequent album, *Okomfoɔ Kwaadɛɛ Mɛtoaso* in a track titled "Kwaadɛɛ." Listeners are not informed as to whether or not this story is the lyricist's rendering of a true account of bewitchment or a fictionalized tale.

The principal character is a woman named Kwaayie, who, with her first husband, has established numerous cocoa farms and cultivates a number of other food crops. Incessant drinking by Kwaayie's first husband—an alcoholic who has earned the nickname Antɔbrɔ—features prominently in the lyricist's description. In the Akan language, the term *antɔbrɔ* refers to people who have a reputation for partaking in the consumption of food or drinks purchased by others, be they family, friends, or acquaintances, but never contributing anything of their own. In light of the success of the couple's farms, the lyricist leaves unanswered the question of whether

Kwaayie's husband is *antɔbrɔ* because he is a spendthrift who is less inclined to spend his own money on food and drinks, or whether he is *antɔbrɔ* because Kwaayie, his wife, controls the purse strings, depriving him of the money to purchase what he desires. Nor does the lyricist explain whether he developed into an alcoholic prior to, during, or after the establishment of the farms and the couple's financial success.

Following one of his drinking bouts, Antɔbrɔ is tragically struck by a car, which kills him instantly. We learn that Kwaayie and her husband have several children. Although it is not revealed precisely how many, it is possible to surmise from the song that there are at least two boys and two girls. After his death, Kwaayie's farm becomes even more productive with larger yields of cocoa and other food crops and the procurement of numerous animals through the traps set up on the farms. Kwaayie amasses unimaginable riches from the sale of crops and animals from her farms. Meanwhile, there is community speculation about the premature death of Kwaayie's husband before he was able to enjoy fully the fruits of his own toil. Was Kwaayie spiritually behind the alcoholism of her husband and his early calamitous demise?

Following the death of this first husband, Kwaayie marries Kwaadɛɛ, ostensibly to support her in caring for her children from the first marriage. A distinguishing characteristic of the second husband is his large, distended belly, which the lyricist describes in grotesque terms. Listeners are told that his abdomen is so striking in appearance that it is the first thing one notices in sighting the man. Kwaadɛɛ is described as a glutton whose eating habits are homologous to that of a pig. In addition, his snore is so deafening that it can be heard from far away. Moreover, listeners are told that Kwaadɛɛ is not only a chronic drunk like Kwaayie's first husband, but is also *y'asa no; ɔnnwo* (sterile). The lyricist states that he has been bewitched (*y'abɔ no dua*), and so is incapable of producing children. It is said that his "children," or the children that he would have actually fathered, are spiritually deposited inside his stomach (*ne mma abɛduru n'afuru*), causing his protruding belly.

Kwaayie uses her wealth to provide for her children, including paying their school fees. Significantly, we learn that her daughters are highly intelligent and gifted while her sons are dull-witted or unintelligent. The girls are so successful academically that they pass all their examinations and proceed to go overseas for advanced education. The boys are so hopelessly dull that they fail academically and become drunks, devoting their time consuming alcoholic beverages at clubs and bars.

The lyricist describes the tragic events that follow when Kwaadɛɛ is caught helping himself to meat from a pot of soup being prepared in the household, a cultural taboo in Ghana. The "theft" was discovered by his stepsons who confront him and force him to spit out the meat in his mouth as evidence of the theft. He is continuously harangued by his stepsons. Kwaadɛɛ plots his revenge to kill the boys. That night, he surreptitiously puts poison in the soup, expecting to kill the stepsons who he expected to be the first to taste the soup the following day. Coincidentally, Kwaayie's daughters who are studying overseas arrive home the following morning. Still nursing a grudge from the previous night's incident, Kwaadɛɛ has left the house. The brothers have put the soup on the stove to warm it up, then leave to go and engage in one of their drinking binges with the intention of returning home later to consume the soup for their afternoon meal. With Kwaadɛɛ's actions unbeknown to anyone else in the household, the soup is warmed up and, in a tragic twist, the girls are served the poisoned soup. Kwaayie's daughters die within minutes of consuming it.

The lyricist describes the public outcry following the death of Kwaayie's cherished daughters. "Yɛse Kwaayie yɛ bayie" (Kwaayie is suspected of being a witch) who has used her witchcraft to kill her children. There are rumors and innuendos among the townsfolk about Kwaayie's *bayi kwasea*. There is reference to the notion of "bayie mpɛ adepa" (witchcraft does not like good things). Kwaayie is alleged to have used her witchcraft to kill and cannibalize her offspring, sacrificing her beautiful, successful girls living overseas rather than the hopeless, alcoholic boys living in the village. Speculations and accusations of witchcraft against Kwaayie are strengthened by references to "ɔno nkoaa abusua deɛ, ɛmaa na ɛye yie; mmarima no, obiara mmɔ bra" (the contrasting success of mother and daughters relative to the failures of the husbands and sons). In determining whether Kwaayie is a witch, the people take a retrospective look at her life: Kwaayie's first husband was *antɔbrɔ*; it was believed that he had been bewitched—if not directly by Kwaayie, then with her connivance; it is speculated that he drank to excess because the witches had put an empty barrel inside his stomach that made it necessary for him to drink gallons of alcohol before he would experience any demonstrable effects ("ankorɛ si ne yɛm; ɔbɛbro nsa a gye ngrawa"). Kwaayie's second husband, Kwaadɛɛ, is also a drunk and a victim of bewitchment. His additional challenge is impotence or sterility. It is rumored that his stomach has grown to grotesque proportions because it is harboring all the children he would have fathered in his life. Furthermore, Kwaayie has used her witchcraft to reduce her sons to alcoholics while simultaneously enabling her daughters to become intelligent and successful. In these contexts, it is typical for others to speculate that the female witch has removed the brains of the male children and added them to the brains of the daughters, a common belief in the witchcraft ideology of the matrilineal Akans, and a claim featured in the confessional statements of some self-proclaimed witches.

Jubilant over her misfortunes and social demise, Kwaayie's enemies fuel the accusations of witchcraft against her. Meanwhile, her sympathizers, lovers, and friends mourn with her, denouncing her accusers and denying the accusations. There are calls of "yɛnnworo no atɔprɛ" (she should be tortured) to get her to confess and settle the matter of whether she is a witch. Meanwhile, Kwaadɛɛ, who was in a drunken stupor in a neighbor's cocoa farm during all the commotion, is found and questioned about the deaths of his stepdaughters. He confesses to having poisoned the soup but says that the girls' deaths were accidental as his stepsons were the intended victims. Is Kwaayie therefore exonerated from the accusations regarding the deaths of her daughters? The lyricist leaves this as an unanswered question. Yes, she did not directly kill them by putting poison in the soup. No, because as a witch she still could have engineered the murders by letting the husband carry it out so as not to suffer the consequences directly. The singer promises again to mɛtoaso (continue) the tale in his next album, which at the time of this writing had yet to be released.

Consistent with Akan beliefs regarding witchcraft, Kwaayie's witchcraft is of two genres: *bayi pa* and *bayi kwasea*. She is alleged to have used her *bayi kwasea* to stymie the efforts of male members of her family; she is said to have used her *bayi pa* to promote the success of her farms and that of the girls in the family. Her malevolent witchcraft is used to further cause the death of her first husband and her daughters, and to promote alcoholism in her husbands and her sons, intellectual dullness in her sons, and impotence in her second husband. With regard to witchcraft suspicions and accusation against Kwaayie, the calamities that befall those around her are accepted as conclusive evidence that she is a witch. According to Akan witchcraft beliefs, malefic witches have no moral feeling or human regard and have no qualms about wreaking havoc on the significant others in their lives. They are vicious, morally impoverished, and ethically bankrupt.

"Enyɛ m'ani a," by Dr. Paa Bobo

The song "Enyɛ M'ani a" ("It is not Deliberate") is featured on a highlife album, *10 Greatest Remix of Dr. Paa Bobo*. In this song, the lyricist laments his general lack of success in life, attributing it to the machinations of the intrafamilial witch. The lyricist argues that his wretchedness, deviant behaviors, and lack of success are not really of his own making, but rather are being dictated by malefic spiritual powers. "Obi na ɛde biribi ayɛ me" (it is somebody who has done something to me) is a lamenting refrain that appears throughout the song, highlighting the lyricist's despair about the role of malevolent spiritual actions in undermining his success in life. He implores his parents not to blame him directly for his failure, his lack of financial prosperity, his abuse of alcohol and other moral lapses because *obi* (somebody else) is hindering his efforts, making it impossible for him to prosper. In the context of the song, the *obi* refers to the witch in the family. He cites a common Akan saying: "Yɛmfa ti bɔne ntu bata" (one should not sojourn with bad luck). He maintains that he carries a pot full of bad luck with him wherever he goes as witches assail him from all angles, trailing him from place to place, ensuring that he does not become successful. He has been sojourning around the world in search of greener pastures, seeking to improve his condition in life. But these efforts have all been to no avail because of what the witch has done to him. He wakes up every morning at the crack of dawn, toiling all day, but his efforts are fruitless. The witch spiritually accompanies him everywhere, thereby spoiling his chances of success in every undertaking. The witch stalks him to ensure that success does not crown his efforts. Then the lyricist provides specific examples of how witchcraft has been utilized to undermine his efforts in life. Most of the time he is penurious, lacking in financial resources to take care of himself. Then on the very day that he finds temporary employment and manages to earn some money, he develops a strong craving for alcohol to which he succumbs. This he attributes to the workings of the witch. In his inebriated state, he ends up squandering what little money remained, thereby reduced to poverty once again.

In another part of the song, the lyricist invokes witchcraft to explain why the protagonist is facing difficulties finding a cure for his illness despite traversing the length and breadth of the entire country in search of a remedy ("yadeɛ baako wo de bɛnenam saa nso wore nnya ano aduro"). He has taken analgesics for many years to relieve the pain of his condition and has taken every other variety of medicine to cure his illness without success. The witches have ensured that medical treatments from a doctor, such as an injection, will be ineffective, preventing the medicine from coursing through his veins; the witch makes the medicine disappear into nothingness. In his dreams, it is revealed that he is being assailed by witches. He laments the fact that he is dreaming about being chased by bulls despite the fact that he does not raise cattle. This is an implied reference to witchcraft consistent with Akan notions where being chased by wild bulls in a dream is symptomatic of bewitchment or imminent bewitchment.

"Efie Mpo Ni," by Dr. Paa Bobo

Representation of witch beliefs in Akan highlife songs finds additional expression in a song by Dr. Paa Bobo, "Efie Mpo Ni" ("Imagine This Being

Home") that appears on the album *10 Greatest Remix of Dr. Paa Bobo.* The lyrics touch on the myriad techniques through which the intrafamilial maleficent witch can be a source of ruin in one's life. While the central focus is the maleficent witches' proclivity for destruction, other prominent features of Akan witch beliefs are also represented, including illness, financial ruination, and conjugal difficulties.

Witchcraft is invoked to explain the protagonist's perpetual suffering in life. Employing Akan linguistic symbolism, he notes that it is better to trust an outsider than a family member: "sɛ efie mmosea twa wo a ɛsen sekan" (when pebbles [*mmosea*] from the houseyard cut you, it is more painful than sustaining a cut from a knife [*sekan*]). *Efie mmosea* symbolizes family while *sekan* represents outsiders.

From the lyrics, one continues to learn about the diverse array of techniques employed by the witch to hamper the success of its victims. The lyricist describes how, as a result of his own bewitchment, he has become a drifter, as the witch has spiritually stuck nails in his chair. The points of the nails are sticking out from under his chair, making it impossible for him to sit down. He analogizes the condition of being at home to the experience of having his body smeared with the poison from an itching plant.

The lyricist bemoans the disastrous results of his concerted efforts to succeed in life. As a vendor, there is no success because the witch "abɔ no kahyire bɔne" (has put a bad carrying pad on her head). When she sells, people refuse to buy from her. Her marriage fails because she cannot have children. He is financially struggling because he cannot find a job. He attributes his overall lack of success to the actions of the intrafamilial witch. This witch was one of the attendants at his birth, which placed her in the position to change his destiny at birth. He was destined for greatness but the witch changed his destiny to one of misery, struggle, and failure. He maintains that his new destiny is incongruous with financial success ("me kra kyiri sika"), which implies a lifetime of penury. He has completed schooling, but due to witchcraft he has no success finding employment. He describes venturing to Accra to seek a white-collar job but *efie abayifoɔ* (intrafamilial witches) have ensured his failure. He is told to "go and come back" or to "come back tomorrow" by the employer. Then he is finally told never to return. He laments mournfully, "This is not the way God created me. My destiny has been changed," adding, "efie abayifoɔ asɛe me koraa" (intrafamilial witches have destroyed me completely).

This chapter examined Akan witchcraft themes depicted in eight Ghanaian songs. The results demonstrate a concordance between images of the witch presented in the lyrical texts and the stereotypes held by Akans concerning the characteristics and behavior of witches. This finding seems to suggest that song lyrics reinforce, and can potentially facilitate the dissemination of witchcraft knowledge. Many Ghanaians are well-versed about witchcraft by the time they reach adolescence or young adulthood as a result of socialization acquired from a range of agents of socialization, including music. Musical lyrics provide insights into the ways of witches and information about their supposed key attributes: they are believed to be cunning, predatory, secretive, treacherous, disloyal, and destructive. Meanwhile, for persons unschooled in Ghanaian witch beliefs, songs about witchcraft provide valuable insights into the basic or rudimentary conceptions of Akan witchcraft.

Popular music is a powerful conveyor of messages, as a medium for further disseminating, or for reinforcing established belief systems. This is indeed the case with witchcraft ideology. In recent years Ghana's print and electronic media have given considerable attention to incidents involving physical attacks on putative witches. While it cannot be determined whether this is a result of increased attacks against alleged witches or expanding media interest in the issue, some observers have surmised that the attacks have been engendered by new developments such as new radio programs with witchcraft themes and songs that lyrically emphasize bewitchment. For this reason, some analysts have gone so far as to suggest that radio presenters whose programs and musicians whose music emphasize witchcraft themes should be held personally liable for violence emanating from witch assaults. Whether songs about witchcraft inadvertently give legitimacy to witchcraft beliefs or embolden some people to take strident action against their perceived witch detractors is ultimately a matter of speculation that warrants further research and exploration.

The next chapter focuses on proverbs, which are another powerful medium that conveys witchcraft ideology. As a repository of witchcraft beliefs, Ghanaian proverbs in general and Akan proverbs in this case have the potential to transmit witchcraft ideology across generations.

Chapter 5

WITCHCRAFT IMAGERY
IN AKAN PROVERBS

Paremiologists, sociocultural anthropologists, and other social scientists have acknowledged the ubiquitous presence of proverbial expressions in many languages around the globe, emphasizing their entrenched use in some cultures, as well as the social functions of proverbial statements (Appiah, Appiah, and Agyeman-Duah 2002; Awedoba 2000; Schipper 2003; Yankah 1989). For example, Schipper's (2003) anthology of gendered proverbs contains more than 15,000 entries drawn from nearly 240 languages in over 150 countries while Peggy Appiah, Kwame Appiah and Ivor Agyeman-Duah's (2002) collection of Akan proverbial sayings yielded 7,015 proverbs.

Defined as terse, concise, pithy, gnomic, or condensed expressions embodying the admitted truths, cherished beliefs, or ageless wisdom of a group of people (Derive 2004; Jackson-Lowman 1997; Schipper 2003; Yankah 1989), proverbs fulfill at least three important social functions noted by proverb scholars. First, proverbial expressions serve as an index for the core values, beliefs, and worldview of a people. Much can be gleaned about a social or cultural group by examining its proverbial expressions, precepts, and maxims. Extant research (e.g., Awedoba 2000; Schipper 2003; Yankah 1989) shows that analyzing the proverbial expressions of a cultural grouping invariably offers a fascinating glimpse into the convictions, hopes, and fears of the group. As Merrick (cited in Jackson-Lowman 1997, 77) aptly puts it, proverbs convey "the virtues most admired, and the vices most despised" by a people.

Another social function of proverbs is to enrich or enliven ordinary or mundane speech. As the famous African novelist Chinua Achebe (1983, 10) notes in his classic novel, *Things Fall Apart,* "Among the Ibo, the art of conversation is regarded very highly, and proverbs are the palm-oil with which words are eaten," a particularly apt expression from an African people noted for their culinary use of the ubiquitous red palm oil. Among the Akan speakers of Ghana, Boadi (1972, 186) notes that rhetoric is an "important part of an adult's linguistic equipment. . . . A mature participant in a dialogue or public discussion always strives to use vivid language because his audience is continually making folk-literary analyses of his speech. The importance attached to brilliance and imaginativeness in public speech leads those who aspire to enter traditional public life and hope to exert influence, especially in the courts and in politics, to cultivate the use of striking images."

Proverbial expressions have yet another major linguistic function: they allow a speaker to indirectly express ideas or statements that would be deemed socially unpalatable if expressed directly (Yankah 1989). Schipper (2003, 10) notes, "Quoting is an art, and quotations can be used to convey something that, for whatever reason, one does not wish to say outright. The proverb creates a sense of detachment and generalization. It allows the speaker to stand back and broach sensitive matters in an indirect artful manner, to express what one has to say, but safely, since the speaker cannot be held responsible personally for a 'traditional' statement. The quote provides a safe way to criticize, mock or even insult."

Proverbs also define and validate societal norms. Given their origins, proverbial sayings and the ideas they convey seemingly represent beliefs that come with the endorsement of elders or ancestors of the society, particularly when introduced with the preface "our ancestors said that" or "in the olden days, it was said that" (Derive 2004; Schipper 2003). Schipper (2003, 10) notes, "The proverb is associated with established wisdom. Its powerful impact is further strengthened by forceful references such as: 'The tradition has taught us . . . ' or: 'As our ancestors used to say . . . ' If the authority has said so, who are we to swim against the tide of so much traditional, religious or sound judgment?"

Finally, proverbs serve as conduits for the transmission of the values and behavioral standards of a society (Oduyoye 1979; Yankah 1989). Like folktales, legends, dances, and music, proverbs are vital educational tools passed down through the generations. Often expressed in the form of advice or warnings, in prescriptive or proscriptive formats, proverbial expressions may serve as a channel for the dissemination of belief sysems and standards of normative conduct of a people. Particularly in parts of the world heavily reliant on oral traditions as a method for transmitting knowledge, proverbs, maxims, and precepts are major vehicles for the dissemination of important ideas of the society. Boateng notes with respect to Africa (cited in Reagan 2005, 64), "Another means by which traditional education promoted intergenerational communication was through proverbial sayings. Proverbial sayings are widespread throughout Africa, and their themes bear strong similarity to one another. The educative and communicative power of proverbs in traditional Africa lies in their use as validators of traditional procedures and beliefs. Children are raised to believe strongly that proverbial sayings have been laid down and their validity tested by their forefathers."

Proverb Use in Ghana

Ghanaian proverb scholars (e.g., Awedoba 2000; Yankah 1989) and other observers of Ghanaian society concur that proverbial expressions are ubiquitous in Ghanaian languages, constituting critical media for the communication and dissemination of values and cultural standards of behavior of the society (see Appiah, Appiah, and Agyeman-Duah 2002; Awedoba 2000; Yankah 1989). A plethora of proverbs in the Akan language can be found in Christaller's seminal collection of Twi proverbs, which yields 3,600 proverbial sayings, while Peggy Appiah, Kwame Anthony Appiah, and Ivor Agyeman-Duah's anthology of Akan proverbial expressions, *Bu Me Bɛ* (2002) comprises over 7,000 proverbs.

Ghana is similar to many African and non-Western societies characterized by a relatively high prevalence of proverb use in daily speech. This contrasts with Western societies in Europe and North America where proverb use in quotidian interaction and discourse is rare or has waned considerably (Derive 2004; Schipper 2003). As later sections of this chapter amply attest, proverb use is revered by Akan speakers and listeners, with those individuals demonstrating exceptional competence in proverb usage accorded great prestige (Yankah 1989). Comparing proverb use in African and European societies, Derive notes,

> The proverb is a highly valued mode of discourse that functions as an indication of cultural status. In Europe, someone who uses or speaks in proverbs is likely to be regarded as backward and intellectually limited for using hackneyed expressions instead of having a more personal and original discourse. In African societies, on the other hand, where an oral tradition of discourse exists, and where memory is the sole guarantee of conservation of this verbal culture, proverbs are held in esteem. The individual who demonstrates a knowledge of proverbs distinguishes himself as the inheritor of his ancestors'

cumulative wisdom, as well as a master of the poetic dimension of the language. (Derive 2004, 374–75)

Proverbs have a deep social significance among Akans. A content analysis of Akan proverbs provides a glimpse into an array of attitudes, convictions, and sentiments significant to Akan society and its people (Boadi 1972; Oduyoye 1979). In remarks prefacing their anthology of Akan proverbs, Peggy Appiah (Appiah, Appiah, and Agyeman-Duah 2002, 1) observes, "proverbs contain the philosophy, humor, symbolism and religion of the peoples who use them. They are imbued with a deep knowledge of the surrounding world, physical and spiritual, and social realities. No one can appreciate the philosophy and beliefs of the Akan without studying their proverbs."

The notion that proverbs are wise sayings that forebears have bequeathed to their progeny is a deeply held belief among Akans. As a consequence, the possession of many proverbs at one's disposal, as well as demonstration of an ability to quote them profusely, eloquently, and appropriately, is emblematic of sagacity and of deep knowledge of one's culture and traditions. According to Yankah (1989, 10), "Knowledge of proverb lore is a valuable social asset; for to speak in proverbs is to exhibit knowledge of tradition—an important tool for social advancement." Similarly, Peggy Appiah (Appiah, Appiah, and Agyeman-Duah 2002, 1) observes, "amongst the Akan, a truly educated and cultured person is one who can make use of proverbs and whose speech is full of the imagery and the innuendo that they make possible." Over the years, in many African societies, there have been concerns raised about the growing loss of traditional culture as a result of Western influences from non-African mass media and other sources. In efforts to reclaim lost traditions and to preserve traditions, a number of African societies have been undergoing retraditionalization to preserve local cultural and customary practices. In Ghana, among Akan speakers, this process of cultural revitalization is called *sankofa* (going back to claim what has been left behind) and has become of particular interest to the country's Ministry of Education. Currently, at the University of Ghana, Legon, students are required to pass a course in African studies (such as a course in African language, African music, African dance, etc.) as a condition for obtaining a university degree. In this era of heightened retraditionalization of the society, efforts are being made in many segments of the society to generate an interest in the learning and use of traditional proverbs as symbols of the past.

Among Akans, as elsewhere, proverbs embody the accumulated experience and wisdom of sages. For this reason, a prolific user of proverbs is highly regarded as *onyansani* or *obadwema* (wise person). As Yankah (1989,

81) puts it, "According to the Akan, a child's ability to decode proverbs is one mark of wisdom." Conversely, a person who does not understand proverbs is perceived as inept, lost, acting as a foreigner, particularly if the person has resided abroad for any length of time. The Akan proverb "oba nyansani, yɛ bu no bɛ na yɛnka no asɛm" (the wise child is spoken to in proverbs, not in long discourse) epitomizes the idea of the proverb user as a wise person.

Relatedly, among the Akans proverb eloquence is emblematic of linguistic wit. As Yankah (1989, 80) observes, "[A] good speaker is expected to embroider his words with appropriate proverbs if need be," and according to Peggy Appiah (Appiah, Appiah, and Agyeman-Duah 2002, 3), "The Akan do not always favor clear and direct statement, and proverbs are used when people do not want to be immediately and directly understood, or where a double meaning or a prevarication is required. . . . [Proverbs] can be used as a polite—and oblique—form of criticism, when direct speech would cause offence, and they are thus a way of avoiding quarrels or conflict."

As with proverbial expressions in other societies, Akan proverbs, when properly cited and used in a timely fashion, have the potential power of driving home or buttressing a point, and contributing to the persuasiveness of an argument. Yankah (1989, 77) notes, "Akan proverbs assert a social truth that is rarely contested by opponents during debates" while Peggy Appiah (Appiah, Appiah, and Agyeman-Duah 2002, 1) notes, "Even today, the use of an appropriate proverb in public oratory is deeply appreciated and is often the final word in an argument. One short proverb can provide the equivalence of pages of philosophical discussion."

Evidence of the high esteem accorded proverbs in Akan culture can be seen in the recent establishment of a weekly radio program on proverbs. This half-hour program, *Sɛ Wo Bu Bɛ a Me Nso Te Bɛ* (if you know how to quote proverbs, I also know how to interpret proverbs), is currently broadcast on Peace 104.3 FM every Sunday evening; it has become one of the most popular weekend evening shows on radio. Contestants compete in a verbal duel of sorts to see who can quote the largest number of proverbs off the cuff and within the allotted time. Misquotation of a proverb leads to disqualification while the panel of judges evaluates the accuracy of the proverbs cited. The competition goes on throughout the year and generous prizes are awarded to the top contestants at the end of the year.

Akan proverbs also fulfill another function noted by proverb scholars in other cultures: as a purveyor of moral and social standards. Among the Akans, Peggy Appiah (Appiah, Appiah, and Agyeman-Duah 2002, 2) asserts, "Education in traditional society involved oral and not written communication; and proverbs were a way of reinforcing moral and social precepts.

They teach the philosophy and way of life of the community, its customs and its prejudices. Before a person can become well versed in customary behavior, they must have a broad knowledge of proverbs to illustrate and emphasize their statements. This knowledge is, and was, learnt by listening to the elders." For this reason, Akans assert, "nea ɔnnim n'ammamerɛ ayera" (he who does not know his customs or traditions is lost).

Witchcraft Themes in Akan Proverbs

Given the widespread belief in the reality of witches among Akan speakers, witchcraft themes are pervasive in Akan proverbs. Yet despite the ubiquity of witchcraft themes in Akan proverbs, at the time of this writing no systematic analysis or otherwise has been conducted or published that focuses on witchcraft imagery or beliefs in Akan proverbs. This chapter provides a targeted analysis of proverbs with witchcraft themes. The objective of the chapter is, first, to demonstrate that Akan proverbs are a repository of information on witchcraft beliefs and practices of the society. Second, the chapter aims to demonstrate that proverbs directly or indirectly serve as a medium for the dissemination of witchcraft ideas. The analysis shows that Akan proverbs on witchcraft reflect a depth and diversity of topics including the nature of witchcraft and the relationship between the witch and the bewitched, the characteristics of witches and how to identify them, child witchcraft, and individual vulnerability or susceptibility to bewitchment.

Methodology

The proverbs that I have analyzed in this chapter were obtained from several sources, including R.S. Rattray's *Ashanti Proverbs* (1914), C.A. Akrofi's *Twi Mmɛbusɛm* (Akan Proverbs) (1958), Richard F. Burton's *Wit and Wisdom from West Africa* (1969), and (4) Peggy Appiah, Kwame Anthony Appiah, and Ivor Agyeman-Duah's anthology of Akan Proverbs, *Bu Me Bɛ* (2002). A review of these hugely comprehensive works revealed a voluminous number of proverbs with witchcraft themes that make it impossible to do a complete analysis within the context of one chapter. I have therefore confined the scope of my analysis to the thirty-four proverbs that focus explicitly and exclusively on witchcraft by making specific references to *obayifoɔ* or *bayifoɔ* (witch) or *bayie* (witchcraft). I extracted these proverbs, then translated them into English and then analyzed them for their themes.

1. Bayie fata aberewa, nanso ɛbia na akɔdaa na ɛnnyɛ.

"Witchcraft (*bayie*) befits the status of an elderly woman (*aberewa*) but a child (*akɔdaa*) may be the bad one (*nnyɛ*)." This proverb is concerned with the issue of the proper identification of witches as well as of children's involvement in witchcraft in Akan society. Extant research shows that in many places across the globe women of advanced age are overrepresented in stereotyped images of witches (Adinkrah 2004, 2011c; Schipper 2003; Ware 2001). In Ghana, for instance, most people accused of witchcraft are elderly women (Adinkrah 2004, 2011c; Bannerman-Richter 1982). The proverb cautions against the rush to judgment against the elderly woman during times of suspected bewitchment.

Indirectly, the proverb confutes the persistent stereotype of the witch as an elderly woman. This proverb also indirectly draws the attention of Akan speakers to the existence of child witches. As indicated earlier, Akan belief concerning witchcraft holds that witches potentially come in any age, sex, or size. Hence, even children can be implicated as perpetrators of malevolent witchcraft. In the three years preceding this writing, an increased involvement of children as putative witches has been noted in numerous self-confessions, from children who themselves claimed to be witches to accused child witches arrested by priests and priestesses of witch shrines or Christian evangelists. Witchcraft confessions by adult witches have occasionally implicated child witches as well, mentioning them as accomplices or describing their influential and powerful positions in the witch companies. Indeed, the testimony provided in some witchcraft confessions has included the claim that some child witches are spiritually mightier than some adult witches. This is particularly the case if a child witch is believed to be a carrier of a witchcraft power that has long been in existence in a family line. Since witchcraft power is believed to be transferred across generations, the witchcraft power borne by a child may be more virulent than that borne by an adult witch. Thus, a child's witchcraft may be regarded as particularly destructive. In a town in the Eastern Region of Ghana, I was told the story of a young girl of nine years who freely confessed to indulging in witchcraft since the moment she began speaking in sentences. She claimed that she was a recipient of a witchcraft spirit from her maternal grandmother whom she regularly accompanied to the witches' secret nocturnal assemblies.

2. Mfomso te sɛ bayie, ebi wɔ abusua biara mu.

This proverb means, "wrongdoing is like witchcraft; some form of it is found in every lineage." As in the English saying, to err is human, this

Akan maxim draws an analogy between the innate propensity of humans to make mistakes and the presumed existence of witches or witchcraft in every Akan *abusua*. Just as wrongdoing is characteristic of human nature, so is the presence of witches in every lineage an unquestionable reality. This maxim confirms the Akan belief that witchcraft exists in all lineages. For this reason, no one is totally immune from bewitchment since there is a witch in every lineage.

One informant related the account of two Ghanaian mothers and their contrasting use of witchcraft to affect the fortunes of their daughters. Given the emphasis on the use of malevolent witchcraft in Ghanaian society, of particular interest is the case of the use of *bayi pa*. In this instance, a middle-aged woman was said to be the mother of eight daughters. It was alleged that through the power of her witchcraft she had managed to secure ideal spouses and marital bliss for all eight daughters. At the time of my field research, I was told that seven out of the eight daughters were living overseas with their husbands, the latter of whom were all holders of professional positions, including a lawyer, a professor, an accountant, a physician, and an engineer. I was told that the youngest daughter had just obtained her travel visa and was about to join her husband in the United States where the husband was employed as a researcher with a major pharmaceutical company. The informant suggested that this amount of success was far too exceptional to have occurred without some type of spiritual intervention, adding that as a beneficiary of her good witchcraft, this woman spent her time shuttling between Ghana and her daughters' homes overseas, enjoying the high standard of living in her children's households. An informant contrasted this story with that of a woman of the same town: None of her six daughters had managed to secure a solid marriage. Their marriages were not only typically of short duration, but were marked with the perpetration of violence against the women. It was surmised that in this instance the mother had used her diabolical witchcraft power to spiritually orchestrate conflicts between her own daughters and their husbands, prompting their short-lived marriages.

3. ɔbayifoɔ anum yɛ nam a, ɔdidi asuogya na ɔntumi mfa ntwa asuo.

Another major theme permeating Akan witchcraft beliefs is that a witch can bewitch only a close lineage member, particularly, a matrilineal relative (Warren 1973). This belief is reflected in this proverb: "However powerful witches' malefic power, they can use the witchcraft power only to 'eat' on the banks of a river without the ability to cross over to the other side of the river to feast on others." Consistent with the Akan witchcraft belief regarding bewitchment of close family relatives, this proverb asserts that regardless of how potent a witch's witchcraft power, he or she cannot use that witchcraft power to directly attack a nonrelative. This may explain why suspicions, accusations, and assaults regarding Akan witchcraft almost invariably involve a victim (the bewitched) and an offender (the witch) who are related to each other matrilineally.

4. ɔbayifoɔ nsuo, ɔbaako nnware.

Another overarching theme in Akan witchcraft beliefs is vulnerability to bewitchment or susceptibility to the evil machinations of the witch. Bewitchment, according to Akan witchcraft beliefs, is not confined to a select few; everyone is at risk. This widely held belief is reflected in this proverb, which likens witchcraft to a flowing stream in which anyone can drown. In other words, everyone is susceptible to bewitchment. As will become evident in subsequent discussions in this chapter, the Akan belief that everyone is vulnerable to bewitchment or that no one is safe from bewitchment is replete in proverbs about witches. Large numbers of proverbs refer directly, as well as metaphorically, to this belief. Other proverbs that express similar sentiments are proverb number 2, "Mfomso te sɛ bayie, ebi wɔ abusua biara mu," and proverb number 5 "efie biara bayie wɔ mu" (there is a witch in every abusua).

The belief that everyone is vulnerable to bewitchment has implications for behavior in the society. With notions of universal vulnerability there is persistent fear of destructive witchcraft; that fear comes with frantic efforts to obtain protection against its effects. Since everyone is vulnerable, witchcraft fears are universal in society. Since no one knows when they may fall victim to bewitchment, everyone takes what are widely regarded as necessary preemptive measures to protect themselves, such as attending church regularly, constantly saying prayers or reciting verses from the Bible, and regularly fasting.

5. Efie biara bayie wɔ mu.

This proverb, "there is witchcraft in every abusua," reflects the same entrenched Akan belief regarding the ubiquity of witchcraft and the susceptibility of individuals to bewitchment. The word *efie* is often used interchangeably with the word *abusua*. Among Akans, it is popularly conceived that there is a witch in every *abusua.* The implications are clear. Since there is at least one witch or wizard in every *abusua,* and since witches can bewitch only matrilineal kinsfolk, there is the presupposition that everyone swims in the stream of witchcraft, and that no one is safe from the machinations of witches. During fieldwork in an urban location in the Eastern Region of Ghana, I learned of an eighty-five-year-old woman whose alleged malefic witchcraft provoked great fear in her own adult children and grandchildren. These relatives not only feared bewitchment by the elderly woman, but also were afraid that she might transfer her witchcraft spirit to them prior to her death. When the elderly woman was admitted to the local hospital for an illness, many relatives, including her own children, refused to visit her at her sick bed. When suspicions deepened that she would not recover, the remaining few who occasionally visited her abandoned her completely. Relatives were apprehensive that facing imminent death, the elderly woman would transfer her witchcraft power to any family relation who made herself or himself available through their physical proximity. Akans believe that witchcraft spirit is not transportable to the netherworld. It was alleged that, as she neared death, the woman confided in her adult male children to take her to a powerful witch shrine so she could confess her misdeeds, be exorcised of her witchcraft power, become free, and then face death with serenity. The financially successful children and grandchildren, many of whose successes had been attributed to the elder woman's witchcraft, were afraid that their reputations would be tarnished by the woman's witch confessions; hence, they directed her to keep quiet, threatening that if she uttered a word about her witchcraft, they would abandon her and not give her a befitting funeral.

6. ɔbayifo kum wadi-wamma-me na ɔnkum wama-me-na-ɛsua.

"The witch kills the person who eats and does not give me any; the witch does not kill the one who eats but gives me only a little." According to Akan conceptions of witchcraft everyone is susceptible to bewitchment. Akans also believe that because the witch is motivated by envy, hatred, and jealousy, those who do not share personal fortunes, riches, or resources with other lineage members are particularly vulnerable to spiritual assaults by witches. While conducting my field research in Ghana, I was provided with several accounts of witchcraft that illustrate this proverb. One elementary school teacher related the story of a man who was killed by his sister through witchcraft. The man's supposed sin or transgression was failure to share a *kenkey* (fermented corn dough shaped into balls and boiled) and sardine meal with his sister, the alleged witch. According to the story, the victim, a Ghanaian who had lived in the United States for a long time, returned to Ghana to establish a very successful business venture. He also established trading ventures for his sisters in their home town that brought them great material prosperity. One Saturday the man traveled from Accra to his hometown to attend a funeral. When he arrived, he did not meet any of his sisters at home; they had presumably left for the funeral. Hungry after his journey, he took out a tin of sardine from his traveling bag and sent a child on an errand to buy him *kenkey*. While eating, one of his sisters returned from the funeral. He resumed eating while the two discussed family matters. A week later, after he had returned to Accra, he fell ill and died suddenly. Some weeks following his funeral, the sister allegedly confessed that she was a witch and was responsible for killing her brother by witchcraft. The rationale she provided was simple: she had wanted some of her brother's *kenkey* and sardine meal but was hurt by his failure to offer her any; she therefore used her witchcraft power to kill him.

Another informant told the story of a Ghanaian returnee from Nigeria who was allegedly killed by his mother through witchcraft because, according to the mother, the son overlooked her while distributing basic provisions such as sardines, milk, and soap to the rest of the family. According to the story, the man returned from his workstation in Nigeria with several pieces of luxury Dutch wax print cloth, one of the most prized cloths in Ghana (locally known as *dumas*). He had purchased the cloth and reserved it exclusively for his mother. For other members of the extended family, he had purchased and distributed basic goods such as milk, sardines, and toiletries. Ten days following his arrival in Ghana, he fell seriously ill and died suddenly. The mother allegedly offered a witchcraft confession shortly after her son's death wherein she claimed that she took offense when the son did not give her any of the sardines, milk, and toiletries.

7. Obi mfa ade kɔkɔɔ nsisi ɔbayifoɔ.

The idea expressed in this proverb is consistent with the Akan conception of the witch as prone to cannibalistic or anthropophagous behavior. The proverb means, "a person cannot cheat or threaten a witch with a red-colored object." The proverb emphasizes the idea that witches have an affinity for the color red. Akan witches are believed to fly through the sky as giant balls of fire to arrive at their nocturnal assemblies. The fire and the associated flames give the witch a connection and identification with the color red. Witches are also deemed to be cannibals, and so are presumed to have an insatiable appetite for human flesh and an unquenchable thirst for human blood. These meals are said to be served at witches' Sabbaths.

Human flesh in its raw form is also tainted with red blood from the victim. For this reason, witches can never be confounded by anything that is red in color. Consistent with the regular association of witchcraft with the color red, persons who show a preference for things red in color are suspected of being witches while those with an exorbitant taste for red meat, red palm oil, *abɛnkwan* (red palm fruit soup) are similarly suspect.

8. Abɔntenso bayie bɛdi wo nam a, na ɛfiri efie.

This proverb stresses the issue of the enemy within. The proverb means, "a cannibalistic, stranger witch can consume your flesh only with the active connivance of a witch or wizard from your own *abusua*." The Akan conception of witchcraft supposes that witches are only able to directly bewitch a close family member, a matrikin. Akan witchcraft ideology, however, recognizes the possibility of indirect bewitchment of a person by a nonfamily member. This includes instances of bewitchment between spouses, friends, or neighbors. For bewitchment to occur in contexts of nonkin relations, the witch must solicit the assistance of a witch from the potential victim's family. Only with the permission and assistance of witch kin is bewitchment of a friend or spouse possible. Akan witches often belong to witch covens. Members of these witches' guilds take turns contributing victims for cannibalistic feasts. Thus, it is possible for nonfamily members to participate in the consumption of the flesh of nonkin that has been contributed by other witches who have bewitched their own matrikin.

9. ɔbayifoɔ ba wu a, ɛyɛ no ya.

This proverb means, "witches are pained or distressed by the death of their own children." Akan witches are typically regarded as anthropophagous or cannibalistic, using their witchcraft powers to kill and feast on their matrikin, including their own children. Given the supposed murderous and cannibalistic activities of witches, one would presume that witches would find the deaths of their own children painless. The proverb, however, asserts that even witches grieve from the loss of their own children. In fact, given the agony associated with such a loss, some Akan witches are said to prefer the status of a herbivorous (plant-eating) or frugivorous (fruit-eating) scavenger, refraining from participation in cannibalistic witch feasts. Consider the case of Abena Kobua, who, in 1975, caused a national sensation by publicly revealing her identity as a witch (see chapter

6). To avoid the torment associated with the loss of her children or other relatives to witchcraft, she made a decision not to participate in nocturnal cannibalistic feasts but only to scavenge on garbage dumps.

That malefic witches are believed to be aggrieved by the death of their own children is confirmed by a story related to me by an informant. In this story, one learns about the extent to which one woman would go to prevent the fatal bewitchment of her son, to no avail. According to the story, the elderly female witch who lived and practiced her witchcraft in a small town in central Ghana, participated in the consumption of the flesh of human victims supplied by members of her witch coven. When it came time for her to supply her own matrikin as a victim, the woman fled the town to go and live with her wealthy son and his family in Accra. This son, the most financially successful and socially influential of the woman's six children, was the preferred victim of the witch coven. After weeks of her stay in Accra, the coven sent a member to Accra to relay the message to the woman that the time for her to contribute her "meat" was past due and demanded immediate supply of her quota for their consumption. Recognizing that her son was to suffer fatal bewitchment, the woman immediately advised her son to attend a spiritual church in Accra that she was convinced would offer him spiritual protection. The son did not heed her advice. On the day of his death, the woman tried vainly to prevent her son from embarking on a journey. He was involved in a car accident and died a few hours later, his mother not having moved a single step from the site where she stood to bid him farewell. Rumors persist to this day in the local community that he was killed, dismembered, and devoured by his mother's witches' guild.

10. Onipa a ne sunsum yɛ duru na ɔbayifoɔ ntumi no.

This proverb means, "the witch is unable to spiritually assault a person with a strong spirit." Proverbs have so far been cited that suggest that everyone is susceptible to bewitchment. However, this proverb suggests that there are opportunities to escape and become immune from the forces of bewitchment. Among Akans, there is a strong belief that people with strong *sunsum* are less likely to experience bewitchment or suffer witch assaults. In terms of behavior, being of strong spirit in the Akan context means being brave, courageous, or fearless or being combative or confrontational. People who exhibit such character traits are said to be feared by witches who are less likely to consider them as candidates for bewitchment. On the contrary, people who have light *sunsum* (*ne sunsum yɛ hare*) (light personalities, spirits, or life souls) or who are otherwise timorous, diffident, or quiet are said to be excellent candidates for bewitchment (Fisher 1998). Why are witches afraid of people with strong spirits? It is believed that such persons are likely to expose the witch's witchery.

This proverb has behavioral implications. Given the popular perception that witches are apprehensive, frightened, or even terrified of individuals with combative dispositions, some Ghanaians tend to adopt a confrontational attitude toward suspected witches, being abusive toward them at the slightest opportunity. The idea behind this demonstration of ruggedness is that by intimidating or striking fear in the putative witch, they are less likely to face spiritual attack from supposed witches. This belief may account for some of the perennial incidents of lethal and nonlethal assaults launched against suspected witches. Consider the following excerpt from Ntim-Korsah's study of witchcraft beliefs among the people of Techiman in the Brong-Ahafo district:

> It was believed by some section of the Techiman community that when witches are subjected to harsh and unkind treatment, they tend to shun from using their witchcraft substance on the people who meted out that treatment to them. The idea was that the witches feared that if their secret activities on such people should be detected, they would not be treated kindly. There was a case of a man called Kofi Gyan who beat his own mother and drove her away from the house for the reason that the mother was a witch and the probable cause of his alcoholism. (Ntim-Korsah 1988, 36)

11. Bayi kwasea na aduro kyere no.

This saying means, "it is the foolish witch that is typically caught or apprehended by the witch fetish." Due to a perceived prevalence and malevolence of witchcraft, fetish shrines staffed by witch-finders have been established throughout the country to catch witches and offer protection from them. Witch finders are available to confirm suspicions of witchcraft and to identify supposed witches. When apprehended, witches allegedly confess voluntarily or are coerced to recount the vices and misdeeds that they have perpetrated through witchcraft. In this era of spiritual churches, the job of arresting witches is shared with apostles, prophets, prophetesses, and other religious personnel. Given the supposedly large number of witches in the country and the small number of witches who are caught each year, this proverb suggests that the savvy witch knows what to do to evade detection and arrest, and that it is the foolish witch who is apprehended.

The proverb lends itself to another interpretation. Akans distinguish between *bayi kwasea* or *bayi bɔne* and *bayi pa*. Malevolent witchcraft is used to kill, maim, cause disease, and wreak other forms of havoc on its victims. Beneficent witchcraft, conversely, is used to provide protection and extend good health and fortune to its beneficiaries. Conventionally, the only types of witches arrested by fetish priests and witch finders in Ghana are malevolent witches, prompting this saying.

12. Sasabonsam kɔ ayie a osoɛ ɔbayifoɔ fie.

This proverb means, "when *sasabonsam* (the forest monster) attends a funeral, it lodges with *obayifoɔ* (the witch)." It is well-acknowledged within Akan witchcraft beliefs that witches are members of witch companies and that the witches of a given village, town, or city often congregate and conduct their activities through the local witches' guild. Members are said to hold regular, secret, nocturnal meetings during which various nefarious activities take place. While the primary activity of these witch gatherings is cannibalistic feasting, the social agenda of these witch assemblies also includes playing soccer, ludo (a board game for two to four players), checkers, and engaging in other forms of conviviality. It is also said that witches seek the company of other witches in other social contexts, such as at funerals.

This proverb also makes reference to the monster-like creature in Akan folk tales called *sasabonsam*, a creature of monstrous size with a penchant for causing wicked deeds (Konadu 2007; Warren 1973). Living in the remotest part of the forest, this creature shares the mischief of the witch (Warren 1973). Thus the proverb says that when *sasabonsam* goes to a funeral, it seeks the company of the witch. In short, and in the words of another maxim, birds of the same feather flock together.

13. Bayie nnim ɔmani.

This popular Akan aphorism means, "witchcraft makes no distinctions among intimates, friends, and complete strangers." In short, the witch will spiritually attack a victim regardless of his or her relationship with the victim. In essence, the proverb reflects one of the central Akan beliefs concerning witchcraft, that bewitchment typically involves intimates both as victims and perpetrators. One does not preempt bewitchment by becoming close to the suspected witch. To the contrary, and as reiterated in this book, Akans regard bewitchment as more likely to involve close relatives than nonrelatives or strangers. On another level, this proverb expresses the heartlessness, ruthlessness, and sheer wickedness attributed to the witch in Akan beliefs. As has been described in previous chapters, the malevolent witch is a perpetrator of violence. The witch's refusal to spare the ɔmani or intimate relative or close friend confirms his or her viciousness and moral degeneration.

Numerous stories abound of witches using their malevolent witchcraft power to commit atrocities against their children and other close family members. According to one account related on the *Etuo Mu Wɔ Sum* program of December 12, 2005, a witch was reported to have sacrificed all ten of her children to cannibalistic witchcraft. She had jointly consumed her children with her witch sister but was now at loggerheads with her because the sister reneged on a deal to sacrifice all five of her own children. The sister had offered four of her children, but refused to offer her fifth and final child for consumption.

14. Bayie mpɛ adepa.

Another major proverbial expression in the Akan witch belief system is "witchcraft does not like good things." This maxim is often quoted in response to news that some form of ill-fortune has befallen a young, successful person. This proverb emphasizes the destructive aspects of Akan witchcraft associated with the malefic witch. *Bayi kwasea* or *bayi tuntum* is often cited as the cause of business failure, auto accidents, impotence in men, barrenness in women, and the destruction of marriages. It is used to afflict illnesses and cause premature death. It can be used to cause kleptomania, blindness, lameness, and madness in witch victims. A malefic witch can precipitate the deportation of an illegal immigrant visiting or residing overseas. Malevolent witchcraft is believed to be so destructive that the malevolent witch will automatically destroy anything good in his or her wake. Malefic witches use their witchcraft to change the fortune of those destined for greatness and turn success into failure and ill-fortune. To this extent, misfortunes and afflictions of any kind suffered by the young and successful are attributed to witchcraft.

In the course of conducting ethnographic research in Ghana for this book, I encountered several individuals who related stories concerning the destructive propensities of witches. Their stories of bewitchment were often about persons who had suffered major business failures; auto accidents; dissolution of seemingly happy marriages; the affliction of strange, inexplicable, and incurable illnesses; sexual impotence; and barrenness. In other contexts, informants drew my attention to highly successful persons whose affliction with AIDS, blindness, tuberculosis, or epilepsy was attributed to witchcraft. These were buttressed by the stories of self-proclaimed witches who offered their own confessionals of using *bayi kwa-sea* to visit a range of calamities upon their matrikin. In one small town in the Eastern Region of Ghana, a self-professed witch claimed responsibility for causing the death of her financially successful son in Accra as well as sabotaging the marriage of her young, newly married niece by causing the latter's barrenness. Another self-avowed witch in another town confessed to having caused a litany of tragedies to one or more members of her family. Given the popularity of this proverbial expression, many people in Ghana who suffer misfortunes are quick to attribute it to the witch. Indeed the number of calamities a witch can afflict on an individual is believed to have no bounds.

This expression is also uttered by Akans to explain why very successful people are most prone to being singled out for bewitchment. It is widely believed among Akans that witches who belong to witch covens take turns in supplying the victims for their cannibalistic feasts. It is believed that when it is the turn for an individual witch to offer a candidate from his or her own *abusua* for victimization, witch colleagues are specifically implored to select the rare, juicy victim. The "rare, juicy victims" is a reference to persons most cherished by the witch or the most exceptional and successful in the lineage. Thus, the only child, the most educated member of the family, the newly married, and the educated professional are regarded as the most prized victims of bewitchment. Concurrently, witch companies are said to repudiate or reject the old, the infirm, the blind, the physically impaired, the financially unstable, alcoholics, and other individuals regarded or perceived as failures, unsuccessful, or unexceptional. For witches to contribute highly valued members of their family as victims is the ultimate sacrifice.

15. ɔbayifo nkum wo a na wo di mfensa.

This proverb means, "when you have not been killed by a witch, you live for three years." Here, three years is actually intended to denote a relatively significant time period. This proverb stresses the murderous nature of Akan witchcraft as well as everyone's susceptibility toward bewitchment. According to the proverb, a person has life and longevity only insofar as he has not suffered bewitchment. Hence, since bewitchment has the effect of unceremoniously cutting short the life of witchcraft victims, one should guard against bragging about one's longevity or taking it for granted. The effect of such a saying is to make individuals conscious of their own mortality. The proverb also reminds people that deaths in youth may be attributable to witchcraft. This explains why the deaths of young people evoke particularly strong emotive responses, often provoking immediate accusations of witchcraft and retributive justice against any suspected witches believed to be responsible.

16. Onipa a wayɛ bayie awuo no, yɛnsu n'ayie ase.

The proverb means, "we do not weep or wail at the funeral of a deceased person who was a witch," and is reminiscent of another popular Akan saying, "onipa bɔnefo wuo nyɛ nnipa ya" (the death of a bad person does not evoke pain in people). This proverb is consistent with the relationship between Akan witchcraft beliefs and Akan funerary rituals. Among Akans, the extent of wailing and weeping that occurs at funerals is suggestive of the value surviving relatives, friends, and neighbors place on the deceased person. Given the widespread belief among Akans that witches are malevolent and cannibalistic, witches are presumed, in the course of a lifetime, to have harmed or killed scores of people through their misdeeds. Because witches are blamed for all manner of misfortune, the witch who is exposed or caught, or who confesses, arouses considerable hatred in the families and communities in which they live. Since Akan funerals are intended to celebrate the life and good deeds of the deceased, it is expected that a witch's death will not engender much sorrow and grief in family members. It is hard to mourn loudly—to weep or wail—for a person who is believed to have done so much mischief with his or her witchcraft. Witches who do receive a funeral do not attract mourning, weeping, or wailing sympathizers. Writing about witches' funerals in the Ajumako area of Ghana, Korankye notes,

> Few people will attend her [the witch's] funeral and those who do attend leave the place early. Most people refuse to wail or to sympathize with the family members. In the [Ajumako] area witches normally do not receive [a] befitting funeral. Final funeral rites mostly follow immediately after burial. During this occasion people are seen gathered at certain quarters in groups. There is less merry making and people, after giving donations, leave the place for their homes. Only the friends of the deceased who may perhaps be members of the witch's society [coven] and some of the family members try to make the funeral attractive. (Korankye 1997, 15–16)

17. Deɛ ne ho adwo no sɛ: deɛ ɔresirepɛ yɛ ayɛn (ɔbayifoɔ).

The proverb means, "the person with all the comforts of life tends to call a person who works or toils at night a witch." This proverb underscores the nocturnal nature of witchcraft activity. Akan witches are believed to fly at night for their secret assemblies during which they participate in a range of activities that includes consuming human flesh and blood. People of wealth and without major personal problems normally do not stay up late into the night to work or engage in any economic activity. They typically go to bed early and wake up late the next morning. So those who awake in the middle of the night and see or hear someone who has stayed up to work may accuse the person who stays up at night as being a witch.

Growing up in a small town in the Eastern Region of Ghana, I knew of a food vendor who was rumored in the local community to be a witch because of the time of day that she prepared her food. The food she sold, *waakye,* consists of rice and beans cooked together and served with hot and spicy stew. The woman worked late into the night to prepare the meat and stew and woke up at dawn to cook the *waakye.* She did this to ensure that the food was ready to be served to the public at 6 o'clock in the morning daily. Her stall was heavily patronized for the exceptional quality of her food. Speculations that she was a witch became rampant both based on her successful business and on the unusual time that she prepared her food. The food preparation that occurred at night was said to be of her nocturnal witch activity. It was pejoratively rumored that spiritually the *waakye* was human excreta and the meat and stew served with it was human blood and human flesh. In the same neighborhood, a *kenkey* vendor whose food was also heavily patronized and who prepared her food at dawn was similarly the focus of rumors about her alleged witchcraft.

18. ɔkɔse-ayie na ɔma wɔkum ɔbayifoɔ.

The proverb means, "the funeral announcer is responsible for the killing of the witch." Among Akans, following the death of a person one or more relatives is appointed to announce the death to other lineage members living near and far. In Ghana a person who is sent to notify relatives about the death of a deceased lineage member may directly or indirectly contribute to the accusation of witchcraft and even the murder of a putative witch. In other words, the herald may suggest that bewitchment was the cause of death and wittingly or unwittingly mention the name of a suspected witch as responsible. This may provoke a lethal assault on the alleged witch.

19. Bayie nnim akɔdaa.

This maxim means, "witchcraft does not spare infants and children and will assault a victim regardless of the latter's age." Expressed differently, a person's risk of bewitchment is not mitigated by young age. In essence, a neonate is just as likely to be a victim of witchcraft as a centenarian. Examined broadly, this Akan proverb alludes to the malevolence and brutality of the witch as lacking mercy even for innocent children and infants. In Ghana, one popular witchcraft belief is that witches and wizards have the capacity to cause miscarriages and stillbirths by removing and cannibalizing the developing fetus from the uterus of an expectant mother. Stories also abound of witches transmuting or altering the *nkrabea* (destinies) of newborns and infants marked for greatness, turning success in such persons into lives of failure. Due to the perceived vulnerability of infants and children to the brutal and even murderous actions of witches, some parents go to considerable lengths to obtain protective medicines to ward off potential evil influences on their wards. Thus, it is common to see newborns, infants, and other children wearing talismans and other protective amulets around their necks, waists, and limbs to ward off the evil influences of witchcraft. In a similar vein, specially patterned protective scarification markings made on the face, around the waist, and on the stomach of children and older adults often reflect a childhood history characterized by illnesses presumed to have been caused by witches and sorcerers. For example, the *dɔnkɔ* design or pattern worn on the face is made to break a cycle of miscarriages, stillbirths, and child deaths believed to be caused by witchcraft and other evil supernatural influences.

20. Sasabonsam te ase dada a, yɛse ɔyɛ ɔbayifoɔ, na akowie sɛ osi odum atifi na odum no nso aso mmoatia.

The proverb means, "*sasabonsam* normally is associated with witchcraft but this association is heightened the more when *sasabonsam* is found seated atop an *odum* tree on which *mmoatia* spirits are seated as well." Akans believe in a creature called *sasabonsam*, a monstrous creature with a human form said to live deep in the forests. In Akan folktales, *sasabonsam* is associated with evil. It stalks and hunts down its victims, killing and eating their flesh and drinking their blood. Given their similarities, Akans are as frightened of witches as they are of *sasabonsam*. *Mmoatia* is the plural form of *aboa tia* (short animal). *Mmoatia* are short, elf-like creatures with supernatural powers in Akan traditional beliefs. They are believed to inhabit the deep forests of the country. An important physical feature of *mmoatia* is that their feet point backwards. Good *mmoatia* are believed to provide spiritual and material assistance to their benefactors in the form of money, knowledge of herbal medicine and magical powers. Bad *mmoatia* can kill, maim and afflict diseases on those who offend them. *Mmoatia* are invisible to the ordinary person. Fetish priests and other spiritualists can communicate with them to elicit their assistance. The proverb lends credence to the association of *sasabonsam* and *mmoatia* with witches, composing the trio of evil and destruction.

In Ghanaian animistic and metaphysical beliefs, spirits are domiciled in the earth, rivers, trees, lakes, and animals, among others. Certain species of trees are identified as sacred groves used by fetish priests to provide shelter for shrines. With a botanical name of *chlorophora excelsa,* the *odum* tree is yellow brown to dark brown in color, potentially reaching a height of up to 160 feet and a diameter of ten feet. Perhaps, due to its imposing size, it is universally considered by Akans as a potential dwelling site of spirits and other supernatural entities. Thus, it is common for offerings to spirits and deities to be placed at the base of an *odum* tree. The top of an *odum* tree is widely believed to be the meeting grounds for nocturnal witch gatherings following from its inaccessibility. Due to its huge size, weight, and height, it is also believed to be a common resting place for the *sasabonsam.*

21. ɔba gyegyefoɔ na ɔma obayifoɔ adidie da adie.

The proverb means, "it is the naughty child who allows the witch's witchcraft to become publicly known." Akans believe that witchcraft is mired in secrecy. The identity of a witch is always a source of speculation while the activities of witches remain hidden from nonwitches. Yet the actions of a misbehaving child often cause people in the community to scrutinize the child's family background, sometimes leading to the discovery of the witch status of the child's mother.

A fitting illustration of this proverb is found in a story concerning witchcraft and bewitchment that aired on Ghanaian radio during November and December of 2005. On November 29, 2005, listeners to the *Etuo Mu Wɔ Sum* weekly radio program on the Peace FM 104.3 dial were shocked by the scandal of an alleged case of bewitchment described by the host of the program. In this case a middle-aged woman residing in a small town in the Eastern Region of Ghana reportedly summoned her lineage together for a meeting during which she informed them that the thirty-four-year-old woman known to everyone as her daughter was not, in fact, her real daughter. She was now prepared to return the thirty-four-year-old woman to her "real" family. According to the middle-aged woman, some thirty-four years previously she became pregnant by her husband but suffered a miscarriage a few months later. While grieving at her loss, she was consoled by her older sister who counseled her to grieve no more. The elder sister assured her that she would replace the lost pregnancy. Later that night, the sister appeared to her in a dream and presented her with a developing fetus. After the purported spiritual implantation of the fetus into her womb, she felt pregnant again, as if she had never miscarried. Meanwhile, a young expectant mother who was also her neighbor suffered a miscarriage. The older sister had apparently removed the fetus from this expectant mother and implanted it in her younger sister's womb. She alleged that for thirty-four years she had kept this matter a secret, hiding it from everyone, including the daughter in question. Additional details of the story were revealed in the December 6, 2005, program after the host of the program traveled to the town in question to investigate the claims in the story. The host of the program aired an interview with the thirty-four-year-old woman now being disclaimed by her mother, as well as with the chief of the town. Both confirmed that these claims had been referred to the chief for resolution. In another interview aired on the show, the queenmother of the town affirmed that she was a sister of the woman whose fetus was purportedly removed. At issue is why the mother waited for thirty-four years to reveal the story to her daughter, risking inordinate publicity. What triggered the revelation? According to the woman at the center of the controversy, the root of the matter was that she had resisted her mother's efforts to control her choice in marriage partners. In three consecutive instances, she had abandoned relationships with prospective suitors at the prompting of her mother. By the time she met her fourth suitor, she had resolved that whether her mother approved or disapproved of the man, she would marry him. Predictably, her mother objected but she married the man anyway. The mother, who felt slighted by the daughter's marriage and intransigence, then asked her to leave her household since she was not her daughter anyway. Thus, it was the daughter's defiant behavior that provoked public revelation of information regarding witchcraft and bewitchment. Had her daughter proven submissive, deferential, and compliant, this information would never have been revealed.

22. ɔbayifoɔ reko o!, ɔbayifoɔ rekɔ o! na wonnyɛ ɔbayifoɔ a, wonntwa w'ani.

The proverb means, "if you are not a witch, you don't turn to look when someone says 'There goes the witch!,' there goes the witch!'" This proverb defines appropriate response to witchcraft suspicions and accusations. In Akan communities, people will typically make indirect remarks or cast insinuations on those whom they suspect of being witches. The proverb suggests that an individual who is innocent of an accusation of witchcraft need not respond to the accusation.

The word ɔbayifoɔ has a deeply pejorative meaning. To be called ɔbayifoɔ is to be denigrated as a contemptible being. Even lingering suspicions tend not to lead to openly confrontational accusations of witchcraft. To brand someone a witch may lead to countercharges of slander and a summons to appear before a local chief and his elders. Failure to prove that the person is indeed a witch may lead to the imposition of compensatory and punitive damages. Direct accusations may also degenerate into direct physical confrontations and violence from the suspected witch and the witch's defenders within a family. For this reason, people who suspect others of witchcraft resort to making their feelings known through innuendos, gossip, and aspersions.

23. Sɛ wo nni adaagye a, yɛnnyɛn bayie.

This proverb means, a person who does not have a lot of free time at his or her disposal is not capable of grooming the witchcraft power and should not undertake to carry and nurture witchcraft. Among Akans, it is believed that nurturing witchcraft power requires considerable commitment and an exorbitant expenditure of energy. Akans believe that witches belong to witch companies that hold Sabbaths on regularly scheduled nights. Membership in these witch companies entails certain responsibilities; every witch occupies a special position in the hierarchically structured witch coven and is expected to perform the specialized roles and tasks associated with that position. They must attend these nightly meetings regularly to remain in good standing with the guilds. Thus, to execute one's tasks diligently, one must have considerable time at one's disposal.

24. Nea w'adidi amee se nea ɔdidi anadwo yɛ obayifoɔ.

This proverb means, "the person whose hunger is sated will say that the one who eats at night is a witch or will brand the night eater as a witch." The proverb, once more, underscores the idea that witches have an affinity for nocturnal activities. Witches fly to night Sabbaths, attend conferences at night, play games at night, do business at night, establish business contacts at night, and kill and feast on their victims at night. Cooking at dusk and nighttime occurs often in Ghana. Particularly in the rural areas, where about 50 percent of the population resides, families leave for their farms at dawn and typically return home just after dusk. Once at home, they immediately proceed to prepare their dinner, which would typically consist of a *fufu* meal. *Fufu* is cooked yam, plantain, or cassava which is pounded into a doughy paste that is formed into balls and eaten with soup. *Fufu* preparation not only takes a considerable amount of time to complete, but also involves much pounding action with the traditional mortar and pestle that creates raucous noise that would be particularly pronounced in the late evening hours. Whether in urban or rural areas, it is common for people to derisively accuse those whose cooking goes late into the night of being a witch.

25. Aberewa a yεbɔ no bayie wɔ fie no, ɔno ara na yεkɔ abɔnten ba bεto no bisa no abakɔsεm.

The proverb means, "the *aberewa* (old woman) who is denounced as a witch by relatives at home is the same person whose relatives turn to for answers to questions about their history and traditions." The proverb provides an important social commentary about the complex views held toward *mmerewa* (elderly women) in contemporary Ghanaian society, noting two contradictory statuses. On the one hand, the *aberewa* in Akan society is highly regarded. She epitomizes the sagacity and wisdom borne from accumulated life experiences. She is respected as a repository of knowledge and is regularly consulted over matters of cultural practices, traditions, and history of her people. She plays a significant role in providing care for and enculturating infants and toddlers while regularly counseling adolescents and young adults away from the paths of waywardness. She helps prepare young women in the family for marriage through her counseling and demonstration of cooking, cleaning, and other domestic tasks. She assists and counsels young mothers about proper prenatal practices, occasionally serving as the traditional birth attendant or midwife. She is also a counsel regarding proper postnatal procedures and activities associated with childrearing. Her family and others in the residential community are also dependent on her for postnatal health of the new mother and the baby, administering proper herbs for a range of illnesses that can afflict mother and child.

In contrast to the indispensable role and high esteem in which the *aberewa* is held, the *aberewa* is castigated for suspicion of being a witch. As noted throughout this book, typical witch suspects in Ghanaian society are elderly women. They are not only ready targets for witchcraft accusation by their kinsfolk, but also stand accused of diabolical witchery by witch-detection oracles. Indeed, the word *ɔbayifoɔ, bayifoɔ,* or *anyεn* in Akan language is virtually synonymous with elderly woman. Elderly women are gossiped about, suspected of witchcraft, thrown out of their homes, and banished from their communities while forced to endure painful and financially exorbitant exorcism rituals. In the worst-case scenarios, some are physically beaten, maimed for life, or even killed (Adinkrah 2004).

The ambivalence with which elderly women are regarded in Akan society provides an example of the sociological concept known as status inconsistency. Status inconsistency occurs when a person occupies a relatively high position on one social ladder but occupies a relatively lower position on another. In this context, social prestige that accrues to the *aberewa* based on her chronological age is vitiated by her simultaneous status as the one who embodies the characteristics most often associated with a witch with all its concomitant stigmatization. Held in higher esteem in one social realm, she is held in contemptible status in another social realm.

26. ɔbayifoɔ na n'ani nsɔ adeɛ.

This proverbial statement means, "a witch is a person who is never satisfied with what she has." Indeed, "ɔbayifoɔ biara ani bere adeɛ" (every witch is covetous) and this proverb are statements that are frequently articulated during popular discussions about witchcraft and witches in Ghana. Many Ghanaians believe that one can discern a witch from a nonwitch on the basis of a number of distinguishing physiological characteristics, behaviors, and character traits. If there is a single behavioral trait that is said to give the witch away, it is *anibrɛ* (jealousy or covetousness). Time and again witches are described as greedy, insatiable, covetous, and envious of other people's success, good fortunes, and material possessions. Witches are never satisfied with what they have and will appropriate what others have. In fact, in Akan witch ideology, *anibre* is synonymous with *bayie* or witchcraft and *onibrefoɔ* (covetous person) is synonymous with *ɔbayifoɔ* or witch. It is common to hear "obayifoɔ biara yɛ onibrefoɔ" (every witch is covetous) or "obayifoɔ biara ani bere adeɛ" (a witch is a person who is covetous).

Consistent with this belief and proverbial expression, fictional dramas on Ghanaian television and in movies typically depict the witch as covetous or envious. Where polygynous unions are portrayed, the witch is the cowife who perpetually complains that the husband is showering more resources on the other wives and their children than on herself and her children. If a story features relations in an *abusua* or extended family, the witch is the one who envies her siblings and their children and wants all good fortune and material wealth for herself and her own children. Where children are portrayed, the child witch is often a female child who is prone to jealousy and who consistently covets what her siblings or peers have, while never satisfied with her share of anything given by her family or friends; adults in the community single out this child for rebukes and she is told to reform her ways lest she grow up to become a witch: "sɛ w'angyae wo suban a, daakye, wo bɛ yɛ obayifoɔ" (if you don't alter your character, you will grow up to become a witch).

It is worth mentioning that the portrait of the witch as jealous and predisposed toward craving what others have coincides with beliefs about the nature of females in Ghanaian gender ideology. The belief is strong among Ghanaians that women are by nature covetous and that this is a defining characteristic of girlhood and womanhood: "ɛmmaa yɛ anibrefoɔ" (women are covetous) and "ɔbaa biara ani bere adeɛ" (every woman has a jealous streak in her) are popular expressions in Ghanaian society. Moreover, the witch in fictionalized dramas is always a woman, which perpetuates the belief that it is primarily women who are witches.

27. Wokyekyere funu soa ɔbayifoɔ a, na ɛte sɛ deɛ wode kɔtorɔbankye abɔ ngo mu.

The proverb means, "tying up a corpse and making a witch carry it is like dipping cassava into palm oil." This proverb suggests that one cannot punish a person by giving them what they desire. *Kɔtorɔbankye* in Akan society refers to an inedible cassava while *ngo* refers to red palm oil obtained from palm fruits. To dip *kɔtorɔbankye* in red palm oil is an attempt to make this inedible food edible. The witch has an affinity for human flesh, that he or she devours after killing a human victim. Thus, to try to punish a cannibalistic witch by tying a corpse to it is like offering her what she already desires; it is not punishment at all.

28. Merensuro bayie na m'agyae bogya.

This proverb means, "I am not going to be afraid of the firefly and am not going to be afraid of the witch." In Akan witchcraft lore, the nocturnal witch flies through the air at night in the form of a giant fireball, emitting a trail of sparks as he or she travels to the nightly witches' Sabbath or to seek out and attack victims targeted for bewitchment. Akans are typically wary of the night firefly, which is closely associated with witches. For many people, the features of this insect, as nocturnal and luminous, are evocative of the witch. Moreover, it is believed that witches are able to transmogrify themselves into fireflies at night in order to gain entry into their victims' bedrooms to bewitch them. Hence, to find a firefly in one's bedroom is considered a bad omen, foretelling that one is about to become a victim of witchcraft, and evoking such terror that every effort will be expended to find and kill the creature before retiring for the night. This proverb accentuates the notion that fireflies and witches are regarded as one and the same thing. In fact, for many people the euphemistic term for a witch is *anadwo bogya* (night-time firefly). One example of witchraft lore is the account of a man who killed a firefly in his bedroom one night only to waken the following morning to the news that one of his relatives died early that morning.

29. Enyɛ bayie nyinaa ne: munku no ma me.

This proverb means, "witchcraft is not exclusively about killing." In practical terms, it references the fact that while witchcraft power may be used to kill its victims, it is not used solely for this purpose. Witches are said to use their witchcraft power to cause nonfatal diseases such as epilepsy and other physical conditions such as blindness and alcoholism in its victims. They can cause barrenness in women, sexual impotence in men, dullness and academic failure in school-age children. *Bayie* can also be used to cause the destruction of property such as arson to the victim's house, farm, or other property. Witchcraft can be used to cause all manner of misfortune.

30. ɔbayifoɔ na ohunu (onim) ne yɔnko ɔbayifoɔ.

This proverb means, "only a witch knows a fellow witch." As noted in chapter 2, many Ghanaians believe that witchcraft and associated activities are secret. People who do not have witchcraft do not have the capacity to know other witches. There is also widespread belief that witch doctors possess witchcraft. Thus, their ability to arrest or apprehend a witch stems from the fact that they are themselves witches. Such witch doctors must also have witchcraft power more powerful than that of the witches they arrest.

31. Bayie nsrama nhye afuo.

This proverb means, "the witch's fire does not burn a farm." In essence, the proverb is a reference to the balls of fire in which witches take form.

As mentioned previously, one of the most common physical signs associated with *bayie* is its manifestation as a giant ball of fire. People who claim to have encountered this telltale sign of witchcraft relate stories of giant balls of fire hopping on a grassy field, sitting atop a tree, or flying through the sky. Soccer fields appear to be a particularly common site for claimants who describe seeing several balls of fire of various sizes, some stationary, others hopping across the field. Some say the fire intensifies, fades, and then reemerges. Some say the fire has the capacity to get intermittently larger and then smaller. Observers usually find no traces of scorched earth or any other signs of a fire the following morning.

32. Yɛnfa nsa pan mpam ɔbayifoɔ.

This proverb means, "we don't use empty hands to drive away a witch." The reference is to a malevolent witch who, given his or her powerful and destructive nature, cannot be driven away with ease. In order to be successful in repelling a witch, one must be well-armed with the requisite spiritual resources, which in the Christian context, includes regular fasting, intense prayers and philanthropic giving.

33. Sɛ bɔne nni fie a anka bayie ntumi nkum nipa.

This means, "if there was no sin in the family, a witch cannot kill a human being." In other words, one should not delude oneself into believing that there is no intrafamily violence, misdeed, or evil. Once again, this is a reference to the cannibalistic witch who kills family members.

34. Sɛ wo nni bayie a wonsuro funusoa (afunsoa).

This proverb means, "if you don't have witchcraft, then you are not afraid of *funusoa*." During Ghana's precolonial and early colonial eras, the Akan ritual of *funusoa* (carrying the corpse) was performed as a form of divination, or necromancy, in cases of suspicious deaths, such as accidental deaths, sudden deaths, or the deaths of young persons, which tended to be attributed to witchcraft, sorcery, or other spiritual forces. *Funusoa* involved the carrying of the corpse of the deceased by a group of selected carriers as the spirit of the deceased is summoned to reveal the identity of his or her killer. The corpse would be expected to direct the carriers in the direction of the person who caused the death of the deceased through spiritual means. For the person the corpse has singled out as the killer, it is said, "efunu no asi no" (the corpse has struck the person). The alleged killer would then be set upon by a relative, usually a son of the deceased, and bludgeoned to death. In some instances, the person identified as guilty was called upon to commit suicide, being provided with materials to effectuate the act. Thus the saying that if you know you do not have witchcraft, you are not afraid of *funusoa* because you know you will never be identified as the source of another person's death (see Brokensha 1966, 204–5).

This chapter demonstrates that proverbs are a major source of Akan witchcraft beliefs. Certain proverbs stress the vulnerability of all persons to witchcraft, suggesting that everyone is vulnerable to bewitchment. Proverbial references that focus on witch cannibalism are also legion. Through exposure to, or analysis of proverbs about witchcraft, one can gain insight into Akan beliefs about witches, witchcraft, and bewitchment. The next chapter focuses on local witchcraft trials as repositories of information on witchcraft accusations and witch hunts.

Chapter 6

WITCHCRAFT TRIALS
IN GHANAIAN COURTS

Much of the extant knowledge regarding witch hunts in medieval Europe and colonial America is based on historical, anthropological, and other social science literature constructed from surviving trial records involving accusations and confessions of maleficent witchcraft (Behringer 1997; Hall 1991; Levin 1960; Roper 2004; Rowlands 2001, 2003). Particularly in Europe, the field of witchcraft studies benefited immensely from the massive records that accumulated on witchcraft trials. Indeed, some of the most notable and significant use of trial records in the study of witchcraft and witch hunts to date can be found in Germany, where the availability of voluminous trial records have aided in the reconstruction and understanding of what transpired during the era of the witch hunts (Behringer 1997; Roper 2004; Rowlands 2001, 2003). For other parts of Europe, including France, Italy, and Switzerland, several studies (e.g., Monter 1976) have utilized witchcraft trial records to examine the major patterns of witch persecution and the contextual characteristics of witch hunts. At present, there are a multitude of studies that have been conducted utilizing witch trial records. Contemporary examples include Lyndal Roper's (2004) *Witch Craze,* Wolfgang Behringer's (1997) *Witchcraft Persecutions in Bavaria,* and Alison Rowlands' (2003) *Witchcraft Narratives in Germany.* In recent years, the publication of witchcraft sourcebooks (e.g., Levack 2004), has afforded scholars and the general reader easy access to rich data on the witch trials in Europe, in particular.

Taken together, this literature has assisted in the identification of the following features of witchcraft in early modern Europe: the sociodemographic profile (gender, age, and social status) of accused witches; the sociodemographic profile of witch accusers or denunciators; temporal and spatial aspects of witchcraft persecutions and trials; the social contexts of the witch trial; triggers of suspicions of witchcraft; the triggering events of violent witch hunts; whether or not witchcraft confessions were given voluntarily or extracted under duress; the maleficent activities of the alleged witches; the methods used to extract confessions, including torture; treatment meted out to convicted witches; reasons for the rise and fall of the witch trials; and the decriminalization of witchcraft.

In Ghana, although some traditional courts contain archival records on witchcraft-related trials from the colonial era (see Danquah 1928, 219–35; Gray 2000), and modern courts hold trial transcripts from contemporary witchcraft trials, very little has been written about witch trials and the significance of witchcraft trials as purveyors of information about witchcraft in Ghana. Barring Gray's (2000) doctoral dissertation, which is based on analyses of data from surviving trial records in the Akim Abuakwa traditional courts, there has been very little systematic analysis of the archival records of witchcraft trials in Ghanaian society. The only other substantive research that exists on witch trials is J.B. Danquah's (1928) analysis of witchcraft-related court hearings at the court of King Ofori Attah I. Presently, no studies exist that consider the extent to which witch trials contribute to the maintenance and perpetuation of local beliefs about witches and witchcraft. It is not known, for instance, whether instances of witchcraft accusations increase following a witch trial or whether witchcraft trials generally heighten or fuel people's fears about witches and witch phenomena. The main purpose of this chapter, then, is to explore the impact of witchcraft trials in Ghanaian society. I will argue that witchcraft trials are of enormous significance in the purveyance of witchcraft ideas in the society, playing a role in fueling violent witch hunts in the society.

Witchcraft Trials in Ghana

In Ghana, as in most countries throughout the world, judicial courts conduct civil and criminal trials and various other types of hearings, making factual determinations and serving as primary settlers of legal disputes (Twumasi 1985). Among the myriad disputations Ghanaian courts are called on to adjudicate are those pertaining to witchcraft. As noted in chapter 3, witchcraft trials in Ghanaian courts constitute a major source of information about witchcraft ideas, beliefs, and practices in the society. With adjudicatory hearings conducted in open court and massively attended by the curious members of the public, journalists, and other media representatives, and with trial proceedings regularly reported in the electronic and print media, witchcraft trials become major public social events with far-reaching social consequences.

It has been previously noted that nearly everyone in Ghana believes in the reality of witchcraft and the threat of witches in the absence of any concrete evidence of the phenomenon. Given the supposed clandestine activities of witches, many Ghanaians clamor for an opportunity to witness firsthand any evidence of witchery. As later sections of this chapter make amply clear, throngs of people take advantage of such public trials to witness firsthand what they believe to be evidence of the reality of witchcraft. The analysis will show that over the past few decades witch trials have come to play a significant role in the formation, perpetuation, and dissemination of witchcraft ideas, attitudes, and beliefs. This chapter profiles four witchcraft trials in contemporary Ghana to illustrate how witchcraft trials unwittingly contribute to the dissemination of information about witchcraft in Ghanaian society. Besides summarizing substantive issues involved in the trial, the chapter examines key elements of witchcraft beliefs revealed during the trials and explores the role played by the local Ghanaian media as well as the general public in disseminating trial proceedings as well as the role of the wider public in purveying information revealed in the trials. Although the main focus of the chapter is on how witchcraft trials contribute to the dissemination of information about witchcraft phenomenon, effort is made throughout to highlight the nature of information purveyed through witchcraft trials.

In completing this chapter, I consulted and analyzed a number of documentary sources. First, I obtained certified court transcripts and trial judgments pertaining to the Accra murder case and the Tamale murder case from the registrars of the Accra High Court and the Tamale High Court. For the defamation lawsuits involving *Kofi Badu v. Abena Kobua* and *Ama Kunta v. Abena Kobua,* I obtained certified copies of judicial proceedings and trial judgments from the Saltpond Magistrates' Court. In addition to documentary records obtained from the courts, I photocopied, read, and analyzed all newspaper reports on each of the four trials discussed in this chapter appearing in the *Daily Graphic,* the *Weekly Spectator,* and the *Mirror.* Additionally, I interviewed a small sample of Ghanaian adults on the subject of witchcraft trials. Many respondents were able to vividly recall the Kobua witch trial, including the issues of contention. The fact that these adults remembered the case some thirty years following its incidence is indicative of the impact of witchcraft trials.

The Nature of Witchcraft Trials in Contemporary Ghana

While most witchcraft-related trials in smaller courts are often unpublicized, those witchcraft-related trials in Ghana that capture media attention—whether they are civil or criminal cases—are always high-visibility cases. Unlike the sparse attendance that characterizes most court proceedings, witchcraft trials are associated with crowded courtrooms. Scores of people from all walks of life converge on the courts to witness firsthand courtroom proceedings and to catch sight of the litigants. Witch trials involving self-confessed witches appear to attract the heaviest volume of spectators. Community residents and residents of neighboring communities are willing to travel long distances, even by foot, to witness trials in the courthouse. These become emotionally charged events with newspaper reports recounting the audible emotions of shock, disbelief, bewilderment, and rage expressed by onlookers in attendance. There are many instances when presiding judges experienced difficulties controlling the proceedings in the courtroom due to the raucous behavior of courtroom audiences. There are reportedly numerous instances when trial judges warn those in attendance to comport themselves in accordance with courtroom decorum or else risk being thrown out of the courtroom proceedings. With a mass of reporters associated with the print and television media often in attendance, witchcraft trials become public spectacles.

What accounts for the animated atmosphere that typically characterizes a witch trial? For most people in Ghana, witchcraft is a spiritual reality that affects or has the potential to encumber a person's life in myriad, positive but, more commonly, negative ways. Many people fear spiritual assaults from witches even though they have never seen a witch at work or do not know a "real" witch. Although they suspect relatives, neighbors, and others of being witches, these are mere suspicions that cannot be ascertained or verified. They believe that witches fly in the night and consume the souls of their victims. They believe that witches can transmogrify into animals and fly through the air. They believe witches can bring disease and death upon their victims. They also believe that witch activities, however, are shrouded in secrecy; witches allegedly conduct their business in clandestine ways, all of them outside the purview of normal individuals. The public trial offers citizens an opportunity to behold a self-proclaimed witch and to listen to his or her own testimony of witch machinations. Being in the courtroom and witnessing the trial firsthand allows one to satisfy one's curiosity about witchcraft and witches. For example, is the witch physically different from a nonwitch? Since witchcraft is shrouded in secrecy, many people see a witch trial as the only opportunity they will have in a lifetime to see a confirmed witch. Many think the most legitimate information about witchcraft comes directly from the mouth of the self-confessed witch.

Impact of Witchcraft Trials

Although it is difficult to assess precisely the full impact of witchcraft trials on witch beliefs and knowledge about witchcraft practices, overall, witchcraft trials appear to be effective mechanisms of socialization into witchcraft beliefs and practices. First, public trials regarding witchcraft appear to validate the belief in witchcraft each time they occur. Courtroom testimonies by self-confessed witches during witchcraft trials yield information that constitutes affirmations of established witchcraft beliefs. The oft-raised questions are: If witchcraft did not exist, then how does one explain, justify, or account for the voluntary and detailed confessions of self-professed witches? How does one also explain the numerous claims of seduction into witchcraft by self-confessed witches? How does one explain seemingly credible claims of bewitchment narrated by witch denunciators who claim they have been bewitched? Witchcraft trials provide opportunities to either confirm or debunk one's beliefs. Testimonial evidence provided by self-accused witches is taken as the indisputable truth of witchcraft since these self-accused witches purport to have had intimate experience with the phenomenon. Trial records often provide a wealth of information about the who, what, where, when, why, and how of witchcraft. The case and the outcome of the trial are usually discussed for days, weeks, months, and even years by the Ghanaian public. In these trials, self-confessed witches tell of attending nocturnal assemblies where witches are said to gather and where human victims are killed and consumed in the spiritual realm.

The period following a witchcraft trial is typically characterized by vibrant public and private discussions and debate on the reality of witchcraft. Given the extent of such public interest in witchcraft phenomenon, witchcraft trials are not easily forgotten. A case in point is the Kobua case, which took place more than thirty years ago and is recalled by many Ghanaians as if it happened only yesterday. Information about witchcraft can be gleaned from the testimonies of plaintiffs and defendants, attorneys representing each side of the dispute, and other participants in the trial, rulings issued by the court, judges handling the case, and lawyers representing the prosecution and defense.

Witchcraft trials tend to spawn numerous journalistic articles in local newspapers. In the weeks during and following a witchcraft trial, local newspapers run news stories, editorials, and feature stories about an assortment of witchcraft topics. Routinely, they also carry interviews with prominent members of the clergy or ministers of religion on witchcraft-related themes. For instance, during the Kobua witchcraft trial in 1976 and its immediate aftermath, the two most popular weekly news magazines of the country, the *Mirror* and the *Weekly Spectator*, published several articles on witchcraft, sorcery, and magic in Ghanaian society, covering such themes as, the fear of witchcraft, the harms witches are believed to cause, confessions of accused and self-professed witches, stereotypes of the witch and how to identify witches, practices believed to be efficacious against witchcraft, and witchcraft exorcisms. In 1985, following the conclusion of the Somanya witchcraft case, the print media published several stories on the subject of witchcraft while in the midst of the extensive coverage of the trial itself. They also surveyed the general public on beliefs in witchcraft and perceptions of the problems of witch hunts.

For all four trials discussed in this chapter, a remarkable degree of public interest in witchcraft was aroused. Public discussions about witchcraft grew immensely as people sought to authenticate the veracity of the courtroom testimonies of the self-confessed witches. Everywhere in the country, in a range of venues, from public markets to university classrooms, discussions focused on the trial. The trials also invariably provided an impetus for ministers of religion to intensify their sermonizing and preaching on the topic. In public venues around the country, such as around lorry stations, freelance preachers loudly denounced witches as wicked and destructive, exploiting the general fear of witches. Sermons frequently emphasized the reality of harmful witchcraft and the need for Christians to prepare for the great danger witches posed. As a counter-strategy to overcome the activities of witches, preachers urged Christians to pray and fast regularly and to attend services regularly.

Songwriters and musicians also responded to public interest in witchcraft trials by recording songs that incorporated themes emerging out of witchcraft trials. In fact, an analysis of lyrics in highlife songs around the time reveals an increase in witchcraft themes, specifically ideas embodied in the trials. Concurrently, the trials also contributed to an increase in the radio airtime devoted to the playing of songs with witchcraft themes. The trials also appeared to be associated with an increase in the production and purchase of music audiocassettes featuring witchcraft songs. The huge public interest that the trials engendered also led to an increase in the number of inscriptions on public transportation and the commercial signs of private shops and businesses.

Crowd Behavior

Detailed reactions of courtroom observers to the dramatic testimony of witches were reported in newspaper reports of court trials. During the Kobua trial, news reports included such references as "laughter in court," "prolonged laughter in court," "murmur in court from the audience." In one report, a court official was noted to have commanded, "Order, order, order, order. You are privileged to hear but not to talk" (Mirror Reporter, May 9, 1975, 6). In another proceeding, it was reported, "Mr Drah, the presiding Magistrate, had to warn the packed court several times for being noisy" (Ocran 1975, 2). In yet another instance, the magistrate is recorded to have said, "If you wish to enjoy the proceedings, you should keep quiet" (Mirror Reporter, May 9, 1975, 12). During the Somanya case, the news media made special note of the giggles during the testimony of the teenaged defendant Afua and during the exchanges between the self-confessed witch and the plaintiff. Many in the audience registered their apparent shock, bafflement, and horror about the tales of diabolical destruction and tragedy perpetrated by the witches.

Media Reports

All major news organizations, including local dailies and weeklies, strove to keep the public abreast of happenings in the courtroom during the witchcraft trials. The major newspapers assigned reporters to cover the trial. Media reports of witchcraft trials provided detailed accounts of the testimony of plaintiffs, defendants, and witnesses, as well as objections raised by and opening and closing arguments of the attorneys, and the rulings of the judge. Stories emanating from witch trials often made front page news. The Kobua trial was particularly striking in the media frenzy it generated. A variety of headlines concerning the trial were plastered across the front pages of national newspapers and weekly magazines. The *Mirror* ran such headlines as, "I'm A Witch . . . I Fly at Night with My Baby" (Ocran 1975), "Court Confessions of a Witch: We Turn Birds, Animals" (Mirror Reporter, May 9, 1975), "Witchcraft Is Hereditary" (Mirror Reporter, June 20, 1975, 1), "Defendant's Plea to Turn into Vulture . . . Court Did Not Allow Kobua: Magistrate Explains" (Mirror Reporter, June 6, 1975, 1). The *Weekly Spectator* similarly gave prominent coverage to the Somanya witchcraft case and ran such headlines as "Witchcraft: I Have Been Defamed, Plaintiff Says" (Bokor 1984a; see also Bokor 1984b, 1984c). In addition to the reports, newspapers published several photographs of the plaintiffs and defendants, as well as of the courtroom audience. Some reports were accompanied by photographs of purported sites of nocturnal witch gatherings and activities. In the end, the amount of detailed media coverage of witchcraft trials keeps witchcraft ideas prominent in the minds of Ghanaians.

The Abena Kobua Case

In 1975 two civil lawsuits were filed at the Saltpond Magistrates' Court against a 25-year-old woman, Abena Kobua, and her mother-in-law, Ama Otuwa. In the lawsuit the plaintiffs, Ama Kunta (a fish vendor) and Kofi Badu (a fisherman) sought compensatory cash damages the equivalent of US$300 and US$800, respectively, against the defendants for defamation of character emanating from an imputation of witchcraft by the defendants. By their civil lawsuits, the plaintiffs also sought to redeem their good reputations they claimed had been sullied by the actions and words uttered by the defendants. The defendant, Abena Kobua, was alleged to have directly made the imputation of witchcraft, and her codefendant and mother-in-law, Ama Otuwa, was also civilly sued because she allegedly goaded Abena Kobua into making the defamatory statements, thereby contributing to the impugning of the plaintiffs' integrity.

According to case records, on the day of the imputation of witchcraft the defendant, Abena Kobua, went to the residences of the two plaintiffs. Banging a spoon against a metal pan to draw the attention of onlookers, she proceeded to announce that she was a witch, and that the two plaintiffs were also witches that belonged to her witch coven. She then accused them both of being maleficent, cannibalistic witches who had spiritually bewitched her eight-month-old infant daughter to death. According to Kobua, even though she had known the plaintiffs to be witches for a while her decision to go public with the information was prompted by the death of her infant daughter, a death caused by the two plaintiffs. Abena Kobua alleged that the two plaintiffs were not only witches, but also lovers in the spiritual realm. According to Abena Kobua, on the evening of her infant daughter's death she had gone for her routine nocturnal witch feasting. Proclaiming herself a scavenging vegetarian and fructivorous witch, Kobua stated that she preferred routine feasts on food obtained from a rubbish dump, rather than on the human flesh of witchcraft victims. While feasting, she had placed her infant baby, whom she regularly took to the nocturnal witches' meetings, by her side. This was to enable her to keep an eye on the infant and still be able to scavenge for food, unencumbered by having to carry the baby around. According to Abena Kobua's account, on that fateful night the two plaintiff witches, who were also feasting, approached her and asked permission to hold her baby. She acquiesced while she kept scavenging for food. Unbeknownst to her, the two witches took the baby away, killed her, and consumed her flesh.

In her testimony before the crowded court, Abena Kobua, the principal defendant in the case, described events consistent with popular beliefs concerning witchcraft in Ghanaian society. By the conclusion of her testimony, she had presented such facets of Akan witch-beliefs as the nature, origin, and purpose of her witchcraft; the activities of witches, including their ability to transform themselves into animals; the reality of witches' guilds and associations; the power structure of witches' associations; nocturnal aerial flights to witches' Sabbaths; the gender composition of witches' guilds; the possibility of child witches; bewitchment of children; cannibalistic witch activities; romantic unions in witch covens; and how to identify a witch.

Abena Kobua told the packed courtroom the ways of witches and their activities in her community. She told the court that before leaving for her nocturnal aerial flights to join the company of witches she would put all the residents of her household to sleep by gently blowing air from her outstretched right hand onto them. She would then transmogrify herself into a vulture. She then opened the closed windows and doors of her house by gently tapping on them. According to her testimony, her nocturnal expeditions began between 11:00 P.M. and midnight, and she usually returned home by the first cockcrow at 4:00 A.M. She claimed that during her flights to the witches' meetings she carried her baby on her back. While at the witches' meeting, she would feed at a garbage dump. She claimed that prior to the death of her child she had been feeding alone as a vulture at night for six months until she met the two plaintiffs, Kofi Badu and Ama Kunta, at the witches' feasting grounds. The two, she alleged, were spiritual lovers who had transformed themselves into animals, Ama into a centipede and Kofi into an owl. Prior to killing her infant, the two plaintiffs had expressed interest in her child. She told them that the child was not available for consumption. However, the two snatched the child away from her after they had overpowered her. Abena Kobua said she took steps to retrieve her baby. Upon consulting a witch doctor concerning how to proceed, she was advised to appease her two cowitches with cash in the amount of about US$5, which she indicated was the normal fee paid to witches in order to secure the release of a captured soul. This she did, but the pacification was to no avail as the two witches still killed and consumed her infant daughter. Abena Kobua told the court that the plaintiffs had killed her baby because they claimed that she (Kobua) had participated in the spiritual consumption of meat that they had contributed to the witches' guild, but had not reciprocated by offering any meat of her own at the appointed time.

During cross-examination in court, Abena Kobua took the opportunity to further educate the magistrate and courtroom audience about witchcraft, witches, wizards, and their nocturnal assemblies. She claimed that witches and wizards regularly assumed the form of animals or birds. Some morphed into snakes or deer but she always assumed the form of a vulture. Concerning the numerical gender composition of witches, Kobua asserted that there were more female witches than male wizards because women outnumbered men in real life. In terms of the relative potency of men and women's witchcraft power, she testified that the spiritual power of female witches was just as potent as that of male wizards. She also maintained that male witches and female witches could be lovers, and could even marry spiritually. She said nocturnal witch gatherings could be presided over by either a male or a female witch.

As to the role that spiritual cannibalism played in causing the physical death of her infant daughter, Abena Kobua asserted that as the witches proceeded to devour her baby, the baby became physically ill. As the physical condition of the child deteriorated, she sent her to a spiritual church for prayers, thinking that the pastor would be spiritually powerful enough to overcome the witchcraft spirit of the plaintiffs. However, the witches' power was stronger and her child died. Regarding how she acquired her witchcraft power, Abena Kobua asserted that she was born a witch. That is, her witchcraft spirit was given to her via intrauterine transfer. Abena Kobua also told the court that witchcraft power was transferable by other means and that she could transfer a portion of hers to anyone who wished to have it. On the matter of whether witchcraft spirit was a burden or an asset to the witchcraft carrier, Abena Kobua asserted that possessing witchcraft was an asset because she had managed to use hers to her advantage. As someone who preferred a large family size, she had used her witchcraft power to assist her in having several children. She claimed she could also use her witchcraft to assist any woman who was barren to have a child. Concerning the reality of witchcraft and the power of witches to hurt their victims, Abena Kobua maintained throughout the trial that witchcraft was real and that those who held skeptical views of witches and witchcraft should recognize the power of witches to harm, destroy, and even kill their victims.

Purported Damages Suffered by Plaintiffs

The plaintiffs submitted that they lived in a small fishing community, Ankaful, and had been tremendously adversely affected by the witchcraft accusations—financially, psychologically, and socially. The first plaintiff, Ama Kunta, submitted that as a fish vendor her business had suffered immensely from the imputation of witchcraft. Her regular and potential customers shied away from her fish, fearing that the fish she sold were not real fish but something else that she had obtained from conjuration. The second plaintiff, Kofi Badu, a fisherman, issued a similar complaint, indicating that as a fisherman he could no longer find market for his catch because of the negative perceptions about him shared by people in the community. The plaintiffs further submitted that witchcraft was a highly stigmatizing phenomenon in Ghanaian society. As a result of the defendants' imputation of witchcraft, they, the plaintiffs, had lost social standing in the community in which they lived. They had been reviled because of the widespread belief in the ability of witches to cause great social harm, such as epidemics, droughts, crop failure, and pestilence, as well as illnesses, injuries, and death to their human victims. The defendants averred that they had therefore suffered emotionally and psychologically. The plaintiffs also noted the stigmatizing impact of the witchcraft allegation on their families. They contended that since witchcraft is considered a heritable trait, imputation of witchcraft impugned the integrity of families who may also suffer the hostility directed toward alleged witches.

Submission by the Defendants

In her own defense, Abena Kobua sought the permission of the court to perform a demonstration that would confirm that she and the plaintiffs were all witches. She led the way as the magistrate, the plaintiffs, counsel for the plaintiffs, and the defendants, accompanied by a large, animated crowd of onlookers, ventured to the supposed spiritual feeding grounds where Abena Kobua claimed the kidnapping, killing, and consumption of her baby occurred. She also sought to demonstrate her witchcraft power by turning into the vulture form that she professed to routinely assume for her nocturnal witch trysts. She also sought permission of the court to prove that the plaintiffs were witches by turning them into vultures as well. To enact these demonstrations, Abena Kobua initially asked the court for a cocoa pod. After the court concurred with this request, Abena Kobua sought additional permission of the court to strip naked in the courtroom and for the plaintiffs to do the same in furtherance of her effort to turn herself and the two plaintiffs into vultures. The court declined this request, leading to the instant abrogation of Kobua's testimony.

The Ruling of the Court

The court found Abena Kobua and her mother-in-law liable for defamation of character and asked them to pay a sum of money the equivalent of US$300 in damages to the first plaintiff, Ama Kunta, whose original claim was about US$800 in damages from the defendants. These constituted substantial monetary judgments at the time. In his ruling, the presiding magistrate asserted that the two defendants, Abena Kobua and Ama Kunta, had made allegations of witchcraft that they were unable to substantiate. In a rhetorical question, the magistrate asked, "How could the plaintiff assist the defendant to prove an allegation which she is making against the plaintiff?" ("Kobua to Pay 300 Cedis" August 1, 1975, 1). He noted in response to the question that whoever makes an accusation of witchcraft must have the ability to prove the allegation. In his ruling, the magistrate noted that when the defendant, Abena Kobua, was asked to prove her case that she was indeed a witch, she requested a cocoa pod to facilitate her transmogrification into a vulture. This request was granted by the court. The magistrate noted, "She did not attach any conditions at all. But strangely enough on the adjourned date she changed her mind like a chameleon and imposed unreasonable conditions which she well knew were impossible. Her counsel's plea that the court made it impossible for her to prove her case was baseless and monstrous" ("Kobua to Pay 300 Cedis" August 1, 1975, 1). Turning to Abena Kobua's claim that she could transform herself into a vulture, the magistrate asked, "But if she turned into a huge snake or serpent and attacked people in the court who would bear the blame? Or suppose she turned into a lioness and attacked people in the court, who would bear the blame? The devil and his agents are liars and should not be taken at their words" ("Kobua to Pay 300 Cedis" August 1, 1975, 1).

Regarding the case of the plaintiffs, Magistrate Drah reiterated that the plaintiff, Ama Kunta, had established a very strong case against the defendants—Abena Kobua and her mother-in-law, Ama Otuwa. In the view of the magistrate, she had proved beyond any reasonable doubt that Abena Kobua uttered the defamatory, slanderous, and disparaging words that formed the basis of the lawsuit and that the court strongly believed that Ama Otuwa, the codefendant, urged Abena Kobua to utter those words. "It is easy to say you are a witch but difficult to prove it," he noted ("Kobua to Pay 300 Cedis" August 1, 1975, 1). In concurring with the plaintiff's request for compensatory damages, the court ruled that as a result of the imputation of witchcraft made against Ama Kunta, a fish vendor by profession, people have shunned her person and her business, paralyzing her trade and thus her income. The magistrate stated, "It appears in order to revive her trade as a fish seller, she would eventually have to leave Ankaful for a locality where she is not known and this will definitely inconvenience the plaintiff who has lived at Ankaful all her life" ("Kobua to Pay 300 Cedis" August 1, 1975, 1). The magistrate ruled that the plaintiff had suffered tremendous financial loss. Moreover, her reputation in the community had been jeopardized by the alleged defamatory words. He therefore awarded her about US$300 in compensatory damages. Her counsel was awarded about US$120 in costs.

In the second civil suit, the court found the defendants guilty of defaming the plaintiff Kofi Badu and awarded the equivalent of US$300 in damages to him. The plaintiff had originally requested about US$600 in damages. In his ruling, Magistrate Drah described the case as fascinating, noting, "She says she is a witch and that is her own matter. What is agitating the mind of the court is this. What useful purpose will be served if the defendant strips herself naked and proves that she is a witch? Surely that does not prove the allegation against the plaintiff, Kofi Badu, that he is a wizard. In fact, nobody is challenging the defendant that she is a witch" ("Sensational Ankaful Witchcraft Case" August 15, 1975, 5). The magistrate remarked that whether Abena Kobua was a witch or not was better known to herself.

The court ruled that Abena Kobua had publicly defamed Kofi Badu by the imputation of witchcraft without a demonstrable ability to prove it. It noted that Abena Kobua was relying on a witch doctor to prove that Kofi Badu is a wizard. Since the onus of proof lay on the defendant, it was her responsibility to demonstrate in a convincing manner that Kofi Badu was a wizard and that he had employed his wizardry to kill her child. The magistrate wrote, "The defendant has miserably failed to prove this. This failure on her part to prove the allegation which she had leveled against the plaintiff with effrontery and unbridled audacity has made her liable" ("Sensational Ankaful Witchcraft Case" August 15, 1975, 5). In justifying the award of the hefty monetary compensation to Kofi Badu for the imputation of witchcraft, the magistrate considered the negative public perceptions of the phenomenon of witchcraft and negative public reaction against persons labeled as witches or wizards. The following excerpt from a local media captures the reasoning of the court:

> Witchcraft is abhorrent to human beings everywhere, particularly in Ghana where the imputation tends to scare people away from anyone so suspected." As a result of the defendants' imputation of witchcraft, the court said Kofi Badu's reputation in the small rural community had been blemished beyond repair. In pointing out the many ways in which the imputation of witchcraft may affect the plaintiff, the magistrate averred that it would be detrimental to his business as a fisherman. He noted: "The plaintiff is a fisherman who made a living by fishing and selling his catch to the public. But now every catch he made was suspected to be tainted with elements of wizardry. People will surely avoid him and his catches. He may be forced by circumstances beyond his control to leave Ankaful and fish somewhere else. Difficulties loom

ahead of him. He is caught up in a whirlpool of events over which he has no control. I give him 300 cedis damages with costs of 120 cedis for his counsel." ("Sensational Ankaful Witchcraft Case" August 15, 1975, 5).

Appeal against Verdict

Following the ruling of the Magistrates' Court, the lawyer for the defendants filed an appeal against the judgment at the Cape Coast High Court. The grounds for appeal included the following: "(a) the judgment of the magistrate is against the weight of evidence; (b) the magistrate misdirected himself on the evidence before him and arrived at an erroneous decision; (c) the magistrate fatally and erroneously prevented Kobua from proving her case; (d) the magistrate's grounds for rejecting Kobua's material evidence were untenable and baseless; (e) the magistrate was prejudiced and biased against the defendants, Kobua and Otuwa." ("Sensational Ankaful Witchcraft Case" August 15, 1975, 1).

Discussion and Implications

The image of witchcraft that emerges from Abena Kobua's court testimony is concordant with dominant discourses on Akan witchcraft described in this book—including cannibalistic witches, maleficent witch acts, corporeal aerial flights, and nocturnal witches' Sabbaths. Her description of witchcraft undoubtedly resonated strongly with courtroom spectators, the newspaper readership, radio listeners, and the general public at large. For those previously unschooled about Akan witchcraft beliefs, it was a pointed lesson. The Kobua case fueled heated public debate. On the one hand, many argued that the presiding judge should have allowed Kobua to strip naked and demonstrate her witchcraft powers. On the other hand, others argued that the judge had made the most appropriate decision. Some argued that Kobua's allegations were unfounded. Some insisted that her testimony was accurate and consistent with other witchcraft confessions they had witnessed. Finally, the very treatment of the case in a court of law and the statements by the magistrate had the effect of giving credence to witchcraft and the existence of witches. In rendering his verdict, the magistrate indicated that the defendant bore the burden of proving that she was, in fact, a witch but that she had failed to do so. This ultimately suggests that one's witch status can be proven, which presumes the existence of witchcraft and witches. Furthermore, the magistrate questioned who would be held liable in the event that the defendant was successful in transforming herself into an animal such as a snake and subsequently harmed members of the court. This, again, implies that such actions are possible. Hence, the magistrate confirmed the existence of witches and witchcraft even while handing down a guilty verdict.

A number of questions emerge from the Kobua witch trial and the public response to it, given the major publicity surrounding the trial. Did the trial heighten anxieties about witchcraft? Did people become more fearful of witches than they had been before the trial? Did the trial promote greater fear of witchcraft? Did the trial promote belief in the reality and threat of witchcraft? Did the punishment for slander imposed on Kobua and her mother-in-law stem accusations of witchcraft in the society? Did the outcome of the case deter other people from making formal accusations of witchcraft against their relatives and neighbors whom they suspected of witchcraft? Did it scare individuals who might otherwise have made accusations of witchcraft against others? Did it spur other accused witches to take legal action against those individuals who have presently or previously accused them of witchcraft?

The Somanya Witchcraft Case

In October 1984 the Magistrate Court Grade One at Somanya, in the Eastern Region of Ghana, was the venue for a civil lawsuit involving the imputation of witchcraft. In this case the plaintiff was Esther Bimpong, described in newspaper reports as a rice vendor, seamstress, and a member of the Church of the Lord (Ghana). Esther Bimpong filed a defamation suit against five defendants, claiming that their imputation of witchcraft against her had sullied her reputation and exposed her family to public ridicule and scorn. In the lawsuit, she petitioned the court to award her a sum of money the equivalent of US$5,000 in compensatory damages against the defendants. She also sought to redeem her name that, she intimated, had been besmirched by the imputation of witchcraft. The defendants who were named in the lawsuit were Eunice Gbadam; Eunice Gbadam's sixteen-year-old maidservant, Afua; Kate Yawson; Kate Yawson's sixteen-year-old maidservant, Akua; and Pastor Samuel K. Ababio. All the defendants were members of the Eternal Life Mission church at Asutsuare.

The plaintiff claimed in her lawsuit that a few months prior to the filing of her lawsuit she became the object of witchcraft rumors in her community and traced the source of the rumor to the five defendants. The two teenage maidservants named as defendants in the lawsuit had apparently confessed to the Eternal Life Mission church that they were witches and had named the plaintiff and one Janet Agbogah as cowitches and accomplices at witches' Sabbaths. Pastor Samuel K. Ababio was named as a defendant in the lawsuit because he allegedly goaded the two teenaged girls into making the accusation against the plaintiff. In publicly admitting that they were witches, the two girls were acting at the behest of the Pastor Samuel Ababio, Eunice Gbadam, and Kate Yawson. The pastor and his church's decision to make the allegation of witchcraft public prompted the plaintiff to file suit.

In her claim for damages, Esther Bimpong indicated that since the imputation of witchcraft had been made against her, rumors circulated freely in the community that she was a witch. She contended that her good name, honor, and integrity in the community had been sullied by the imputation of witchcraft. She and her family had been forced to endure tremendous emotional anguish and social stigma. She noted that she had been defamed because wherever she went, people called her a witch and her children were being referred to as *akoo mma* (the children of a parrot), in reference to an accusation that she routinely assumed the form of a parrot at the witches' Sabbath. She further argued that the allegation that she was a witch had caused substantial damage to her reputation as a businesswoman, threatening her livelihood. She noted that potential customers were shunning her, reluctant to purchase her wares, following the witchcraft accusations. She argued that the lawsuit was necessary to counter the false and defamatory statements leveled against her as well as to compensate her for her loss of livelihood and the mental anguish she had suffered as a direct result of the witchcraft accusations.

The Hearing

The Somanya witchcraft saga began when a young girl revealed to her mother, Eunice Gbadam, a dream she had in which she claimed she saw the family's maidservant, Afua, standing beside her bed as she slept at night. Eunice Gbadam, the mistress of Afua, interpreted the dream as a sign that Afua was a witch who was intending to remove the young girl's brain in the middle of the night. Confronted with this allegation, Afua vehemently denied it, insisting that she was not a witch. In response, she was threatened by her mistress and Pastor Samuel K. Ababio of the Eternal Life Mission church that unless she confessed her involvement in witchcraft and recounted the details of witchcraft activities of the witches' coven in Asutsuare, she would be forced to undergo a trial by ordeal in which she would be taken to a cemetery, stripped naked, smeared with fecal matter, and sprayed with a pasty concoction made of hot chili peppers. Responding to additional pressures from the two defendants for her to "testify to the glory of God," the teenager relented, agreeing to make a witchcraft confession at an open religious service conducted by the church on May 30, 1984 ("The Witchcraft Case at Somanya" October 20, 1984, 1). During the open air sermon, she issued a confession declaring that she was a witch. She was then pressed to name her witch accomplices. She proceeded to name Akua, another sixteen-year-old maidservant; Esther Bimpong; and Janet Agbogah (Bokor 1984a, 1984b, 1984c). Angry over the imputation of witchcraft and the negative potential impact of the accusation on her reputation and that of her family, Esther Bimpong filed a civil lawsuit in the Somanya Magistrate Court.

At the time of the trial, sixteen-year-old Afua was the mother of a nine-month-old baby girl. During her courtroom testimony, she brought the infant to court. She told the jam-packed court that she and her nine-month-old daughter were both witches and that the plaintiff, Esther Bimpong, was also a witch who belonged to their witch coven. She described the plaintiff as a witch who was guilty of several reprehensible spiritual deeds and should be publicly censured. She described to the court how she left her house each night for nocturnal witches' Sabbaths. Before going on the nightly expedition, she would wait for a sign—a unique sound of the wind. On hearing this particular sound, she would press her right shoulder on the ground three times. Then she would swing her arms over the house to induce the residents of her household into deep slumber from which they would not awaken until she and her daughter had returned from their nocturnal tryst. She then transformed into a cat and her baby daughter into a lizard, and left the house through a crack in the wall. Afua testified that at the witches' Sabbath Esther Bimpong, the plaintiff, routinely changed into a parrot; Akua, one of the three defendants in the lawsuit, transformed herself into a goat while Janet Agbogah, another defendent, assumed the form of an elephant.

Afua testified that she and Akua were previously beneficent witches but that Esther Bimpong and Janet Agbogah taught them the art of malevolent witchcraft. According to Afua, their nocturnal witches' meetings took place atop the Osudoku Mountains, a large, expansive and famous mountain range in the locality, which was transformed at night by witches into a bustling township. She told the court that at the witches' Sabbath they would prepare elaborate meals for nocturnal feasting. The defendant told the court that she regularly arrived at the witches' meetings with such ingredients as salt, garden eggs (eggplant), tomatoes, pepper, and rice that the plaintiff asked her to bring. She testified that the prepared food was eaten by Esther Bimpong and Janet Agbogah. She and Akua were not allowed to partake in the feasting but obtained their fill of the food when Janet and Esther rubbed their soiled hands against the mouths of the maidservants. She further testified that following the nightly dining, the plaintiff and the other witches in her coven would wipe their soiled hands in the hair of her infant daughter. To buttress her testimony, she displayed her baby's hair to the court and explained that its reddish-brown color was the direct result of the plaintiff and other witches routinely using it to wipe their hands after eating.

The defendant further testified that the plaintiff asked her and Akua to use their witchcraft power to steal money from their mistresses. This, they were to do by waving their hands over the money. This act would cause the money to lose its value. The money and its real value would then transfer to Bimpong and Agbogah. She and Akua often complied but whenever they refused to comply, Agbogah and Bimpong caned them. This defendant also told the court that the plaintiff had asked her on one occasion to tie up her mistress's daughter and turn her into a frog to be killed for a witches' feast. Bimpong, the plaintiff, also asked her to remove the brains of her mistress's daughter. She was to do this by waving her hand over the youngster's head while she slept at night. This she once tried to do, but was caught in the act when the mistress's daughter had a dream and told her mother of seeing the defendant standing by her bed. The defendant also testified in court that on a number of occasions Bimpong and Agbogah sucked her blood and that of Akua as they traveled to the top of the Osudoku Mountains for the witches' Sabbath. Afua also told the court that on one occasion the plaintiff ordered her to take her master's car to the Osudoku Mountains. This she did spiritually, which was why her master's car developed engine troubles and had been sitting inoperably in the garage for six months. Afua reiterated that the plaintiff was being flagrantly untruthful in denying her witch status and her regular involvement in witchcraft activities. She questioned the motive of the plaintiff in seeking court action instead of going to a fetish priest who has the power to determine the veracity of witchcraft and witch involvement. She told the plaintiff, "If one is accused of witchery, the case is not brought to court but to the shrine of some fetish" (Bokor 1984a, 1).

The trial judge asked Afua to demonstrate to the court how some of the actions described in her testimony, such as removing the victims' brains and causing money to lose value, were accomplished. She responded by claiming that she had been exorcised of her witchcraft powers by the pastor of her church and so could not demonstrate any of her former witchcraft feats.

In a rebuttal, Esther Bimpong reiterated her assertion that she was not a witch. She described the defendant's testimony as pure fabrication concocted to impugn her integrity and to further bolster the aims of their church. She argued that Afua's daughter's reddish-brown hair color was symptomatic of *kwashiorkor* (the disease of a malnourished child), and that consumption of nutritious foods would reinstate the child's proper hair texture and color.

The Courtroom Atmosphere

Like the Kobua case, the Somanya case attracted national attention and became a media sensation. The courtroom where the trial occurred was described as crowded during the duration of the trial. One media report described how "an electrifying atmosphere engulfed the court-room" as the plaintiff described her alleged role in the witchcraft saga (Bokor 1984a, 1). On one occasion it was reported that Afua's testimony "drew cries of amazement from the crowded court" and that "the courtroom was full of cat-calls and jeers" (Bokor 1984a, 1). The crowd that gathered to watch the trial consisted of people of all ages. In the small community where the trial took place, the trial was a constant topic of conversation. People were fascinated by the idea of seeing a real witch and were captivated by tales of extraordinary witch activities engaged in by the alleged witches.

Discussion

The Somanya witchcraft case confirms several elements of witch beliefs and responses in Ghana. First, both persons accused of witchcraft in the case were female. As earlier sections of the book make clear, in Ghana witchcraft accusations are most frequently directed toward elderly and middle-aged women. Second, the case reinforces Akan beliefs in the use of malevolent witchcraft power to cause misfortune, disease, and death. Witches are considered inherently evil and dangerous. They cause enormous amounts of physical and social harm. The stories that Afua recounts regarding her nocturnal activities and those of her cowitches are consistent with Akan witch lore: witches cause financial misfortune, remove their victims' brains, and cause car troubles. Third, the mention of dreams in Afua's testimony reinforces the common belief in the ability to foretell one's bewitchment or imminent bewitchment in dreams. Dreams are one of the most important triggers of witchcraft accusations in Ghana. Fourth, testimony concerning the witchcraft power of Afua's nine-month-old infant daughter as well as that of the two sixteen-year-old maidservants are congruent with Akan beliefs about the capacity of young children and teenagers to be witches. Next, from the court testimony we see examples of the extent to which witchcraft accusations create a social stigma in Ghanaian society. As a result of the imputation of witchcraft, people in the community gossiped about the plaintiff and even began calling her children *akoo mma.*

From the testimonies in court, we are given additional information regarding the presumptive motivations of witches in bewitching others. The witch is a woman who wants everything for herself and envies others.

The plaintiff, Esther Bimpong, is a wealthy businesswoman with significant financial resources, yet the defendants portray her as coveting the financial resources of others less fortunate than herself. She instructs her cowitches, the maidservants and Janet Agbogah, to use their witchcraft power to steal money from their mistresses and pass it on to her.

Afua's description of nocturnal flights to witches' Sabbaths and of witches' activities at the witches' assemblies is consistent with Akan witch lore, including the nightly revels of witches that involve cooking, feasting, and general merriment. The trial supported the notion that witches have the capacity to transport themselves through the air. Consider Afua's testimony regarding how she and her cowitches flew to nocturnal witches' Sabbaths. The trial perpetuated beliefs about witches' ability to transform themselves into animals. Afua describes the transformations: her into a cat, her daughter into a lizard, Janet Agbogah into an elephant, Akua into a goat, and Bimpong into a parrot. Recall that in Kobua's testimony she claimed that she turned into a vulture, Badu into an owl, and Otuwa into a centipede. In their confessions, many accused witches in Ghana report that they received their witch power from family members. Afua never revealed the source of her witch power. She claimed that her original witchcraft power was benign but that Bimpong instructed her in maleficent witchcraft.

Like the Kobua case, the Somanya case stirred debates between fervent believers in witchcraft and those who rejected the existence of witchcraft. The trial became a recurrent focus of public and private conversations for several weeks after the conclusion of the trial. Nonbelievers in witchcraft saw the case as yet another example of inanity. Testimony by Afua was described as a mere illusion and discounted as a figment of her imagination. Nonbelievers sided with Bimpong in the assertion that Afua's testimony constituted lies and slander and that any monetary damages awarded Bimpong would be justified.

The Accra Murder Case

In August 1999 a 35-year-old carpenter, Gbenyo Quarshie, was prosecuted in a criminal court, convicted, and sentenced to death by hanging for murdering his 32-year-old wife, Ruth Geh, whom he suspected of being a witch. The man made a confession to police interrogators that he was awakened from sleep in the middle of the night to find a fierce lioness charging at him, attempting to kill and devour his body, as well as that of his young daughter. He alleged that in his panic, he grabbed a large club and bludgeoned the animal to death. He was astounded to discover that the animal that threatened his life and that of his daughter immediately reverted to his wife's body. Implying that his wife was a witch who had transmogrified herself into a fierce lioness to kill and devour him and his daughter, he petitioned the court to acquit him of the charge of murder since he had killed his wife in self-defense. In court, however, he put up a defense of demented mental state and mental delusion, claiming that his wife was indeed alive and living somewhere but had refused to contact him.

The case became the subject of intense media coverage in newspapers, radio, television, and on the Internet based on its combined elements of sensationalist speculations and facts. Extensive media attention throughout the trial ensured that a significant number of Ghanaians became acquainted with the case. That a man had killed his wife was not the focus of interest, given the high incidence of uxoricide in the country (Adinkrah 2008b, 2014b). What fascinated the public was the alleged circumstances of the murder. Some speculated that the murder was entirely and intricately orchestrated by the defendant. Others surmised that the murder was an instrumental or goal-oriented behavior by the defendant designed to pave the way for remarriage to a new lover. Still others speculated that the murder was the result of an argument that escalated to an unplanned lethal assault. Many more speculated that the assailant was a chronic wife beater who finally killed his victim after years of abuse. Although it took five years for the murder case to be finally legally disposed of in the courts, public interest in the murder did not wane. The judicial outcome of the case was transmitted via local newspapers, television, radio, and the Internet where it reached thousands of Ghanaians at home and abroad (Amanor 1999a; Sah 2004).

According to evidence presented in court, at the time of the murder the assailant and his wife had been married for six years. The relationship between the couple had become strained in the years immediately prior to the homicide, with the defendant recurrently picking quarrels with the wife, whom he blamed for his supposed financial woes and lack of progress in life. In the months leading to the homicide, the assailant alleged that he had experienced several recurrent nightmares in which he saw his wife transformed into several fierce creatures before attempting to devour him and his daughter. He consulted a witch doctor who told him that his wife was a witch and her malevolent witchcraft was responsible for his economic difficulties and his recurrent nightmares. The witch doctor offered him a powdery substance with instructions that he sprinkle the substance in his bedroom for three consecutive days. The assailant asserted that following the administration of the substance, his nightmares grew more vivid and intense. According to his statement to police, on the third night he was awakened from a deep slumber to the raucous sound of a wild lioness in his bedroom. He grabbed a handy crossbar and bludgeoned the lion to death but was flabbergasted when the form of the lioness immediately reverted back into his wife's body.

Although the defendant had voluntarily confessed to murdering his wife, during custodial interrogation with police and in court he sought to contest or fight the charges against him by claiming psychological delusion. The trial jury, however, believed that the uxoricidal killing was premeditated, and sentenced him to die by hanging. The judge concurred and imposed the mandatory sentence of death.

A major and recurrent theme in public debates surrounding this witchcraft case was the issue of whether a person could legitimately kill another person and then go to court to invoke a purported witch assault as a defense for the murder. Some opined that because the assailant genuinely believed that he was defending himself against a charging lioness, he should not have been convicted of the crime of murder, but, at most, negligent or reckless homicide. Others argued that the court's acceptance of such a legal defense would set a dangerous precedent, opening a floodgate of crimes in which defendants killed with malice while claiming imaginary witch assaults as justification.

Discussion and Implications

The Accra murder case trial drew hundreds of spectators from all quarters of Accra and beyond. Accounts by journalists covering the trial described hundreds of spectators surrounding the courthouse, attempting to catch a glimpse of the defendant or to listen to his testimony. In this trial, as in the previous two cases, we see snippets of witchcraft ideology.

First, we see the very prominent role of dreams. In the nights leading up to the homicide, the defendant had been having dreams in which he saw his tormentor morph into several vicious animals that tried to kill him. This case exemplifies the power of dreams to act as catalysts to witch hunts. As reiterated throughout this book, in Ghana dreams are considered a window for deciphering the identity of witches and revealing their activities. Gbenyo Quarshie's dream was interpreted as symbolic of his wife's witch status and of bewitchment. Both interpretations served as triggers for the husband's suspicion of his wife's identity as a witch and her ill intentions toward him. All came to a head on the night of the homicide, when he claimed that he saw his wife transmogrify into a vicious lioness that threatened to kill him, and against whom he allegedly took action to protect himself and his daughter. Second, as is usually the case with violent witch hunts, the defendant felt aggrieved by the witchcraft activities of the accused witch. In this case the wife, whom he suspected of using her witchcraft to cause him serious financial misfortune, was the victim. Gbenyo's attribution of his wife's alleged witchcraft to his lack of socioeconomic advancement is also consistent with Ghanaian beliefs about witchcraft. Ghanaians often attribute misfortune to the machinations of witchcraft.

The case also confirms the role of soothsayers, herbalists, witch doctors, and Christian ministers in making witch accusations. The defendant went to a soothsayer who confirmed that the nightmares in which his wife morphed into violent creatures were evidence of her witchcraft and his bewitchment. He gave him a powdery substance to sprinkle in his room with a promise that he would see wonders. Later he approached a pastor believing that he had been bewitched by his wife. In Ghana, as in many societies, an important role of soothsayers is to confirm suspicions of witchcraft and to identify the witches. Corroboration by a Christian minister is another important method of dealing with suspicions of witchcraft.

The Tamale Murder Case

In April 2001 a middle-aged woman was fatally assaulted by a gang of four men who accused her of using malevolent witchcraft to afflict a potentially fatal illness on one of their family members. One of the assailants was convicted and given the death penalty while a coconspirator in the murder plot was convicted and sentenced to prison for life. Two other assailants fled the town; at the time of this writing, they have not been apprehended by law enforcement authorities. The murder occurred in Tamale in the Northern Region of the country where there is rampant fear of witches and where general ill-treatment of putative witches is particularly pronounced. According to the facts surrounding the case, an ailing woman told her husband that she had a dream in which she was being bewitched by a neighbor. Following the disclosure of the dream, the ailing woman's husband, together with the couple's three adult sons, all farmers, went to the house of the suspected witch and made an accusation of witchcraft against her. The four men then ordered the suspected witch to accompany them to the local chief's palace to ascertain the veracity of their charges. The alleged witch, who was in the company of her husband and children when the accusation was made, agreed and followed her accusers to the chief's palace, where the assailants made a formal accusation of witchcraft. The woman offered a formal statement denying an involvement in witchcraft, or of being the source of the woman's illness. Following the testimonies, the chief informed the two factions that he had made prior arrangements to travel to Koforidua, a town in southern Ghana, on that day. The chief advised both factions in the dispute to return home and live amicably while he vowed to resolve the matter after his return.

Later that same day, when the victim's accusers realized that the chief had embarked on his journey, they entered the alleged witch's home armed with clubs, machetes, and other lethal weapons and informed her that they had returned to kill her. By this time, the victim's husband had left for his farm. When the victim's son intervened to protect his mother, the assailants threatened to kill him as well. They dragged the victim to the outskirts of the town where they bludgeoned her to death with clubs and the other objects with which they had armed themselves. The victim's son followed stealthily behind and witnessed the mauling of his mother and fled. Unaware that the victim's son had witnessed the brutal murder, the assailants returned to the son's home and ordered him to go to the outskirts of the town to retrieve his battered mother's body. A post-mortem report revealed multiple bruises on the body of the victim. Following a report of the incident to the local police, two of the assailants were apprehended and remanded to stand trial for the murder while the other two absconded and remain on the run from justice.

Following a jury trial, one of the defendants was convicted of one count each of conspiracy to commit murder and of murder. He was sentenced to death by hanging. His father, a codefendant, was convicted of conspiracy to commit murder and sentenced to life imprisonment. While delivering the judgment before a packed courtroom audience, the presiding judge, Victor Doegah, was moved to express his disgust at the spate of witch killings and the way elderly women were being treated in northern Ghana and the rest of the country. The Northern Region of the country is the scene of some of the most brutal acts committed against suspected witches. Here, witch hunts are characterized by brutal and degrading acts, including torture, lynchings, violent exorcisms, trials by ordeal, and banishment from communities. The judge sounded a stern warning to Ghanaian citizens to refrain from wanton accusations of elderly women as witches and to end physical assaults on alleged witches. He warned that the justice system would take drastic measures against individuals who resorted to vigilantism against suspected witches. In his own words, "The court will not spare anybody caught taking the law into his or her own hands to mete out instant justice to people, especially women perceived as witches" (Orhin 2003, 1).

General Discussion

This chapter has explored the role of witchcraft trials in the dissemination and perpetuation of witchcraft beliefs in Ghana. The analysis shows that witch trials contribute to the dissemination of information about witchcraft. It also confirms many of the extant beliefs about witch phenomena in Ghanaian society. For example, in Ghana females predominate as victims in witch hunts and imputations of witchcraft. In both the Accra and Tamale murder cases, those who suffered lethal victimization were female. In the two civil cases—the Somanya witchcraft case and the Kobua case—concerning witchcraft imputation, all but one of those accused of being witches were female.

Second, these cases demonstrate the importance of dreams in revealing imminent bewitchment and in encouraging imputations of witchcraft. In the Accra murder trial, the assailant's dream of his wife transmogrifying into vicious creatures led to a dream interpretation that imputed witchcraft to the wife, an event that subsequently led to him murdering her. In the Somanya case a young girl's dream of seeing her family maidservant near her bed led to an imputation of witchcraft against the young woman and several other people in the community and generated a defamation lawsuit. In the Tamale murder case, an ailing woman's dream led to a witchcraft allegation against a neighboring woman and the subsequent lynching of the latter.

From the trials, we also learn about the malevolent activities of alleged witches who are blamed for a range of misfortunes. In the Accra murder case, a man's economic woes were blamed on the alleged witchcraft activities of his wife. In the Tamale case, a woman's illness was blamed on the accused witch. In the Somanya witchcraft case, the mechanical troubles of a man's car were among a myriad of mishaps blamed on witchcraft. The trials also perpetuated long-held beliefs about nocturnal witches' meetings. Both Kobua and Afua provided details about secret nocturnal revelries. During her oral testimony, Kobua described nocturnal witch activity, including feeding at a refuse dump on witches' feeding grounds. Similarly, Afua, the self-confessed witch in the Somanya case described vibrant witch activities, including partying, nocturnal cooking, and feasting atop the Osudoku mountains. She related how she and the accused witches traveled to their meeting grounds. Kobua confessed to having participated in witches' assemblies. In short, information from trial testimonies helped perpetuate existing popular beliefs about the powers of witches.

The following chapter addresses lethal victimization of accused witches as the ultimate form of witch persecution. In addition to providing a general analysis of witchcraft-related homicides, the chapter provides case summaries of homicides that involved witchcraft accusations against the victim.

Chapter 7

WITCH KILLINGS

This chapter explores witch killings in contemporary Ghana as the ultimate form of witchcraft persecution. Data obtained through content analysis of local Ghanaian newspapers, news agencies, and Web sites were used to describe the scope and patterns of witch homicides in the country over a thirty-three-year period, from 1980 to 2012. These data allow for a criminological analysis of cases of violent witchcraft persecution that had lethal outcomes, including identifying victim and offender characteristics, victim and offender relationships, and the situational contexts of Ghanaian witch killings. A primary aim of this chapter is to understand witchcraft-related homicides with a view to diminish their incidence. A thorough understanding of witch hunts in Ghana requires that we capture the central features of the phenomenon including the situational elements and contexts of these crime events. Ultimately, the root causes of witch killings must be identified if this phenomenon is to be eliminated.

Data Sources

The data analyzed in this chapter were collected in Ghana between 2004 and 2012 during several research trips to the country. In the absence of comprehensive and reliable official data on homicide in general and witchcraft-related homicides in particular in Ghana, the study relied on content analyses of homicide case reports appearing in the leading Ghanaian national daily newspaper, the *Daily Graphic,* as the primary source of information for incidents of witchcraft-related homicides. Founded in

1950, the *Daily Graphic* is one of only two national dailies in the country. A readership survey conducted in 2001 by an independent research organization revealed that the *Daily Graphic* was the most widely read newspaper in the country (see "*Graphic* Still No. 1" 2001). The paper's favorable reputation is attributed to its accuracy of reporting and depth of news coverage. Regarding crime coverage, trained investigative reporters from the paper are usually at crime scenes and are often in attendance at court trials, which gives them access to reliable crime data in the reportage of crime stories. For this research, all stories on witchcraft-related homicides appearing in the *Daily Graphic* from 1980 to 2012 were selected, photocopied, and systematically analyzed to identify the sociodemographic profile of offenders and victims, precipitating circumstances, the mode of killing, and, where available, the criminal justice outcomes in each case. In Ghana, with a homicide rate of about 2.0 per 100,000, lethal violence is relatively rare and therefore generates considerable media interest (Adinkrah, 2014a). Homicide events receive extensive publicity in both the local print and electronic media. Given the widespread public interest in witchcraft phenomena in the society, witchcraft-related homicides engender even greater levels of interest and readership, with newspapers selling particularly rapidly when carrying stories involving the killing of alleged witches.

I obtained supplementary information from extensive reviews of other Ghanaian dailies and weeklies, including the *Mirror,* the *Ghanaian Times,* and the *Weekly Spectator.* In addition, I scoured Web sites featuring Ghanaian news and information (e.g., Ghanaweb.com, Myzongo.com, Ghanatoday.com and Ghanamma.com) for corroborative information whenever necessary.

Extent of Witch Murders

This study identified forty victims of witchcraft-related homicides in published media sources. However, the actual number of witch murders that occurred in Ghana during the study period cannot be determined precisely and it is highly probable that this figure grossly underestimates the real scope of witch-related killings. There are several reasons for this. First, the various print and electronic media may not have reported all instances of witch homicides. Second, some witchcraft-related homicides might have been misclassified as accidents, suicides, mortality from illnesses, or deaths from undetermined causes. The police force in Ghana is underresourced and does not have sufficient tools for solving crime (Adinkrah 2005). Currently many deaths in Ghana are not autopsied due to the lack of logistical resources. There is also a shortage of pathologists to perform autopsies in cases of suspicious death. In 2008 it was reported that only four hospitals in Ghana had practicing pathologists; it was not uncommon for one pathologist to perform thirty post mortem examinations in a single day (Darko-Mensah and Lartey 2008). This makes it difficult to ascertain the exact cause of death in many instances of suspected homicides. Third, because murder is a capital offense in Ghana, perpetrators of witchcraft-related homicides often go to extensive lengths to conceal their crime. In 2009 it was estimated that only 62 percent of births and 24 percent of deaths occurring in the country were reported to the Births and Deaths Registry (Bentil 2009). These factors may contribute to the underreporting of witchcraft-related homicide cases.

Public Reaction to Witch Murders

In Ghana, information about witch killings typically reaches other parts of the country. The data show a recurrent tendency for witch homicides in the society to generate substantial public interest and widespread media attention. This is due, in large part, to the already strong public interest in the phenomenon of witchcraft. Interestingly, each of the forty homicides identified for the study and profiled in this chapter gained national notoriety. While a few of the cases were featured in televised news broadcasts, all of the cases received either front-page newspaper coverage or coverage in the crime news section of the newspaper. As is typical of homicide cases in Ghana, newspaper journalists and reporters followed the cases from the initial report to the final disposition of the case, regularly issuing updates of arrests, courtroom appearances of witnesses and suspects, and excerpts from trial proceedings. From the moment of initial reportage of the homicide episode to the apprehension of the assailant to the conclusion of the trial and final sentencing, each criminal justice phase was marked by the appearance of massive crowds that converged on the local police station and trial court.

Apart from individual and personal reactions of repulsion, witch killings—particularly those involving multiple victims—typically fueled public concern over witchcraft-related violence. Many Ghanaians that I encountered in the course of this research found this type of murder, especially its vigilante features, particularly disturbing. Some argued the need to deter witch killings by sentencing offenders to long prison terms and by imposing capital punishment for heinous crimes associated with witch hunts. Some advised the courts to utilize draconian punishment to effectively control and prevent the crime. Some urged the government to implement the death penalty by actually executing those sentenced to death for murder. Others raised questions about witchcraft-related murders. Some of the questions posed included, Is witchcraft-related violence more serious today than it was in the past? Are there more witch killings now than there were before, or have the media merely sensationalized a few lethal acts? Why are women more likely than men to be accused of witchcraft? Why are men more likely than women to engage in witch killings?

The data show that vigilante or collective acts of violence against putative witches generally received greater media attention than lethal acts committed by a solitary offender against a lone accused witch. Additionally, attacks on suspected witches resulting in multiple lethal victimizations received greater public attention than those on a single victim. To illustrate, following the outbreak of a cerebrospinal meningitis epidemic in 1997 that claimed over 540 lives in the Northern Region of Ghana, witches were blamed for using witchcraft to cause and spread the disease. In response, several elderly women in the affected community were stoned, burned, or bludgeoned to death by marauding public lynch mobs in a bid to purge the community of witches. Over a period of about six months the incidents garnered massive and sustained coverage in the print and electronic media. As news of the massacre sent shockwaves across the nation and the globe, international pressure soon mounted on the government to take action. In response, the Commission on Human Rights and Administrative Justice organized a roundtable conference in 1998 to collate ideas on the proper way to solve the problem of witch persecution and human righs abuses against putative witches (see "Round Table Conference" 1998).

Sociodemographic Profile of Victims

An inspection of the data revealed that the vast majority of victims of witch killings were female, comprising thirty-four out of the forty victims, or 85 percent. Only six out of the forty victims, or 15 percent, were male. In Ghana females are more likely than males to be accused of witchcraft. The question that arises is, Why are females more likely to be victimized than males?

The data also reveal that the elderly faced a much higher risk of witchcraft homicide victimization than did younger people, although children were also at risk of lethal violence at the hands of family members who accused them of witchcraft. However, the very young had lower rates of homicide victimization in witchcraft-associated homicides. Information regarding the ages of thirty-four out of the forty victims were available in media reports of witchcraft-related homicides. Victims ranged in age from four years old to one hundred years old. The median age was sixty-two years old. In Ghana the common perception is that most witches are elderly and female. Thus, elderly women run a particular risk of being accused of witchcraft. By contrast, a young male has a particularly low chance of being accused of witchcraft.

Sociodemographic Profile of Assailants

Examination of the data revealed that witch-hunting is an overwhelmingly male activity. Most assailants in witchcraft-related homicides were men. Concurrently, a review of the data showed that females were less disposed to commit witch homicides than males. Forty-five persons were arrested by police in connection with the forty witch murders. Of these, thirty-eight, or 84.4 percent, were male.

The ages of assailants were available in twenty-five of the cases. Assailants ranged in age from eighteen to sixty years old. It is notable that in all witch homicides in which the ages of the assailant and victim were provided a younger assailant killed an older victim. The notion in Ghanaian witch lore that witches are disproportionately elderly contributes to a pattern where the young are more likely to regard elders as potential witches.

Social Class and Occupational Status of Victims and Offenders

Most of the victims and offenders in the witchcraft-related murders reviewed here came from low socioeconomic backgrounds. Victims often lacked formal education and were unaware of the legal resources and assistance available for dealing with accusations of witchcraft. Poor, elderly women faced the greatest risk of being victimized. This may also be partly explained by the difficulty that elderly women face in defending themselves against physical assaults. In contrast, the wealthy were never targets of witch homicides.

On the other hand, poor, working-class, young, men tended to be disproportionately represented in the population of assailants. Prevalent among these were unemployed youths, peasant farmers, and casual laborers. It is possible that their unmet needs contributed to frustrations that festered into murder against relatives they suspected or considered responsible for their social or economic woes. The homicide was often the final encounter in protracted conflicts and disputes between the assailant and the victim.

Victim-Offender Relationships

The analysis of data included examining the relationship between the victim and the offender in each case of witchcraft-related homicide. Intrafamilial killings dominated the list of homicides reported during the study period. Twenty-four out of the forty cases, or 60 percent, depicted some form of intrafamilial relationship between the victim and the offender. Perpetrators were usually close kin, including husbands, sons, daughters, nephews, and grandchildren. Ten out of the forty cases (25 percent) involved killings in which the assailant killed his or her mother. In nine out of these ten cases of matricide, the son was the culprit. Two out of the forty cases (5 percent) involved patricide. In both of those cases sons were culprits. In another two cases (5 percent), grandsons killed their grandmothers. In another case of intrafamilial killing, a man murdered his wife. In another two cases (5 percent) of intrafamily murder, brothers killed their sisters, and in another case a man killed his aunt. One man killed his daughter. In one case, a couple was charged with the murder of their son. In the only two cases where the killings were perpetrated by a lone woman, a 65-year-old woman killed her ninety-year-old mother and a 26-year-old woman killed her four-year-old niece. In another incident a man killed his stepson.

Sixteen (40 percent) out of the forty cases involved extrafamilial murders in which neighbors and strangers murdered persons they suspected to be witches. Even in most extrafamilial witch killings, victims and offenders had some kind of relationship with each other.

Witch Killings by Mob Violence

Most witch homicides involved a lethal assault on a single victim by a single offender. Collective acts of violence against putative witches constituted about 20 percent of the cases profiled in this chapter. Nine (22.5 percent) out of the forty persons were killed by a public lynch mob. Mob violence often involved arson where the assailants, in addition to committing the murder, torched the victim's property. Victims of mob violence were often found dead, having suffered lethal assaults with knives or blunt objects. Witchcraft-associated homicides that were perpetrated by a public lynch mob were typically carried out by young males. In all cases of mob violence examined in this chapter, males constituted the overwhelming majority of the arrested mobsters.

Instances of vigilante style mob violence were highest in the northern regions of the country. This must be placed within the context of witchcraft beliefs in these regions that make mob violence a more accepted method of dealing with witches. In contrast to Akan beliefs where direct bewitchment is only possible within the matrikin, witchcraft beliefs among ethnic groups in northern Ghana include the belief that witches have the capacity to directly bewitch any nonrelatives, which would include complete strangers. This means that droughts, famine, plagues, and other calamities affecting entire communities can be caused by one witch or a cadre of witches who have no relationship with their victims. Entire communities, then, come together to extirpate the witch in order to alleviate the witchcraft spell inflicted on them. Because Akan witchcraft beliefs focus on bewitchment of matrikin, witchcraft accusations are more likely to be considered a family matter best confined to and resolved within the privacy of the family. Compared with a marauding mob of neighbors and strangers, relatives may also exercise more restraint in dealing with a family member accused of witchcraft—an accusation that may itself meet with controversy as individual family members dispute a witchcraft charge leveled against another family member and come to the defense of the accused witch.

Location of Witch Killings

Regarding the settings of homicides, a large proportion of victims were slain in their homes or adjacent environs. The predominance of domestic settings among homicide scenes stems from the intrafamilial nature of many conflicts. Four witch killings involving mob action occurred in public arenas. Two witch homicides occurred in fetish groves of fetish priests following the performance of purification rituals associated with exorcisms.

Homicides associated with witchcraft accusations were more common in rural communities. Only two incidents occurred in urban locales—one in Accra, the capital, and another in Kumasi, the second-largest city in the country. Hence, living in a rural area was a key risk factor in witchcraft-related homicide victimization. The data were further analyzed into spatial distribution based on Ghana's ten administrative regions. Regarding regional distribution of witch killings, the three administrative regions in the northern part of the country (Upper East, Upper West, and Northern Regions) had a disproportionate share of the witch killings. Vigilante violence in pursuit of witches was also more common in this part of Ghana.

Temporal Aspects

In the northern regions of the country, an increase in witch killings is associated with periods of epidemic disease (e.g., buruli ulcer, cerebrospinal meningitis) and periods of natural catastrophes (e.g., droughts) in which cases putative witches are blamed for the calamities. Following the outbreak of a cerebrospinal meningitis epidemic in 1997 in the Northern Region, the people in the afflicted territory scapegoated elderly women in the community, resulting in the massacre of elderly women suspected to be witches.

Modus Operandi

The data reveal that witch homicides were perpetrated by a variety of methods, including beating with blunt objects, cutting with knives, stoning, and shooting with a firearm. Two victims died when they were forced to drink a poisonous concoction in a purificatory ritual. Three accused witches sustained fatal injuries from machete attacks, whereas another three victims were bludgeoned to death with sticks and pieces of timber. The relatively small number of homicides committed with firearms stems in part from the strict licensure laws on the ownership and possession of firearms in Ghana.

Extent of Premeditation and Prior Planning

The study examined the extent to which planning and premeditation preceded the commission of witchcraft-related homicides or whether they were spontaneous acts done in the heat of passion, committed with little forethought. In some cases longstanding animosities and suspicions of witchery degenerated into accusations of witchcraft and verbal altercations erupted into violent physical assaults. A few were meticulously planned.

Motivations behind Witch Killings

This research examined offender motivations for committing homicide against a putative witch. In this section I examine the many facets of motivation in witchcraft-related homicides.

In a significant number of cases, the motivation for witch killings was to avenge some grievance harbored against the witch. As was elaborated in chapter 2 on witchcraft beliefs in Ghana, witches are blamed for inflicting all manner of physical ills and misfortune on their victims. In Case 7.8, a Ghanaian citizen who had been living in West Germany flew back to Ghana and committed matricide; spiritual authorities he consulted while in Ghana attributed his physical ill-health to his mother's witchcraft. Determining that only the physical elimination of his mother would lead to his recovery, he fatally wounded his mother with a machete. In Case 7.11, a patient with epilepsy brutally mauled to death a sixty-year-old woman in his community after linking his disease to the victim's witchcraft. In Case 7.14, a young man blamed his sexual impotence on his sister whom he lethally assaulted.

Accused witches were also blamed for causing, spreading, or intensifying disease epidemics and illnesses in their communities. Alleged witches were blamed for droughts, crop failure, famines, auto accidents, premature deaths, unemployment, and other economic hardships. In other words, alleged witches were cast as the architects of every form of misfortune. In Case 7.4 a violent mob fatally assaulted three women accused of using witchcraft to cause and spread cerebrospinal meningitis in the local community. In Case 7.5, a group of eight masked men fatally attacked two elderly women in their community who were accused of using malevolent witchcraft to cause the death of a young man in the community. In Case 7.22, residents in a local community, unable to explain a number of mysterious deaths in the area, approached a local witch doctor to provide divinatory services. When the diviner identified a local resident as the purported witch, an irate mob lynched the person.

Analysis of data revealed that suspicions over the use of witchcraft to afflict some form of physical malady or illness was the single most cited reason for perpetrating lethal violence against an alleged witch. Examples of physical ailments attributed to witchcraft in homicide cases include epilepsy, abdominal pains, physical paralysis, sexual impotence, AIDS, alcoholism, and barrenness. In Case 7.6, the offender placed the blame for his alcoholism on his mother and grandmother. Their protracted conflict climaxed into a verbal altercation that culminated with a lethal assault. Fear and suspicion that the accused witch had used witchcraft to cause mental illness ranked second among the list of motivations inciting lethal violence against the suspected witch. Perpetrators acted to avenge the affliction or to cause the victim to cease bewitching them.

One of the central charges leveled against alleged witches is that they inflicted bad luck on the assailant. Victims in witchcraft-related murders were also blamed for the assailants' lack of financial or material success in life. In nine of the forty cases (22.5 percent), the assailants blamed the victims for their failure to obtain stable employment or to progress in life. In Case 7.28, a farmer killed his elderly aunt and threatened to deal similarly with two other family members upon his release from prison. According to him, the trio had caused his financial and other woes in life through their witchcraft.

Analysis of data further shows that several assailants killed suspected witches to avenge the deaths of relatives and friends they believed had been caused by witchcraft. In Case 7.21, the assailant attributed a centenarian's long life to the latter's witchcraft, blaming the victim for several deaths in the assailant's family. He killed the elderly man for his exceptional longevity that he could only explain as the result of his spiritual sacrifice of several family members that had passed away over the years.

Some witch homicides were fueled by a dream or nightmare in which the assailant claimed to have seen the homicide victim bewitching the assailant or in which the assailant believed his bewitchment was imminent. In Case 7.1, profiled in chapter 6 on witchcraft trials, a husband who killed his wife attributed his homicidal behavior to a nightmare in which he saw a lioness charging at him. He bludgeoned to death what he thought was a lioness only to find that the lioness he killed had morphed into the body of his wife. In Case 7.16, a young man interpreted a dream in which he saw his body parts being shared by a group of witches as a premonition of his physical demise, accusing his stepmother of witchcraft. He confronted her with the information; when she denied the accusation, he butchered her with a machete.

Some assailants were suspected by family members or police investigators of abusing drugs and alcohol at the time of the homicide. Some witch killings were suspected to be the work of emotionally or mentally disturbed youths. Cases 7.3 and 7.20 involved assailants who attributed their psychiatric illnesses to the witchcraft of their mothers, subsequently killing them. In Case 7.3, a young man absconded from a psychiatric facility where he was a patient and lethally assaulted his mother whom he blamed for using witchcraft to cause his chronic mental illness. Case 7.10 involved an assailant who attributed his epilepsy to his mother.

Dispositional Outcomes

In Ghana, premeditated homicide constitutes murder and a conviction of the charge elicits a death sentence, but no execution has taken place in the country since 1993 (Adinkrah 2008b). Dispositional outcomes were available for only three of the forty (8 percent) homicides profiled in this book. In two cases the assailants were convicted of murder and sentenced to death. In one case the assailant was convicted of manslaughter and sentenced to life imprisonment. A number of factors contribute to the absence of information on the dispositional outcome of the majority of cases. First, the legal outcome for some cases was not reported in the *Daily Graphic* or in other media. Second, in Ghana there is a significant time lapse between the time of initial arrest of a murder suspect and the final disposition of a homicide case in a court of law. Homicide cases in the country are routinely referred by local police to the Attorney General's Department in Accra for legal advice. It is not uncommon for a case to be held in abeyance in that department for ten years or longer. Third, in many murder cases assailants are referred to psychiatric hospitals for evaluation to determine their fitness to stand trial. Such evaluations typically take considerable time. There is evidence that in some cases, even after the psychiatric hospital makes its evaluation and finds the defendant mentally fit to stand trial, the referring police are reluctant to arrest the defendant. In 2008 the medical director of the Accra Psychiatric Hospital cited the Ghana Police Service's dereliction of duty in these cases. In December 2008 the acting medical officer of Pantang Hospital noted that "patients referred to the hospital by court for observation, evaluation and treatment were often forgotten by the authorities and they become a burden on the hospital" (Ohene-Asiedu 2008b, 31).

Case Information

Below are case histories of forty of the witch murders that occurred in Ghana from 1980 to 2012. In these stories we see examples of homicide as the ultimate form of witchcraft persecution and also see how the beliefs about witchcraft, bewitchment, and witches drive this form of homicide.

Case 7.1. "I Thought I Was Killing a Lion"

This case was briefly described in the introduction of this book and profiled more extensively in chapter 6 on witchcraft trials. In this case a carpenter bludgeoned his wife to death with a piece of timber (Amanor 1999a). Days before the incident, the man had taken the couple's five-year-old daughter to a local pastor for spiritual healing after the child fell ill. When meeting with the pastor, the carpenter told him about nightmares he had been having in which his wife morphed into different creatures and tried to kill him. The pastor gave him a powdery mixture with the instructions to sprinkle it around his bedroom. But after administering the substance in his room, his nightmares worsened. According to the carpenter, the night of the murder, a lioness entered his room and charged at him while he slept. He fatally clubbed the animal in defense of his life and that of his wife and daughter. It was only after the animal lay dying that he realized it was actually his wife.

Case 7.2. The Exorcism Ritual That Turned Fatal

The murders of the elderly women described in this vignette sparked a heated discussion in the Ghanaian legislature, prompting calls for "an immediate investigation into the circumstances leading to the death of two elderly women at Klomadaboe, a village near Akosombo" (Buabeng and Kofoya-Tetteh 1998, 11). In November 1998 the *Daily Graphic* reported a story in which two women, both eighty-five years old, were pronounced witches by a prophet of a healing church (Buabeng 1998; Buabeng and Kofoya-Tetteh 1998). According to the report, the two women were subsequently forced to drink concoctions prepared by the prophet in a bid to exorcise them of the witchcraft. The two women died shortly after consuming the potion.

Case 7.3. Mentally Ill Son Kills the Mom He Blamed for His Illness

A 58-year-old woman sustained fatal machete wounds at the hands of her 24-year-old son ("Son Butchers Mum" 2001). The son, allegedly a psychiatric patient, lethally assaulted his mother on suspicion that she was a witch and that the genesis of his mental maladies lay in his mother's evil witchcraft. Media reports indicated that the assailant had been committed to a psychiatric hospital but absconded. A day prior to the matricide, the victim had sought assistance from relatives to return her son to the hospital. Siblings of the assailant disputed the witchcraft accusation made by their brother.

Case 7.4. Mob Lynches Three Elderly Women

As is typical of witch persecutions that involve mob action, the lethal violence against women contained in this case occurred during a period of great crises and misfortune. In March 1997 an irate mob physically attacked and subsequently lynched three middle-aged women in the village of Yoggu in the Northern Region (Safo 1997). The angry crowd accused the three women of using witchcraft to spread disease in the community. The murders coincided with a cerebrospinal meningitis epidemic that claimed over five hundred lives.

Case 7.5. Two Women Stoned to Death

In Ghana there is a common perception that death is unnatural unless the deceased was aged. Witchcraft is often suspected when a person in the prime of life falls seriously ill or dies. Consistent with these beliefs, bewitchment was invoked to explain the death of a young man in Kumbungu in the northern division of the country in January 1998 (Hushie and Al-hassan 1998). Three days after his death, about eight masked vigilantes avenged his death by bludgeoning and stoning to death two women, aged fifty-five and sixty years, on suspicion that the pair were witches and had caused the man's death by malevolent witchcraft.

Case 7.6. Man Kills Grandmother over His Alcoholism

In this case a man's chronic alcohol abuse appeared to have played a piv-otal role in his inability to secure gainful employment (Ephson 2001). He was convinced that his economic failures were due to witchery. The assail-ant, a 35-year-old university graduate, chronically abused alcohol and lost several lucrative jobs. He sought the services of a witch doctor for explana-tion into his financial hardships. Upon divination, the fetish priest stated that he had been afflicted with these misfortunes by the evil witchcraft of his aging mother and maternal grandmother. Determined to transform his luck, the assailant drank heavily on the day of the murder, grabbed a machete, and assaulted his mother and grandmother with it. The grand-mother perished but his mother survived with severe lacerations.

Case 7.7. "My Mother Killed My Son"

This case shows that accusations of witchcraft as well as fatal assaults against a supposed witch are not always made by men against women. In this case a 65-year-old woman fatally assaulted her ninety-year-old mother on the grounds that the elderly mother had killed her own grand-son through bewitchment (Ablekpe 1996). The son, a Ghanaian émigré to Guinea, returned home to visit his family but died a few days later. Follow-ing the final funeral rites, the assailant branded her mother a witch, an accusation vehemently denied by the victim. Enraged and unconvinced of her mother's denials, the assailant grabbed the victim's walking stick and assaulted her with it, hitting her on the head and killing her instantly.

Case 7.8. Son Kills His Mother, Who He Blamed for His Chronic Abdominal Pain

This case demonstrates that residence in a Western, industrialized society does not preclude the retention of traditional witchcraft beliefs. In this case the assailant had been living in Germany for thirteen years prior to returning to Ghana (Sam 1996). While in Germany, the offender developed acute stomach pains as well as pains in one leg for which medical doctors could find neither a cause nor a cure. After returning to Ghana he made another round of visits to doctors without receiving a diagnosis for his condition. It is not uncommon in Ghana for doctors who have difficulties diagnosing a condition to inform patients that their illness cannot be treated through conventional medical procedures. This is widely interpreted as meaning that the illness has been caused by witchcraft or sorcery and requires spiritual remedies. It was with this interpretation in mind that the assailant attended several spiritual churches to seek treatment for his mysterious ailment. He was advised by some members of the clergy that his ailment was of a spiritual nature and that his mother was to blame. On the day of the homicide, the assailant invited his mother to accompany him to a church in a neighboring village. Along the way, the assailant turned to his mother, accusing her of being the source of his illness, and demanded that she cure him. The victim denied her son's charges of witchcraft and told him she would be unable to alleviate his condition. He then produced a hidden machete and butchered his mother on the spot.

Case 7.9. Man Kills Pair He Blamed for His Bewitchment

A 34-year-old man killed his stepmother and her sixteen-year-old son because he was convinced that the two had cast a spell on him (Kyei-Boateng 1996). The assailant accused the pair of inflicting incurable diseases on him and for making it impossible for him to succeed financially. The assailant told police that a week prior to the murders he was physically attacked by a hawk while working on his farm. He claimed he fell ill after returning home and lost his appetite. He imputed the hawk attack to witchcraft. According to the assailant, a day prior to the murder, he overheard the two victims discussing their victory in successfully "overpowering him through spiritual intervention." Infuriated by what he allegedly overheard, he grabbed a rifle the next morning, loaded it, and shot the two, killing both instantly.

Case 7.10. "Free Me from Mental Illness"

A 23-year-old man clubbed his 56-year-old mother to death on suspicion that she was responsible for causing his mental illness (Ablekpe 2000). The homicide occurred at a church healing center where the assailant, accompanied by his mother, was receiving spiritual healing for a psychiatric condition. The assailant had been behaving abnormally for a period of two years prior to the homicide and had sought psychiatric help to no avail. He had been referred to a healing center where his condition had allegedly improved considerably. On the day of the murder, the assailant helped his mother prepare the local *fufu* meal. After the meal, his mother retired to a section of the healing center to converse with other women. The assailant grabbed the pestle, a long, thick, and heavy wooden club-shaped implement used to pound the *fufu,* and assaulted his mother with it. The victim died from massive bleeding due to a ruptured spleen. In his statement to police, the assailant attributed his psychological ailments to his mother's witchcraft and justified his murderous action as a design to extricate himself from the snares of her sinister witchcraft power.

Case 7.11. "You Are Responsible for My Epilepsy"

In March 1999 the *Mirror,* a Ghanaian weekly newspaper, reported the brutal slaying of an elderly woman accused of witchery (Aziz 1999). According to the story, "Farmer Clubs Woman, 60 to Death," a thirty-year-old man fatally assaulted a sixty-year-old woman with a pestle. The assailant, who had earlier in the day been performing community service with a group of men in his village, was believed to have abandoned the work party during their lunch recess. He went into the victim's compound where he brutally killed her through "merciless pounding" with the pestle. Following an alarm for help raised by the victim, other members of the work crew rushed to the victim's aid. However, their assistance came too late: the victim had been battered to death. The assailant's actions were based on the suspicion that the victim was a witch who had used her witchcraft to afflict him with a number of physical ailments. Prominent among the list of physical ailments purported to have been inflicted on the assailant by the victim was epilepsy. He allegedly killed her "as a means to liberate myself from the bondage of the evil spirit of the old lady." Following a charge of murder, police authorities arranged for the defendant to undergo a psychiatric assessment to ascertain his state of mind.

Case 7.12. "You Are Hindering My Prosperity"

A story, "Man Beats Grandma to Death," reported the case of how neighbors' efforts to rescue a frail, elderly woman from a fatal beating from a young grandson, proved futile (Asare-Buakyi 1994). Indeed, so incensed was the crowd that congregated near the scene of the crime that the assailant was nearly lynched. According to the *Mirror* of June 11, 1994, a 21-year-old man beat his ninety-year-old maternal grandmother to death because he saw her "as hindering his prosperity" in life. The assailant, who had regularly accused the elderly woman of being a witch, was alone with her in the family home on the day of the murder, and used this occasion to perpetrate the crime. The report further noted that the victim had persistently and vehemently refuted the assailant's consistent claims that she was a witch.

Case 7.13. "One of the Conspirators Is Dead"

In this 1994 case, a 64-year-old-woman was beaten to death by a marauding lynch mob (Fuseini 1994). Her alleged crime was using witchcraft to inflict several incurable diseases, along with paralysis, on a twelve-year-old boy. The murder victim was one of three villagers aged sixty-four, sixty-five, and sixty-seven, who had all been accused of conspiring to kill the young boy by using supernatural means to capture and imprison his soul. Eight years prior to the homicide, the victim had been accused of bewitching the boy when the boy accompanied his grandmother to a funeral at the victim's home. The decision of the community to avenge the boy's ailments and avert his potential death came when, a week prior to the murder, the boy started mentioning the name of the victim during nightmares he purportedly had. In those nightmares, the boy claimed he saw the victim charging at him with a knife. His shouts of "[name of the victim] leave me," "[name of the victim] don't kill me" were interpreted as evidence that the victim was bewitching the boy. Following persistent nightmares and the incessant calling of the victim's name, the matter was referred to the chief of the village who summoned a sorcerer to use divination to determine the alleged witch. Following divination, the sorcerer allegedly confirmed the bewitchment, claiming the twelve-year-old boy had been turned into an antelope for an imminent witch cannibal feast. When the accused witches denied the bewitchment, they were set upon by a public lynch mob and beaten severely enough to result in the death of one of the women and the hospitalization of the other two.

Case 7.14. "Give Me Back My Manhood"

A 24-year-old man lethally assaulted his sister whom he accused of using malevolent witchcraft to make him impotent (Tetteh 1996). In a story captioned "Give Back My 'Power,'" which appeared in the March 9, 1996, edition of the *Mirror*, a young man reportedly killed his forty-year-old sister when his ultimatum that she "restore my manhood or be killed" was not heeded. According to the media report, two years prior to the murder, the man, who had been experiencing persistent nightmares in which he dreamed he was copulating with his sister, consulted a fetish priest about his sexual impotence. The fetish priest is alleged to have blamed the man's sister for his physical condition. The sister was brought before the fetish priest and was alleged to have admitted responsibility for her brother's condition, claiming that she belonged to a witch coven that killed and consumed its victims. Due to her love for her brother, she had decided to exchange her brother's manhood for his soul in order to spare him physical death. The victim was summoned to perform some rituals with local herbs to restore the man's sexual potency. When after the ritual the man had not regained his sexual potency, the man pounced on his sister, hitting her on the head with a cudgel, killing her instantly.

Case 7.15. "My Mother Is a Witch"

A man who blamed his mother for his general lack of success in life and for the death of his six-year-old son, bludgeoned the 45-year-old woman to death (Bekoe 1992). The 29-year-old man intervened during a violent altercation between his wife and his mother. The altercation had been sparked by his wife's allegation that her mother-in-law had bewitched their son to death. The man, who had also harbored a similar suspicion all along and therefore nursed a grudge against his mother as a result, darted into his room, retrieved a sharp machete, and brutally slashed his mother to death. After temporarily escaping into the bush, the assailant turned himself in to a local police station, claiming he had been under the influence of drugs at the time of the crime and did not know what he was doing.

Case 7.16. "My Stepmother Is Out to Destroy Me"

In an article captioned "Death Dream," the *Weekly Spectator* of October 28, 1995 reported the incident of a 24-year-old farmer who killed his stepmother who he claimed was a witch and was about to destroy him spiritually (Atta 1995). According to the story, prior to the homicide, the assailant had a dream in which he saw his body parts being shared by a group of witches that included his stepmother. The next day, the assailant paid a visit to his stepmother at her home. Upon arrival, he saw the victim preparing palm-fruit soup. Because in Ghanaian witchcraft beliefs palm fruit soup, with its concomitant red palm oil, symbolizes the blood of whoever a witch consumes, the assailant became convinced that the previous night's dream was denotative of his stepmother's apparent attempt to destroy him by malevolent witchcraft. Without hesitation, he grabbed a machete and inflicted several knife wounds on the victim, killing her instantly. The screams of the victim attracted an elderly neighbor to the scene. The older woman was also assaulted with the machete, sustaining severe knife wounds in the process.

Case 7.17. "My Grandmother Is Responsible for My Mental Illness"

An eighteen-year-old student murdered his 86-year-old grandmother on the grounds that the victim was a witch who had been haunting him spiritually (Ankamah 1995). According to the facts of the case, the assailant, who resided in the same home as the victim along with several other family members, had, for some time, been acting strangely. During his interrogation by the police, the assailant claimed that the night prior to the lethal assault he had had a dream in which he saw a group of people including his grandmother pursuing him, with some spiritual forces urging him to pick up a pestle to bludgeon the elderly woman. The assailant, who had always suspected his grandmother of being responsible for his mental condition, acted on the urgings of the forces in his dream, grabbing a pestle and battering the grandmother's head and legs, killing her instantly.

Case 7.18. Lethal Consequences of a Nightmare

A 29-year-old farm laborer awoke from a nightmare and killed his four-year-old daughter (Haizel 2003). His intended victim was his wife, whom he claimed to be a witch. She managed to sneak out of the family bedroom to avoid the assault. Following the lethal assault on his daughter, the man fatally assaulted two dogs and two fowls in his compound. On the day of the murder, the assailant's wife was awakened at 1:30 A.M. in the morning by the piercing screams of her husband. The man, apparently having a nightmare, accused his wife of being a witch and threatened to kill her and their two children if they did not leave the house immediately. Fearing an imminent assault, the wife managed to flee the house with one of the children. She returned shortly with the assistance of a neighbor to retrieve the other child only to discover that her husband had carried out the lethal threat.

Case 7.19. "Because of My Father, I Can't Find a Wife"

In this case of patricide, a thirty-year-old farmer struck his father on the head with a stick, sending the elderly man into a coma; he died without coming out of the coma (Seini 1998). The lethal assault was precipitated by the assailant's suspicion that his father was a wizard who had used his witchcraft to cast a spell on him, an accusation that the father repeatedly denied. The young man had attributed his difficulties in successfully finding a wife to his father's evil witchcraft. The man had nursed considerable resentment toward his father over this and when a quarrel ensued over another matter, the man responded by striking his father. A postmortem examination revealed that the victim died from severe head injuries sustained in the attack.

Case 7.20. "My Mother Is Responsible for My Mental Illness"

In this case of matricide, a mentally deranged thirty-year-old man killed his 52-year-old mother whom he suspected of causing his mental illness (Asare 1999). Sources close to the assailant reported that the young man developed a mental illness about five years prior to the homicide, and had been in and out of a mental hospital. On the day of the murder, witnesses claim they saw the assailant sharpening a machete for more than six hours. However, no one approached him or enquired about his intentions regarding the knife. At about 10:30 P.M. that evening, the assailant made a visit to his mother with the machete hidden in his clothes. While there, he asked her if he could borrow some kerosene for his lamp. When his mother crouched to pick up the kerosene, he attacked her with the machete, and she sustained severe and fatal injuries. In an interview with police, the man revealed that in killing his mother, he believed that his mental illness would abate.

Case 7.21. The Centurian Wizard

A 34-year-old farmer shot to death his neighbor, a 100-year-old blind man, whom he suspected of causing the deaths of several members of his family (Boateng, 1997). The incident occurred in the afternoon while the victim was enjoying fresh air under a shade tree in his compound. According to witness accounts, the blind victim was guided into his room by a live-in caregiver when it threatened to rain. At around the same time, the assailant, armed with a shotgun, came into the victim's compound and entered his room under the guise of obtaining shelter from the rain. He immediately opened fire, killing the victim instantly. When questioned by police, the assailant confessed to the crime, stating that the victim was a wizard who had used his malevolent witchcraft to kill many people in the assailant's family, including his father. At the time of the killing, a woman who lived in the assailant's village was ill and at the point of death. The assailant blamed the victim for the woman's illness and claimed that he killed the elderly blind man in a bid to avert her death.

Case 7.22. The Vigilante Murder of a Wizard

A 56-year-old man was lynched by an angry mob that accused him of using witchcraft power to cause several mysterious deaths in his village (Mensah 1997). The man was lynched shortly after a fetish priestess, whose divinatory services had been engaged by the townsfolk, pronounced him culpable for several baffling deaths that occurred in the town. The townsfolk mobilized the equivalent of about US$40 in public donations to be used to engage the services of the diviner. After performing divination rituals, the priestess announced that the victim was the wizard and had been responsible for the previous deaths. The news report noted that the fetish priestess was taken into police custody and interrogated for her role in the death of the victim.

Case 7.23. Housewife Lynched

This case was profiled in Chapter 6 as the Tamale Murder Case. In this case that occurred in a suburb of Tamale, a forty-year-old housewife was lethally assaulted by an angry mob that accused her of causing the death of her husband's sixteen-year-old nephew ("Housewife Lynched" 1995). Following the lynching, the victim's body was dragged to a nearby refuse dump where it was collected the following morning by the city police. Not satisfied with the lynching, the enraged mob set fire to the victim's house, completely destroying it .

Case 7.24. "You Are Responsible for My Lack of Progress in Life"

This case occurred in a small rural community in the Central Region of Ghana (Nuhhu-Billa 2005). A nineteen-year-old man hacked his eighty-year-old grandmother to death on suspicion that the octogenarian victim was a witch responsible for his lack of progress in life. According to the story, the assailant had on numerous occasions accused his grandmother of responsibility for his financial difficulties. At the time of the murder, the victim was returning home from a church-related choral program at about 9 P.M. when she came upon her grandson, who lived in another house. He offered to walk his grandmother home since, according to him, it was too late for her to travel by herself. Upon reaching her home, the assailant bade the woman goodnight and decided to take another footpath back to town. The woman in turn offered to see the assailant off, but just about nine meters from the house, the assailant pulled out a knife hidden in his clothes and stabbed the woman repeatedly. He then fled the scene of the crime, packed a few belongings, and took refuge in the home of another relative in Kumasi. The family members who learned about the murder turned the assailant in to the police. Following his apprehension by law enforcement authorities, the assailant feigned mental illness, claiming that he butchered an antelope that later turned out to be his beloved grandmother.

Case 7.25. The Child as Accused Witch

A 26-year-old woman locked up her four-year-old niece in a small bedroom and inflicted multiple knife wounds on the child that proved fatal (Penni 1984). The assailant believed that the toddler was a witch who was responsible for her personal difficulties in life, including her inability to conceive more children. At the time of the incident, the assailant had been residing with her sister, brother-in-law, and the victim for about six months. There were no apparent signs of acrimonious family relations. The assailant, a divorcee, however, had lost her only child eight months prior to the murder. On the day of the incident, the father of the four-year-old child had left for work in the morning while the child's mother, the assailant's sister, stepped out to run an errand, entrusting the child to the care of the assailant. Returning about ten minutes later, the mother found that her daughter and her sister were locked up inside the assailant's bedroom. She called out for her daughter and received a response followed by a piercing scream. The assailant refused to open the door despite several pleas from the mother. By the time the door was forced open, the assailant had snuck out and fled into the woods. The victim was found unconscious in a pool of blood and died on arrival at the local hospital.

Case 7.26. "You Are a Young Wizard!"

An elder in a faith healing church was arrested for the murder of a congregant whom the assailant suspected of being a wizard (Mensah 1989). According to the facts of the case, one month prior to the murder, the assailant had lost a child, accusing a 29-year-old male congregant of causing the death through his wizardry. The young man denied the charge. However, unbeknownst to anyone, the elder decided to teach him a lesson. On the day of the lethal assault, the elder was praying for the suspected wizard when he took out a bottle of kerosene, poured it on the victim, and set him ablaze. The victim was rushed to the hospital with severe burns but died "as a result of severe shock, occasioned by severe dehydration due to fluid losses as a result of the burns."

Case 7.27. The Judge's Plea to Ghanaians

A 28-year-old man and his father received a death sentence and a prison life term, respectively, from the Tamale High Court for their roles in murdering a woman whom they accused of witchcraft ("Court Sentences Man" 2003). According to court records, the older man's wife fell ill. A few days later, the ailing woman awoke from sleep and told her husband about a dream in which she was being bewitched by the victim. The husband told his three adult sons about their mother's dream. The sons reacted swiftly, grabbing sticks and besieging the victim's house. They demanded that the alleged witch leave the village immediately. The woman's husband pleaded with the assailants for patience, requesting that they go to the village chief for his wife to prove her innocence. At the chief's palace, the woman vehemently denied the accusation of bewitchment and declined a request to go into a shrine to prove her innocence. To resolve the impasse and determine the veracity of the accusation, the chief asked for a deferment of the case as he needed to travel out of town for a few days. The chief advised the husband to remove his accused wife from the village pending resolution of the case. Before the accused wife could leave, and taking advantage of the chief's departure, the men seized clubs and other implements and raided the suspected witch's house while her husband was away on his farm. They dragged her to the outskirts of the village, then beat her to death with their weapons. Facing imminent arrest, two of the assailants fled from the village, leaving the police to arrest the husband of the ailing woman and one of his sons. Charged with murder, the two were tried by the local High Court. While the son was convicted of murder and received a death sentence, the older man was convicted of conspiracy to commit murder and given a life sentence. During sentencing, the presiding judge seized the opportunity to issue a stern warning to Ghanaians about witchcraft accusations against women, stating that they "should stop accusing innocent women as witches and murdering them." He said the court "would not spare anybody caught taking the law into his or her own hands and meting out instant justice to people, especially women they perceive as witches."

Case 7.28. "My Aunt Is a Witch"

A forty-year-old farmer bludgeoned his 75-year-old aunt to death on suspicion that the aunt was a witch who was responsible for his financial situation and other woes in life (Otchere 2005). As a member of a local spiritual church, the assailant had been attending special prayer sessions organized by the church some weeks prior to the homicide. It was allegedly revealed to him during one of the prayer sessions that three of his relatives, including the victim, were witches and responsible for his problems in life. Following the revelation, the assailant planned the physical annihilation of the accused witches to rescue himself from their clutches. At 8:00 A.M. the following morning, the assailant armed himself with a club and went to his aunt's home where he attacked her, opening a deep gash on her forehead. The victim was rushed to the local hospital but died shortly after arrival. Following his apprehension, the assailant allegedly informed police during interrogation that two additional relatives, whom he also accused of being witches, would suffer a similar fate after his release from jail. He was quoted as saying, "I have finished with one; I am left with two more to complete my task."

Case 7.29. For Refusing to Leave

In this September 2005 case that occurred in the Northern Region, a man who attributed the death of his younger brother to fatal bewitchment, avenged his brother's death by bludgeoning to death the 48-year-old woman he presumed to be responsible ("Yendi Police Arrest Farmer" 2005). According to the facts of the case, a week prior to the murder, the assailant went to the house of the victim and accused her of using witchcraft to kill his brother. He subsequently warned her to leave the village for the neighboring witch sanctuary for her own safety. Insisting on her innocence of the charge of bewitchment, the victim ignored the threat and maintained her residence in the village. On the day of the murder, the assailant arrived at the victim's home with a heavy club and beat her repeatedly over the head, causing her death.

Case 7.30. "My Stepfather Is a Wizard"

A 22-year-old man killed his seventy-year-old stepfather who had been married to his mother for sixteen years ("Man, 22 Allegedly Kills" 2005). The young man suspected that the older man was a maleficent wizard and the source of his physical, social, and economic woes. Having threatened to kill his stepfather on two previous occasions, the young man finally made good on his threat one morning as the elderly victim was bathing. The assailant entered the bathroom with a machete, then proceeded to inflict deep cuts on the victim, slashing and disemboweling him. After the crime, the assailant proclaimed that he had finally extricated himself from the clutches of his witch-tormentor. While fleeing the scene, the young man brandished the blood-soaked murder weapon, threatening to bludgeon anyone who came near him. After he turned menacingly toward his mother and threatened to kill her as well, the assailant was finally overpowered by a gathering crowd and taken to the local police station. What was the impetus for the homicidal attack? Police records show that the assailant, who was epileptic, had returned home from a spiritual healing camp a day prior to the homicide. He was supposed to be receiving treatment for his condition at the camp. Apparently, this was where he was led to believe that he was the victim of the maleficent wizardry of his stepfather.

Case 7.31. The Soccer Incident

The tragic circumstances surrounding this case demonstrate the capriciousness of witchcraft accusations whenever accusers attempt to link disasters or misfortunes to the machinations of an alleged witch. On May 9, 2001, in a tragedy widely reported in the local and international media, 126 Ghanaian soccer fans were crushed and trampled to death in a sports stadium in Accra during a soccer match ("Two Arrested" 2001). After the home team Accra Hearts of Oak scored two late goals to beat the opposing team, Kumasi Asante Kotoko 2 to 1, Kotoko fans reportedly registered their protest by destroying the plastic seats in the tiers of the stadium, throwing them on to the running track surrounding the soccer field. Police personnel on duty at the stadium responded by firing tear gas into the crowd, which led some spectators to retaliate by throwing bottles at the police. Eyewitness reports indicate that the police then intensified the firing of tear gas canisters. As the concentration of tear gas increased in intensity, a panic ensued, causing a stampede in the 40,000-capacity stadium. As spectators scrambled for the exits, they found them locked shut, which led to the suffocation and trampling of victims. A few weeks later, in June 2001 a 54-year-old woman was beaten to death by a group of eight youth at Abutia-Kloe in the Volta Region of the country. According to police, the assailants accused the victim of using witchcraft to cause the stadium disaster. Their accusations stemmed from an incident that reportedly occurred the day of the stadium disaster. Among the spectators who lost their lives was a 25-year-old nephew of the woman. The assailants claimed to have witnessed the woman engaged in a fiery verbal altercation with her nephew hours before he left for the soccer match in Accra. During the burial and funeral of the young man, one of the youths who was a friend of the deceased and who witnessed the quarrel announced that he was possessed by the spirit of the young man. He then proclaimed that the aunt, also in attendance at the funeral, had bewitched him and was responsible for his death. The youths then set upon the woman and beat her to death. The assailants surmised that the deceased woman spiritually followed the young man to the stadium to unleash vengeance on him, setting in motion the events that led to the stadium disaster with the specific intent to kill him.

Case 7.32. Farmer Kills His Sister

A 25-year-old male farmer had for many months been obsessed with the idea that his 45-year-old sister's malevolent witchcraft was impeding his ability to achieve financial prosperity in life (Aklorbortu 2009). In April 2009 he decided to take action to reverse the perceived curse on himself.

In a gruesome assault, he used a machete to decapitate his elder sister. The unrepentant assailant then walked to the local village chief's house and reported his homicide. He was immediately apprehended and turned over to police. According to the case report, prior to the homicide the assailant had confronted his sister and reported her reputed witchery to other family members. He had made persistent demands on his father and other family members to prevail upon the sister to use her mystical powers to reverse the curse and ensure his financial success. When these efforts failed, he decided to take matters into his own hands and put an end to her witchery in the manner he deemed most effective—decapitation of the witch. The incident reportedly occurred on a Sunday afternoon, in full public view of the rest of the family.

Case 7.33. Leaving a Child Wizard to Die

Police in a major city arrested a couple for negligently causing the death of their nine-year-old son (Dotsey 2008). The husband and wife, both aged thirty-five years, refused to obtain medical treatment for their ailing son on the orders of a spiritualist who had counseled them that the boy was a wizard whose supposed illness was symptomatic of spiritual torment associated with his witchcraft. The chain of events surrounding this case began with the son complaining to his parents that he was feeling ill and felt heat in his body. The parents took him to see the spiritualist at a healing center for prayer. Here, the boy was branded a wizard and asked to confess to the misdeeds he had executed through his witchcraft powers. The boy allegedly confessed to being a wizard who had participated in the consumption of human flesh donated by other members of his witches' guild. He claimed that he was now being tormented by his cowizards and witches for failure to reciprocate an offering of a human victim from his own lineage. The fetish priest advised the couple that their son would never recover from his malady and that the only course of action was to lock him up in a room and leave him to die. The parents acted in accordance with the fetish priest's advice, leaving their son alone to die of starvation and neglect.

Case 7.34. Because of a Dream

On July 14, 2010, police in a northern Ghanaian village arrested a sixty-year-old father and his 23-year-old son, charging them with murder for masterminding the lynching of a 62-year-old widow and neighbor to the assailants ("Woman Lynched" 2010). According to police sources, on the day of the murder, the son related to his father a dream he had during the preceding evening in which he saw himself being chased by their neighbor. The father quickly interpreted the dream as proof of bewitchment or impending bewitchment by the elderly woman. He immediately walked over to the widow's home, narrated his son's dream to her, accused her of witchcraft, and then warned that he would kill her if his son died. When the elderly woman denied the imputation of witchcraft, the father became incensed by the denial and quickly mobilized the youth in the community to kill a witch. The assembled mob battered the elderly woman to death and then set her body on fire. A family spokesperson for the victim described the elderly woman as a person who lived in peace with her neighbors.

Case 7.35. Witch Grandma

In this case, featured in the introduction of this book, a 72-year-old woman was brutally killed by a group of vigilantes who had deemed her to be a witch. The elderly woman had left her village by bus to visit her son in a suburb of Accra (Ocloo 2010a, 2010b). The woman was unaware that her son had just moved, and so was unable to locate his home. As she wandered through the neighborhood looking for her son, she became distraught, appealing to strangers for water, food, and then money for transportation to return to her village. She wound up in the living room of a 37-year-old woman who had left her house to take her children to school. The woman's brother, a pastor, was the first to come upon the elderly woman sitting alone in a room in the house. The pastor raised an alarm that drew the attention of his sister's neighbors and his sister as she returned home. The pastor declared that the older woman was a witch who had wound up in the housing compound after her flight to her witches' Sabbath had been diverted. The elderly grandmother was then detained by six assailants—the pastor, his sister, and three other women and a man from the neighborhood. The six vigilantes tormented the victim for four hours, coercing her into confessing to malevolent witchcraft activities. They then drenched her in kerosene and gasoline and set her alight. A student nurse came upon the scene and intervened, conveying her to a local hospital. But the older woman died hours later. Family members of the victim denied the charges of witchcraft against the older woman, noting that she was an upright citizen who had been suffering mild symptoms of dementia. The assailants were tried for murder. In court, they admitted to performing a ritual to exorcise the victim of witchcraft, but denied dousing her with kerosene and gasoline. They claimed that they had only rubbed her with anointing oils that had spontaneously ignited into flames amidst their intense prayers and chants of "Holy Ghost Fire!" and that this was what ended her life.

Homicide constitutes the most dramatic expression of witch persecution in Ghanaian society. Using data obtained from various media sources, the present chapter examined withcraft-related lethal violence that were made public from 1980 to 2012, illuminating the extent and nature of witch killings in Ghana. The data show that certain demographic groups—particularly older, low-income women—were statistically more vulnerable than others to be victimized in witchcraft-related homicides. Conversely, young upper-class women and men were the least at risk for witchcraft accusation and murder. The next chapter explores forms of witchcraft persecution in Ghanaian society that do not result in the lethal victimization of the putative witch. Several actual cases are also provided in that chapter for purposes of illustration.

Chapter 8

NONLETHAL TREATMENT
OF ALLEGED WITCHES

The preceding chapter examined several cases of lethal violence perpetrated against persons accused of being witches. But violence perpetrated against suspected witches does not always end in death. Indeed, in terms of the total volume of violence committed against alleged witches, witch killings represent only a minuscule proportion of such violence. Evidence obtained from the same sources suggests that each year hundreds of alleged witches are physically and psychologically abused by relatives and other aggrieved individuals. In this chapter, I examine thirty-eight cases of nonlethal violence perpetrated against alleged witches and the circumstances under which the acts occurred.

A close examination of the data of these thirty-eight cases shows that nonlethal violence against alleged witches took a variety of forms. These ranged from serious episodes of physical assault and battery in which the victim suffered life-threatening injuries, to cases of psychological torment and verbal abuse. In the pages that follow, an attempt is made to examine the who, what, where, when, why, and how of nonlethal violence perpetrated against suspected witches. Information about the cases are cited throughout the discussion section of the chapter for purposes of illustration, and actual case profiles are presented after the discussion to illuminate the drastic nature of these assaults and to illustrate witchcraft beliefs and ideas discussed earlier in the book. As was the case with the previous chapter on witch killings, the analysis of cases of nonlethal victimization of accused witches in this chapter derives from content analysis of reports from leading Ghanaian newspapers and Web sites covering the period from 1980 to 2012.

Publicity

In the preceding chapter, it was observed that although incidents of lethal violence against alleged witches are few, they make headlines when they do occur. By contrast, because incidents of nonlethal violence are more common, they do not receive the same degree of publicity when they occur. Occasionally, a few of these incidents become highly publicized. However, unlike acts of witch killings, very few of these events received front-page coverage.

Nonreporting of Cases

Each year, scores of people suspected or accused of witchcraft in Ghana become victims of nonlethal violence. Most of such crimes, however, are not reported to the police. It is therefore difficult to determine the full scope of the problem. The reasons for not reporting vary. Many victims and their families tend to treat nonlethal victimization by family members as private family matters that do not concern the police and criminal justice officials. Some assault victims fear reprisals if they complain. Some are ashamed to admit that they are abused by their family members. While some victims or their representatives do report serious cases of assault to the police, many acts of physical and psychological intimidation such as threats and emotional and psychological abuse go unreported. Even some cases that are reported to the police are later withdrawn as victims prefer to have the matter resolved privately. When such crimes are reported to the police, the victim may be pressured to withdraw the case by family members wishing to avoid negative publicity. Moreover, despite physical and psychological trauma, victims may be reluctant to report crimes committed by relatives, troubled by the prospect of their son, daughter, nephew, or niece being arrested, remanded in jail, prosecuted, convicted, and sent to prison. Nonreporting may also be due to the low literacy levels of many of the victims of witch persecution. In Ghana, as in many societies, illiteracy is associated with ignorance of, or lack of knowledge about, the law and one's human rights.

Sociodemographic Characteristics of Victims

Victims of nonlethal violence who were accused of witchcraft were over-whelmingly female. Of the forty victims, thirty (75 percent) were female and ten (25 percent) were male. The accused male witches tended to be children or elderly men. Five males were children aged between seven years and fifteen years; the older male was seventy-five years old. The victims ranged in age from four years to 110 years old. The median age was seventy-two years old.

In the majority of cases, information regarding the occupational background of victims was not provided. Of the cases where occupational information was available, accused witches were of low socioeconomic background, including a peasant cocoa farmer, a seamstress' apprentice, and an unemployed. While the occupational statuses of the elderly victims were not mentioned in the case stories, it is plausible to surmise that they were retired from active economic activities.

Sociodemographic Characteristics of Assailants

Like witch killings, nonlethal acts against alleged witches were typically perpetrated by men. Twenty-eight out of the thirty-eight assailants (73.7 percent) were men, while ten (26.3 percent) were female. Mob violence or vigilante assaults on putative witches were almost invariably by a mob consisting of males. The assailants ranged in age from twenty-seven to fifty-five years old.

Victim-Offender Relationship

The victims and the assailants were often acquainted as family members or neighbors. In four instances, men attacked their mothers; in one instance, a woman attacked her mother; in five instances, parents or other close family members, such as an aunt, physically assaulted suspected child witches; in one instance, an adult grandchild attacked his grandmother, whom he suspected of being a witch; in one instance, a man attacked his brother-in-law whom he accused of bewitching him; in a case involving siblings, a brother assaulted a sister he accused of bewitching him; in two instances, nephews attacked their aunts. In one instance, a child was assaulted by his mother and uncle. Of the instances where the victim and offender were not related by blood or marriage, typically the assailants were pastors, prophets, and fetish priests. Assaults by mobs occurred in four cases. In one instance, the village chief was arrested for the physical and psychological abuse and mistreatment of a putative witch.

Spatial Aspects of the Crime

Rural areas had the highest number of reports of nonlethal witchcraft-related violence. Rates of such violence also varied by region of the country. The northern regions had consistently higher rates of reported cases of nonlethal witchcraft-related violence.

Motive

This study attempted to identify the motives behind nonlethal witch attacks. In most cases the motive for mistreatment was revenge and retaliation. Some nonlethal assaults were to avenge the deaths of loved ones. In Case 8.15 a fourteen-year-old girl was blamed for causing her own father's death through witchcraft. In Case 8.21 the alleged witch was assaulted after being accused of masterminding a car accident that claimed several lives, including the assailant's two wives. In Case 8.27, for example, a young man attacked an aunt whom he suspected of being responsible for his mother's death.

In some instances the alleged witches were blamed for the assailant's physical or mental illness. Violence and intimidation were used to force alleged witches to remove their spells on those thought to be bewitched. For example, in Case 8.4, a man blamed his brother-in-law for his physical afflictions; in Case 8.5 the assailant blamed his grandmother for his sexual impotence; in Case 8.19 the assailant blamed the victim for being the source of his chronic headaches; in Case 8.23 the alleged witch was attacked for using her witchcraft power to cause her brother's asthma; and in Case 8.28 the alleged witch was alleged to be the source of a man's hypertension and stroke.

In a large number of cases, the alleged witches were blamed for the assailants' lack of financial success. Frustrated and angry at their inability to achieve economic prosperity or even the means to earn a living, assailants found a witch as a scapegoat. In Case 8.2 the assailant attacked his 75-year-old mother, blaming her for his deportation from Libya and subsequent financial difficulties. In Cases 8.6, and 8.24, the assailants blamed the alleged witch for their financial or economic difficulties. In Case 8.26, the assailant attacked the alleged witch for his past job losses and his current long-term unemployment. In Case 8.30, two young girls were whipped with canes and made to confess responsibility for their grandmother's failed business.

In cases of mob action, the violence and mistreatment followed the labeling of the victim as a malevolent witch and evildoer in their midst. Community members felt impelled to deal with those who failed to conform to the precepts of good neighborliness in the society. Hence, the motivation appeared to be to put pressure on the alleged witch to abide by the rules of society. In Case 8.3, residents of a village nearly publicly lynched an elderly woman and her grandson, who confessed to have caused a guinea-worm infestation in the village.

In a few instances, alleged witches were attacked when found to be out late at night or in the early morning hours. For elderly men and women, being out at night or at dawn provokes accusations of witchcraft from neighbors who assume that the victim is returning from a witches' Sabbath. In Case 8.7, an eighty-year-old woman was accosted by a group of vigilantes who said they had witnessed her transform from a bird into an elderly woman. In Case 8.25, a 95-year-old woman was subjected to a harrowing ordeal after she was spotted sitting in front of a residential building around one o'clock in the morning. In Case 8.31, a 110-year-old woman was accosted, interrogated, and then beaten by a group of young people who spotted her taking a walk through their neighborhood.

Types of Mistreatment of Accused Witches

Verbal Abuse

The data showed that persons who were accused of witchcraft were often verbally assailed. A common form of verbal abuse consisted of name-calling in which alleged witches were referred to by one or more of a myriad of names used to describe a witch in local languages: *obayifo, adze, kayere kayere, anadwo bogya, ayɛn, atufaa*. Relatives of the alleged witch, such as children, were often subject to the same form of abuse. Other forms of verbal abuse include cursing, threatening, and other expressions of ill-will. Alleged witches were yelled at, hooted at, and insulted while out in public. A review of Cases 8.7, 8.25, and 8.31 shows that verbal abuse was regularly heaped on alleged witches. Along with name-calling, victims of verbal abuse faced the consequences of verbal denigration and stigmatization in the community that came with being publicly labeled as a witch. In Ghana the stigma suffered by persons accused of witchcraft is enormous. There is evidence that some putative witches develop emotional disorders, while others attempt or actually commit suicide (see "Grandma, 85, Commits Suicide" 2007).

Trial by Ordeal

A common form of violence committed against suspected witches was trial by ordeal. A trial by ordeal calls for the performance of some task or feat—usually one involving the endurance of significant pain or humiliation—to determine one's guilt or innocence of a charge. Refusal to submit to an ordeal is tantamount to an admission of guilt.

Although trials by ordeal are prohibited by the Constitution of the Republic of Ghana (1992), the data show that in many communities throughout the country, persons who were suspected of witchcraft were taken to fetish shrines to have their guilt or innocence verified by religious personnel via a trial by ordeal ("Herbalist in Trouble" 2005; "Trial by Ordeal" 1998). In Cases 8.14, 8.16, 8.20, 8.21, and 8.22, the alleged witches were made to undergo such trials by ordeal. Part of the verification process usually entailed the subjection of the alleged witch to some form of physical or psychological torment. Some of the more popular trials by ordeal involved subjecting the accused witch to cruel, demeaning practices such as forcing victims to drink their own urine and consume their own feces; forcing them to handle a snake; pouring a concoction over their face; smearing charcoal powder over their naked body; and placing them in a room filled with noxious smoke from burning peppers.

In the Gambaga area of northern Ghana, following an accusation of witchcraft a trip to the *gambarana* (custodian of the witch sanctuary in Gambaga, or witch doctor) by the alleged witch and her accusers is required. Here, identifying a witch through divination involves the strangulation of a fowl. The chicken or fowl ordeal requires the suspected or accused witch to bring a fowl to the *gambarana*. The person can purchase one in town or buy one from the witch doctor. The witch doctor strangles the fowl and lets it loose on the ground as it dies. The chicken typically flutters around until it dies. If in its death the chicken falls on its back, the accused is determined to be innocent of a witch charge and is free to go. If it falls on its face, the accused is confirmed to be a witch.

Physical Abuse

Persons who were suspected of witchcraft were often beaten by their accusers. Victims were assaulted with sticks, pelted with stones, kicked, pushed, or shoved. The data show that victims of physical abuse suffered a range of physical injuries, ranging in severity from minor cuts and bruises to critical and life-threatening injuries. Reported injuries included fractured jaws, dislocated shoulders, broken arms, severed hands, ruptured internal organs (such as liver, spleen, and kidneys), bruises, lacerations and scars, and the loss of teeth. In many instances, protestations of innocence by the alleged witch were met with increased brutality. Although such assaults did not eventuate in death, they did leave victims with major physical and psychological scars. Even in those episodes where only minor physical injury occurred, victims reported feeling apprehensive about future harm. Some forms of physical abuse occurred as part of the process of obtaining confession from the alleged witch. In Case 8.26, for example, a man severed the hands of his aunt because he suspected her of being responsible for the difficulties he faced in life. Physical abuse against alleged witches was particularly severe in cases of mob or vigilante justice. Mob violence or acts of vigilante justice were committed with fists, feet, sticks, stones, or other objects.

Banishment of Accused Witches

Another common method of punishment to which alleged witches were subjected was banishment. The data show that in many communities in northern Ghana suspected witches were forced to abandon their homes and their local communities after being accused of witchcraft. The accused were forced to abandon their families and friends and take up residence at a witch sanctuary or refuge center. At present, there are several witches' sanctuaries in the northern regions of Ghana. In 1997 a public uproar ensued following publicity about the camps, leading the Commission on Human Rights and Administrative Justice and women's groups to request measures be taken to abolish the camps. Women's groups also called for government to systematically address the dire social conditions of the women living in the camps, including the nature of their victimization as accused witches. It is estimated that these refuges are collectively accommodating as many as eight thousand suspected witches. While some accused witches are banished without physical battery, some are allowed to leave only after enduring merciless beatings and other forms of ill-treatment at the hands of their accusers. A condition for acceptance into many camps is submission to a dewitching or exorcism regimen. This is to ensure that the witch will permanently be divested of any capacity to bewitch others.

Most accused witches spend several years in witches' camps. Indeed, some spend the rest of their lives in such camps upon admission. When I visited the Gambaga Witches' Camp in 2005, I learned that the longest-serving resident had resided there for thirty consecutive years. The psychological and economic hardships that banishment imposes often reach crisis levels, in a few instances leading to suicide. Critics of banishment contend that it is unjust to imprison and thereby deprive accused witches of their liberty. Moreover, the squalid conditions in witches' sanctuaries have been a matter of concern for many years, with advocacy groups taking it up as a human rights issue. The deprivations of liberty and freedom faced by camp residents have been of particular concern to local women's groups that are sensitive to the overrepresentation of women among inmates of witches' camps ("NGO Launches" 2010).

On successful completion of the exorcism or dewitching rituals, the accused witches in the camps are released back into their communities. However, many elect not to leave the sanctuary for fear of reprisal at the hands of aggrieved family members or other community members. During a visit to the camp, I was told that some of the women had been dewitched but were being detained for their inability to pay for the costs associated with the exorcism ritual.

The abandonment of alleged witches in these witches' camps and the failure of family members, the community, and the government to provide adequate food, clothing, shelter, and medicines to the residents allows caretakers or custodians of the witches' sanctuaries to exercise extensive discretion in the exploitation of the residents. Some caretakers have created a system of indenture where the labor of camp residents is rented out to local farmers in the cultivation and harvesting of their crops. Part of the rent goes toward the provision of food, clothing, and other necessities for the residents.

Critics charge that one of the greatest complications facing the witches' camps is the problem of reintegrating camp residents back into their communities. While the initial goal and primary function of the camps is to provide sanctuary for accused witches and to keep them out of harm's way, perceptions of the threat that accused witches pose to their communities make reintegration difficult at best and impossible at worst.

To avoid the insults, ridicule, gossip, taunts, jeers, gawking, shame, and embarrassment attendant to witchcraft accusations, some alleged witches voluntarily withdrew from society, avoiding going out in public during the day. In the northern regions, some elderly women voluntarily checked themselves into the witches' camps when they believed that they would be branded witches and physically battered or even killed.

In some cases, accused witches have faced a form of exile or expulsion known as denaturalization. This entails being permanently banned from entering one's former community, including being barred from attending funerals, and being refused a burial of one's own in the community—the latter being two highly important exclusions symbolizing disconnection from a community. In Case 8.20, a woman was denaturalized from her native town following her refusal to submit to a trial by ordeal. She had been accused of using witchcraft to inflict illnesses on some relatives and to kill others.

Prayer Camps

At present, witches' sanctuaries are confined to the country's northern regions. In the rest of the country, accused witches are often conveyed to prayer camps and spiritual healing centers where they may be temporarily detained for "treatment," or exorcism of their witchcraft. With the rapid spread of Christianity and the emergence of Pentecostal or spiritual churches, pastors, apostles, prophets, and other personnel, prayer camps have spread rapidly in Ghana (see Figures 8.1, 8.2, and 8.3). Because most prayer camps are located in rural areas, there is no oversight of their activities. There are numerous reports of a range of abuses perpetrated against accused witches in such prayer camps. The combination of the removal of the accused witch from her place of residence and a range of degrading treatments are intended to create harsh conditions for extracting confessions from the accused witch. Indeed, the data show that persons

Figure 8.1. Advertisement for a Christian Prayer Camp (1)

Figure 8.2. Advertisement for a Christian Prayer Camp (2)

Figure 8.3. Advertisement for a Christian Prayer Camp (3)

accused of witchcraft are often subjected to a regimen of mistreatment. This ranges from corporal punishment to other indignities that include having the head shaved and a combination of varied forms of physical and psychological abuse, all in order to extract confessions. Victims are beaten with sticks, canes, belts, ropes, and electrical cords. Alleged witches who do not make a "proper" confession receive merciless beatings, often requiring medical intervention (Osei 2008).

Among the most publicized forms of mistreatment meted out to suspected witches was exposure to the elements. Some suspected witches who were referred to traditional antiwitchcraft shrines for divination, trial by ordeals, exorcism, and other related rituals were put in chains and tied to a tree or heavy log while exposed to the elements (Sackey 2010). The expectation was that this ordeal would force them to confess to witchcraft allegations. Many of the victims were traumatized, suffering severe emotional and psychological effects from such treatment. Witch suspects were also often denied food and water by their accusers and other custodians. In Case 8.11 the alleged witch was denied food and water, as part of her ordeal. The motive for denying the accused witch food and water was to force her to confess her involvement in witchcraft. The combination of the removal of the individual from his or her place of residence and denying her food and water under degrading conditions can have severe emotional and physical toll on the victim.

Shaving of the hair was yet another recurrent form of violence perpetrated against putative witches, and was often used in prayer camps. In the Ghanaian context, forcibly cutting the hair of an adult is one of the most heinous acts of degradation to which a person can be subjected. The forced shaving of the hair of an adult individual is shameful and tantamount to a serious form of abuse and degradation. Among other forms of degradations, the 73-year-old female accused of witchcraft in Case 8.11 had her hair forcefully shaven. In Case 8.12 the 21-year-old alleged witch had hair on her head, armpits, and pubic regions forcefully shaven. In Case 8.14, the 65-year-old victim had hair on her head shaven off, besides suffering other forms of indignities at the hands of her accusers. In Case 8.21, a middle-aged woman suspected of witchcraft had her hair shaven, among other indignities.

In Ghanaian culture, nudity is frowned upon while forced nudity is a form of extreme degradation. Information concerning the activities of witch doctors suggests that many of the confessions were obtained through torture. Part of the torture process included stripping the accused witch naked and subjecting her to other degrading treatments. In Case 8.11 the 73-year-old victim was stripped naked, tied to a tree, and repeatedly caned while being denied food and water and being exposed to the elements. In Case 8.21 a middle-aged woman was stripped naked, smeared with charcoal powder, and had a noose put around her neck. In Case 8.23, a 65-year-old woman was stripped naked and forced to sit on a huge boulder in full public view. In Case 8.31 the 110-year-old female victim was stripped naked and brutally beaten by a public mob.

Other Contexts for Nonlethal Victimization of Accused Witches

Accused witches were subjected to similar forms of mistreatment in other venues as well. Detention of people believed to be witches inside their own homes was a frequent occurrence. Imprisonment, forced isolation, and confinement were initiated by family members of the accused witch who were motivated to keep that person from public view. In many instances the confinement was preceded by an incident or series of incidents in which the confined individual was subjected to a torturous ordeal. The duration of the confinement varied. The data show that children who experienced such detention were particularly traumatized by the experience.

Corporal punishment was also meted out by family members. Case 8.9 involved an instance of corporal punishment in which a 42-year-old man caned his mother, seventy-two, who was an alleged witch, until she lost consciousness. Additionally, the data show that it was not only in prayer camps that accused witches were placed in physical restraints and exposed to the elements. The fifteen-year-old accused wizard profiled in Case 8.1 was put in dog chains, tied up in the sun, and beaten. Similarly, in Case 8.2, a man took his 75-year-old mother, an alleged witch, to a healing camp. There she was tied up, exposed to the elements for three months, and intermittently denied food. She was also caned thirty-six times daily on her bare back. Her son participated in some of the caning incidents.

Other forms of nonlethal victimization that witchcraft suspects were subjected to included such indignities as being spat upon. In many Ghanaian ethnic communities, to be spat upon is a form of cruel degradation. Such treatment was meted out with striking regularity toward alleged witches. This was most common, but not confined to, contexts of mob violence where other acts of degradation were enacted by lynch mobs. In Case 8.10, a 32-year-old woman spat in the face of her 55-year-old mother whom she accused of being a witch.

More serious forms of sublethal violence were also perpetrated against accused witches. Evidence suggests that some witch accusers who were frustrated by the alleged witch's refusal to confess to committing acts of malevolent witchcraft resorted to more severe punitive and deterrent strategies. In Case 8.4, a man poured acid on his brother-in-law whom he suspected of being a wizard and responsible for his physical afflictions.

There were cases of physical assault in which the suspected witch was burned as a form of torture to elicit a confession of witchcraft involvement or witch misdeeds. In Case 8.18, a father burned the heels of his two sons whom he suspected of being wizards. The burning of the heels was to ensure that the boys did not have the supposed capacity to fly to witches' Sabbath.

Reports of knife attacks against alleged witches recurred with striking frequency, in many such cases only avoiding what would otherwise have been lethal assaults. Accused witches bludgeoned with machetes typically suffered severe lacerations. Some had limbs such as hands chopped off as a result of knife attacks. In Case 8.5, a man used a machete to sever his grandmother's wrist, accusing her of using witchcraft to cause his sexual impotence. In many of these cases, the injuries sustained from the knife attacks were so severe that it was impossible to determine whether the intent was to physically eliminate the victim or simply to punish her.

Economic Boycott and Destruction of Property

As noted in this and the preceding chapters, accusations of witchcraft often had the effect of injuring the character or reputation of the person against whom the allegation was directed. Accused witches who made a living as professional traders tended to suffer economic hardships and financial ruination as their wares were boycotted. For some, witchcraft accusations were accompanied by stories alleging that their displayed wares were spiritual counterfeits. Persons labeled as witches experienced great difficulty regaining financial success once they were accused of witchcraft. In the case of the Kobua case profiled in chapter 6, buyers boycotted the wares of both Kofi Badu, the fisherman, and Ama Kunta, the fish seller following the imputation of witchcraft.

The data show that destruction of property constitutes a common reprisal perpetrated against people alleged to be witches. Accused witches had their houses burnt down and farms razed, culminating in vast economic losses to the victim. In many instances, the value of the property destroyed was enormous. In Case 8.27 a man destroyed the kitchen of an aunt he suspected of causing his mother's death.

Special Mortuary Rites for Witches and Wizards

Further evidence of the repulsion Ghanaians have towards witches and witchcraft is seen in the denial of befitting burials for putative witches. In some ethnic communities, persons who are accused of witchcraft, then purportedly verified to be witches through divinatory procedures or personal confessions, are summarily buried after their deaths without ceremony; they are also denied funeral obsequies (Nkrumah 1984). In some communities, affirmed witches are buried in special cemeteries reserved for persons who have committed suicide, or suffered other so-called bad deaths (Nkrumah 1984). To illustrate, the local media in 1995 reported a case in which the interred remains of a 72-year-old woman identified as a witch within her community was exhumed from a public cemetery by a vigilante group who reburied the remains in a small cemetery designated for persons who suffered bad deaths. In this case family members had performed a conventional burial and funeral for the decedent in a public cemetery (Atsu 1995). In another case, an embittered writer to the "Letters to the Editor" of a local newspaper wrote about two cases in which the corpses of purported witches were denied normal funerary protocols and buried in dishonorable circumstances. The following is an excerpt from the letter:

> In 1989, my family suffered gross injustice at the hands of the rulers of my town, Katakyiease, near Fante Nyakomase. . . . In the year referred to, my grandmother aged about 89, died. While we were preparing for the funeral and making other arrangements to bury her, the rulers of the town came to inform us that the old lady had been branded a witch so they would not permit her to be buried in the normal way. We were ordered to put her in a coffin at the mortuary and bury her quietly at sunset. We were ordered not to weep, not to perform any funeral ceremony and not to play any musical instrument. We were simply told that that was the custom for burying witches. We were forced to comply and my old grandmother was buried like a dog. I was very bitter, but felt at the time that nothing could be done. In October 2006, history repeated itself. An 85-year-old lady, Obaapanin Yaa Koduah, died at Katakyiease. The rulers informed her family that she had been declared a witch so she would not be permitted to be buried like a normal corpse. (Mensah 2007).

Case Information

The following are actual cases that illustrate nonlethal forms of mistreatment meted out to suspected witches in contemporary Ghana.

Case 8.1. The Wizard Is Now in Chains

In this harrowing case, family members brutalized a fifteen-year-old boy on suspicion that he was a wizard responsible for their failures in life (Biney 1994). The boy's 36-year-old mother, a born-again Christian, had come to believe that her son was a wizard. She recurrently tied up her son with a dog chain, beat him, and left him kneeling in the sun for hours on end. As a result, the boy suffered scars on his body and would have died if not for his timely rescue by a witness. The boy's mother, who sold goods in the market, claimed that each time she went to collect money from her debtors, they rained insults and innuendos on her. She attributed this to the witchcraft of her son. An older sibling of the victim noted, "Anytime my mother decides to go out to collect her monies, the [witchcraft] spirit of the boy precedes her and this makes it difficult for her to get her money." In recounting his ordeal, the boy noted, "I have been made to stop schooling and have become the target of scorn and gossip amongst even the members of the prayer group who visit the house regularly to pray."

Case 8.2. "Help! My Son is Abusing Me"

In this case a 75-year-old mother made an urgent appeal to the security agencies to rescue her from the wrath of her son, a businessperson, who had subjected her to various forms of physical and psychological indignities because he suspected her of being a witch (Nsowah-Adjei 1994). In this case the son suspected that his business had suffered because of his mother's evil machinations. According to the news report, the assailant, an émigré to Libya, was deported back to Ghana for lack of relevant immigration documents. Upon his return, he established a transportation business, hoping to recoup substantial savings to embark on another trip to Libya. However, the sole vehicle he operated experienced chronic mechanical problems, causing the business venture to fail. When the son consulted several oracles to determine if there was a spiritual basis for his business predicaments, some self-styled prophets attributed his business difficulties to his mother's alleged witchcraft. According to the case report, the son, wielding a sharp machete, confronted his mother with the claim of her diabolical witchcraft. When the mother denied the witch claim, he slapped her across the face with the side of the machete. After persistent denials, the son took his aging mother to a prayer healing camp several miles away in anticipation that she would come around and confess to her witchery. At the camp the elderly woman was tied against a wooden log with hands and legs bound together. For three months, she was regularly exposed to the elements, including being placed in the open sun and left in the frequent rainfall. She was also periodically denied food. Her son participated further in her torment, administering thirty-six strokes of the birch each day on her bare back, while imploring her to confess to being a witch. Unable to induce any confession from his mother, the assailant took his mother back to her village where the physical assault against her continued.

Case 8.3. Who Is Responsible for the Plague?

A young boy's alleged self-confession of witchcraft practice nearly cost him and his grandmother their lives at the hands of an enraged mob (Mirror Reporter 1991). A guinea worm infestation had afflicted and incapacitated residents in a small village community for a period spanning two years. The intervention of public health officials did little to dissipate the plague. It was noted that a number of bore holes and hand pumps had been provided by the health authorities for potable water but all to no avail. While the community continued to combat the affliction, a nine-year-old boy allegedly confessed to being a member of a local witch coven that was responsible for causing and spreading the disease. According to the boy, the witchcraft had been given to him by his maternal grandmother. He confessed that, as a member of a witch coven, he had participated in the mixing of a bluish substance that was subsequently introduced into the town's drinking water. He claimed that as a result anyone who drank the town's water, excluding the members of the witch coven became afflicted with the disease. The boy's alleged confession raised the ire of the entire community, which descended on the boy and his grandmother. But for the timely intervention of law enforcement personnel, the entire community would have lynched the boy and his elderly grandmother.

Case 8.4. An Acid Assault

A man who suspected his brother-in-law of being a wizard and of being responsible for a number of physical afflictions, retaliated by pouring acid on the alleged wizard (Azu 1990). According to the facts of the case, the victim was the assailant's brother-in-law. The two men had not been on speaking terms for over three years, a situation fueled by a prior legal dispute in which the assailant was sued by the victim and convicted for physical assault. It was alleged that, following the legal battle, the assailant suffered a stroke and sought spiritual assistance and treatment at a fetish shrine in the neighboring country of Benin. While in Benin, he was told that his brother-in-law was a wizard who had been haunting him spiritually and was responsible for causing his stroke. After his return to Ghana, the assailant fell ill again and was rushed to Benin again for treatment. It was again suggested that the assailant's affliction was caused by his brother-in-law's wizardry. The assailant was told that he would develop rashes on his genital area that would herald his imminent death. A few days prior to the acid assault, the assailant discovered the predicted rashes and decided to retaliate against the victim before his impending death. He purchased sulphuric acid from a local store and went to lay ambush at the victim's house from 4 P.M. until 9:30 P.M., at which time he saw the victim returning home from work. He struck the victim from behind with a club and, when he fell, sprayed his face with the acid. The assault with the acid caused severe burns to the victim, necessitating hospitalization.

Case 8.5. "Reverse the Spell!"

A man who believed that his seventy-year-old grandmother was a witch who had used her witchcraft to cause sexual impotence in him, demanded that she reverse the spell (Addoteye 1992). When she was unable to reverse the spell, he retaliated by using a machete to sever the woman's right wrist. The incident sent ripples of horror through the entire neighborhood as the victim's screams attracted residents in the area to the scene. They overpowered the assailant and subjected him to a severe beating that broke a bone in his arm. According to the story, about ten years prior to the wrist-slashing incident, the assailant alleged that when he was first introduced to the victim at a family gathering, their handshake generated a funny feeling in him "as if a spirit was departing my body." He had since nursed this grudge against the old woman, suspecting that she had used her witchcraft to cause his sexual impotence.

Case 8.6. The Witch Pair

In this case two elderly women, the oldest of eighty residents in an Accra homestead, were brutalized and forced to publicly admit that they were witches while being detained against their will in a Christian prayer and healing camp for three days (Afful and Ankamah 1994). The women gained their release only after police raided the healing camp, following a complaint to police that some of the accused witches were being held in the camp against their will. According to the news story, a resident of the homestead brought a Christian pastor to the homestead to expel the witchcraft power responsible for their lack of success in life. The pastor was said to have exhumed a black pot that was allegedly the cause of the lack of economic success among tenants in the homestead. Following this, tenants in the homestead were forced to drink a concoction that, it was further alleged, would identify the supposed witches in the homestead. Following the ingestion of the substance, the two elderly women collapsed and were transported by bus to the church healing center where they were beaten and coerced into confessing their alleged misdeeds as witches. For refusing to confess, the pastor stripped the women naked and ritually bathed them against their will. They were also taken to the beach where they were repeatedly dunked into the ocean in a cleansing ritual.

Upon return to the healing center, they continued to be detained against their will.

Case 8.7. "That's No Bird, That's a Witch"

An eighty-year-old woman was physically assaulted by a mob of pedestrians who claimed that the woman was a witch who had transformed herself into a strange bird and held up traffic (Azumah 1993). According to the assailants, the strange bird appeared in the middle of a busy Accra street while pedestrians threw sticks to drive it away. Then the bird turned into a gray-haired, elderly woman. According to the story, "it was when they started to hit the bird, which could not fly and was disturbing traffic that it allegedly turned into a gray-haired old woman." A mob congregated rapidly, taking the old woman for a witch and beating her with sticks amid shouts of *aye! aye!* (witch! witch!). The bleeding woman was rescued from the assaulting mob by a good Samaritan who took her to a nearby police station. However, the police directed that she be sent to a hospital. In a terse statement, the woman indicated that she left home for a funeral but was pounced upon by a mob as she was returning to the house. Family members corroborated the woman's story about leaving the house for a funeral. Family members suggested that the woman left the house on a Saturday morning to attend a funeral but did not return until about 7 A.M. the following day when they received reports that she was assaulted and accused of being a witch.

Case 8.8. "I Hit a Snake That Was Eating My Baby"

A seventeen-year-old girl became comatose for twenty-one days after being hit in the head with a piece of cement block (Tetteh 1997). The assailant was a friend who believed that the victim had transformed herself into a snake and was about to devour her one-month-old baby. The 21-year-old mother left her baby in the bedroom with her sleeping friend to go to the lavatory at dawn. According to the young mother, upon her return she did not see her friend. Instead, she found a huge snake wrapped around her baby. Terrified and shaken, she found a piece of cement block, hit the reptile's head with it, and then picked up the baby. Surprisingly, the snake had morphed back into her friend.

Case 8.9. "My Witch Mother Should Leave my Business Alone"

In an article, "He Canes Mother, 72," a local weekly newspaper described the ordeal of an elderly woman beaten into unconsciousness by her 42-

year-old son who accused her of being a witch (Gmanyami 1996). According to the story, the assailant, a marijuana peddler, had been asked by his mother to desist from this illicit activity. The woman had also asked her son's accomplice in the drug trade to refrain from coming to the house. Enraged, the assailant accused his mother of being a witch and subsequently caned her until she fell unconscious. When two other relatives rushed to the aid of the elderly victim, the assailant was alleged to have attacked them with a machete.

Case 8.10. Jail Time for Assaulting "Witch" Mother

In an apparent move by judicial authorities to stem the tide of witchcraft accusations and violence against alleged witches in the community, a 32-year-old woman who physically assaulted her mother after accusing her of witchcraft was sentenced to a six-month jail term for "offensive conduct" (Gmanyami 1998). According to the story, the assailant, a trader, gave money to her mother for safe-keeping. She alleged that when she went back to retrieve the money, her mother gave her substantially less money than she had given her mother. From then on, the enraged assailant hurled insults at her mother at the least provocation. On one occasion, the assailant, after waking from bed in the morning, accused her mother of being a witch and subsequently spat in her face. The mother, bitter from the experience, reported the matter to the local police, resulting in the assailant's arrest, prosecution, conviction, and sentencing.

Case 8.11. "Not Until She Confesses"

A 73-year-old woman branded a witch by a 39-year-old fetish priest was severely beaten and tormented in an apparent effort to get her to confess to using diabolic witchcraft to inflict a variety of misfortunes on her family (Afful 1995). The woman was labeled a witch after her nephew's child fell seriously ill. In an effort to get the ailing child well, the father went to the shrine of the fetish priest where he was told that the woman was a witch and was the source of the child's physical afflictions. The fetish priest sought permission to take the old woman to his shrine in order to exorcise her of the witchcraft. At the shrine, the old woman denied the witch allegation leveled against her, whereupon she was stripped naked, had her hair shaven, was tied to a tree, caned, abandoned in the scorching sun, and denied food and water for eight hours in an apparent effort to elicit a confession of witchery. Distressed by the abuse, one of the elderly woman's granddaughters reported the incident to the police. Police officers who arrived at the scene described the woman as "lying on the bare ground, pale, weak, and having contusions and blood stains all over her body."

Case 8.12. Prophetess Flogs Seamstress

A story, "Seamstress Flogged by Prophetess," described an incident in which a 21-year-old apprentice seamstress was subjected to a harrowing ten-day ordeal in which she was held captive and physically assaulted (Spectator Reporter 2000). According to the story, the victim, a regular member of her church, attended service one Sunday morning. During a prayer interlude, the prophetess in charge of the congregation announced that the 21-year-old woman's right hand was a snake with which she planned to cause mischief. She also alleged that the hair on her head, eyebrows, armpits, and in her pubic region were all snakes. The victim was then dragged away to another location in the church, had the hair all over her body shaved, and was subjected to severe flogging to elicit a confession. When she denied the witch claim, the victim was locked up in a room for ten days. According to the report, she was deprived of food and water. A distraught church member leaked the matter to the parents of the victim who reported the matter to the police to secure their daughter's release from the church.

Case 8.13. The Haunted Room in the House

In this case two self-styled pastors were arrested by police for beating a man who refused to allow them to enter his bedroom to exorcise the room of witchcraft and other evil spirits (Boaten 1998). According to the story, a sister of the man attended a local church where she complained about her lack of financial success. The pastors informed her that through prayers they had established that her financial predicament could be traced to a room in her house that "contained the problems of the family." The room, the pastors alleged, housed the spirit of the woman's deceased mother and a gold bar that "contained witchcraft which was spiriting monies of the family away." When the man became suspicious of the pastors' intentions, he refused them entry into the room. The two pastors, together with the man's sister, pounced on him and severely beat him.

Case 8.14. Trial by Ordeal

A fetish priest and his wife were apprehended by police and charged with aggravated assault for subjecting a 65-year-old woman to a trial by ordeal intended to prove that she was a witch (Abban 1998). According to the story, the elderly victim was summoned to appear before the local fetish priest. Upon her arrival, she was asked whether she had ever given a loaf of bread to someone as a gift. Upon answering affirmatively, the priest accused her of being a witch and asked her to pay a sum the equivalent of about US$200. When she refused to pay, the priest subjected her to a series of humiliating ordeals to force a confession of witchcraft out of her, including shaving her head, beating her, and pouring a concoction over her face. According to the story, an onlooker who could not withstand the inhumane treatment being meted out to the elderly woman reported the priest to the police. Police personnel were dispatched to the crime scene to investigate the crime. Upon sighting the police, the fetish priest was alleged to have attempted to escape the scene by climbing through a window. In his statement to police, the priest admitted the offense, saying "though I shaved a woman to enable me to perform a trial by ordeal, I was forced to do so by some spirits."

Case 8.15. Locked Up for Five Years

An article in the *Daily Graphic* reported that the Women and Juvenile Unit of the Ghana Police Service was conducting an investigation into the case of a fourteen-year-old girl who had been locked up in a room for five years based on suspicions that she was a witch ("Girl Locked Up" 2004). At the time of her rescue by police, the physically handicapped victim was isolated, neglected, and unkempt. At age nine, shortly after her father's death, the young girl had been struck by an enigmatic ailment one night and began screaming uncontrollably. She was then rushed to a local psychiatric hospital for treatment. The victim was discharged the next day after being given some medication. Shortly thereafter, the nine-year-old victim became paralyzed. The victim's mother, who had eight other children, dispatched the child to the hospital four more times, finally obtaining herbal treatment for her daughter. With still no improvement in the child's condition, the mother presumed the child was a witch and confined her to the room until her rescue five years later.

Case 8.16. "Those Boys Killed the Chief"

Two brothers were detained at a fetish shrine for sixteen days following a trial by ordeal (Dzamboe 2004). A confession was extracted from the pair during which they were forced to admit culpability in using witchcraft to kill the chief of the town. Following the verdict, the pair was asked to pay a financial penalty of about US$100 and provide one goat each to the shrine. The pair was freed from detention only following the intervention of the local police and the Commission on Human Rights and Administrative Justice, a statutory body charged with protecting the human rights of Ghana's citizens. After the pair was rescued, residents of the town harassed, intimidated, threatened, and banished the boys from the town; townspeople also poisoned their drinking well. The pair was to be readmitted into the community only on condition that they undergo spiritual cleansing as demanded by the customs of the traditional area in a trial by ordeal.

Case 8.17. "You Can't Live Here Anymore"

In this case a self-professed prophet who claimed to have used his spiritual powers to identify and expose witches in a rural community incurred the wrath of that same community (Hope 2004). According to the news story, the 43-year-old prophet who made the allegation on a local radio station, claimed that about 90 percent of the residents of the community were wizards and witches who had bewitched the youths of the town to prevent them from becoming prosperous. The allegation created considerable tension in the community, resulting in the community's decision to send him into exile, with threats of reprisal should he return. At the time of the report, the man was being investigated for two criminal cases involving fraud. According to the story, "[T]wo women from the town had dragged him to court for allegedly duping them under the pretext of exorcising them of evil spirits that he said were haunting them." He allegedly collected the sum the equivalent of US$30 and US$6 from them to release them from their spiritual chains but absconded shortly thereafter.

Case 8.18. For Flying at Night

A father who blamed his lack of financial success on the malevolent witchcraft powers of his two young sons burned the heels of the children in his apparent bid to curtail the kids' nocturnal flights to witches' Sabbaths (Odoi 2003). The assailant, the proprietor of an auto mechanic shop in a major city, attributed the lack of financial success in his business to witchcraft, claiming that he saw the two boys flying in his dreams. The boys adamantly denied being wizards or having any involvement in witchcraft. To curtail the children's alleged activities and to set himself on a course for financial success, he started a fire and, while the two boys slept, woke them up one by one, then burned their heels in the fire.

Case 8.19. A Threat to Kill

In February 2005 a Ghanaian magistrate court imposed a two-year incarcerative sentence on a 28-year-old unemployed man found guilty of threatening to kill his middle-aged mother with a machete ("Court Jails Man" 2005). Case information showed the man had previously consulted an oracular priest to inquire about the cause of his chronic headaches. The oracle allegedly told him that his mother was a witch and her witchcraft was spiritually the cause of the headaches. Upon his return from the consultations, the defendant demanded a sum of money the equivalent of US$700 from his mother to be used by the oracle to effect his treatment. When the mother told him she could not come up with the requested amount, the man became offended, grabbed a machete, and threatened to kill her.

Case 8.20. For Refusing to Submit

A seventy-year-old woman suspected of witchcraft was denaturalized and deprived of her rights as a citizen of a major ethnic group in the country ("Witchcraft Case Put Off" 1980). She had refused to submit to a trial by ordeal ordered by the chiefs and elders of the community to determine whether she was a witch. According to the story, the victim was ordered to appear at the chief's court to assist in the investigation of a case of witchcraft against her. When the court ordered that she submit to a trial by ordeal to determine her innocence or guilt, the woman refused to comply on the grounds that she was a Christian and that such a trial violated her Christian ideals. Consequently, she was denaturalized. In addition, she was barred from attending any funeral in the area and "on her death, she would not be accorded a fitting burial." The case received national attention when the woman filed suit at the Koforidua High Court requesting that the court quash the order of denaturalization.

Case 8.21. No More Ordeals

A middle-aged woman accused of using witchcraft to cause the death of two women killed in a motor vehicle accident was subjected to a harrowing trial by ordeal ("Trial by Ordeal" 1981). According to the facts of the case that were revealed to a trial court, an automobile accident occurred on the Accra-Ashieye road in January of that year, claiming a number of lives, including the two wives of one man. Convinced that the deaths were caused by witchcraft, the husband consulted a local herbalist. Following divination, the herbalist named a middle-aged woman who lived in the same village as the accident victims as the party responsible for the deaths. Despite her denials, she was apprehended and dragged to the home of the herbalist to undergo a trial by ordeal to prove her innocence. Here, the herbalist forcefully shaved her head, stripped her naked, and smeared her body with charcoal powder. Acting upon the instructions of the herbalist, aides put a noose around her neck as the herbalist recited incantations. It was alleged that following the incantations, the noose tightened against the alleged witch's neck, which was interpreted as a confirmation that the accused woman was indeed a witch and was guilty of causing the accident through witchcraft. Following her release by the herbalist, the woman lodged a complaint with the local police. The herbalist and witnesses who were present at the trial were all arrested, tried, convicted, and fined for the unlawful trial by ordeal. In his remarks following the conviction of the criminal defendants, the trial magistrate noted that it was a serious breach of the law for a licensed herbalist to conduct a trial by ordeal and warned that the court would deal seriously with anyone brought before it again on the same offense.

Case 8.22. The Exorcist Goes to Prison

A renowned local fetish priestess and alleged exorcist was sentenced to four years imprisonment by a Ghanaian magistrates' court (Okaitey 1985). She was charged with conducting an unlawful trial by ordeal, larceny, unlawful imprisonment, and causing damage. According to court records concerning the case, two brothers consulted a fetish priestess following suspicions that the recent death of their sister was caused by witchcraft. Confirming the brothers' supicions, the priestess led the pair to the house of a 77-year-old woman—the landlady of the deceased—proclaiming her complicity in their sister's death. While in the house, the priestess allegedly performed a short ritual that identified the 77-year-old woman as a witch and the cause of the young woman's death, then produced a snake compelling the accused witch to handle it. The priestess then entered the elderly woman's closet and took out a white kente cloth, saying it was the woman's duty apparel, or witchcraft garb. She then arrested the alleged witch, took her to her fetish shrine, stripped her naked, beat her, and subjected her to other forms of inhumane treatment. When the woman persistently denied that she was a witch, the fetish priestess locked her up in an isolation chamber and denied her food. The woman was later rescued after her relatives lodged a complaint of unlawful detention with the local police. During sentencing, the presiding magistrate of the court described the fetish priestess as "a wicked and notorious woman who had brought confusion into many homes." The priestess' lieutenant and the two brothers who sought the services of the fetish priestess were also criminally charged. The priestess had previously pleaded with the court to have mercy on her.

Case 8.23. Blamed for Asthmatic Condition

A 65-year-old female cocoa farmer was accused by her asthmatic brother of being a witch and using her witchcraft to cause his ill-health (Nehemia 1988). The victim's ordeal began when she arrived at the home of her brother, living in the same town, to bid him farewell because she was en route to her farming village. The brother asked her to accompany him to another village under the pretext of collecting a debt owed to him. Upon reaching this village, her brother accused her of being a witch and of spiritually tormenting him. When she would not yield to their accusations, she became the brunt of an assault by three men. Following the witchcraft accusations, her assailants stripped her naked, forced her to sit on a huge boulder in full public view, beat her, tortured her, and forced her to confess to bizarre witchcraft activities, including the bewitchment and spiritual torment of her accusing brother. The accusers and the assailants included her 45-year-old brother and two other male accomplices—a 27-year-old fetish priest and his twin brother, who was also the priest's page-boy. According to police records, the assaults resulted in deep cuts and bruises all over the victim's body. But for her timely rescue by her son and armed police, the victim would have perished. By the time the series of assaults on her ended, she had been deprived of her gold jewelry and several pieces of clothing believed to be the repository of her witchcraft. The three were arrested and put before a court for "causing harm, trial by ordeal and abetment of crime."

Case 8.24. The Octogenarian Mother as an Alleged Witch

A 55-year-old man was apprehended by police for inflicting severe knife wounds on his eighty-year-old mother on suspicion that the elderly woman was a witch who had been an obstacle in his effort to achieve economic prosperity (Yamoah 2005). According to police records, a few weeks prior to the attack, the defendant, an unemployed drifter, visited his mother's home and pleaded with her to allow him to stay in her house. The elderly woman not only acquiesced to the request, but also showed him a piece of farmland and purchased a machete for him, with the understanding that the defendant would engage in farming for his upkeep. On the day of the knife assault, the defendant returned home drunk and started insulting his mother. He then pulled the machete, entered his mother's bedroom and dealt her several blows on the head, neck, and back. Screams for help from the elderly woman attracted neighbors who rushed to the scene. With the aid of a long club, the neighbors managed to disarm the assailant. Police arrived later on the scene to convey the comatose woman to the local hospital. The attack sent the elderly woman to the hospital with wounds on the head, neck, and back and in a comatose state.

Case 8.25. Returning Home?

In August 2005 a woman in her mid-nineties was nearly mauled to death by a band of neighborhood youths in Kumasi, the second-largest city in the country, on suspicion that she was a witch ("Labeling People Witches" 2005; Nunoo 2005). The incident occurred when the youth came across the frail, haggardly, and distraught woman sitting atop a big boulder in front of a residential building around one o'clock in the morning. The youth surmised that the woman was returning home from a nocturnal witches' Sabbath and that her journey had been derailed by their witch-sighting. After subjecting her to four hours of torment, including verbal abuse, the youth frogmarched the woman to the local police station where police personnel detained her for another three hours while attempting to disperse a fractious crowd that had congregated in front of the police station clamoring to mete out "instant justice" to the woman. In the middle the commotion, relatives of the elderly woman arrived at the police station to appeal for calm and to secure her release to their care. They informed the police that the woman was psychiatrically impaired and a member of the royal family of a nearby town. She sometimes wandered from home, occasionally at odd hours. It was during one of those absences that she was accosted by the youth and branded a witch. Following publicity given the story, the Board of Directors of Help Age Ghana, a nongovernmental organization, called for the criminalization of witchcraft accusation in the country as a measure to combat violence toward elderly persons in the name of witchcraft suspicions and accusations.

Case 8.26. A Private Matter?

In January 2001 a 25-year-old, unemployed man in the village of Tongor in the Kpandu District of the Volta Region used a machete to slash the head and sever the hands of his 75-year-old paralyzed and bedridden aunt (Ephson 2001). He suspected the elderly woman of being a witch responsible for his prior job loss, current protracted unemployment, and general lack of economic advancement in life. The attack was perpetrated amidst shouts of "witch, witch" by the assailant at the victim. In a post hoc crime interview with police the man claimed that he had been informed "upon consultations" with various witch doctors that his father's sister was the cause of his woes. Despite the man's heinous actions, the incident was not reported to police until a month had elapsed because the victim and her family regarded the assault as a family problem and a private matter. The assailant was later sentenced to prison for six years of hard labor.

Case 8.27. "You Killed My Mother!"

In this 2005 case a 22-year-old unemployed man found himself on the wrong side of the law when he attempted to avenge the death of his mother ("Man in Custody" 2005). According to police records, the assailant blamed his mother's sisters for having spiritually caused her death through witchcraft. In his determination to avenge his mother's death and punish the culprits involved, he physically assaulted one of the aunts with whom he shared a home and caused extensive damage to the wooden structure the aunt used as a kitchen. At the time of the media report on this story, the man, who had been arraigned in court on a charge of causing unlawful damage, had pleaded not guilty to the charge and was to appear in court at a later date for trial.

Case 8.28. The Polygynous, Hypertensive Man

The deteriorating physical health of a hypertensive man who later suffered a stroke was attributed to the witchcraft of his seventy-year-old mother ("Woman, 70, Accused" 1998). Unbeknownst to the victim that she was the prime suspect in a witchcraft divination case in which she was identified as the source of her son's hypertension and a stroke, the woman made a trip to visit her sick, bedridden son at a Christian prayer camp and healing center. There she endured a harrowing experience that nearly cost her her life. According to case records, the polygynous man with four wives and ten children had been diagnosed with hypertension by a local doctor and prescribed hypertensive drugs for his treatment. However, the family was unable to afford the cost of the medication, which was therefore discontinued. A few months later, the man suffered a stroke and was admitted to a local hospital for treatment. Unable to afford the financial expenses associated with the hospitalization and medical care, the family abandoned medical treatment at the hospital, transferring him to the custody of two male, self-proclaimed spiritualists who purported to have the ability to use traditional herbal cures and spiritual power to effect a cure for his physical conditions. As partial payment for their care, the spiritualists collected money the equivalent of US$300 and several other items from the family, then conducted a divination that allegedly implicated the man's septuagenarian mother as the cause of his physical ailments. The spiritualists then lured the victim to their operational base under the guise of encouraging her to visit her sick, bedridden son. Upon arrival at the healing center, she was bundled up and thrown into "a room engulfed in a thick cloud of 'pepperish' choking smoke" and urged to confess to being the culprit in her son's bewitchment. She collapsed, recovering only later at a local hospital where she was taken by some neighbors who responded to her screams for help. Following her release from the hospital, the victim reported the matter to the local office of the Commission on Human Rights and Administrative Justice, where it was directed that the ailing man be returned to the hospital, that no further money be paid to the self-proclaimed spiritualists, and that family members refrain from their accusations of witchcraft against the victim.

Case 8.29. Eight Years of Confinement

A girl with epilepsy who was suspected of being a witch was confined by her family to a barricaded room for eight years, forced to share the dark, cramped space with the family's chickens and goats (Gbolu 2006). Barred from all human contact, the girl was only occasionally fed with table scraps and only periodically bathed. Confined at the age of nine, she was rescued eight years later by a child advocacy group. When the girl was found as a seventeen-year-old, she could barely speak coherent sentences, was unkempt, and had broken bones and twisted limbs from the years of physical neglect and abuse and from constant crouching and lying on the bare floor. According to the facts surrounding the case, at age six the girl began to suffer from the symptoms of epilepsy, including recurrent seizures. To the family and wider community of the small town in which she lived, these presented as an inexplicable illness. When she did not recover from the ministrations of doctors at the local hospital and the herbal cures of indigenous healers, her family grew suspicious that her illness derived from a spiritual cause. Her father's death two years later appeared to confirm the family's suspicions. She was pronounced a witch by her mother and accused of being spiritually responsible for her father's death.

Case 8.30. Two Grandchildren and Financial Woes

A grandmother who believed her vending business was faring poorly and who suspected that money was disappearing mysteriously from her home sought the assistance of a local cleric to determine the cause of her financial woes (Gbolu 2006). The pastor determined that her financial problems were due to the malevolent actions of witches. He then accused the woman's two female grandchildren of being the witches responsible not only for their grandmother's financial difficulties, but also for the general lack of financial prosperity of the entire village. Upon the orders of the pastor, the girls were taken to a local prayer camp and healing center where they were formally accused. The girls, aged twelve and fourteen years, were repeatedly whipped with canes as part of an exorcism ritual intended to cast out demons and were ordered to surrender their witchcraft powers for destruction in order that they would be freed from the "bondage of witchcraft." When they denied the witch accusations, they were repeatedly beaten. Information regarding the abuse reached the child welfare and human rights authorities, who rescued the two victims. By then, the young girls had been forced to drop out of school as the imputations of witchcraft led members of the community to ostracize them. Stigmatized, despised, and shunned, they were found living in seclusion from family and friends.

Case 8.31. Beaten into a Coma

The principal and students of a local computer and secretarial school detained an elderly woman, verbally abused her, stripped her naked, and beat her into a coma ("Party Official Helps Police" 2006). The assailants suspected that the older woman was a witch who was returning home from a nocturnal witches' rendezvous. According to the facts of the case, a man brought his 110-year-old mother from the village of Bunkpurugu in the Northern Region to live with him at Wiawso where he lived and worked. The man had lived together with his mother in the community without incident for three months. The elderly woman had been advised to take regular walks to maintain her physical fitness and overall health. This she did every morning by walking a few yards away from her home. The day of the incident, she set off for her regular walk at 6:00 A.M. When she did not return soon after, the man and his son went in search of her. About two hundred meters away, they found the woman surrounded by a hostile mob. She had been stripped naked and brutally beaten by a mob that included the principal and students of the computer and secretarial school. The crowd claimed that they had apprehended a witch and were in the process of saying prayers for her. The first to discover the mistreatment of the elderly woman was the victim's grandson. When he attempted to rescue the woman, the crowd set upon him and beat him as well. The woman's son and other members of her family arrived in time to avert a tragic escalation of the violence. They managed to rescue the old woman and rushed her to the local hospital where she was treated for her comatose condition and multiple injuries sustained from the brutal beating.

Case 8.32. Those Force-Feedings

In this case which was profiled in the introduction of the book, a 44-year-old woman was charged with cruelty for subjecting her seven-year-old nephew to force-feedings of human urine and excreta (Tenyah 2009). Police investigations into the case revealed that this abuse was part of a systematic pattern of torture that the victim had endured at the hands of an aunt with whom he was residing. The force-feedings were intended to extract a confession from the boy that he was a malevolent wizard. The aunt began leveling witchcraft allegations against her nephew following claims by her pastor, who told her that her nephew was using witchcraft powers to afflict her mother with ailments that the older woman had been suffering from that were resistant to medical treatment. In addition to using force-feedings to coerce a confession, the aunt also applied a heated pressing iron to the face, hands, legs and chest of the victim.

Case 8.33. To Confess or Not to Confess?

Four persons, including a self-proclaimed fetish priest, were arrested at Odortia, a village in the Greater Accra Region, by law enforcement officials for subjecting a middle-aged woman to a harrowing trial by ordeal for one month ("Four Arrested" 2001). The victim, forty years old, was accused of being a witch and subjected to severe physical maltreatment. The four assailants comprised the fetish priest who made the imputation of witchcraft, the father of the victim, as well as a brother and a sister of the victim. Details of the case indicate that as part of her ordeal the victim was asked to squat for several days beside a deep hole that had been dug. A thick rope was tied around her neck while the other end of the rope was pegged down to a stick in the hole. Whenever the victim attempted to stand up, the rope squeezed her neck, forcing her back into the squatting position. The victim was said to have remained in the squatting position from 6:30 A.M. to 9:00 P.M. daily for three consecutive days. On the third day, she succumbed to the pressure to confess to being a witch. Following the confession, she was freed from one ordeal only to begin another. In the second phase of the ordeal, the fetish priest shaved the victim's hair with crude metal objects. He then sentenced her to penal servitude as a laborer on his farm during the day while doing domestic chores in his house in the mornings and evenings. The victim's family was asked to supply certain materials for her exorcism before he would release her. The victim continued to be subjected to this form of servitude until her husband, who was unaware of his wife's whereabouts for a month, finally traced her to the fetish priest's shrine and secured her release. Upon reaching the bus terminal, the victim's brother, who was complicit in her detention, attempted to abduct her and return her to the fetish priest. The ensuing commotion caused the police to intervene and arrest the brother and all the assailants involved in the woman's ordeal.

Case 8.34. Two Pastors Convicted in Court for Child Abuse

Two male pastors of a local pentecostal church were arrested by police for subjecting three children to a harrowing ordeal involving torture, ostensibly to exorcise them of evil spirits (Yamoah 2009). The victims, a boy and two girls aged eleven, six, and four, respectively, had accompanied their parents to the church's healing center for worship. During the sermon the children were singled out and identified as witches. Following the accusation, the children were prepared for exorcism. The pastors forced all three victims to kneel down and hold up a piece of cement block in their palms while being whipped with brooms across their backs and buttocks by the pastors, ostensibly to exorcise them of the witch spirits. Only the timely intervention of a witness who was in the vicinity of the church prevented the situation from degenerating further. Upon hearing the loud and agonizing cries of the children, this witness went to investigate, and upon surveying the scene, immediately called the police. The pastors were arrested and tried. They pleaded guilty to charges of assault and child abuse. The court imposed a fine the equivalent of about US$3,000 on each of the defendants. In default of payment of the fine, they were to receive a custodial sentence of twelve months of imprisonment.

Case 8.35. "You Are Responsible for my Sleepless Nights"

A 25-year-old male mason was arraigned before a magistrate court on a charge of causing harm when he physically assaulted a friend that he accused of bewitching him (Kumi 2008). According to the facts of the case, the two had been good friends for years. A few weeks prior to the assault, the assailant complained to some other friends that he was suffering from insomnia. He blamed the victim for bewitching him and for being spiritually responsible for his sleepless nights. On the day of the violent assault, the assailant confronted his friend and accused him of being responsible for his insomnia. The assailant vehemently denied any responsibility for his affliction. The assailant, further incensed by the denial, grabbed a stick and struck the victim twice in the head. At the time the assailant was arraigned before court, the victim was still in critical condition at a local hospital, having become unconscious from the vicious attack.

Case 8.36. A One-Month-Old Infant Declared a Witch

This case demonstrates the far-reaching repercussions of witchcraft imputation not only for the alleged witch, but also for subsequent generations of the accused. In this case a one-month-old female infant was branded a witch ("One-Month-Old Baby" 2008). Community sanctions against her, her mother, and other caregivers were so severe that she was subsequently abandoned in a dungeon, ostensibly to die so family members could live their lives, unencumbered by community ostracism. However, she was rescued by a member of the community who turned her over to government authorities.

The witchcraft allegation against the infant stemmed from the fact that both her mother and grandmother had, in prior years, been branded witches. The facts of the case indicate that several years prior to the infant's birth, her maternal grandmother was branded a witch by community members and tortured to death. At that time, the infant's mother was a young girl in the community. She was also branded a witch while a fourth-grade elementary school student. Due to the discrimination leveled against her and her family, she was eventually expelled from her school. When other schools in the area refused to grant her admission, she was forced to drop out of school completely. At the age of twenty-two, she became pregnant by a young man in the community. When her boyfriend learned about the witchcraft accusations against her, he abandoned the expectant mother. After the woman gave birth, the harassment against her and her infant intensified, and included physical attacks on the two. In grief about her circumstances, the mother died when her infant baby was barely a month old. With the infant girl now left in the care of her uncle, community sanctions extended onto him, with accusations that the uncle was a wizard. Public lynch mobs subjected him to severe beatings and forced him to confess to being a wizard to spare his own life. The infant girl and anyone who assumed the role of her caregiver continued to endure taunts and stigmatization. According to the report, "whoever carried the infant in the house or community was shunned and hooted at by community members and even immediate neighbors." However, community members stopped short of killing the baby. Community members held religious beliefs that the killing of any infant, even an infant witch, would provoke the wrath of the gods. However, community harassment made the care of the infant an ordeal for the relatives. Family members then decided to abandon the infant in a dark dungeon. That was when government officials intervened to save her life. The infant was moved out of the community and into another town where she was renamed to hide her identity and taken into a foster home.

Case 8.37. The Girl in the Wooden Cage

In January 2012 a joint team of law enforcement officers and officials of Ghana's Department of Social Welfare stormed a local Christian prayer camp to rescue a sixteen-year-old girl being forcefully detained there (Aklorbortu 2012b). The junior high school student had been involuntarily held in the camp for four years during which she was physically assailed and psychologically abused on suspicion that she possessed maleficent and contaminating witchcraft. According to reports by a leading local daily newspaper, the sixteen-year-old was asthmatic and had been taken by her mother to the prayer camp for prayers and spiritual healing. While at the camp, the prophetess and overseer of the camp spiritually diagnosed and attributed her condition to witchcraft, saying her asthmatic condition was a manifestation of witchcraft possession. She professed to have the capacity to exorcise the girl of the witchcraft but the teenager would have to await her turn at the facility until the time came for her exorcism. She was then put in seclusion in a specially constructed wooden cage without light, bath, or toilet facilities. At night, she was forced to sleep on the wooden floor of the makeshift structure. To further emphasize the extent of her contaminating witchcraft, the wooden structure was positioned several yards away from the main premises of the prayer camp. Her food and water were placed a distance from the cage as a person shouted at her to collect her food and water. According to the teenager, due to the location of the cage next to bushland, she was exposed to snakes and other reptiles. Government officials learned that in addition to her exclusion, her mother had been placed in perpetual bondage to the camp, forced by the prophetess to pledge her services to the prayer center for the rest of her life as a condition for the healing of her daughter.

Case 8.38. Forced Landing of an Aerial Flight?

In September 2011 a frail 85-year-old woman residing with her extended kinsfolk in Accra wandered away from home. When she did not return after several hours, her family mounted an intensive search. It took the family several days to locate her. Family members described her as suffering from dementia and Alzheimer's disease. During the four days she was missing, she was passed off between four governmental agencies, shunted from one to another as each claimed lack of jurisdictional authority over her. Meanwhile, a group of bystanders who were among the first to encounter her after she wandered away subjected her to intense questioning. According to these interrogators, when they discovered her lying helplessly by a dirt road in a suburb of the city the elderly woman confessed to being a witch whose nocturnal aerial flight with fifteen other witches in her witch coven had been derailed. After this alleged witchcraft confession, her interrogators pelted her with stones with the intention of lynching her. When Red Cross personnel rescued her from her attackers and took her to the local police station, police personnel refused to take her, saying that she was not a criminal. When she was taken to a psychiatric hospital, she was refused admission by staff who said they could not admit or treat her since she had not been formally diagnosed as mentally ill. When she was taken to a hospital, she was refused admission because she was not suffering from any demonstrable illness. It was at this hospital that a patient on admission indicated that she knew the elderly woman and was able to notify her relatives. By the time the family arrived to take her home, a fractious crowd of onlookers had gathered to catch a glimpse of a witch whose aerial flight had been aborted (Arthur 2011).

This chapter, the preceding chapter, and the case studies depict the extent of the physical and psychological maltreatment mounted against accused witches. The level of mistreatment reflects the social abhorrence toward witchcraft in Ghanaian communities. The data further show a preponderance of females among accused witches. The following chapter provides a discussion and analysis of the gendered nature of witchcraft ideology.

Chapter 9

GENDERED VICTIMIZATION
Patriarchy, Misogyny, and Gynophobia

The preceding analysis of data regarding witchcraft accusations and violent victimization of putative witches clearly demonstrates the gendered nature of witchcraft beliefs and practices in contemporary Ghanaian society. On the one hand, the data reveal the predominance of females among the victims of witchcraft suspicions, accusations, and accompanying aggression; on the other hand, the data demonstrate that males account for a disproportionate percentage of accusers and victimizers. In many instances, accusations of witchcraft were made by young men against women who were much older than the men. Further evidence of the disproportionate representation of females as victims of violence associated with witchcraft accusations in Ghana is found in the special refuges or asylums established for accused witches fleeing physical retribution from their attackers (Adinkrah 2004; Badoe 2011; "Report on the Round Table Conference on the Treatment of Suspected Witches in Northern Ghana" 1998). Indeed, available data demonstrate that in the Northern Region of Ghana where these witches' sanctuaries are disproportionately sited, over 95 percent of the residents in the camps are women. To illustrate, in 1997 the Commission on Human Rights and Administrative Justice, Ghana's constitutionally mandated local human rights organization, conducted investigations into the witches' camps and found disturbing evidence of gender-based violence and displacement, noting, "out of a total population of 815 persons found in witches homes in four districts of the Northern Region, only 13 were males" ("Report on the Round Table Conference on the Treatment of Suspected Witches in Northern Ghana" 1998, 16). In 2001 it was estimated that some five thousand to eight thousand suspected witches, mostly women, had been banished to live in servitude under physically dehumanizing conditions in these sanctuaries ("Round Table Conference on the Treatment of Suspected Witches" 1998; Wiafe 2001). During a February 19, 2004, research trip to the Gambaga Witches' Camp, a refuge for women fleeing witch persecution, I found that all but one of the eighty-three residents were women (see Figures 9.1 and 9.2). In addition to those sequestered in witches' sanctuaries, the majority of alleged witches undergoing exorcism rituals in Christian prayer camps and Christian spiritual churches are women (Amoah 1987). Similarly, the vast majority of persons undergoing antiwitchcraft cleansing rituals in fetish shrines and traditional healing centers in the southern regions of the country are women (Amoah 1987).

Such female overrepresentation among the victims of witchcraft persecution is particularly vexing considering that witchcraft beliefs of the various Ghanaian ethnic groups plainly demonstrate that both males and females can be witches and male witchcraft power tends to be far more potent and sinister than female witchcraft power (Adinkrah 2004; Bannerman-Richter 1982; Debrunner 1961). The lingering question, then, is why more women than men are victims of witch hunts.

There is nothing novel about the idea of a female witch. Witchcraft historiography indicates that accused and executed witches in seventeenth-century European and American societies were predominantly female (Bailey 2002; Behringer 1997; Brauner 1995; Roper 2004; Rowlands 2001). Jensen (2007, 5) notes, "most studies estimate somewhere between 70 and 90 percent of the targets were women." The literature on witch persecutions also indicates that witch hunts were largely conducted by men. Among explanations offered for this observed pattern was the deeply mi-

Figure 9.1. The Author at a Witches' Camp in Northern Ghana

Figure 9.2. Women Inmates at a Witches' Camp in Northern Ghana

sogynistic attitudes that pervaded American and European societies during the era of the witch hunts (Brauner 1995; Roper 2004). Male hegemony and female subordination were well established in patriarchal norms. Despite the profusion of literature on the topic, particularly with references to medieval Europe and the British colonies in the New World, the issue has received paltry attention in the professional literature on non-Western societies.

At present, it is unclear whether the strong association between witchcraft and gender described for early modern Europe and colonial United States is similar to or different from the observed patterns in non-Western societies and, if so, what accounts for the similarities and differences. Given the noted gap in the literature, this chapter concentrates explicitly on answering the question of why witchcraft-related violence in Ghana has been most often directed against women. It contends that to answer this question, one needs to examine fully Ghanaian society's attitudes toward males and females as well as notions of masculinity and femininity. For instance, I will argue that female overrepresentation among suspected and accused witches is traceable to deeply held misogynistic attitudes and gynophobic beliefs, which are the effects of patriarchal arrangements and ideology embedded in the society. In Ghana there is a strong, general expectation that males must conform to cultural norms of masculinity and that females must abide by the norms of femininity. Witchcraft accusations and related violence are most often directed toward the female whose behavior is interpreted as deviating from cultural expectations around gender norms. I further argue that women's social and economic positions provide an important backdrop for understanding women's victimization in witch hunts in Ghana. Evidence of the backlash hypothesis is evident. As the backlash hypothesis posits, "changes in women's working lives, and in attendant cultural norms about family responsibilities and even sexuality, have made women more vulnerable to physical violence" (Heimer and Kruttschnitt 2006, 9). It is further argued that elderly women in Ghana experience witchcraft-related violence at the highest rate in the society because of their latent, predisposed, or vulnerable status. Presently, they are less capable of repelling their assailants than are men.

Notions of Masculinity and Femininity in Ghanaian Society

This section of the chapter explores local notions of masculinity and femininity in Ghanaian society and their implications for witchcraft suspicions, accusations, and the treatment of accused witches. As is the case in many societies, all ethnic groups in Ghana maintain that there are core differences between males and females that result in unique features of femaleness and maleness. At present, most Ghanaians believe that there are male and female human natures fundamentally distinct from each other. Male and female behavioral differences are said to be governed by the interaction of biological and social influences. For example, Akan culture acknowledges the biological distinctions between the sexes, including differences in primary sex characteristics such as external genitalia and secondary sex characteristics that include the larger breasts and broader hips of women, and the deeper voice and presence of facial hair of men. So entrenched are recognized biological distinctions between males and females in the society that any deviation from this pattern, however slight, engenders suspicion and censure. When a female is identified as having behavioral or physiological characteristics normally associated with males, society views her with the greatest negativity. For instance, many Ghanaians believe that the presence of facial hair and a deep voice in a female is symptomatic of witchcraft. By contrast, males who exhibit female attributes such as larger breasts or soft voices are only occasionally the subject of suspicion and ridicule in their community. Consider the following statement from a fifteen-year-old informant:

> In my small village, there is this middle-aged woman called Yaa Dansoa. She is married and has four children. Several people in the village, including older people and young children, males and females, regard her as a witch. Some people treat her with disrespect; some even harass her children and call them names. Why? Because they say she has hair on her chin and on her upper lip. She even has what some people called "sideburns." I don't think she behaves differently from other women in the village. All we know is that women who become witches tend to grow beards and moustaches. To many people, she is a witch because she has a beard, moustache and sideburns, something which only men are supposed to have; a woman is not supposed to have a beard or moustache.

This quotation corroborates the observations of other witchcraft scholars who have written on Ghanaian witchcraft. Consider, for example, an excerpt from Bannerman-Richter's biography of a self-proclaimed witch in Ghana:

> One day my husband noticed a strand of hair on my chin and he exclaimed, "Ama Ninsin, you are growing a beard! Any woman who grows a beard is a witch!" Of course, it is not necessarily true that any such woman is a witch as it is commonly believed in Ghana. My husband was just saying that in jest, for he neither suspected nor knew at the time that I was indeed a witch. He continued, "Ama Ninsin, look, here is a strand of hair on your chin! What is

becoming of you? You better watch out, for you seem to be on your way to becoming a witch." (Bannerman-Richter 1984, 43)

In addition to the primary and secondary sex characteristics, Ghanaians acknowledge additional physical differences between males and females. For example, the average male is expected to be relatively taller, physically larger, heavier, more muscular, and physically stronger than is the average female. Consistent with these supposed physical traits, males in the society are often assigned tasks requiring physical strength. In former times when the various tribes waged punitive expeditions and wars of territorial expansion, men performed the duties associated with combat. Even today, Ghanaian men perform the more risky and dangerous communal tasks such as house-building and road construction. Men also work in the more hazardous occupations such as hunting and mining. They dominate, as well, in the more powerful, high-status professional and managerial positions in the society. In contrast, females, who society considers to be less capable of physical exertion, are assigned tasks closer to hearth and home, including collecting firewood, cooking, cleaning, sewing, and laundering clothes. Such rigid adherence to notions of gender and physiology has implications for witchcraft accusations and witchcraft-related violence. Since boys and men are expected to be relatively larger and physically stronger than girls and women, Ghanaian females who deviate from this normative expectations of gender physiology—such as females who are generally bigger, taller, and stronger than males—are mockingly referred to as witches. Similarly, girls and women who are strong enough to physically fight and dominate male compeers are suspected of being witches.

Among Ghanaians, there are also important recognized behavioral differences between males and females that are believed to be innate. What are Akan conceptions of feminine and masculine behavior? Being female is being gentle and cooperative whereas being male means being forceful and competitive. Men are expected to be strong, aggressive, and decisive; women are expected to be weak, passive, and indecisive. Women who deviate from the normative expectations of gender are accused of witchcraft and subjected to violence as a way of keeping them in check. Thus girls who are perceived to be more physically aggressive than boys are believed to be witches. Although expectations about gender are changing, girls who display athleticism or excel in sports events are looked upon with suspicion. For example, during my childhood in southern Ghana, females who excelled in stereotypically male sports such as soccer were teased and derided as witches.

Another example concerns male and female emotional expression. Throughout Ghana, among the various ethnic groups, there is less acceptance of emotional expression in men. Boys are socialized to suppress such feelings as fear, anxiety, and sadness. "Obarima nsu" (males don't cry) is a constant refrain or exhortation to boys and men who have been hurt physically or emotionally, discouraging them from expressing an emotional response. For example, while women are expected to weep or wail uncontrollably at funerals, and may in fact be taught the art of wailing, men are discouraged from shedding tears or crying at the funerals of even the closest of family relations. By contrast, of the stoic woman who does not weep or wail at funerals, it is said, "n'ani ase yɛ den" (she does not cry easily), and must be a witch. Not only would such a woman be accused of being a witch but, for her lack of tears, would most likely be accused of being the source of the deceased's demise. Ghanaians also regard women as having maternal instincts and as being naturally nurturing. Thus, gender norms for girls include a strong expectation that they marry and bear children. Consequently, females who are reluctant to marry and are uninterested in children are deemed deviant and may experience enormous pressures to alter their behavior to fit within the normative expectations. Witchcraft accusations are among the negative sanctions imposed on women and girls for their lack of compliance with gender norms.

Gynophobic Attitudes and Beliefs about Women

The ubiquity of gynophobic attitudes and beliefs in Ghanaian society and culture appears to be another major factor influencing the tendency to perceive, suspect, and accuse females of being witches, which contributes to their subsequent violent victimization in witch hunts.

Gynophobia refers to the fear or hatred of women. Among the languages for all ethnic groups in Ghana, there are maxims or proverbial expressions that convey variable levels of gynophobia. For example, among the Akans, there is the saying that "sɛ w'ansuro ɔbaa a, worennyin nnkyɛ" (if you don't fear a woman, you will not live long). There are several other related Akan sayings that describe women in phobic terms. Some common sayings are "ɛmaa ho yɛ hu" (women are terrifying beings), "ɛmaa yɛ awudifoɔ" (women are murderers), and "asɛm bɔne bɛba a, na ɛfiri ɔbaa" (all evil things originate with a woman). Such phobic expressions about females are based on rigid, generalized perceptions that females are cunning, sly, covetous, avaricious, acquisitive, materialistic, treacherous, gossip-mongerers who are full of intrigues. Numerous Akan folktales and song lyrics perpetuate similar stereotyping of women. Similar messages are inscribed on commercial motor vehicles plying Ghana's streets. While there is societal recognition of women's contributions as wives, child-bearers, caregivers, and homemakers, these contributions are countered with ideas about female predisposition toward mischief. Men are exhorted to exercise circumspection in their associations and dealings with women lest they be led astray, suffer economic ruination, or social disgrace. For married men there is the expression, "sɛ wonya asɛm a, ɛnnka nkyerɛ wo yere" (don't share secrets with your wife). It is often said "ɛnnye obaa nni" (don't trust a woman), because they may beguile a man into com-mitting evil deeds. In many of these expressions, fearing women and be-ing guarded in one's relations with women are prescriptions for a man's peace and longevity on this earth and for achieving social and economic success. One Akan proverb tells men, "sɛ wopɛ wo yere bebrebe a, oma wo bɔ dam" (if you love your wife too much, she'll make you go insane). Another says, "sɛ wo fa ɔbaa yɔnko a, ɛhia wo" (if you take a woman for a companion, you live in poverty). Still, another, "wo di mmaa akyi a w'afuo ka adwooguo" (if you associate with women too much, your farm will be up to no good). A popular inscription on commercial vehicles and other commercial sign posts warns men directly to "suro ɔbaa" (fear woman). A more poignant inscription implicitly warns of the consequences of not fearing women: "sɛ w'ansuro ɔbaa a, worennyini nkyɛ" (if you don't fear women, you won't live long).

Gynophobic characterizations of women have major implications for witchcraft-related violence. First, there is the mistrust that such beliefs breed. Males who have been exposed to these ideas potentially develop highly prejudicial views of women, including scapegoating them for per-sonal and societal problems. These attitudes can reinforce or provide an ideological rationale or justification for the mistreatment of women that often includes full-fledged violence. It is small wonder, then, that many Ghanaian men have come to see women as the cause of their personal or social problems. In chapters 7 and 8 of this book we found numerous instances where men looked to female relatives—their mothers, aunts, sisters, and wives—as the source of their sexual impotence, financial ruin-ation, and myriad physical and mental ailments.

Covetousness as Part of Women's Nature

To fully understand female overrepresentation among suspected and ac-cused witches, one also needs to examine the motivations that Ghanaians ascribe to those persons accused of witchcraft. According to Ghanaian witchcraft lore, witches spiritually assault their victims out of envy, jeal-ousy, and covetousness. In Akan, jealousy and covetousness are known as *anibrɛ*. Females are said to be *anibrɛ* or to harbor jealous or envious tendencies. A popular saying is "ɛmaa ani bere adeɛ kyɛn mmarima" (females are more covetous than males). It is also believed that the *anibrɛ* of females is innate or inborn, and thus cannot be shed, discarded, or jettisoned. Women and girls are said to covet whatever others have, especially the marks or symbols of success, both material, such as money or children, and immaterial, such as status, power, or prestige. It is the females who display *anibrɛ bɔne* (extreme covetousness) that are most likely to become witches. Witches are also considered naturally inclined to use their witchcraft power to cause the social or economic downfall or physical demise of the object of their envy and jealousy. Inasmuch as Ghanaian society views women as innately covetous, and covetousness is identified as a motivating factor for the bewitchment of others, a woman is more likely than a man to be suspected and accused of witchcraft whenever there is suspicion of bewitchment.

Women's Spiritual Weakness

Many Ghanaians attribute the greater tendency of women to become witches to women's supposed spiritual weakness and their natural proclivity for evil (Amoah 1987; Bannerman-Richter 1982, 1984). A recurrent theme that emerged during interviews with Ghanaians about the relationship between female status and witchcraft accusations was presumptions about the physical, mental, spiritual, and moral inferiority of females. From the perspective of some Christian Ghanaians, these inferiorities made women susceptible to the temptations of the devil and consequently more prone to become witches than males. According to several Christian informants, God created man in his own image. Because people often view God as male, a man therefore has God-like features. He is mentally strong, spiritually firm, and morally superior. A woman, on the other hand, sprang from a man's body, represented in Eve's creation from Adam's rib. A woman is therefore only a fraction as strong as a man—mentally, morally, and spiritually. This is reflected in women's lesser physical and mental constitution. Relative to men, women are said to be more malleable, impressionable, gullible, and easily corrupted. Their supposed weaker constitution that makes them more prone to envy, covetousness, greed, demonic deception, and seductions also makes them more inclined to turn to maleficent witchcraft.

Traditionally, Akan gender ideology holds the female to be spiritually inferior to her male counterpart. Males are said to have stronger *sunsum* than females, who have light or weak *sunsum* (Amoah 1987, 86). Males are born with stronger *sunsum* because they will need a relative surplus of the spiritual substance to pass on to their children. It is believed to be transferred from the father to his progeny at or during birth. It is averred that this gender differential in male and female spirituality manifests itself in men's relatively greater courage, bravery, stoicism, and ruggedness.

Given their presumptive spiritual weakness, Akan women are precluded from participation in certain religious practices. For example, among Akans an important religious practice is the pouring of libation. Here, on religious holidays and special occasions, alcoholic drinks are poured onto the bare earth. Then male Akans summon ancestral spirits buried within the earth and resident in the netherworld to come and accept the drink offering in exchange for bountiful crop yields, good health, and reproductive fertility. Women are generally barred from pouring libation or participating in any other way during this ceremony. In the rare instances when women are allowed participation, it is confined to women who have reached menopause.

This perception of women as mentally, spiritually, temperamentally, and morally weak and untrustworthy has major implications for witchcraft accusations. Given their perceived inferior spiritual and moral strength, females are considered more susceptible to manipulations by and temptations from malevolent spiritual forces. This accounts, in part, for the disproportionate representation of women among witches and their greater susceptibility to witchcraft accusation and violent victimization.

Scapegoating

The concept of the scapegoat is relevant in explaining the predominance of women and girls among suspected, accused, and violently victimized putative witches. According to Jary and Jary (1991, 549), a scapegoat is "a person or group made, unjustifiably, to bear the blame for the problems and misfortunes of others." Jensen (2007, 61) defines scapegoating as "the displacement of blame, anger, or anxiety on people who are not actually responsible for a problem but provide convenient targets of attack because of other characteristics that they possess." There are a number of features that characterize a scapegoat. First, scapegoats are often visibly identifiable groups such as racial and ethnic minorities. Second, scapegoated individuals or groups are typically the most vulnerable persons or beleaguered groups in the society, having the least social, political, economic, and, in some cases, physical power. As a result of their condition or status, they are incapable or limited in offering effective resistance to their victimization. Third, central to the scapegoat concept is the notion that scapegoats are blamed for the misfortunes of others in ways that mask, distract, or draw attention away from the actual underlying causes of societal woes.

Earlier sections of this book have documented the subordinate status of Ghanaian females vis-à-vis their male counterparts in every societal domain. In Ghana, as in other patriarchal societies, females occupy marginalized positions in all major institutions throughout the society. This is particularly the case for elderly women, many of whom suffer the quadruple jeopardy of being female, elderly, poor, and widowed. With their marginalized status, they are easy targets for others to blame them for personal and social ills, hardships, and misfortunes. They then become vulnerable to violent victimization as others direct their hostility toward them. To illustrate, in 1997 elderly women in the Northern Region of Ghana were accused of employing witchcraft to cause and spread a cerebrospinal meningitis epidemic that claimed the lives of more than five hundred people. Unschooled in the etiology and trajectory of disease transmission, residents in the afflicted communities imputed the disease and its spread to witchcraft. Elderly women were, then, identified as the culprits in a community that vented its rage on the women. Many elderly women were lynched by angry mobs as the public attempted to extirpate the alleged maleficent witches in their midst. Analyses of data in chapters 7 and 8 also demonstrated several cases in which elderly women were blamed for the misfortunes or shortcomings of their relatives or communities and were lethally and sublethally assaulted. Consistent with scapegoating theory, people experiencing severe difficulties or frustrations in their lives lashed out against elderly female relatives whom they accused of witchcraft to rationalize or explain away their own shortcomings or failings.

Family Stress Theory and Caregiver Burden

Family stress theory and the concept of caregiver burden provide additional plausible explanations for the disproportionate representation of elderly women among accused witches in societies such as Ghana where witchcraft beliefs and witch persecutions result in the violent victimization of elderly persons. Social gerontologists Morgan and Kunkel (1998, 245) define caregiver burden as the "degree of strain reflecting lower life satisfaction, depression, and a decline in health among care providers to dependent relatives or friends." In another definition, Hill and Amuwo (1998, 204) emphasize the "physical, emotional, financial and other problems encountered by persons who provide services to the impaired elderly." Family stress theory, a widely accepted perspective for explaining elder victimization, suggests that providing care for an elderly person produces tensions within the family and frustrations for the individual caregiver. According to the theory, the time and financial investment in providing care for elderly persons may lead to economic hardship, frequent interruptions of privacy, and other stresses that may cause the caregiver to feel resentment toward the elderly person.

Family stress theory and the concept of caregiver burden are particularly salient to discussions of the elderly and their violent victimization in the industrializing nations of Africa. Here, the absence of governmental social security programs has shifted elderly caregiver responsibilities onto adult offspring and other relatives. In Ghana, for example, adult offspring and other extended family members routinely provide a wide array of care, including assistance during illness, financial support, health-care expenditures, housing needs, emotional support, and housekeeping assistance for the aged. Indeed, with the absence of governmental social insurance programs, all of the care of frail and disabled elders is invariably provided by kin. The greater life expectancy of women, coupled with higher female unemployment rates vis-à-vis men in the wage economy means that elderly women are more likely to be recipients of caregiving assistance than are men. Men tend to require less material support from their offspring and other kinfolk because of prior work experience in the monetized economy where retired males subsist on pension benefits.

Research by social gerontologists suggests that family members who assume caregiver responsibilities regularly experience stress and caregiver burden while combining their caregiving role with their other activities and responsibilities. Caregiver burden is greatest for persons providing caregiving responsibilities to patients with cognitive impairments (Morgan and Kunkel 1998). Some caregivers begrudge the considerable amount of time and financial investment that the tasks of caregiving entail. Consistent with the frustration-aggression thesis, some caregivers take out their frustrations on the elderly relatives in their care. In Ghana, with its wage economy of limited employment opportunities, many adults with caregiving obligations face financial constraints providing the material resources for themselves and their immediate families and become resentful about having to support aged parents or other adult relatives. In multigenerational household settings, grandchildren may also become resentful of having to provide assistance for daily living to elderly, frail, and disabled grandparents and elders. Brown's (1999, 34) extensive study of elderly persons in Ghana revealed the following: "While most Ghanaians are still willing to take responsibility for their aged parents, young people frequently complain of their own financial inability to care as much as they would wish for their aged relatives. Indeed, the overall effect of the modernization process has been pressure on the nuclear family of young wage earners to provide for themselves, with little resources available for aged parents." In the Ghanaian context, it seems plausible to argue that the caregiver burden may culturally manifest itself in the form of witchcraft accusations and related physical and psychological abuse toward dependent adult relatives given the prevalence of witchcraft ideology in the society. Our analysis of data in chapters 7 and 8 shows that in Ghana the perpetrator of witchcraft-related violence is typically a close relative, especially an adult offspring, niece, nephew, or grandchild. The typical victim is a woman sixty years old and older, feeble, and in poor physical health. In most cases, the victim and the abuser shared the same household. It is plausible to infer that in some of these cases those making the witchcraft allegations are overburdened or depressed caregivers hostile to the long-term prospect of tending to a mentally and physically impaired, isolated, and dependent individual. The disproportionate percentage of elderly women among accused witches stems from women's greater life expectancy and the greater association of advanced age with physical and mental impairment. According to Hill and Amowu (1998, 206), "the older the person, the higher the risks of abusive behavior, because advanced age is associated with disabling mental and physical conditions that may lead to an inability to resist or defend himself or herself from abusive treatment."

Useless Women, Disposable Women

Elderly women can be considered a burden in some families, stemming from the notion that such women can no longer sustain the productive roles generally assigned to women in Ghanaian society. In Ghana, as in many traditional patriarchal societies, women's social status is defined in strictly productive and reproductive terms. Women are to assist as farm hands, or engage in local industry as workers. In terms of sexual reproduction, they are defined largely in terms of their ability to bear children and to provide primary care for them, particularly given the high premium placed on having children. In such societies, elderly women are regarded as having outlived their usefulness. As menopausal or postmenopausal women, they can no longer bear children. They are also unable to contribute much, if any, productive labor to the family or community and become dependent on their adult children and other family members for their daily sustenance and needs. They are therefore perceived to be expendable. Given their dispensable status, they are more likely to be blamed for misfortunes occurring in the family, labeled as witches, and forced to flee from their homes. The argument finds considerable support from societies and tribes in the northern regions of Ghana. Here, the majority of the women in the witches' camps are elderly, many having arrived there in poor physical health.

Academic Work, Occupational Segregation, and Witchcraft Accusations

In Ghana there is a tendency to cast academically talented and successful female students as witches. This stems in large part from a belief that females are inherently less intelligent than males. As Amoah (1987, 85) observes, "in most of the deliberations concerning the welfare of the community women are left out. If men are present, the views of women are not needed; it is said, *ɔbaa deɛ ɔnim nyansa bɛn?* 'What wisdom has a woman?' It is precisely because women are considered unintelligent that their views are rarely sought in decision making." Hence, while male academic excellence is considered normal, female academic excellence is deemed an aberration. Popular stereotypes of the girl witch include the academically brilliant female student. In elementary and secondary schools, males who are outperformed by females on examinations are mocked by their peers with taunts challenging their masculinity for allowing a female student to exceed their academic performance. Such mocking may come from teachers and even parents as well as from classmates. In the same context, girls who excel academically are suspected of being witches. In her analysis of women who were accused of being witches, Amoah (1987, 87) provides the account of a woman professor of a local university who was labeled a witch by family members because "she is the only one of the ten children who could study up to a University level. In other words, she used her witchcraft to collect other people's intellect and added them to hers to be able to achieve what even men find difficult to do, that is, obtain a doctorate."

Girls are generally ostracized for excelling in mathematics and the physical sciences beginning in elementary school, given that these fields are regarded as male domains. This may include being labeled a witch. Women who pursue degrees in medicine, law, and engineering are similarly labeled for the same reason.

Indeed, traditional Ghanaian society socializes girls and women to choose marriage and motherhood over the pursuit of a career outside the home. Thus, women who embark on doctorate or professional degrees, which require extensive years of study, are seen as deviant, and are likely to be labeled as witches.

Sex stereotyping in occupations contribute to a similar pattern. Occupational sex segregation is very strong in Ghana, with a concentration of women in occupations such as nursing, clerical work, social work, and elementary school teaching. Given the gendered nature of work, women pay a heavy price for not pursuing those professions deemed "female." For example, women who are employed as auto mechanics, painters, lawyers, doctors, or engineers—presumably male professions—are stereotyped as witches. In this context, the witch label is a tacit way of discouraging females from entering professions in which men are dominant, thereby perpetuating men's monopolization over such fields. Currently, men remain overrepresented in undergraduate and graduate science programs.

Witchcraft Accusation as a Weapon for Enforcing Patriarchal Norms

A number of witchcraft scholars have argued that women's greater susceptibility or vulnerability to witchcraft accusations and witchcraft-related femicide is a manifestation of patriarchal social structures (Bever 1982; Rowlands 2001; Roy 1998; Skaria 1997). It is posited that men employ witchcraft accusations and the threat of witchcraft accusations to assert and maintain their elevated and privileged status in society while keeping women in a subordinate position. In this case women whose behavior departs from expected social patterns elicit a witch label—a potential deterrent to ambitious women and a mechanism to ensure their subservience. In short, witchcraft accusations are one means by which men try to control female behavior in patriarchal social structures.

This perspective finds substantial empirical support in the Ghanaian context, where the witch label is often applied to females who challenge gender norms. Women's social, political, and economic subordination in Ghanaian society has been highlighted throughout this book, yet it should be stressed that women's economic position has been on the rise and women continue to make strides in their educational status. Still, resistant males who feel aggrieved by the growing independence of females have mounted opposition to these changes, in some instances invoking witchcraft accusations in response. Susan Drucker-Brown's (1993) analysis of witchcraft accusations among the Mamprusi of northern Ghana illustrates how men in this highly patriarchal society use accusations of witchcraft to maintain their sociopolitical status. Adduced evidence suggests that witchcraft accusations increased in intensity when men's privileged position in the society was threatened. Women who became economically more successful than husbands and other significant males in the family and society were accused of witchcraft and were physically chastised for defying patriarchal norms that mandate the obeisance and servility of females. Drucker-Brown writes,

> Women are expected to be submissive and subservient to men and to senior women, but economic necessity decrees that they must farm, travel, and trade to provide for their families. This increasing autonomy is paralleled by frustration among men, who see their own activities threatened as those of their wives expand. Belief in the increased frequency and virulence of witchcraft, as well as new ways of dealing with witches, reflects not so much a change in the

nature of female power as a loss of control by Mamprusi men over their own economic and political environment. The need of men for women's economic support, and the increasing autonomy of women which that implies, conflict with the traditional definition of women as ideally controlled by men. Mamprusi have always regarded women as potentially subversive. . . . [T]he fear of witchcraft has grown as men's dependence on women has increased, and the increasing autonomy of women threatens both men's control of women and the control by senior women of their juniors. (Drucker-Brown 1993, 547–48)

There are several parallels between Drucker-Brown's observations of the Mamprusi and my own observations in southern Ghana where, over the past few decades, growing numbers of women have established or maintained successful economic ventures, in many instances hiring men as employees. Against the background of expected male economic dominance and female economic dependence, financially successful women are often accused of securing economic success for themselves through witchery (Amoah 1987). In her study, "Women, Witches and Social Change in Ghana," Elizabeth Amoah identified a group of women who had attained tremendous success as entrepreneurs but whose achievements were negated by accusations of witchcraft. She concluded, "The success of women in business is attributed to their use of witchcraft. Women, it is believed, are not capable of achieving anything without the help of an external power or outside influence, such as witchcraft. . . . When women depart from tradition by owning fishing boats or employing men in their businesses, for example, witchcraft accusations against women increase" (Amoah 1987, 93).

In the domestic sphere, growing demands by women for greater gender equality with men have also contributed to an increase in witchcraft allegations. The view is widely held in some circles that witchcraft accusations have grown directly in response to a gradual but increasing emancipation of women in Ghanaian society. For example, men with working wives are said to be increasingly emasculated and made insecure by their spouses' demands for more power in the domestic sphere pursuant to their increased levels of education, their capacity to earn money through paid employment, and their ability to exercise a greater degree of personal autonomy. It is contended that in response to this situation, more men have been willing to resort to physical battering of wives to compensate for feelings of inadequacy. Increased levels of domestic violence, then, have been one means by which males have sought to maintain control and dominance in the name of patriarchy. Economically successful women are particularly singled out for chastisement and censure for challenging patriarchal norms that require economic and social dependence on males.

Latent, Vulnerable and Predisposed Victims

It is possible to draw from criminology when considering factors that contribute to the prevalence of elderly women as victims of violent witchcraft accusations. Because elderly women are among the most physically vulnerable groups in the society, it is useful to apply Rasko's criminological concept of latent or predisposed victims to the analysis of the elderly female victim. Latent or predisposed victims are those who are "not able to defend themselves because of their general state" (Rasko 1976, 398). These include children, the infirm, the severely ill, the inebriated, and those who are sleeping. Elderly women fit this definition of latent victim since their physical fragility often leaves them vulnerable to physical victimization. Women, particularly elderly women, have limited physical strength. Witchcraft accusations in Ghana, as elsewhere, are often accompanied by torture and other forms of physical and psychological abuse in which those accused of being witches are pressured to make confessions of witchcraft activities or deeds. To avoid violent physical encounters with their accusers, most elderly women concede to, or agree with, their labelers or accept the witch label. Males, on the other hand, are unlikely to countenance an accusation of witchcraft without active resistance to the charge. A witchcraft accusation against an adult male is likely to not only invoke vigorous denials, but also to provoke physical retaliation. In addition to being physically vulnerable, females, particularly elderly women, tend to occupy an economically marginalized position in their families and in society at large. In Ghana, as in many societies, most of the accused women tend to be poorly educated, tend to hail from low-income backgrounds, and to be indigent. Consequently, they typically lack the knowledge or the financial resources to embark on civil lawsuits for defamation against their attackers.

Elderly Women's Social Role as Caregivers and Family Counselors

The predominance of elderly women among suspected and accused witches can also be linked to their prominent social role as caregivers and counselors to young people in the Ghanaian family structure. Here, as in most traditional societies, women carry a disproportionate responsibility for child care. Although patterns are gradually changing, Ghanaian men are not as involved as women in the daily tasks and responsibilities associated with child care and maintaining the home. In multigenerational Ghanaian homes, elderly females oftentimes play the triple role of mother, grandmother, and great-grandmother of the family. This often involves supplementing the caregiving role of the birth mother, who is typically the daughter in residence in a matrilineal system. In this combined role, they teach children domestic duties, including cleaning and cooking. They also play active roles as counselors and disciplinarians. Grandmothers are often there to issue warnings about potential consequences that will befall the errant individual should her advice go unheeded. Recalcitrant youths are urged to reform their ways or else face negative consequences as adults. When the child suffers an illness or misfortune consequent to failing to follow the counsel of the elder woman, or if several years later the person suffers economically or fails to thrive in life, that person tends to attribute his or her woes directly to the female elder who issued the warning. Her foresight becomes not the counsel of a wise elder but evidence of her witchcraft. It may be asked, "If she were not a witch, how did she know that this calamity would befall me?" It is presumed that she could only have known because she was directly responsible for causing the calamity, employing her witchcraft to bring it to fruition. This leaves elderly women vulnerable to regular witchcraft accusations. There are numerous potential scenarios where counseling and warnings from elders could lead to accusations of witchcraft. Consider the example of a young woman who had unprotected sex, and after multiple pregnancies that ended in abortions, found herself unable to bear children later in life; or consider the young man who abused alcohol and drugs in his youth and suffered a premature death. In these instances, typically an elder woman would have advised the individuals about potential consequences of their risky behaviors, only to be accused of witchcraft by the now childless woman and relatives of the deceased youth.

This chapter has concentrated on identifying the economic, social, cultural, and even psychological factors that lead to the predominance of females among those accused of witchcraft. A review of the literature dealing with witchcraft amply demonstrates that there are indeed parallels between the witch hunts of medieval Europe and colonial America and those in contemporary Ghana. In all three cases, misogynistic, gynophobic, and patriarchal views and practices were significant contributing factors in the perpetration of witchcraft accusations against women, largely by men. Many scholars of witchcraft and witch-hunting in Europe stress women's vulnerability to accusations of witchcraft and as witch-hunt victims. Given the dearth of information on the topic in Ghanaian witchcraft historiography, this chapter adds considerably to our overall understanding of the gendered nature of witchcraft persecution in Ghana.

Conclusion

CURBING WITCHCRAFT-RELATED VIOLENCE IN GHANA

I have approached the study of violence that emanates from witchcraft accusations as not only an issue of academic interest, but also as a social problem that warrants attention and redress in Ghana. This book has identified a systematic relationship between witchcraft beliefs and violent persecution of accused witches in ways that provide a potential starting point for considering strategies for curbing the incidence of such violence in the country. This essay revisits a number of contexts in which witchcraft accusations operate as a means to explain a range of misfortunes and difficulties that individuals experience in life, and become precipitants for the type of scapegoating that leads to violence. However, here I go a step farther, proposing measures for preventing, ameliorating, or lessening the incidence of problems that tend to lead to witchcraft accusations. Another objective of this book is to generate public awareness about secular-based explanations for conditions and challenges that afflict individuals and communities.

It should be emphasized here that, given the multiple dimensions of witchcraft beliefs and their relationship to violence, tackling witchcraft-related violence and homicides will require more than public service announcements that simply confront witchcraft beliefs as a product of faulty reasoning. In fact, such a pointed strategy would likely prove ineffectual and be dismissed offhand, given the magnitude of witchcraft ideology's integration into Ghanaian society. A likely more-effective strategy would be to approach the myriad issues that relate to witchcraft beliefs and address them individually, involving a range of relevant professionals in the process, including those in the health professions, criminal justice system, and the educational system.

Witchcraft Accusations and the Health Professions

This book has identified how all manner of health disorders and illnesses, from the most minor to the gravest, are attributed to witchcraft. The cerebrospinal meningitis outbreaks that led to the lynching of elderly women in northern Ghana were one of the more dramatic and tragic examples of this phenomenon. More common illnesses endemic to the country such as malaria and a range of minor common discomforts may also be attributed to witchcraft. Public service announcements and other educational programs would have to be directed toward addressing causes of, symptoms of, and treatments for the range of illnesses, disorders, and other health issues attributed to witchcraft. The health professions could also play a particularly constructive role in alleviating witchcraft-related violence by stepping up campaigns to educate the public about the symptoms and etiology of various health disorders and illnesses that are relatively novel but that are becoming increasingly prevalent in Ghana. These include lifestyle diseases or diseases of affluence more often associated with the industrialized West but that are emerging as health problems in Ghana following changes in dietary consumption patterns and other lifestyle changes. Hypertension and diabetes are some of these illnesses of relatively recent vintage (Abugri 2009; Kwamin 2008; Yeboah 2008). These recent diseases are far more likely to be attributed to witchcraft compared with diseases and disorders that have been endemic to Ghana and for which there have been a range of traditional treatments and remedies. Since these new disorders have no precedence and the public has limited experience with them, these health problems readily enter the realm of the unknowable and inexplicable, which then translates into interpretations of witchcraft as the cause (see Ghana News Agency 2012). Furthermore, diagnostic procedures in many clinics and hospitals in the country are highly deficient due to limited medical resources. Many health facilities are unequipped to deal with such medical emergencies as appendicitis and other health crises and complications that require immediate treatment. Moreover, some doctors with neither the technical means nor the skills to diagnose the conditions of acutely or chronically ill patients have been known to dismiss patients with the news that their condition cannot be treated through conventional medicine. This is widely interpreted as meaning that the source of the illness is witchcraft, sorcery, or some other supernatural force. An investment in technological developments in the national medical infrastructure, including equipping hospitals and clinics with the requisite medical resources and skilled personnel needed to improve diagnostic procedures, needs to be made a greater national priority.

The causes of infertility and sexual impotence also need to be more widely communicated to the public. Often, a woman who faces difficulties conceiving or bearing a child will blame members of her *abusua* while a male will blame his own female kin when he is presumed to be impotent or sterile. Information about the physiological bases for these problems, including hormonal imbalances, as well as the potential sources of treatment need to be made more readily available to the citizenry. Infertility, barrenness, and male sexual impotence are particularly emotive issues given the cultural emphasis on fecundity and the stigma attached to childlessness. In effect, there is much cultural investment in childbearing, all of which, in some way, are tied to witchcraft beliefs. Infant and maternal mortality lead to a significant number of deaths annually in Ghana, the etiology of which includes a range of environmental factors and the limited availability of prenatal care. The death of a mother or child due to complications from childbirth is often attributed to bewitchment. However, when the mother dies and the child survives, the surviving child is typically accused of being a witch who caused the death of his or her own mother through bewitchment. The stigmatization and ostracism of such a child by the wider community is all but guaranteed. The government needs to play a more active role in making prenatal care a national priority to promote the health of mother and child through safer and healthier pregnancies, deliveries, and postnatal care of infant and mother. Midwifery should involve more formal training in identifying the signs of complications during deliveries and measures for responding appropriately where they occur, while there needs to be an effort to standardize a high quality of care in maternity wards and neonatal units of hospitals in particular, given the special vulnerabilities of patients in these wards. At present, there is a great deal of variation in the quality of care in such wards across the country, with those in rural and semirural clinics having inadequate measures to protect newborns from malaria-carrying mosquitoes and other disease-causing agents. These conditions must be recognized as a major contributing factor in infant mortality and are a matter of national urgency.

Autopsies

The foregoing discussion has noted that sudden deaths of infants and seemingly healthy adults tend to be attributed to the spiritual attacks of malevolent witches. Individuals deemed to be responsible for such deaths become the object of witch hunts, and are physically chastised, occasionally with lethal outcomes. Given the current dearth of medical resources and personnel to perform autopsies in the country, the underlying primary or biological causes of many sudden deaths are never established, with the consequence that witchcraft is invoked to explain many deaths with no apparent cause. For this reason, it is highly recommended that all deaths in Ghana be autopsied by qualified physicians to determine the exact cause of morbidity. Autopsy results should then be communicated to family members and other surviving relatives. This measure would help allay fears and anxieties that a death is the result of supernatural causes such as witchcraft.

Illicit Drugs

Media reports indicate that the use of recreational drugs has increased in Ghana since the mid-1980s. In March 2014, the Executive Secretary of Ghana's Narcotics Control Board, Mr. Akrasi Sarpong, called for the legalization of marijuana, saying that the use of the drug was prevalent throughout the whole country (Appiah, 2014). Despite this, individuals witnessing the unusual behavior of those using illicit drugs often attribute their behavior to bewitchment. Systematic campaigns that specifically target youths, describing the dangers of using illicit drugs, are needed. There is also the need to establish treatment programs geared toward rehabilitation. Finally, in addition to limiting the demand for illicit drugs, efforts need to be directed toward stemming the supply, discouraging farmers in their production and dealers in their distribution, and exacting penalties for production and distribution.

Road Fatalities

Road deaths are one of the major causes of mortality in Ghana, which warrants attention as an urgent public health issue. Drunk-driving, faulty vehicles and vehicle parts such as threadbare tires, and speeding combined with the common practice of passing other vehicles, the overloading of buses and trucks for higher profits, and roads in various states of disrepair are among the litany of causes of fatal road accidents that cost roughly seven hundred Ghanaian lives annually. Yet fatal accidents involving trucks, buses, and cars are often blamed on witchcraft. The attribution of road fatalities to witchcraft will ensure that such loss of life will continue in the absence of any interventions. Indeed, the rate of death on the nation's roads will likely increase with the growing number of vehicles on the road and with the rapid expansion of Ghana's roadway system. Ghana's Ministry of Road and Transport must impose more rigid standards of motor vehicle inspections. Meanwhile, mass media could be enlisted to help change behaviors, attitudes, and the level of awareness regarding the lethal combination of alcohol and driving.

Spiritualists and their Churches

Many Ghanaians respond to limited health facilities by seeking out spiritualists, some of whom may have genuine capacities for healing (Appiah-Kubi 1981). Still, there remain many spiritualists with solely pecuniary interests who regularly engage in fraudulent behavior, bilking the most vulnerable of clients seeking their assistance. Such self-styled spiritualists typically initiate their encounters with clients through demonstrations of variable forms of trickery, including activities designed to show gifts of clairvoyance or the performance of miracles. These are intended to give legitimacy to their capacity and skills as spiritualists and to establish a following of loyal clients.

Some observers of Ghanaian society have blamed the increasing incidence of witchcraft accusations on the proliferation of spiritual churches that profess to have the power to conquer witches, cure witchcraft-related diseases, and perform other forms of healing through prayer and fasting (Dornoo 2009). Many people suffering from HIV/AIDS, tuberculosis, epilepsy, and other potentially fatal diseases are kept in prayer camps following the claims of spiritualists that their illnesses have spiritual origins. In many instances, this also involves the labeling of relatives of clients as the source of the illness. When innocent persons are identified as witches, often the aggrieved party in the alleged bewitchment seeks retaliation in the form of physical assaults on the alleged witch. Imputations of witchcraft by spiritualists is often what sets in motion much of the witchcraft-related violence that culminates in lethal assaults on alleged witches. To stem the violence, the government must play an active role in regulating the activities of spiritual churches that specialize in the exploitation of vulnerable persons seeking their services of healing. The tricks of the trade of fraudulent spiritualists should also be exposed so that potential clients can identify their strategies of deceit. Furthermore, such practitioners should be held criminally accountable as accomplices when their accusations of witchcraft lead to assault and homicide.

Mental Health Issues and Witchcraft

In Ghana, an indeterminable percentage of the population suffers from undiagnosed mental disorders. This constitutes a major public health issue. The mentally ill are typically stigmatized and abandoned in society, and are left to live on the streets with little hope for treatment in a nation with limited psychiatric care. Those who have been treated in psychiatric hospitals face problems regarding integration into society as relatives abandon them at these hospitals. While the implications are particularly dramatic for those suffering from misdiagnosed mental illnesses, there is a serious lack of public knowledge about the impact of even minor conditions that impact mental health, such as mild depression. The degree of misdiagnosed mental health problems is further compounded by the stigma associated with seeking treatment for mental illness in psychiatric facilities. This is relevant to the issue of witchcraft since psychiatric disorders such as schizophrenia, depression, and senility-related dementia are associated with many symptoms that are identified as stereotyped witch behaviors. Talking to oneself, irritability, absent-mindedness, and other behaviors are all considered characteristics of witch-like behaviors. Those with severe schizophrenia may present with symptoms that lead others to label them as witches. These include delusional behaviors and hallucinations. Furthermore, if these individuals are accused of being witches, they may in turn actually engage in witchcraft confessionals, providing elaborate details of nocturnal flights or accounts of bewitchment. In severe cases of schizophrenia, for example, afflicted individuals make claims of having visions; being able to communicate with disembodied beings, spirits, or gods; or having the capacity to perform magnificent superhuman feats. In addition, mental health care professionals need to identify culturally specific symptoms of mental illnesses as well as how witchcraft beliefs contribute to the persecution and labeling of the mentally ill as witches. In exploring culturally specific manifestations of schizophrenia, mental health care professionals need to consider the confessionals, delusions, and hallucinations of individuals claiming to be witches as a cultural expression of socialization into witchcraft ideology.

Economic Hardship and the Scapegoating of Accused Witches

The tendency to attribute financial difficulties, unemployment, poverty, and other material hardships to bewitchment is also common in Ghana. The explanations that individuals invoke to justify their own material deprivations and difficulties often center on blaming alleged witches in their midst. In seeking such external sources, individuals cannot foresee, and therefore do not seek, concrete and constructive courses of action to ameliorate poverty and other material hardships; instead their energy is vested in identifying and seeking out the witch on whom to vent their frustrations. For Akans, this leads individuals to identify members of their own matrikin—perhaps an elder woman such as an aunt, mother, or grand-mother—as the source of their troubles. These scapegoats then become the target of myriad forms of persecution, including potentially lethal violence.

On the other hand, the wealth or prosperity of an individual is attributed to the beneficial use of witchcraft. It was noted that witchcraft beliefs in Ghana also include notions of *bayi fufuo* in contradistinction to *bayi tuntum*. In this vein, the economic and overall material prosperity of Western industrialized nations is attributed to Europeans' tendencies to use their highly powerful benevolent witchcraft in the service of technological advancement and development. Prosperity and misfortune both are attributed to the machinations of witchcraft. It is also said that as witches use *bayi fufuo* to advance opportunities and create good fortune for their beneficiaries, they also divest others of opportunities and create misfortunes for nonbeneficiaries of their good witchcraft. This zero sum game notion of achievement not only ends in negating the role of effort in achieving or acquiring material well-being and wealth, but also defines wealth as something that is always achieved at the expense of others. This makes those with wealth not only the target of rumor and innuendo regarding the use of witchcraft, but also the target of hostility on the part of those less well-off who perceive the economically better-off as directly or indirectly responsible for their own economic plight. In this vein, it can actually lead individuals, in their own pursuit of wealth and prosperity, to consider ritualistic means as the only viable means to acquire wealth themselves, which limits constructive effort in improving their economic difficulties.

Mass Media and the Dissemination of Witchcraft Beliefs

The mass media has been identified as an institution that has played a major role in reinforcing the types of witchcraft beliefs and stereotypes that generate witchcraft-related violence. The films regularly viewed by Ghanaians have emerged in Ghana not only as a significant medium of entertainment, but also as sources of news and information. Many viewers regard videos, television programs, and films as actual recorded events rather than mere dramatizations. Many consumers of such media believe they are not observing actors and actresses putting on performances for the benefit of an audience, but rather real-world events providing a slice of life. For many viewers, films and videos are reality shows. This means that they will regard the images depicted as significant and powerful in their messages. It is beholden, then, to producers of video dramatizations to include disclaimers at the introduction and conclusion of such programs, emphasizing the fictional nature of the program.

The power of mass media has captured interest and generated concerns among representatives in government and the media itself. In a newspaper report, one government representative reported that roughly 70 percent of the dramas and movies aired on Ghanaian television are Nigerian imports that focus on witchcraft themes, ritual homicide, and other topics related to black magic. As reported in 2005 in the article "African Movies Demean African Culture," Ghanaian legislator Josephine Addoh noted that most African films "portrayed aged persons as witches responsible for the misfortunes of the youth and portrayed wealthy people as ritual murderers and corrupt, as if to say that for one to be rich and successful one necessarily had to take dubious and obnoxious means." In suggesting the broader implications of the values promoted, including the notion that material success derives from mystical or corruptive action, she noted further that such media "discourages our youth from even trying to make money through fair means because the movies also point to fair means of succeeding as very difficult and in some cases unfruitful." A media representative in that same article similarly observed, "African movies and drama series on the television dampened the spirits of viewers and discouraged hard work as the means for success and wealth." The report described representatives in government and the media urging filmmakers to heed the call to become responsive in the types of messages and themes portrayed in their films given the power of their media to reinforce, influence, and even shape societal values. As Addoh indicated, "Our film makers must be more creative and nationalistic in their work to ensure that the films promote good values and motivate our youth to aspire to succeed through hard work and also to respect the elderly in society." One actor, speaking on the influence of his own role, is reported in that article as stating, "I believe the media has moved from being the fourth to the second estate of the realm and we need to make use of the power we wield responsibly to ensure that we capture the minds of society for good values."

Menopause, Older Women and the Witch Label

Although accusations of witchcraft may be directed against young women, young men, and even children, these are exceedingly rare phenomena.

The overwhelming majority of those accused of witchcraft are post-menopausal women. When most people envision a witch, they envision an elderly female. It is important to point out that the behavioral characteristics and features that people associate with witches are similar to the complex of symptoms linked to menopause. These behavioral and physiological signs associated with "the change" include hot flashes, headaches, mood swings, night sweats, irritability, anxiety, insomnia, and changes in short-term memory. In Ghana an understanding of menopause and its symptoms has not entered the realm of public awareness. It is more often the case that physiological and physical characteristics that are considered unusual in older women are explained away as witch behavior. Indeed, it is highly likely that these characteristics have become part of the repertoire of witch-like features by virtue of their association with older women. For example, among the physiological characteristics often identified with witches is a red discoloration of the eyes, which is regarded as a symptom of cannibalistic witchcraft. Yet, one major cause of such discoloration of the eyes is traditional styles of cooking or food preparation in Ghana. In many parts of the country, the traditional *bukyia* (house stove) involves the regular use of firewood in the close quarters of small kitchens. In many instances, women—who are virtually exclusively responsible for using such stoves in the context of performing what is known as women's work—use their mouths to blow air into the stove to ignite the flames when using the *bukyia*, which stirs up smoke and fumes that irritate their eyes. Elderly women have endured years of exposure to this form of cooking that induces redness of the eyes. Other physiological symptoms of aging include loss of body weight and a stooping posture often associated with osteoporosis. As with menopause, these symptoms are often interpreted in Ghana as signs of witchery. Health care professionals should inform the public about the physiological signs that are normative to the aging process, particularly as life expectancy continues to rise (see Figure C.1 and Figure C.2).

Longevity and the Witch Label

As in most societies currently experiencing increases in standard of living, life expectancy is increasing in Ghana. It is also the case that the aged are revered in Ghana as sources of wisdom and traditional knowledge. Yet there are limits to the accepted levels of agedness beyond which one becomes a source of suspicion in witchcraft matters. In an irony of sorts, the so-called excessively aged are presumed to have attained their exceptional longevity via their own witchcraft. This book examined numerous

Killing Is A Crime

Branding or lynching women alleged of witchcraft is a crime

ANTI WITCHCRAFT ALLEGATION

JOIN US!!!

Sponsored by:
German Development Service (DED)
Box TL 341 Tamale, NR, Ghana
Tel:071-22832
E-mail: eotamale@africaonline.com.gh

Contact Address:
The Human Help & Development Group (THUHDEG)
P. O. Box 273 E/R Tamale NR. Ghana
Tel:071-25977/024-298195
E-mail: thuhdeg@yahoo.com

Produced by Teaching for Freedom Foundation

Collaborators: CAD, CENSUDI, CHRAJ, CRS, FISTRAD, GAMBAGA OUTCAST HOME PROJECT, GUB-KATIMALI, ISODEC, MAATA-N-TUDU, MAID, RUMNET, SEND FOUNDATION, SINGLE MOTHERS ASSOCIATION, THUHDEG, TUN-TEEYA DRAMA GROUP, TVTC & WIDOWS MINISTRIES, ETC

Figure C.1. Anti–Witchcraft Violence Campaign Poster (1)

cases where aged women were identified, blamed, and physically attacked for misfortunes in their communities by virtue of their exceptionally old age. Gerontological studies of physical aging suggest that higher life expectancy is associated with genetic factors, nutritional practices, the minimization of stress, limited alcohol consumption, and other lifestyle practices and habits. Presently, many Ghanaians are unaware of the fac-

Figure C.2. Anti–Witchcraft Violence Campaign Poster (2)

tors that contribute to a greater life expectancy and longevity. We need to demystify the increased life expectancy of a growing aged population by educating the public about factors that have promoted a higher life expectancy in the country.

Concluding Thoughts

This book was intended to elucidate witchcraft ideology in Ghana, its dissemination and its consequences, particularly for those who are the victims of witchcraft accusations. Socialization into witchcraft ideology and its perpetuation through family, schooling, mass media, music, and proverbial expressions show the level of pervasiveness of particular beliefs about witches, including their personal and behavioral characteristics and their activities. In the description of witchcraft trials and case histories of lethal and nonlethal incidents of witchcraft persecution, we also see the social dynamics of witchcraft accusations and how they lead to violence. The book also placed witchcraft ideology within a broader social context, including providing a detailed analysis of the gendered nature of witchcraft ideology and witchcraft accusations. In Ghana, we see that, as is the case for many other contemporary societies as well as in the historical epoch of some societies, there are far more witches than there are wizards. The female witch is the most common image of the practitioner of witchcraft in Ghana. Also, as in many other societies, the Ghana case demonstrates how witchcraft ideology makes certain marginalized members of society even more vulnerable through the scapegoating of its most disenfranchised members—children, the elderly, women, the disabled, and the poor—as witches. Rarely are socially or economically powerful individuals accused of being witches or wizards. Distinctive patterns were identified in witchcraft in northern and southern Ghana but in both regions elderly women were identified as the vast bulk of the victims of violent witchcraft accusations. Elderly women are a particularly vulnerable segment of Ghanaian society. Interestingly, as advocacy for elderly women has increased with growing public awareness campaigns by women's groups, human rights organizations and NGOs generating increased recognition of their victimization, children are increasingly being accused of witchcraft. Children are yet another highly vulnerable and marginalized segment of society. And while the scale of violence against children has not reached the levels that elderly women have experienced, the incidence of child victimization in witchcraft-related violence is on the increase in the country. The popular witchcraft radio shows increasingly feature on-the-air confessionals by children claiming to be witches and recounting their witchcraft misdeeds. Perhaps we will face the unfortunate scenario where the victimization of children will increasingly call for advocacy on their behalf as well in the future. It is hoped, however, that instead of finding new targets, that increasing public awareness will stop making any violent witchcraft accusations of any segment of society.

Finally, the government of Ghana is currently a signatory to several major international treaties granting certain human rights protections. These include the Universal Declaration of Human Rights; the International Covenant on Economic, Social and Cultural Rights; the UN Convention on the Rights of the Child; and the Convention on the Elimination of All Forms of Discrimination against Women. By ratifying these international treaties, the government pledges to align its domestic laws, policies, and programs to conform to the ideals enshrined in these treaties. Concurrently, the current Constitution of the Republic of Ghana (1992) makes the abridgement of citizen human rights inviolate. It is therefore incumbent on the government to marshal all available resources to design and implement programs and policies that advance the realization of these principles and standards, as well as enforce laws that promote the human rights of all its citizens. Anything short of this constitutes an injustice.

GLOSSARY

The following is a list of vernacular words used in the text. Words are in Twi (Akan) forms, except where indicated in parentheses.

abisa—divination

abusua—matrilineage

abonsam yareɛ—a disease of the devil; used in reference to stigmatized diseases like leprosy, tuberculosis, epilepsy

abusua—matrilineage

abɔsɔɔ—a string made from cloth that serves as a belt, used by women and girls to tie a local type of skirt .

aduro—sorcery; also refers to traditional medicine

adze—witch (Ewe, Ghana)

adziwowo—witchcraft (Ewe, Ghana)

ahweneɛ or *aheneɛ*—stringed beads that women wear around the waist

anibrɛ—covetousness, envy

animguaseɛ—shame, disgrace, dishonor

anyɛn—witch; also *aye* and *ayɛn* (Fante, Ghana)

aperɛwa—a child with speech patterns akin to an adult

aprapransa—a meal consisting of beans, red palm fruit oil and corn meal cooked together

asaman bɔne—bad or malevolent ghosts

asaman twɛntwɛn—wandering spirits of persons who died "bad deaths" *asamando*—a place where departed spirits reside

atufaa—flies smoothly, in specific reference to the flight of a witch

aye—see *anyɛn* (Fante, Ghana)

ayɛn—see *anyɛn* (Fante, Ghana)

badudwan—a sheep given by a husband to his wife to honor her after she has borne her tenth child

bare—barrel

baribonsam—wizard; also *barima bonsam*

barima bonsam—see *baribonsam*

bayi—witchcraft; also *bayie* and *beyie*

bayi borɔ—bad or malevolent witchcraft; also *bayi bɔne*

bayi bɔne—see *bayi borɔ*

bayi fufuo—white witchcraft

bayi kuku—a pot that contains witchcraft substance; also *bayi kukuo* and *bayi sɛn*

bayi kukuo—see *bayi kuku*

bayi kwasea—foolish witchcraft

bayi pa—good witchcraft

bayi sɛn—see *bayi kuku*

bayi tuntum—black witchcraft

bayiboa—an animal familiar, or an animal that accompanies or assists witches

bayie—see *bayi*

beyie—see *bayi*

beyifo—witch; also *ɔbayifo* and *ɔbayifoɔ*

bukyia—locally made house stove, usually made of clay or bricks, in which firewood is burnt

chera—witches (Kasena, Ghana)

chorro—witch (Kasena, Ghana)

cherro—witchcraft (Kasena, Ghana)

church healing center—see prayer camp

dracunculiasi—Guinea worm

ebge—witch (Gonja, Ghana)

faith healing center—see prayer camp

feiticeira -witch or sorceress (Portuguese, Sao Tome and Principe) fetish priest—a person endowed with spiritual powers to detect and cure diseases and other afflictions caused by spiritual forces using various traditional medicinal regimens

fɛkuo—association; also *fɛkuw*

fɛkuw—see *fɛkuo*

fufu(o)—a popular Ghanaian meal in which boiled cassava, plantain or yam is pounded into a doughy paste, formed into small balls and eaten with soup

garifɔtɔ—grated, dried and fried cassava mixed with cooked beans and red palm oil

grawa—a metal container capable of holding one-gallon or multiple-gallons of liquid

kindoki—witchcraft (Democratic Republic of the Congo)

kisi kuro—a sore that is chronic or slow to heal

kolo—old-fashioned

kra—soul, spirit

matrikin—members of a matrilineage

mpanyinsɛm—a child who has the mannerisms of an adult

mpatuwuo—a death that is sudden or unexpected

nsamanwa—ghost cough; often used to describe tuberculosis

omununkum—sleep paralysis

onchocerciasis—river blindness

onwansan—bushbuck

onyina—silk cotton tree

owabɔne—bad cough; often used to describe tuberculosis

prayer camp —a residential center operated by a Christian church pastor for spiritual healing; also referred to as a church healing center, faith healing center, prayer center, and spiritual healing center

prayer center—see prayer camp

pɛ nsɛmkeka—a person who is loquacious; also someone who is prone to gossip

schistosomiasis—bilharzias

soog—matrilineal kinfolk (Tallensi, Ghana)

spiritual church—place where prayers are used to heal physical and spiritual afflictions

spiritual healing center—see prayer camp

sunsum—spirit

trokosi—traditional cultural practice in which virginal girls are given to traditional fetish shrines to live as servants to fetish priests to atone for deviant acts committed by the girl's clansmen (Ewe, Ghana)

witch finder—traditional priest whose duty is to identify witches and exorcise them of their witchcraft

yarebɔne—bad disease; used to refer to stigmatized diseases such as leprosy, tuberculosis and epilepsy

etwa—epilepsy; also *etwerɛ*

etwerɛ—see *etwa*

ɔbaabarima—tomboy, or a masculine female

ɔbaafadie—sissy, or male considered to have feminine interests or characteristics *ɔbayifo*—see *beyifo*

ɔbayifoɔ—see *beyifo*

ɔpanyin—elder

BIBLIOGRAPHY

Abban, Peter. "Trial by Ordeal." *Weekly Spectator,* June 13, 1998, 16.

Ablekpe, Boniface. "Woman Beats Mother to Death." *Daily Graphic,* March 5, 1996, 3.

———. "Man Clubs Mother to Death in Kumasi." *Daily Graphic,* August 18, 2000, 17.

Abugri, George S. "Rate of Cholesterol-Related Deaths Worrying." *Daily Graphic,* September 15, 2009, 31.

Achebe, Chinua. *Things Fall Apart.* New York: Ballentine Books, 1983.

ActionAid. *Condemned Without Trial: Women and Witchcraft in Ghana.* London: ActionAid International, 2012.

Addoteye, Eunice. "70-Year Old Woman's Wrist Chopped Off." *Mirror,* January 25, 1992, 1.

Ademowo, Adeyemi J., G. Foxcroft, and T.D. Oladipo, eds., *Suffereth Not a Witch to Live: Discourse on Child Witch Hunting in Nigeria.* Ibadan, Nigeria: Mufty Prints Concepts, 2010.

Adinkrah, Mensah. *Military Ideology and Social Control: A Study of Military Regimes in Ghana, 1957-1982,* M.A. thesis, Queen's University, Kingston, Canada 1983.

———. "Political Coercion in Military-dominated Regimes: A Subcultural Interpretation." Ph.D. diss., Washington University, St. Louis, U.S.A. 1988.

———. "Africa: Myths and Realities," *African Voice* 1, no. 1 (1992): 10–12.

———. "Witchcraft Accusations and Female Homicide Victimization in Contemporary Ghana." *Violence Against Women* 10, no. 4 (2004): 325–56.

———. "Ritual Homicides in Contemporary Ghana." *International Journal of Comparative Criminology* 5, no. 1 (2005): 29–59.

———. "Vigilante Homicides in Contemporary Ghana." *Journal of Criminal Justice* 33, no. 5 (2005): 413–27.

———. "Analysis of Inscriptions on Ghanaian Motor Vehicles." (unpublished manuscript, August 7, 2006) Microsoft Word file

———. "Witchcraft Themes in Popular Ghanaian Music." *Popular Music & Society* 31, no. 3 (2008a): 299–311.

———. "Husbands Who Kill Their Wives: An Analysis of Uxoricides in Contemporary Ghana." *International Journal of Offender Therapy and Comparative Criminology* 52, no. 3 (2008b): 296–310.

———. "Spousal Homicides in Contemporary Ghana." *Journal of Criminal Justice* 36, no. 3 (2008c): 209–16.

———. "Criminalizing Rape within Marriage: Perspectives of Ghanaian University Students." *International Journal of Offender Therapy and Comparative Criminology* 55, no. 6 (2011a): 982–1010.

———. "Epidemiologic Characteristics of Suicidal Behavior in Contemporary Ghana." *Crisis: The Journal of Crisis Intervention and Suicide Prevention* 32, no. 1 (2011b): 31–36.

———. "Child Witch Hunts in Contemporary Ghana." *Child Abuse & Neglect: The International Journal* 35, no. 9 (2011c): 741–52.

———. "Better Dead Than Dishonored: Masculinity and Male Suicidal Behavior in Contemporary Ghana." *Social Science and Medicine* 74, no. 4 (2012): 474–81.

———. "Homicide-Suicide in Ghana: Perpetrators, Victims and Incidence Characteristics." *International Journal of Offender Therapy and Comparative Criminology* 58, no. 3 (2014a): 364–387.

———. "Intimate Partner Femicide-Suicides in Ghana: Victims, Offenders, and Incident Characteristics." *Violence Against Women* 20, no. 9 (2014b).

Adjetey, Fitnat, and Gloria Ofori-Boadu. *FIDA Handbook on Domestic Violence in Ghana.* Accra, Ghana: Friedrich Ebert Foundation, 2000.

Adjokatcher, Ivan D. "Evangelist Jailed for Stealing." *Mirror,* December 30, 1989, 3.

Afful, Loretta. "Woman 73, Tried by Ordeal." *Weekly Spectator,* 1995, 1.

Afful, Loretta, and D. Ankamah. "Two Forced to Confess to Witchcraft." *Weekly Spectator,* October 22, 1994, 1.

African Movies Demean African Culture-MP. Modernghana.com, November 2, 2005. http://www.modernghana.com/music/1431/3/african-movies-demean-african-cul ture-mp.html

Afrifa, Adjepong. "The Problem of Child Abuse and Neglect in Ghana." In Mensa-Bonsu and Dowuona-Hammond, *The Rights of the Child in Ghana,* 10–17.

Agyako, Bossman. "The Scourge of Superstition." *Daily Graphic,* January 31, 1998, 9.

Agyekum, Kofi. *Akan Verbal Taboos in the Context of the Ethnography of Communication.* MPhil thesis. Norwegian University of Science and Technology, 1996.

Agyeman, Nana K. "'Don't Be Obsessed with Material Wealth.'" *Daily Graphic,* April 3, 2009, 24.

Ahinful, Kwamena Apostle "Don't Beat Witches." *Mirror,* February 20, 1999, 12.

Aklorbortu, Moses D. "Farmer Chops off Sister's Head." *Daily Graphic,* April 21, 2009, 48.

———. "Spiritualist Arrested for Fraud." *Mirror,* May 26, 2012a, 3.

———. "JHS Pupil Rescued From Prayer Camp." *Daily Graphic,* January 12, 2012b, 1.

Akosah-Sarpong, Kofi. "Dangerous! When Medical Doctors Believe in Witchcraft." *Newstime Africa,* October 23, 2012. http://www.newstimeafrica.com/archives/

Akrofi, Clement A. *Twi Mmebusem (Twi Proverbs).* London: Macmillan and Company Limited, 1958.

Akrong, Abraham. "A Phenomenology of Witchcraft in Ghana." In Ter Haar, *Imagining Evil,* 2007, 53–66.

Akyea, Peter. "Ending Child Abuse: The Way Forward." *Daily Graphic,* June 27, 2009, 11.

Alhassan, Zakaria. "Guinea Worm Cases Go High in NR." *Daily Graphic,* July 14, 2004, 40.

Amanor, Eric. "Reflections on Int. Literacy Day." *Daily Graphic,* September 8, 2008, 30.

Amanor, Millicent. "Man, 39, Clubs Wife to Death." *Daily Graphic,* August 19, 1999a, 1.

———. "Two More Suspects Arrested." *Daily Graphic,* September 4, 199b, 12.

Amoah, Elizabeth. "Women, Witches and Social Change in Ghana." In D. Eck and D. Jain, eds., *Speaking of Faith: Global Perspectives on Women, Religion and Social Change,* Philadelphia: New Society Publishers, 1987, 84–94.

Ampofo, Akosua A. "Controlling and Punishing Women." *Review of African Political Economy* 20 (1993): 102–11.

Amuzu, Margaret. "Female Genital Mutilation Exists in Accra." *Daily Graphic,* February 1, 2000, 14.

Anderson, Norma J. "Come through the Door, Not the Window: Tracing Akan Witchcraft Perceptions and the Deterioration of Social Balance from a Pre-Colonial Ideal to the Present." B.A. honors thesis, Mount Holyoke University, South Hadley. 1999.

Ankamah, Divine. "J.S.S. Boy Kills Grandma." *Weekly Spectator,* 1995, 1.

Ansong, R.A. "Child Labor and its Effects." *Daily Graphic,* June 18, 2009, 11.

Appiah, Dorcas, and Kathy Cusack. *Violence against Women & Children in Ghana.* Accra, Ghana: Gender Studies & Human Rights Documentation Centre, 1999.

Appiah, Edwin. (2014). "Ghana Should Consider Legalizing Marijuana—Nacob Boss." Myjoyonline.com, March 12, 2014. http://www.myjoyonline.com/news/2014/march-12th/ghana-should-consider-legalising-marijuana-nacob-boss.php

Appiah, Peggy, Kwame Appiah, and Ivor Agyeman-Duah. *Bu Me Be: Akan Proverbs.* Accra, Ghana: The Center for Intellectual Renewal, 2002.

Appiah-Kubi, Kofi. *Man Cures, God Heals: Religion and Medical Practice Among the Akans of Ghana.* Totowa, NJ: Allanheld, Osmun, & Co. Publishers, 1981.

Appiah-Poku, J., Laugharne, R., Mensah, E., Osei, Y., and Burns, T. "Previous Help Sought by Patients Presenting to Mental Health Services in Kumasi, Ghana." *Social Psychiatry and Psychiatric Epidemiology* 39, no. 3 (2004): 208–11.

Armah, Golda. "'Experts Must Advise on Rape Menace.'" *Daily Graphic,* November 13, 1999, 1.

Arrests over Malawi Witchcraft Violence. BBC News, April 14, 2001. http://news.bbc.co.uk/1/hi/world/africa/1277820.stm

Asamoah, Williams. *The Witches and the Hunter.* Kaneshie, Ghana: Knowledge Source Publications, 2004.

Asante-Darko, Nimrod, and Sjaak van der Geest. "Male Chauvinism: Men and Women in Ghanaian Highlife Songs." In *Female and Male in West Africa,* edited by Christine Oppong. London: Allen & Unwin, 1983.

Asare, B. Interview. February 2, 2004.

Asare, Kwame. "Man, 30, Butchers Mother to Death." *Daily Graphic,* May 10, 1999, 1.

Asare-Buakyi, E. "Man Beats Grandma to Death." *Mirror,* June 11, 1994, 3.

Ashforth, Adam. *Witchcraft, Violence and Democracy in South Africa.* Chicago: University of Chicago Press, 2005.

Ashiagbor, Platini C. "Spare the Rod and Guide the Child." *Daily Graphic,* November 17, 2008, 27.

Asiedu, P. "Let's Protect Children from Risk of Ritual Killings." *Daily Graphic,* May 8, 1992a, 1.

———. "Press Reports on Ritual Murders—Matters Arising. *Daily Graphic,* July 9, 1992b, 7.

Asmah, Gladys. "Ministry of Women and Children's Affairs: Meet the Press Series." *Women & Children's Affairs News Bulletin,* April–June, 2003, 26–35.

Assani, Tampuri S.M. "Witchcraft and its Effect on Women in East Mamprusi." B.A. long essay, University of Ghana, Legon, 1996.

Assimeng, Max. "The Witchcraft Scene in Ghana: A Sociological Comment." *Ghana Social Science Journal* 4 (1977): 54–78.

Assimeng, Max. *Social Structure of Ghana.* Accra-Tema. Ghana Publishing Corporation. 1981.

Atakpa, V.P. "DOVVSU Worried over Violence Against Children." *Daily Graphic,* February 27, 2009, 30.

Atitsogbe, Famous Kwei. "Don't Chain Humans Like Monkeys-Dr. Akwasi Osei." *Joyonline,* August 25, 2014, 1.

Atta, Kwame Amoako. "Death Dream: Farmer Butchers Woman to Death." *Weekly Spectator,* October 28, 1995, 1.

Atsu, Kodjo. "Woman's Body Sent Off to Witches Cemetery." *Mirror,* July 22, 1995, 1.

Avoiding Accidents During the Easter. *Daily Graphic,* April 7, 2004, 17.

Awedoba, Albert. *An Introduction to Kasena Society and Culture through Their Proverbs.* New York: University Press of America, 2000.

———. *Culture and Development in Africa with Special References to Ghana: Some Basic Issues Volume 1.* Accra, Ghana: Institute of African Studies, 2002.

Awenva, A.D., U.M. Read, A.L. Ofori-Attah, V.C.K. Doku, B. Akpalu, A.O. Osei, and A.J. Flisher. "From Mental Health Policy Development in Ghana to Implementation: What Are the Barriers?" *African Journal of Psychiatry* 13, no. 3 (2010): 184–91.

Aziz, Abdul. "Farmer Clubs Woman, 60 to Death." *Mirror,* March 6, 1999, 4.

———. "Ministry to Close Down 125 Brothels in a Bid to Check Child Prostitution." *Daily Graphic,* June 21, 2008, 17.

Azu, Vance. "Rev Osei Kofi: The 'Wizard' Dribbler." *Mirror,* March 27, 2004, 31.

———. "Allow Us to Drive—Hearing Impaired Cry Out." *Mirror,* October 15, 2011, 21.

———. "Man Sprays Acid on in-law for Alleged Bewitchment." *Mirror,* December 8, 1990, 1.

Azumah, Vincent. "Strange Bird Turns into Woman?" *Mirror,* December 18, 1993, 1.

Badoe, Yaba. "The Witches of Gambaga: What it Means to be a Witch in the Northern Region of Ghana." *Jenda: A Journal of Culture and African Women Studies,* 19 (2011).

Bailey, Michael D. "The Feminization of Magic and the Emerging Idea of the Female Witch in the Late Middle Ages." *Essays in Medieval Studies* 19, no. 1 (2002): 120–34.

Bannerman-Richter, Gabriel. *The Practice of Witchcraft in Ghana.* Elk Grove, CA: Gabari, 1982.

———. *Don't Cry! My Baby Don't Cry: Autobiography of an African Witch.* Winona, MN: Appollo Books, 1984.

BBC News. "Congo Witch-hunt's Child Victims." December 22, 1999. http://news.bbc .co.uk/1/hi/world/africa/575178.stm

Beacom. E, "Brain Drain: How it is Affecting our Health." *Daily Graphic,* December 15, 2008, 43.

Behringer, Wolfgang. *Witchcraft Persecutions in Bavaria.* New York: Cambridge University Press, 1997.

———. *Witches and Witch Hunts: A Global History.* Cambridge, U.K.: Polity Press, 2004.

Bekoe, Dwamena. "Man Butchers Mother to Death." *Mirror,* May 16, 1992, 1.

Bentil, Naa L. "Register Births, Deaths Promptly." *Daily Graphic,* July 31, 2009, 51.

Bever, Edward. "Old Age and Witchcraft in Early Modern Europe," in P.N. Stearns, ed., *Old Age in Preindustrial Society.* New York: Holmes & Meier Publishers, 1982, 150–90.

Beware of False Prophets. *Daily Graphic,* August 22, 2000, 7.

Bierlich, Bernhard. "Notions and Treatment of Guinea Worm in Northern Ghana." *Social Science and Medicine* 41, no. 4 (1995): 501–9.

Biney, S. Andrews. "Boy, 15, in Dog Chains." *Mirror,* February 12, 1994, 1.

Blair, David. "Starved and Beaten with Nails: Kinshasa's Young 'Witches' Cast Out by Slum Preachers." *The Telegraph,* September 24, 2005. http://www.telegraph.co.uk/news/ worldnews/africaandindianocean/democraticrepublicofcongo/1499111/Starved- and-beaten-with-nails-Kinshasas-young-witches-cast-out-by-slum-preachers.html

Blay, Benibengor. *Operation Witchcraft.* Aboso, Ghana: Benibengor Book Agency, 1968.

Boadi, A. Lawrence. "The Language of the Proverb in Akan." in Richard M. Dorson, ed., *Akan Folklore.* Bloomington: Indiana University Press, 1972, 183–191.

Boadu-Ayeboafoh, Yaw. "The Media and Disability." *Daily Graphic,* February 7, 2004, 7.

Boakye-Sarpong, Kwame, and K. Osei-Hwedie. *Witchcraft: Myth or Reality.* Lusaka, Zambia: Multimedia Publications, 1989.

Boaten, Abayie B. "The Trokosi System in Ghana: Discrimination against Women and Children" in Apollo Rwomire, ed., *African Women and Children: Crisis and Response.* Wesport, CT: Praeger, 2001, 91–104.

Boaten, Gyamfi. "2 Pastors in the dock." *Weekly Spectator,* August 8, 1998, 16.

Boateng, K. "Farmer Held over Blindman's Death." *Daily Graphic,* July 7, 1997, 1.

Boateng, Mavis K. "Ugly Face of Commercial Sex Trade." *Daily Graphic,* March 14, 2009, 11.

Bokor, Michael Kodjo. "Witchcraft: I Have Been Defamed—Plaintiff Says." *Weekly Spectator,* October 6, 1984a, 8.

———. "The Witchcraft Case at Somanya." *Weekly Spectator,* October 20, 1984b, 1.

———. "The Somanya Witchcraft Case." *Weekly Spectator,* November 8, 1984c, 8.

Boneh, Galia. *Why Whites Are Richer: Images of White People and Explanations for their Economic Advantage as Perceived by the Gonja of Northern Ghana,* M.A. thesis. University of California, Los Angeles, 2004.

Bonsu, F. "TB Is Not a Curse from the Gods." *Daily Graphic,* April 5, 2005, 11.

Brauner, Sigrid. *Fearlesss Wives and Frightened Shrews: The Construction of the Witch in Early Modern Germany.* Amherst: University of Massachusetts Press, 1995.

Brempong, Owusu. *"Akan Highlife in Ghana: Songs of Cultural Transition."* Ph.D. diss., Indiana University, Bloomington, 1986.

———. "They Have Used a Broom to Sweep My Womb: The Concept of Witchcraft in Ghana." *Research Review* 12, no. 1 & 2 (1996): 42–50.

Brenya, Kofi. *The Ungrateful Friend.* Accra, Ghana: Kwamfori Publishing, 1992.

British Medical Association. "Mental Health-Ghana." 2013. http://bma.org.uk/working-for-change/international-affairs/humanitarian-fund/ghana-mental-health

Brokensha, David. *Social Change at Larteh, Ghana.* Oxford: Clarendon Press, 1966.

Brown, C.K. *Caring for the Elderly: Perspectives from Ghana and Japan.* Cape Coast: Catholic Mission Press, 1999.

Buabeng, C.S. "House on Plight of Women Accused of Witchcraft." *Daily Graphic,* March 11, 1998, 1.

Buabeng, C.S., and Abraham Kofoya-Tetteh. "Parliament Calls for Probe into Death of Two Women." *Daily Graphic,* November 21, 1998, 11.

Burton, Richard. *Wit and Wisdom from West Africa.* New York: Negro Universities Press, 1969.

Chao, Shiyan. *Ghana: Gender Analysis and Policymaking for Development.* Washington, DC: World Bank, 1999.

Chavunduka, Gordon. *Witches, Witchcraft, and the Law in Zimbabwe.* Harare: Zimbabwe National Traditional Healers Association, 1980.

Clark, Gracia. "Gender and Profiteering: Ghana's Market Women as Devoted Mothers and 'Human Vampire Bats'." In*"Wicked" Women and the Reconfiguration of Gender in Africa.* eds. Dorothy L. Hodgson and Sheryl A. McCurdy. Portsmouth, NH: Heinemann, 2001, 293–311.

Clay, Clayton. "The Horror of Rape." *Daily Graphic,* July 17, 1999, 8.

———. "When People Die Suddenly." *Mirror,* July 12, 2003, 11.

———. "Epilepsy Can Be Controlled." *Mirror,* June 12, 2004, 12.

Clegg, Sam. "This Insatiable Craving for Wealth Must Cease." *Daily Graphic,* September 15, 1981, 3.

Clemence, Hollie. "Empowering the Physically Challenged: Is Legislation Alone Enough?" *Daily Graphic,* July 25, 2009, 16.

Collins, John. *Highlife Time.* Accra, Ghana: Anansesem Publications, 1994.

Commonwealth Human Rights Initiative. *A Simplified Version of Disability Rights in Ghana.* Accra, Ghana: Commonwealth Human Right Initiative, Africa, 2007.

Constitution of the Republic of Ghana. Accra, Ghana: Ghana Publishing Company, 1992.

Court Jails Man for Threatening to Kill His Mother. Ghanaweb.com. 2005. http://www.ghanaweb.com/GhanaHomePage/NewsArchive/artikel.php?ID=74786#

Court Sentences Man to Death for Murder. GhanaWeb.com, August 1, 2003. http://www.ghanaweb.com/GhanaHomePage/NewsArchive/artikel.php?ID=40360

Crawford, Angus. "Congo's Child Victims of Superstition." BBC News. July 30, 2005. http://news.bbc.co.uk/2/hi/programmes/from_our_own_correspondent/4727745.stm

Dankwa, V.O. Emmanuel. "The Constitutional Provisions of the Fourth Republic: The Tasks Ahead." In Mensa-Bonsu and Dowuona-Hammond eds., *The Rights of the Child in Ghana,* 59–65.

Danquah, John B. *Cases in Akan Law: Decisions Delivered by the Honorable Nana Sir Ofori Atta, Omanhene of Akim Abuakwa.* London: George Routledge & Sons Limited, 1928.

Darko-Mensah, D. and N.L. Lartey. "Police Hospital Needs More Pathologists." *Daily Graphic,* April 1, 2008, 48.

Darkwa, Osei. "Toward a Comprehensive Understanding of the Needs of Elderly Ghanaians." *Ageing International* 25, no.4 (2000): 65-79.

Davies, Julie-Ann. "Witch-Hunt." *New Humanist,* March 1, 2004. https://newhumanist.org.uk/articles/706/witch-hunt

Debrunner, Hans. *Witchcraft in Ghana: A Study on the Belief in Destructive Witches and its Effect on the Akan Tribes.* Accra, Ghana: Waterville Publishing, 1961.

de Graft-Johnson, K.E. "The Child and the Welfare Agencies." In Mensa-Bonsu and Dowuona-Hammond, *The Rights of the Child in Ghana,* 40–49.

Department of Sociology and Social Work. B.A. Sociology Course Objectives. September 2014. http://sociology.knust.edu.gh/undergraduate/ba-sociology-course-objectives

Derive, Jean. "Proverbs." In *African Folklore: An Encyclopedia,* edited by Philip M. Peek and Kwesi Yankah. New York: Routledge, 2004, 374–75.

Dodds, J Scott., D. M. Warren, T. Wallace, and D. D. Ohl. *Healers of Ghana.* Princeton: Films for the Humanities & Sciences. 1996.

Donkor, Salome. "One-third of Ghanaian Women Victims of Violence." *Daily Graphic,* February 21, 2000, 16.

———. "Problems of Suspected Witches." *Daily Graphic,* February 21, 2008, p. 17.

———. "Belief in Witchcraft and the Effects on Human Rights." *Daily Graphic,* December 2, 2010, 11.

———. "Disbanding Witches Camps: Our Collective Responsibilities." *Daily Graphic,* September 11, 2011, 11.

Dorkenoo, Efua. *Cutting the Rose, Female Genital Mutilation: The Practice and its Prevention.* London: Minority Rights Group, 1994.

Dornoo, Jennifer. "Superstitious Belief: its Impact on Development." *Daily Graphic,* May 30, 2009, 11.

Dotsey, Moses. "Couple Arrested for Death of Son on Orders of Maame Osofo." *Daily Graphic,* April 14, 2008, 1.

Dovlo, Elom. "Witchcraft in Contemporary Ghana," in Ter Haar, *Imagining Evil,* 67–92.

Dowuona-Hammond, Christine. "Introduction," in Mensah-Bonsu and Dowuona-Hammond, ed., *The Rights of the Child in Ghana—Perspectives,* 1994, vii–xiv.

Drucker-Brown, Susan. "Mamprusi Witchcraft, Subversion and Changing Gender Relations." *Africa* 63, no. 4 (1993): 532–49.

Duff, Oliver. "Tanzania Suffers Rise of Witchcraft Hysteria." Worldwide Religious News, November 28, 2005. http://wwrn.org/articles/19669/?&place=eastern-africa&section=occult

Duodu, Samuel. "Reform Customs Affecting Women, Children." *Daily Graphic,* March 25, 2008, 11.

Dykes, Emma B. "Child Labor." *Daily Graphic,* November 17, 2008, 20.

Dzamboe, Tim. "Exiled Couple Petition CHRAJ." *Mirror,* February 7, 2004, 22.

Edmonds, James, and Josie Morley. "A Report into the Psychiatric Situation in Ghana." GhanaWeb.com, November 28, 2010. http://www.ghanaweb.com/GhanaHomePage/NewsArchive/artikel.php?ID=198318

Enos, K. Samuel. "Badu guan: A Celebration of High Fertility among the Akan People of Southern Ghana," in Caroline Bledsoe, ed., *Discovering Normality in Health and the Reproductive Body: Proceedings of a Workshop.* Evanston, IL: Northwestern University, 2002, 91–101.

Ephson, Ben. "Trouble Brews for Ghanaian 'Witches.'" *Daily Mail and Guardian.* April 16, 2001. http://wwrn.org/articles/7674/?&section=native-religions

Ewusi-Mensah, Isaac. "Post Colonial Psychiatric Care in Ghana." *Psychiatric Bulletin* 25 (2001): 228–29.

Field, Margaret. "Witchcraft as a Primitive Interpretation of Mental Disorder." *Journal of Mental Science* 101 (1955): 826–33.

Fisher, Robert B. *West African Religious Traditions: Focus on the Akan of Ghana.* Maryknoll, NY: Orbis Books, 1998.

Foster, Ohene. "Witch Gets AIDS after Eating AIDS Victim." *P & P People and Places,* February 26, 2004, 3.

Fuseini, A.B.A. "Suspected Witch Beaten to Death." *Mirror,* April 23, 1994, 1.

Gbolu, Florence. "Bewitching Ghana's Children." *Chronicle,* January 11, 2006, 3.

Gentilcore, David. "Witchcraft Narratives and Folklore Motifs in Southern Italy." In Oldridge *The Witchcraft Reader,* 97–108.

Ghana Education Service. *Cultural Studies for Junior Secondary Schools.* Accra, Ghana: Ministry of Education and Culture, 1988.

Ghana Health Service. *Annual Report.* Accra, Ghana: Ministry of Health. 2007.

——. *Annual Report.* Accra, Ghana: Ministry of Health. 2010.

Ghana News Agency. "Witches not to Blame for Cocoa Disease—District Cocobod Manager." Ghana News Agency, April 24, 2011. http://www.modernghana.com/news/326027/1/witches-not-to-blame-for-cocoa-disease-district-co.html

——. "Do Not Attribute Breast Cancer to Witchcraft—Vice President." Ghana News Agency, May 25, 2012. http://www.ghananewsagency.org/details/Health/Do-not-attribute-breast-cancer-to-witchcraft-Vice-President/?ci=1&ai=44026

Ghana Statistical Service. *Demographic and Health Survey.* Accra, Ghana: Statistical Service, 1998.

——. *Demographic and Health Survey.* Accra, Ghana: Statistical Service, 1999.

——. *2000 Population & Housing Census.* Accra, Ghana: Statistical Service, 2002.

——. *2010 Population and Housing Census: Summary Report of Final Results.* Accra, Ghana: Statistical Service, 2012.

Ghosh, R. Palash. "Black Magic Woman: Young Mother Burned Alive for Practicing 'Sorcery' in Papua New Guinea." *International Business Times,* February 7, 2013. http://www.ibtimes.com//black-magic-woman-young-mother-burned-alive-practicing-sorcery-papua-new-guinea-1069136

Ghunney, K. Joseph., Greer, M. Joanne, and John Allen. "African Spiritual Worldview: Its Impact on Alcohol and Other Drug Use by Senior Secondary School Students in Ghana." *Research in the Social Scientific Study of Religion* 10 (1999): 191–216.

Ginzburg, Carlo. "Deciphering the Witches' Sabbat," in Oldridge, *The Witchcraft Reader,* 120–28.

Girl Dumped in Witch Camp for Being Brilliant. Ghanaweb.com, April 2, 2012. http://www.ghanaweb.com/GhanaHomePage/NewsArchive/artikel.php?ID=234749

Girl Locked Up for 5 Yrs. on Suspicion of Being a Witch? *Daily Graphic,* March 15, 2004, 3.

Gmanyami, Jonathan. "He Canes Mother, 72." *Weekly Spectator,* April 27, 1996, 1.

———. "Jailed for Calling Mom a Witch." *Weekly Spectator,* June 20, 1998, 1.

Gobah, Timothy. "Prez Visits Accra Mental Hospital." *Daily Graphic,* April 6, 2010, 1.

Gocking, Roger. "A Chieftaincy Dispute and Ritual Murder in Elmina, Ghana, 1945–46." *Journal of African History* 41, no. 2 (2000): 197–219.

Graham, Ronnie. *The Da Capo Guide to Contemporary African Music.* New York: Da Capo Press, 1988.

Grandma, 85, Commits Suicide. Myjoyonline.com, August 6, 2007. http://edition.myjoyonline.com/pages/news/200710/9278.php

Graphic Still No.1. *Daily Graphic,* June 16, 2001, 1.

Gray, Natasha. *The Legal History of Witchcraft in Colonial Ghana: Akyem Abuakwa, 1913–1943.* Ph.D. diss., Columbia University, New York, 2000.

Grindal, Bruce T. "Witchcraft, Authority, and the Ambiguity of Evil in Sisaland." In *Ghana's North: Research on Culture, Religion, and Politics of Societies in Transition,* edited by F. Kroger and Barbara Meier. New York: Peter Lang, 2003, 45–59.

Gyan-Apenteng, Kwasi. "Witchcraft, Theory of Power Shedding." *Mirror,* January 13, 2007, 15.

———. "Who Killed Amma Hemmah? *Daily Graphic,* December 4, 2010, 10.

Hagan, E.B. "Disabled Persons in Society." *Daily Graphic,* June 4, 1981, 3.

Haizel, Joe I. "Labourer Butchers Daughter." *Mirror,* February 22, 2003, 1.

Hall, David. *Witch-Hunting in Seventeenth-Century New England: A Documentary History, 1638–1692.* Boston: Northeastern University Press, 1991.

Heimer, Karen, and Candace Kruttschnitt. *Gender and Crime: Patterns of Victimization and Offending.* New York: New York University Press, 2006.

Hemmings, Annette. "The 'Hidden' Corridor Curriculum." *The High School Journal* 83, no. 2 (2000): 1–10.

Herbalist in Trouble for Conducting Trial by Ordeal. Ghanaweb.com, July 6, 2005. http://www.ghanaweb.com/GhanaHomePage/NewsArchive/artikel.php?ID=85241

Hill, B. Jacqueline, and Shaffdeen A. Amuwo. "Understanding Elder Abuse and Neglect," in Nicky A. Jackson and Gisele C. Oates eds., *Violence in Intimate Relationships: Examining Sociological and Psychological Issues.* Boston: Buterworth-Heinemann, 1998, 195–223.

Hope, K.E. "Prophet Banished." *The Spectator,* February 21, 2004, 1.

Housewife Lynched. *Ghana Review International.* February 6, 1995. http://www.ghanaweb.com/GhanaHomePage/NewsArchive/artikel.php?ID=259

Hudson, K. "More Rape Cases in Tema." *Daily Graphic,* January 7, 1999, 23.

Hushie, Brilliant, and Zakaria Alhassan. "3 Arrested for Lynching." *Daily Graphic,* January 27, 1998, 20.

Ingram, Rick E., Walter D. Scott, and Sarah Hamill. "Depression: Social and Cognitive Aspects." In Paul H. Blaney and Theodore Millon, eds., *Oxford Textbook of Psychopathology.* New York: Oxford University Press, 2009, 230–51.

International Center for Nigerian Law. "*Ezekiel Adekunle v. The State.*" http://www.nigeria-law.org/Ezekiel%20Adekunle%20v.%20The%20State.htm

Integrated Regional Information Networks (IRIN). "Benin: Fears of Witchcraft Lead to Widespread Infanticide in Remote North." IRIN News, July 15, 2005. http://www.irin

news.org/report.asp?ReportID=48175&SelectRegion=West_Africa&SelectCountry =BENIN

Jackson-Lowman, Huberta. "Using Afrikan Poverbs to Provide an Afrikan-Centered Narrative for Contemporary African-American Parental Values." In *Language, Rhythm, & Sound: Black Popular Cultures into the Twenty-First Century*, edited by Joseph K. Adjaye and Adrianne R. Andrews. Pittsburgh, PA: University of Pittsburgh Press, 1997, 74–89.

Jary, David, and Julia Jary. *Collins Dictionary of Sociology*. Glasgow: Harper Collins Publisher, 1991.

Jensen, F. Gary. *The Path of the Devil: Early Modern Witch Hunts*. New York: Rowland and Littlefield Publishers, 2007.

Jesus One Touch Jailed 10 Years. ModernGhana.com. January 20, 2011. http://www.mo dernghana.com/news/312986/1/jesus-one-touch-jailed-10-years.html

Kabba, Muctaru. "Ritual Homicide in Sierra Leone." In *Criminology in Africa*, edited by Tibamanya M. Mushanga, 127–152 Rome: UNICRI, 1992.

King, Rosemary Ofeibea Ofei-Aboagye. "Domestic Violence in Ghana: An Initial Step," in Adrien K. Wing, ed., *Global Critical Race Feminism: An International Reader*. New York: New York University Press, 2001, 317–31.

Kofoya-Tetteh, Abraham. "More Children Die of Malaria." *Daily Graphic*, April 27, 2005, 48.

———. "Prosecute Pastors Who Keep AIDS Sufferers." *Daily Graphic*, March 25, 2008, 21.

Konadu, Asare. *The Wizard of Asamang*. Accra, Ghana: Waterville Publishing House, 1964.

Konadu, Kwasi. *Indigenous Medicine and Knowledge in African Society*. New York: Routledge, 2007.

Kondor, Daniel. "Witchcraft and Apparitions: What is the Linkage?" *People's Daily Graphic*, February 20, 1991a, 7.

———. "Witchcraft and Faith-healing." *People's Daily Graphic*, July 3, 1991b, 7.

Korankye, M. Ferguson. "Witchcraft Beliefs and Practices in Ajumako Traditional Area." B.A. long essay, University of Cape Coast, Cape Coast, Ghana. 1997.

Kpiebaya, E. Gregory. "The Endless Conflicts in Northern Ghana: A Worry for All." *Daily Graphic*, April 1, 2009, 7.

Kuada, John, and Yao Chachah. *Ghana: Understanding the People and Their Culture*. Accra, Ghana: Woeli Publishing, 1999.

Kumi, M.J. "Mason Charged for Causing Harm to Friend." *Mirror*, September 20, 2008, 27.

Kwamin, Francis. "Hypertension and Monitoring at Home" *Daily Graphic*, October 28, 2008, 7.

Kwawukume, E.Y. "Understanding Infertility." *Mirror*, June 5, 2004, 17.

Kwawukume, Victor. "'HIV/AIDS Not Spiritual Curse.'" *Daily Graphic*, October 9, 2008, 17.

Kyei-Boateng, Samuel. "Murder: Farmer Nabbed." *Daily Graphic*, December 24, 1996, 24.

———. "Farmer Held over Blindman's Death." *Daily Graphic*, 1997, 1.

———. "Herbalist Jailed Seven Years for Fraud." *Daily Graphic*, June 10, 2000, 24.

———. "Pupil, 14, Dies From Teacher's Cane." *Mirror*, March 7, 2009, 3.

———. "Pastor Jailed 20 Years for Raping 5 Sisters." *Daily Graphic*, August 31, 2011, 3.

Lamptey. J. J. "Patterns of Psychiatric Consultations at the Accra Psychiatric Hospital in Ghana." *African Journal of Psychiatry* 3 (1977): 123–127.

Latimore, Carolyn. *Gender, Justice and Development: Women and Development in Ghana*. Ph.D. diss., University of Pennsylvania, 1997.

Laugharne, Richard, and Tom Burns. "Mental Health Services in Kumasi, Ghana." *Psychiatric Bulletin* 23, no. 6 (1999): 361–63.

Leprosy Ambassador Targets Discrimination. Ghanaweb.com. March 10, 2010. http:// ghanaweb.com/GhanaHomePage/health/artikel.php?ID=178169&comment=5556815 #com

Levack, Brian, ed. *The Witchcraft Sourcebook.* New York: Routledge, 2004.

Levin, David. *What Happened in Salem?* New York: Harcourt, Brace & World, 1960.

Locals Bitter. *The New Vision,* April 21, 2005. http://www.newvision.co.ug/D/8/19/4303 42/witchcraft

Mair, Lucy. *Witchcraft.* New York: McGraw-Hill, 1973.

Mambule, Ali. "Mob Raids Rakai Police, One Killed." *The New Vision,* August 18, 2005a. http://www.newvision.co.ug/detail.php?mainNewsCategoryId=8&newsCategoryId= 19&ne...

———. "40 Evicted from Rakai Village." *The New Vision,* September 21, 2005b. http://www .newvision.co.ug/detail.php?mainNewsCategoryId=8&newsCategoryId=19&ne...

———. "Uganda: Mob Hacks Man to Death over Witchcraft." *The New Vision,* November 7, 2007. http://allafrica.com/stories/200711080064.html

———. "Masaka Residents Attack Colleague over Witchcraft." AllAfrica.com, November 12, 2009. http://allafrica.com/stories/200911130132.html

Man, 22, Allegedly Kills 70-Year-Old Stepfather. Ghanatoday.com. http://ghanatoday .com/index.php?option=news&task=viewarticle&sid=13441

Man in Custody for Accusing a Relative of Being a Witch. Ghanaweb.com, September 9, 2005. http://www.ghanaweb.com/GhanaHomePage/NewsArchive/artikel.php ?ID=89762

Mantey, Ivy. "Occultism on the Rise in Schools." *Public Agenda,* December 20, 2004, 1.

Martin, L. "Three Charged with Witchcraft Killings of Boys: Father and Two Female Relatives Admit 'Heavenly Rituals.'" *Herald Scotland,* November 14, 2002. http://www .heraldscotland.com/sport/spl/aberdeen/three-charged-with-witchcraft-killings-of-boys-father-and-two-female-relatives-admit-heavenly-rituals-1.133997

McCarthy, Leslie. "Depression Is the Leading Mental Problem in Ghana and Not Madness." Kintampo Health Research Center. http://www.kintampo-hrc.org/khrcnews/ depression_problem.html

Medical Association Advises Against Bad Lifestyles. *Daily Graphic,* December 24, 2003, 17.

Mends, Emmanuel H. "The Rights of the Child in Ghana: The Socio-Cultural Milieu." In Mensa-Bonsu and Dowuona-Hammond, *The Rights of the Child in Ghana,* 3–9.

Mensa-Bonsu, Henrietta J.A.N. "Protecting the Child through Criminal Legislation in the Fourth Republic." In Mensa-Bonsu and Dowuona-Hammond, *The Rights of the Child in Ghana,* 96–119.

———. *The General Part of Criminal Law: A Ghanaian Casebook. Volume 1.* Accra, Ghana: Black Mask Limited, 2001.

Mensa-Bonsu, Henrietta J.A.N., and Christine Dowuona-Hammond, eds. *The Rights of the Child in Ghana—Perspectives.* Accra, Ghana: Woeli Publishing, 1994.

Mensah, A. "Re: Disbanding, Dismantling of Witches Camps in the North." *Daily Graphic,* October 4, 2012, 7.

Mensah, Agnes Kutin. "Magistrate Rules Against Obnoxious Custom." *Daily Graphic,* January 12, 2007, 9.

Mensah, F. "'Holy Fire' Victim Dies." *Mirror,* August 19, 1989, 3.

Mensah, Mary. "Man 56 Lynched at Asemko." *Daily Graphic,* May 7, 1997, 12.

———. "Spiritualist, Accomplice on Fraud, Rape Charges." *Daily Graphic,* February 1, 2000, 1.

———. "'Spiritual Factor Should Not Be Discounted in Accidents.'" *Daily Graphic,* October 10, 2011, 51.

Mettle-Nunoo, E.A. *Ahitophel's Series: West African Traditional Religion.* Accra, Ghana: Ahithophel, 1994.

Meyer, Birgit. "The Power of Money: Politics, Occult Forces and Pentecostalism in Ghana." *African Studies Review* 41, no. 3 (1998): 15–37.

_____. "Pentecostalism, Prosperity, and Popular Cinema in Ghana," *Culture and Religion*, 3, no.1 (2002): 67–87.

Mfumbusa, Bernadine. "Witch Killings: Tanzania's Silent Holocaust." *Africanews*, June 1999. http://web.peacelink.it/afrinews/39_issue/p7.html

Midelfort, H.C. Erik. 2002. "Heartland of the Witchcraze." In Oldridge, *The Witchcraft Reader*, 113–19.

Minister Condemns Porn Material on TV. Ghana News Agency, November 10, 2009. http://ghananewsagency.org/social/minister-condemns-porn-material-on-tv--9288

Ministry of Education. *Education Sector Performance Report*. Accra: Ministry of Education. 2010.

Ministry of Health. *The Ghana Health Sector: 2008 Programme of Work*. Accra: Ministry of Health, 2007.

Mirror Reporter. "Court Confessions of a Witch: We Turn Birds, Animals." *Mirror*, May 9, 1975, 1.

———. "Defendant's Plea to Turn into Vulture . . . Court Did Not Allow Kobua: Magistrate Explains." *Mirror*, June 6, 1975, 1.

———. "Witchcraft Is Hereditary." *Mirror*, June 20, 1975, 1.

———. "Kobua to Pay 300 Cedis as Damages." *Mirror*, August 1, 1975, 1.

———. "Sensational Ankaful Witchcraft Case . . . Kobua Appeals Against Verdict." *Mirror*, August 15, 1975, 1.

———. "Confessions of a Witch." *Mirror*, April 6, 1991, 1.

———. "2000 People Perish in Road Accidents." *Mirror*, October 18, 2008, 35.

Misra, Neelesh. "Few Women Survive in India Villages after being Branded as Witches." *Los Angeles Times*, September 17, 2000, 1.

Monter, William. *Witchcraft in France and Switzerland: The Borderlands During the Reformation*. Ithaca: Cornell University Press, 1976.

Morgan, Leslie, and Suzanne Kunkel. *Aging: The Social Context*. Thousand Oaks, CA: Pine Forge Press, 1998.

Mullings, Leith. *Therapy, Ideology and Social Change: Mental Healing in Urban Ghana*. Los Angeles: University of California Press, 1984.

Nabila, M. "Rehabilitation of the Witches in Gambaga: The Role of the Presbyterian Church of Ghana." B.A. long essay, University of Ghana, Legon, 1997.

National Road Safety Commission (NRSC). "Spotlight on Road Safety." *Daily Graphic*, June 16, 2005, 7.

Nehemia, K. "Suspected Witch Subjected to Indecent Treatment." *Mirror*, December 17, 1988, 1.

NGO Launches Witches Camp Integration Project. Ghanaweb.com, March 20, 2010. http://ghanaweb.com/GhanaHomePage/NewsArchive/artikel.php?ID=178855

Niehaus, A. Isak. "Witch-hunting and Political Legitimacy: Continuity and Change in Green Valley, Lebowa, 1930–91." *Africa* 63 (1993): 498–530.

Nkrumah, J. McBob. "Woman, 43, Refused Christian Burial." *Weekly Spectator*, October 6, 1984, 8.

Nkrumah-Boateng, A. "Emile Short and the 200 Witches." *Daily Graphic*, October, 20, 1997, 9.

Nsowah-Adjei, Thomas. "Son Harasses 75-year-old Mother." *Mirror*, February 19, 1994, 3.

Ntim-Korsah, Yaw. "Witchcraft and Its Influence: A Study of the Belief of the People of Techiman District in the Brong-Ahafo Region." B.A. long essay, University of Cape Coast, Cape Coast, 1988.

Nuhhu-Billa, Hadiza. "Boy, 19, Butchers Grandma 80." *Mirror*, March 5, 2005, 22.

Nukunya, G.K. *Tradition and Change in Ghana: An Introduction to Sociology.* Accra, Ghana: Ghana Universities Press, 2003.

Nunoo, Chris. "You're a Witch: Youth Subject Woman, 90, to 3-Hour Humiliation." *Mirror,* August 27, 2005, 1.

Obeng, S. Cecilia. *Voices of Affliction: Aspects of Traditional Healing and Their Implications on Akan Families in Ghana.* Koln, Germany: Rudiger Koppe Verlag, 2004.

Obeng, J. Pashington. *Asante Catholicism: Religious and Cultural Reproduction among the Akan of Ghana.* New York: E.J. Brill, 1996.

Obour, S.K. "500 Cured Lepers Can't Go Home." *Mirror,* January 28, 2012, 3.

Obugyei, Abraham. (n.d.). *Bayie Ho Asem.* Audiocassette Recording.

Ocloo, R. Della. "Grandma Set Ablaze to Exorcise Witchcraft." *Daily Graphic,* November 26, 2010a, 1.

——. "'My Mum Is Not a Witch.'" *Daily Graphic,* November 29, 2010b, 1.

Ocran, J.K. "Sensational Revelation in Court: I'm a Witch . . . I Fly at Night with My Baby." *Mirror,* May 2, 1975, 1.

Odoi, A., S.P. Brody, and T.E. Elkins. "Female Genital Mutilation in Rural Ghana, West Africa." *International Journal of Gynecology & Obstetrics* 56 (1997): 179–80.

Odoi, A.K. "The Practice of Female Genital Mutilation in Bolgatanga." *Sisterwatch,* 1 (2002): 1.

Odoi, Victoria. "Father 'Roasts' Feet of Sons for Flying at Night." *Mirror,* July 26, 2003, 6.

Oduyoye, Amba. 1979. "The Asante Woman: Socialization through Proverbs (Part 1)." *African Notes* 8 (1979): 5–11.

Offei-Aboagye, Rosemary O. "Altering the Strands of the Fabric: A Preliminary Look at Domestic Violence in Ghana." *Signs* 19, no. 4 (1994): 924–38.

Ohene-Asiedu, Leticia. "'Help to Demystify Mental Health.'" *Daily Graphic,* November 17, 2008a, 38.

——. "Pantang Admits More People with Substance, Alcohol Abuse." *Daily Graphic,* December 19, 2008b, 31.

Oheneba-Mensah, Evans. "Ghana: Mental Health in Crisis." Allafrica.com June 18, 2010. http://allafrica.com/stories/201006220659.html

Oheneba-Sakyi, Yaw. *Female Autonomy, Family Decision Making, and Demographic Behavior in Africa.* New York: The Edwin Mellen Press, 1999.

Okaitey, Samuel. "Okomfo Nyamekye Jailed." *Mirror,* November 9, 1985, 3.

Okine, Vicky. "The Surveillance Strategies of Poor Families in Ghana and the Role of Women Therein," in Joycelin Massiah, ed., *Women in Developing Economies: Making Visible the Invisible.* Providence, RI: Berg Publishers, 1993, 167–94.

Oldridge, Darren. "Witchcraft and Gender," in Oldridge, *The Witchcraft Reader,* 268–71.

Oldridge, Darren, ed. *The Witchcraft Reader.* New York: Routledge, 2002.

Oliver-Commey, Joseph. *The Disabled Child in Ghana: Whose Fault and Who Cares?* Accra, Ghana: Ghana Universities Press, 2001.

Oloya, Opiyo. "Witchhunting Must Be Stamped Out in Uganda." *New Vision,* October 4, 2005. http://www.newvision.co.ug/D/8/20/459169

One-Month-Old Baby Declared a Witch? Northernghana.com April 1, 2008. http://www.northernghana.com/news/i/?n=534

Opoku, Kofi Asare. "The World View of the Akan." In *Akan History and Culture,* edited by I. Anthony Asiwaju, and John K. Fynn. Essex, UK: Longman, 1982, 61–73.

Oppong-Ansah, Albert. "Traditional Beliefs and Fate of Deformed Children." *Daily Graphic,* October 15, 2011, 11.

Oppong, R. Joseph. "Ghana: Internal, International, and Transnational Migration," in M.I.

Toro-Morn and M. Alicea, eds., *Migration and Immigration: A Global View*, Westport, CT: Greenwood Press, 2004: 81–96.

Orhin, Isabella Gyau. "The Witch Menace: Judge Joins Campaign as he Warns Perpetrators." Ghanaweb.com August 10, 2003. http://www.ghanaweb.com/public_agenda/article.php?ID=1675

Osei, Akwasi. "Facts and Myths about Prayer Camps." *Daily Graphic*, 2008, 27.

———. "The State of Mental Health in Ghana." *Daily Graphic*, January 14, 2010, 9.

———. "Confab on Witches Camps." *Daily Graphic*, September 7, 2011, 19.

Osei, A.O. "Witchcraft and Depression—A Study into the Psychopathological Features of Alleged Witches." *Ghana Medical Journal* 35, no.3 (2001): 111–15.

Osei, A.P. *Ghana: Recurrence and Change in Post-Independence African State*. New York: P. Lang, 1999.

Osei-Boateng, Rebecca. "Leading the Legal Battle: Gender Rights in Ghana," in Nana Araba Apt., Naana Agyemang-Mensah, and M. Grieco, eds., *Maintaining the Momentum of Beijing: The Contribution of African Gender NGOs*. Brookfield: Ashgate, 1998, 64–70.

Osei-Edwards, R "PLWHA Advised not to Spend Time in Spiritual Homes." *Daily Graphic*, July 16, 2004.

Otchere, Frank. "Man Clubs Aunt to Death." *The Ghanaian Times*, August 1, 2005, 15.

Owusu, Morgan. "Woman Sells Baby for GHc20." Modernghana.com January 16, 2010. http://www.modernghana.com/news/259508/1/woman-sells-baby-for-gh20.html

Owusu-Ansah, David. "Prayer, Amulets and Healing," in Nehemia Levtzion and Randall L. Pouwels, eds., *The History of Islam in Africa*. Athens: Ohio University Press 2000, 477–488.

Palmer, Karen. *Spellbound: Inside West Africa's Witch Camps*. New York: Free Press, 2010.

Parish, Jane. "The Dynamics of Witchcraft and Indigenous Shrines among the Akan." *Africa* 69, no. 3 (1999): 426–48.

———. "From the Body to the Wallet: Conceptualizing Akan Witchcraft at Home and Abroad." *Journal of the Royal Anthropological Institute* 6, no. 3 (2000): 487–500.

Party Official Helps Police in Case of Manhandling Old Woman. Ghanaweb.com February 27, 2006. http://www.ghanaweb.com/GhanaHomePage/politics/artikel.php?ID=100079

Pellow, Deborah. "Work and Autonomy: Women in Accra." *American Ethnologist* 5, no. 4 (1978): 770–85.

Penni, K. "Child Slashed to Death." *Mirror*, April 7, 1984, 1.

Plange-Rhule, Gyakua. "What Price for a Child's Life?" *Daily Graphic*, August 16, 2008, 25.

Prah, Mansah. "Women's Studies in Ghana." *Women's Studies Quarterly* 24, no. 1 & 2 (1996): 412–22.

Psychiatrist Calls for Collaboration in the Treatment of Mental Health Cases. Ghanaweb.com, 2005. http://www.ghanaweb.com/GhanaHomePage/NewsArchive/artikel.php?ID=76301

Quaye, George F., and Chris Nunoo. "Only Two New Doctors Accepted Posting to Upper West Region in 2008." *Daily Graphic*, May 26, 2009, 20.

Raghavan, Sudarsan. "Children Tortured in Congo Witch-hunt." *Detroit Free Press*, October 21, 2003.

Rasko, Gabriella. "The Victim of the Female Killer." *Victimology* 1 (1976): 396–402.

Rattray, Robert. *Ashanti Proverbs*. Oxford: Clarandon Press, 1914.

Rawlings Slams at False Prophets. Ghanaweb.com, August 25, 1997. http://www.ghanaweb.com/GhanaHomePage/NewsArchive/artikel.php?ID=1635

Razak, Abdul. "Did She Bewitch Me?" *Mirror*, December 6, 2003, 13.

Reagan, Timothy. *Non-Western Educational Traditions: Indigenous Approaches to Educational Thought and Practice.* Mahwah, NJ: Lawrence Erlbaum Associates, 2005.

Rice, Xan. "Gambian State Kidnaps 1,000 Villagers in Mass Purge of Suicide." *The Guardian,* March 18, 2009. http://www.guardian.co.uk/world/2009/mar/19/gambia-witch-craft-hallucinogenics

Roper, Lyndal. *Witch Craze: Terror and Fantasy in Baroque Germany.* New Haven, CT: Yale University Press, 2004.

Round Table Conference on the Treatment of Suspected Witches in Northern Ghana: Report on the Round Table Conference on the Treatment of Suspected Witches in Northern Ghana. Commission on Human Rights and Administrative Justice and US-AID. Tamale, Ghana, 1998.

Rowlands, Alison. "Witchcraft and Old Women in Early Modern Germany." *Past & Present* 173 (2001): 50–89.

———. *Witchcraft Narratives in Germany: Rothenburg, 1561–1652.* New York: Manchester University Press, 2003.

Roy, Puja. "Sanctioned Violence: Development and the Persecution of Women as Witches in South Bihar." *Development in Practice* 8, no. 2 (1998): 136–47.

Sackey, Emmanuel. "Human Right Abuse at Prayer Camps." Ghana Federation of the Disabled February, 2010. http://www.gfdgh.org/right%20abuse%20at%20prayer%20camps.html

Sad Case of Cured Mental Patients. Modernghana.com January 13, 2011. http://www.modernghana.com/news/312035/1/sad-case-of-cured-mental-patients-600-face-ejectio.html

Safo, Margaret. "Making 'Witches' More Powerful." *Daily Graphic,* December 4, 1997, 9.

Sah, Stephen. "Carpenter to Hang for Murder." *Daily Graphic.* August 24, 2004, 3.

———. "Bishop in Custody for Alleged Visa Deal." *Daily Graphic,* May 10, 2005, 46.

Salia, K. Albert. "Ghana Marks Day Against Drug Abuse." *Daily Graphic,* 2009, 16.

Salifu, Nurudeen. "Supporting Persons with Mental Illness." *Daily Graphic,* March 2, 2010, 20.

Sam, B. "International Women's Day." *Daily Graphic,* March 4, 2004, 11.

Sam, Eben C. "Driver Butchers Mum for Being a Witch." *Mirror,* May 25, 1996, 3.

Sanders, Todd. "Save Our Skins: Structural Adjustment, Morality and the Occult in Tanzania." In *Magical Interpretations, Material Realities: Witchcraft and the Occult in Postcolonial Africa,* edited by H.L. Moore and Todd. Sanders. New York: Routledge, 2001, 160–83.

Sarpong, Peter K. *Ghana in Retrospect: Some Aspects of Ghanaian Culture.* Tema, Ghana: Ghana Publising Corporation, 1974.

———. *Girls' Nubility Rites in Ashanti.* Tema, Ghana: Ghana Publishing Corporation, 1977.

Schipper, Mineke. *Never Marry a Woman with Big Feet: Women in Proverbs from Around the World.* New Haven, CT: Yale University Press, 2003.

Seini, Iddrisu. "Farmer Charged for Murder." *Daily Graphic,* August 6, 1998, 16.

Shroeder, R.M., Danquah, S.A., & Mate-Kole, C.C. "The Therapeutic Significance of Widowhood Rites in a Ghanaian Society." In *African-Centered Psychology,* edited by Dauda Ajani ya Azibo, 145–53. Durham: Carolina Academic Press, 2003.

Simpson, Noble. *Unravelling the Mystery of Witchcraft.* Accra, Ghana: Combert Impressions, 2009.

Six Forty Nine Died in 14,000 Road Accidents Last Year Ghanaweb.com. January 31, 2005. http://www.ghanaweb.com/GhanaHomePage/NewsArchive/artikel.php?ID=74456

Skaria, Ajay. "Women, Witchcraft and Gratuitous Violence in Colonial Western India." *Past & Present,* 155 (1997): 109–41.

Smith, J. Daniel. "Ritual Killing, 419, and Fast Wealth: Inequality and the Popular Imagination in Southeastern Nigeria." *American Ethnologist* 28, no. 4 (2001): 803–26.

Soko, Boston, and Gerhard Kubik. *Nchimi Chikanga: The Battle against Witchcraft in Malawi.* Blantyre, Malawi: Christian Literature Association in Malawi, 2002.

Soku, Leonard. *From the Coven of Witchcraft to Christ.* Vol.1. Accra, Ghana: Unknown Publisher, 2000.

Son Butchers Mum. *Daily Graphic,* June 16, 2001, 18.

Sosywen. *The Wasted Years: The Reality of the "Witches Camps."* Accra, Ghana: Southern Sector Youth and Women's Empowerment Network, 2012.

Spectator Reporter. "Seamstress Flogged by Prophetess." *Weekly Spectator,* January 8, 2000, 1.

Ssejjoba, Eddie. "Masaka Woman Lynched." *New Vision.* September 28, 2005. http://www.newvision.co.ug/D/8/13/458170

Tandoh, Ike. *One Blow: You Devil, Leave Me Alone!* Kumasi: Unknown Publisher, n.d.

Tangumonkem, Eric, T., and R.T. Ghogomu. Combating Witchcraft Beliefs by Accessing and Reconstructing the History of Heavy Rainfall–Triggered Landslides and Related Hazards in the Bamumbu Region, South West Cameroon. *Geological Society of America Abstracts with Programs* 36 (2004): 168.

Tebug, E. Olive. "Witchcraft Suspect Lynched, 2 Others Wounded." 2004. http://www.postnewsline.com/2004/11/strongwitchcraf.html

Tenyah, Linda. "Woman Feeds Boy with Shit, Urine." Modern Ghana.com, October 3, 2009. http://www.modernghana.com/news/241927/1/woman-feeds-boy-with-shit-urine.html

Ter Haar, Gerrie. 2007. "Ghanaian Witchcraft Beliefs: A View from the Netherlands." In Ter Haar, *Imagining Evil,* 93–112.

Ter Haar, Gerrie, ed. *Imagining Evil: Witchcraft Beliefs and Accusations in Contemporary Africa.* Trenton, NJ: Africa World Press, 2007.

Tetteh, Ransford. "Give Back my 'Power'." *Mirror,* March 9, 1996, 1.

Tetteh, Vicky. "I'm Not a Snake—Kate." *Weekly Spectator,* April 5, 1997, 1.

Time to Eradicate TB. *Daily Graphic,* March 26, 2009, 7.

Trial by Ordeal. *Daily Graphic,* March 21, 1981, 1.

Trial by Ordeal Fading Out in Upper West Region. Ghanaweb.com. November 30, 1998. http://www.ghanaweb.com/GhanaHomePage/NewsArchive/artikel.php?ID=4362

Two Arrested for Lynching Woman. Ghanaweb.com. June 22, 2001. http://www.ghanaweb.com/GhanaHomePage/entertainment/artikel.php?ID=16133

Twumasi, Paul. *Criminal Law in Ghana.* Tema, Ghana: Ghana Publishing Corporation, 1985.

United Nations Childrens Fund (UNICEF). Situation Analysis of Children & Women in Ghana 2000. Accra, Ghana, UNICEF. 2002.

U.S. Agency for International Development (USAID). USAID Country Health Statistical Report. Ghana, September 2004. http://www.usaid.gov/our_work/global_health/home/Countries/africa/ghana.html

van der Geest, Sjaak. "The Image of Death in Akan Highlife Songs of Ghana." *Research in African Literatures* 11, no. 2 (1980): 145–74.

———. "Death, Chaos, and Highlife Songs: A Reply." *Research in African Literatures* 15, no. 4 (1984): 583–88.

———. 2002. "The Toilet: Dignity, Privacy and Care of Elderly People in Kwahu, Ghana." In S. Makoni and K. Stroeken, eds., *Ageing in Africa.* Burlington, VT: Ashgate, 2002, 227–43.

Vervynckt, Mathieu. "Mental Patients Suffer Violation in Prayer Camps." *Daily Graphic,* May 1, 2009, 16.

Ware, Michael. "Season of the Witch." *Time Pacific.* May 7, 2001. http://www.time.com/ time/pacific/magazine/20010507/witch.html

Warren, Dennis. *The Akan of Ghana: An Overview of the Ethnographic Literature.* Accra, Ghana: Pointer, 1973.

Wiafe, Eric O. *Christianity and African Traditional Religion's Approach to Issues of Life and Death.* Accra, Ghana: Reokey Commercials, 2008.

Wiafe, Samuel. "Witch's Curse: Poor Living Standards Banish Older Women from Their Communities." *New Internationalist.* March 2001, 7.

Witch Killings in India. CNN.com. September 5, 2000. http://www.cnn.com/2000/ ASIANOW/south/09/04/witchkillings.ap/ url does not work: leads to CNN home page.

Witchcraft Case Put Off. *Daily Graphic,* December 10, 1980, 1.

Wojtas, Olga. "Witch Hunts on Agenda at Conference. Gendering the Millenium Conference at University of Dundee." *The Times Education Supplement.* September 11, 1998, No. 1349.

Woman, 70, Accused of Witchcraft. *Ghana News Runner,* March 5, 1998, 1.

Woman Lynched for Denying She Is a Witch. ModernGhana.com, July 14, 2010. http://www.modernghana.com/news/284374/1/woman-lynched-for-denying-she-is-a-witch.html

World Factbook 2003. Washington D. C., Central Intelligence Agency. 2003.

World Factbook 2012. Washington D. C., Central Intelligence Agency. 2012.

Wozuame, Benedictus. "'Madness' and Mental Health Redefined." *Daily Graphic,* May 12, 2010, 23.

Wyllie, Robert W. "Introspective Witchcraft among the Effutu of Southern Ghana." *Man* 8, no. 1 (1973): 74–79.

Yamoah, Ekow. "Man, 55, Attacks Mother 80." *Mirror,* August 20, 2005, 1.

——. "Two Pastors in Court for Child Abuse." *Daily Graphic,* January 3, 2009, 32.

Yankah, Kwesi. "The Akan Highlife Song: A Medium of Cultural Reflection or Deflection." *Research in African Literatures* 15, no. 4 (1984): 568–82.

——. *The Proverb in the Context of Akan Rhetoric: A Theory of Proverb Praxis.* New York: Peter Lang, 1989.

——. "Narrative in Times of Crisis: AIDS Stories in Ghana." *Journal of Folklore Research* 41, no. 2 & 3 (2004): 181–98.

Yeboah, A. Lucy. "Mental Health in Crisis: Only 4 Doctors in Public Service." *Daily Graphic,* March 23, 2009, 1.

——. "Relief for Psychiatric Hospitals." *Daily Graphic,* April 6, 2010, 1.

Yeboah, I. "Woman, 70, Confesses Killing Eight People." *People and Places,* 391, 2001, 1.

Yeboah, Kofi. "Witchcraft is Not Compatible with Religion." *Weekly Spectator,* February 12, 1977, 3.

——. "Cancer Cases Too High—Cardio Centre." *Daily Graphic,* April 12, 2008.

Yendi Police Arrest Farmer for Murder. Ghanaweb.com October 2, 2005. http://www.ghanaweb.com/GhanaHomePage/NewsArchive/printnews.php?ID=91336

Yirenkyi, K. "The Indiscipline Confronting Our Society." *Daily Graphic,* March 12, 2009, 9.

Cases Cited

Ezekiel Adekunle v. The State. 1989. http://www.nigeria-law.org/Ezekiel%20Adekunle%20v.%20The%20State.htm

Kofi Badu v. Abena Kobua. District Court Grade 2. Saltpond. July 29, 1975. Suit No. 224/74.

Ama Kunta v. Abena Kobua. District Court Grade 2. Saltpond. July 8, 1975. Suit No. 209/74.

The Republic v. Kwabena Wayom and 3 ORS. High Court of Justice. Tamale. July 31, 2003.

The Republic v. Gbenyo Quarshie. High Court of Justice. Accra. B/Ind. 1159/01. August 23, 2004.

INDEX

CPSIA information can be obtained
at www.ICGtesting.com
Printed in the USA
JSHW021432300420
5426JS00004B/96